MW00823859

peace
toWAR

The C Henry Smith Series

T he C. Henry Smith series is edited by J. Denny Weaver. As is expected to be true of many future books in the CHS series, volumes published to date are being released by Cascadia Publishing House (originally Pandora Press U.S., a name some of the earlier series books carry) and copublished by Herald Press in cooperation with Bluffton University as well as the Mennonite Historical Society. Bluffton University, in consultation with the publishers, is primarily responsible for the content of the studies.

p e a c e
to WAR

SHIFTING ALLEGIANCES
IN THE ASSEMBLIES OF GOD

Paul Alexander

Foreword by Glen Stassen

The C. Henry Smith Series
Volume 9

Cascadia
Publishing House
Telford, Pennsylvania

copublished with
Herald Press
Scottdale, Pennsylvania

Cascadia Publishing House orders, information, reprint permissions:
contact@CascadiaPublishingHouse.com
1-215-723-9125
126 Klingerman Road, Telford PA 18969
www.CascadiaPublishingHouse.com

Peace to War
Copyright © 2009 by Cascadia Publishing House,
Telford, PA 18969
All rights reserved.
Copublished with Herald Press, Scottdale, PA
Library of Congress Catalog Number: 2008041483
ISBN-13: 978-1-931038-58-4; **ISBN 10**: 1-931038-58-9
Book design by Cascadia Publishing House
Cover design by Merrill R. Miller

The paper used in this publication is recycled and meets the
minimum requirements of American National Standard for Information
Sciences—Permanence of Paper for Printed Library Materials, ANSI Z39.48-1984.

Except when otherwise indicated,
Scripture quotations are based on the author's translation.

Library of Congress Cataloguing-in-Publication Data
Alexander, Paul, 1972-
Peace to war : shifting allegiances in the Assemblies of God / Paul Alexander.
    p. cm. -- (The C. Henry Smith series ; v. 9)
ISBN-13: 978-1-931038-58-4 (pbk. : alk. paper)
ISBN-10: 1-931038-58-9 (pbk. : alk. paper)
1. Assemblies of God--Doctrines. 2. Pentecostal churches--Doctrines. 3. Peace--
Religious aspects--Assemblies of God. 4. Peace--Religious aspects--Pentecostal
churches. I. Title. II. Series.

BX8765.5.Z5A44 2009
241'.624208828994--dc22

2008041483

16 15 14 13 12 11 10 09   10 9 8 7 6 5 4 3 2 1

To my wife, Deborah;
To my children, Nathan and Kharese; and
To my parents, Jerry and Sharon Alexander,
who continually encourage me
to "seek Jesus"

CONTENTS

FOREWORD

Accurate diagnosis by a good doctor who is loyal to your health can provide the gift of new life. I know Paul Alexander well. His whole life shows his deep loyalty to the health of Pentecostalism. In *Peace to War*, he has paid impressively extensive and accurate attention to the health that is intrinsic to Pentecostalism, and his diagnosis is full of suggestions for the direction of new life. *Peace to War* is not only about recovery of the peacemaking witness; it points the way to spirit-filled, Christ-centered, faithful-to-God new life.

Alexander shows how strikingly biblical and Christ-centered early Pentecostalism has been. And this life is still in the body. Pentecostals generally and Assemblies of God in particular were wonderfully biblical in their initial ethics on peace and war. Alexander (p. 301) quotes John Howard Yoder's foreword for Jay Beaman's book, *Pentecostal Pacifism*: Pentecostalism "becomes rather directly and simply pacifist in the first generation. The simplest reason is that they take the whole Bible straight."

Alexander (p. 305) helps us hear Roger Robins on the difference between original Pentecostalism and later, culturally compromised Pentecostalism:

> Where there is argumentation in favor of pacifism, that argumentation is biblically rooted, eschatologically informed, and it frequently appeals to the work of the Spirit in sanctification, conversion, and in the creation of a new people or of a new age. . . . On the other hand, argumentation against pacifism is characterized by political considerations, rationalism and humanism. . . .

Those "political considerations" overwhelm the biblical teachings.

Murray Dempster diagnoses the shift similarly. Alexander sets the stage by noting (p. 306) that "neither the authority of Scripture nor any specific biblical texts were mentioned. . . ." He then quotes Dempster's analysis that thus "The Pentecostal believer's conscience on war no longer needed to be formed specifically by biblical teaching but was now to be informed by knowledge of certain political, theological and ethical propositions."

Paul Alexander shows that pacifism without practical proactive practices that help solve these "political considerations" may be too weak to carry the day. But with practical just peacemaking practices, pacifism has an answer to those political questions. That is why John Howard Yoder moved in his last writings to proactive practices that make for peace, especially in his *Body Politics, For the Nations,* and his forthcoming *The Lamb's War.*

Peace to War suggests that if we are to lead Christians to witness consistently to the way of Jesus for peacemaking, we need to deal with those "political considerations." We need to specify practices that are faithful to Jesus and that solve problems practically. We need to elaborate the practices of just peacemaking that form consciences to resist authoritarian nationalism.

The first generations of Pentecostals were wonderfully biblical in relation to what we should *not* do: engage in killing. But they seem not to have developed a sufficiently articulate ethic of the dangers of nationalistic power nor proactive alternatives to warmaking that could solve injustice without making war. As Yoder wrote (according to Alexander's quotation, p. 302), "But this originality (both the pacifism and the racial integration) was not deeply rooted. . . . The Pentecostals . . . had no alternative view of the meaning of power, the meaning of nationalism. . . . " So when World War II obtained strong nationalistic support, many pacifists had no clear answer pointing to the initiatives pacifist Christians could be taking.

The book of Acts is a call to repentance for narrow nationalism that hinders the gospel. The Holy Spirit again and again moves people *outside Judaism* to repentance and to new life in the gospel—Samaritans, Gentile God-fearers, Gentiles who have no relationship to Jewish faith, jailers, the Ethiopian eunuch. The Holy Spirit called Paul and calls us to repentance for closing the gospel off from people who do not share our nationalistic loyalty.

Paul Alexander shows us we need to think deeply about making both pacifism and just peacemaking "biblically rooted, eschatologically informed, and appealing to the work of the Spirit" in sanctification, conversion, and creation of a new people. His accurate diagnosis points us the way to this new life.

—*Glen Stassen*
 Lewis B. Smedes Professor of Chrisian Ethics
 Fuller Theological Seminary

SERIES PREFACE

C. Henry Smith began his teaching career at Goshen College, 1903-13, and then taught history at Bluffton College (now Bluffton University) from 1913-48, except for the 1922-23 year he spent at Bethel College. The first Mennonite in North America to earn a Ph.D. and remain in the Mennonite church, Smith was the premier North American Mennonite historian of his era. He wrote many articles for Mennonite periodicals and was a central figure in planning the *Mennonite Encyclopedia*. He published five major works over thirty-five years, more full-length writings than any other Mennonite historian of his time. Also a church leader, Smith was on the publication board of the General Conference Mennonite Church and the Peace Committee of Middle District.

Producing the C. Henry Smith Series (CHS) with cosponsorship of the Mennonite Historical Society is one dimension of the service Bluffton University seeks to provide the Mennonite church as well as Anabaptists at large and the wider Christian tradition. Smith's historical expertise, commitment to pacifism and nonresistance, commitment to the church, and wide-ranging interests beyond the discipline of history all represent the values and interests that characterize the series bearing his name. Naming the series for an individual of multiple interests and talents signals a vision to publish works that use a variety of disciplines and modes of inquiry to serve Anabaptist and Mennonite churches.

Works in the CHS Series reflect the assumption that a peace church worldview holds potential to shape discussion of any issue. These books present no consensus view, however, since none exists. Instead, they address aspects of Anabaptist and Mennonite studies pertinent to the future of these churches. Precisely that future dimension compels CHS publication.

SERIES EDITOR'S FOREWORD

The first time I read this manuscript it shocked me. It still shocked me when I read this final, revised version a few years later. The antiwar, Christian, pacifist sentiments of the Assemblies of God that Paul Alexander describes in chapters three and four juxtaposed in close proximity to their pro-war and anti-pacifist passion and identification with America in chapters six and seven is simply striking. It should get any reader's attention. The plot line of *Peace to War: Shifting Allegiances in the Assemblies of God* exposes the transition from one to the other of these contradictory stances within the space of three or four short decades.

The recounting of this story has two distinct audiences. One is the Assemblies of God, Paul Alexander's denomination. His address to the denomination is direct. It is Alexander's hope and prayer that telling this story of transition from peace church to pro-war church will bring questions about pacifism and Jesus' ethic of nonviolence once again to the fore within the Assemblies of God and invite them to renewed Assemblies consideration of Jesus' call to nonviolence.

A particular question implied by the description of the transition is "Did it have to be?" The narrative shows that it did not have to happen. With other decisions taken and choices made, the Assemblies of God could still be a peace church. Another question immediately follows: "Do conditions now have to continue the way they are?" Again the answer is no. Change is possible. And Alexander cites some recent voices to show that in fact more change is possible and that the Assemblies of God could once again become a peace church. This book now becomes a major voice in that movement. I commend it for that purpose and pray for its success.

The Historic Peace Churches, and in particular Mennonite Church USA, compromise another distinct audience for this book. The peace churches should read and note the ease with which the Assemblies of God ceased being a peace church. The transition was not inevitable, but neither was it because a conscious decision was made to abandon the teaching of Jesus. It happened through a combination of forces that included acculturation and espousal of individualism as the ultimate authority for ethics. It occurred through "drift" rather than specific decisions.

With that sliding in mind, Mennonites as a peace church should think, for example, of the many concerns raised about the denomination's peace stance being a hinder to evangelism; or of the letters and articles in church publications apologizing for having made an idol of our peace tradition; or the letters of support in Mennonite periodicals for the administration that invaded Iraq; and the letters that proclaim either invasion of Iraq a "just war"; or the pastor who told me that being a peace church is hard work, and "my people are tired being different, they just want to blend into American society;" or the recent arguments that as an acculturated church, we need to be willing to get our hands dirty and get involved in armed security forces; or the fact that only twenty-three per cent of Mennonites believe that it is "always wrong" to enter the military.[1] Sadly, this list could be extended. Just as the Assemblies of God can see that "it did not have to be," Mennonites can examine this drift and decide that "it does not have to be." Paul Alexander's book can serve as a warning for Mennonites. I pray that the book may fulfill that potential.

Other valuable learnings emerge from *Peace to War: Shifting Allegiances in the Assemblies of God*. One concerns the decision of the Assemblies of God to make "individual conscience" the ultimate test with regard to military participation. As Alexander notes, when individual conscience is defined as the ultimate test, then any answer is acceptable—and that becomes a stance that no longer considers the rejection of violence intrinsic to the gospel of Jesus Christ.

More than once Alexander mentions that one reason for the loss of pacifism by the Assemblies of God was the failure to develop a broadly based biblical and theological defense of pacifism beyond the injunctions to obey the commands of Jesus. Nonviolence was not integrated into their early message of the gospel they preached, and they did not develop an ongoing tradition of pacifism. That observation pertains both to those seeking to recover or restore this teaching as well as to those in longstanding peace church traditions. A commitment to the nonviolence of Jesus dare not be taken for granted. When it is believed that rejection of violence is intrinsic to the good news of Jesus, then that commitment and confession should be part of any message about Jesus. This teaching should be renewed and restated in every generation, and it is quite appropriate and important to extend the appropriation of nonviolence into new areas of theology, as in current discussions about violence in atonement theology and in our understandings of God and the nonviolence of God.

The need to renew and restate peace theology in every generation points to another learning from this book. The Christian commitment to peace, pacifism, and nonviolence does not depend on a particular view of the Bible nor on a particular brand of hermeneutics. In this book, contemporary readers who have benefited from seminary education will encounter pacifism based on views of the Bible and a hermeneutic not learned in a modern Anabaptist seminary. But the point is that although Christian pacifism does depend on taking the *story* of Jesus seriously as the place where God is revealed in the historical arena in which we live, pacifism does not depend on a particular hermeneutic or theory of biblical inspiration. It is the story of Jesus that orients believers in discipleship, and any number of theories of interpretation—hermeneutics—arrive at the conclusion that Jesus rejected the sword even as they differ on many other issues.

Placing the importance of the story ahead of a particular hermeneutic points to another implication of Alexander's narrative. Christians do not need to agree on some supposed beginning presuppositions to agree that Jesus' example and his teaching—his story—enjoin his followers to reject killing. The identifying practice of the Assemblies of God provides one stellar example. As Paul Alexander notes, although speaking and praying in tongues is a definitional aspect of the Assemblies of God, only half their members actually speak and pray in tongues.

Mention of speaking in tongues points to a valuable learning for Mennonites as a peace church. Alexander points out that speaking in tongues became separated from social contexts and social issues, and became only a practice for worship. It ceased being a practice that undergirded social concerns or social ethics and became essentially a definitional but empty practice. In recent years, many Mennonites have come to stress spirituality and prayer retreats, to call for a higher view of sacraments to undergird a more experiential worship, and to call for increasingly experiential worship as a means of church renewal. Such practices are not harmful in and of themselves. However, the experience of the Assemblies of God provides a warning. The commitment to the nonviolence of Jesus needs to be a visible and intrinsic element of these experiential practices, in which case they become practices that nurture the witnessing of the peace church in the world. But if Jesus' rejection of violence is not made intrinsically visible in these practices, they are already on the way to becoming practices devoid of social relevance for the ethic of the peace church.

Paul Alexander's manuscript was challenging and thought-provoking as I worked with it. In our working together, I came to appreciate this manuscript greatly, and to experience Paul as a Christian brother. I am grateful for his willingness to enact changes, to develop suggested new material, and to implement the revisions and additions suggested by the anonymous reviewers. Those efforts show in the quality of this book. It has been a growing experience as well as a pleasure for me to work with him on this manuscript. The volume is a fitting addition to the C. Henry Smith Series, which publishes material from a variety of disciplines in support of a peace church agenda. I am grateful to the Mennonite Historical Society for its generous support of the publication of this manuscript.

—*J. Denny Weaver*
 C. Henry Smith Series Editor

NOTE

1. Conrad Kanagy, *Road Signs for the Journey: A Profile of Mennonite Church USA* (Scottdale, Pa.: Herald Press, 2007), 127.

AUTHOR'S PREFACE

I was a freshman in a Pentecostal college in early 1991 when the United States ousted Saddam Hussein from Kuwait. I cheered as Operation Desert Storm began and the missiles rained down. My friends and I enjoyed watching the war on television, and I thought the song, "Bomb, bomb, bomb . . . bomb, bomb Iraq" (to the tune of "Ba Ba Ba . . . Ba Barbara Ann" by the Beach Boys) was hilarious. I was a tongues-talking, pro-war, hardcore patriotic, Assemblies of God follower of Jesus. If somebody had told me that the Assemblies of God, the denomination of my four generation heritage, had been officially antiwar for its first fifty years, I would have thought they were crazy.

Six years later, when I found out most early Pentecostal denominations had been "pacifist," I did indeed think it was about the dumbest thing I had ever heard.[1] But it so intrigued me that I was drawn to the topics of Pentecostals, war, violence, Americanism, and patriotism as a moth to the proverbial flame.

The study eventually destroyed me; I went mad. Okay, that is an overstatement, but the early Pentecostal testimony against war that was firmly rooted in a radical fidelity to Jesus of Nazareth destroyed my illusion of Christian faith. My understanding of Christianity died, my understanding of God died, my faith died, I died. I was murdered, crucified, with Christ . . . and yet somehow I am still alive. I am a walking dead man—fully alive but having died to my old gods, allegiances, and ways of life. It is no longer I that live, it is Christ who lives in me. And the life I now live, I try to live by faithfulness to the son of God. And now I am going to share with you the story that spurred the transformation of my understanding of Jesus of Nazareth.

So how in the world did I get here? More importantly, why should anybody care? I am an Assemblies of God boy of Kansan and Texan descent who is telling a story about Pentecostals and pacifism. The Lord does work in unexpected ways, and I never would have guessed that this book and my life would be fitting into God's kingdom in this way. But it is, and this work is a result of the journey I have been on for the last several years. It has been painful and extremely frustrating at times, but it has also renewed my faith and my hope.

While researching for a paper on sanctification (tracing the concept from John Wesley to the early Assemblies of God) I stumbled across a commitment to nonviolence in the nineteenth-century holiness movement. This interested me because I had hardly heard of such a witness among Christians, perhaps the Amish or something, but nothing that I could relate to or had ever seriously considered. But then, to my horror, I found pacifism, official pacifism even, in the Assemblies of God itself. In 1917 the Assemblies of God, my own fellowship, had declared itself conscientiously opposed to Christian participation in war. Now this was something new. I had never been told that the Assemblies of God had been a pacifist denomination. I had attended and served in Assemblies of God churches my entire life and had graduated from an Assemblies of God university and an Assemblies of God seminary. But now I was hearing some early Pentecostal voices that in my experience at least had ceased to speak.

This unanticipated discovery left me both concerned and full of questions. Why did early Pentecostals think war was wrong? Why would they refuse to kill, even for America? How did they defend this stance? Why did this official position last fifty years? Why did it change? Why had I never heard of this stance? I started digging deeper and found a few articles, one short book, and a portion of a dissertation that had addressed pacifism among early Pentecostals. I then realized that this was exactly what I wanted to tackle in my own dissertation.

And that is when it got good, or bad, depending on how one looks at it. I started reading the early *Pentecostal Evangels* (the official magazine of the Assemblies of God) and heard ideas coming from those Pentecostals that I had never heard from any Pentecostal I knew. At the same time much of it was very familiar, very Jesus focused, very biblical, very Spirit-filled. But I was unconvinced. I read everything they had to say about war, peace, patriotism, and loyalty to government. There were differences of opinion and disagreements, but the themes of nonviolence and heavenly citizenship consistently rose to the top. Tracking these themes from the 1920s through the 1990s revealed the colossal change the Assemblies of God had experienced.

That is when I had to think it through for myself. My historical survey of this one Pentecostal fellowship forced me to go to Scripture and think. I had to reconsider my own theology and ethics in light of what I had found. I wrestled and argued and fought, I justified and explained and rationalized—but little by little the power of the biblical and theological case for Christian nonviolence persuaded me. I came to realize that it is not idealistic, not passive, and not naïve. I learned that Jesus' way of making peace is aggressive and that it addresses conflict, but I also realized that taking up the cross to follow the Christ is to submit to one's own death at the hand of an enemy. My journey through the history of the Assemblies of God had been linked with the witness of the early church—and I embraced the way of self-giving love that is the way of the crucified and resurrected Messiah.

As I researched and wrote this story of Pentecostals and war, I was motivated to consider my identity in relation to the births and deaths of nations, to racism, to the use of violence in defense of justice, and to nationalism. As important as my Spirit baptism is my confession that Jesus from Nazareth, and no other, is the Messiah. So, I am still very Pentecostal. But since this book is for Pentecostals and non-Pentecostals alike, I should make it clear that I locate my identity firmly in the long story of Israel, the Messiah, and the church.

I taught at an Assemblies of God university for nine years and labored alongside sisters and brothers, faculty and administration, who sincerely believe that Christian nonviolence is misdirected at best and foolish at worst. They think that pacifism is perhaps a matter of conscience that an individual may choose, but realistically it is irresponsible and not the wisest choice. There are many others in my denomination and among American Pentecostals in general who honestly cannot fathom how a Christian could believe in Jesus and renounce violence as a tool for helping the world. This has been especially true in the United States since September 11, 2001. I understand that line of reasoning, it is exactly what I used to think, and I used to argue for it quite effectively. Now I have to admit that the arguments of the first-generation Pentecostals convinced me I needed to reconsider.

But this book is not about my biblical and theological arguments for why Christians should follow Jesus' example of enemy love and forgiveness even when it includes a renunciation of violence. That book is coming. Instead, my hope is that this telling of the story in an accessible way will foster careful thinking and dialogue about this immensely significant issue. This book is in large part for those who disagree with, or were unaware of, the early Pentecostal (particularly the Assemblies of God) theology and practice of nonviolence. Those who are comforted that the position was changed from pacifism in 1967 will find some support for their perspective all the way back to the beginning of the Assemblies of God. Those who are unsure will find all sides represented in their own words and with their own explanations to be considered.

I am an American Pentecostal who accidentally found this heritage and then wrestled with its implications. The ensuing battle with Christian pacifism resulted in this book and a very different life than expected. So this is a conversation among friends: a Pentecostal who has never heard this part of her story, another who may have heard it but was at least a little embarrassed by it, and members of traditional peace churches who may be questioning the continuing relevance of their church's peace witness.

This narrative invites Pentecostal and Charismatic brothers and sisters, particularly the Assemblies of God friends with whom I have worked and served my entire life, to interact with a forgotten part of their nonviolent heritage. I will respectfully and honestly engage the history and theology and encourage prayerful consideration of who we are and who we aspire to be on the basis of this analysis of Assemblies of God pacifism and our interaction with nationalism and war during the last century. ·

It has been nine years since I wrote the dissertation version of this book, and I have engaged in hundreds of conversations about these issues with family members, pastors, missionaries, students, district and national officials, and colleagues. I am very aware that the majority of Assemblies of God people in the United States support Christian combatant participation in warfare, although I have found Assemblies of God crucifists in all of the groups mentioned above.

For Mennonites, Brethren, Friends, and others who may be considering whether or not they still want to be a peace church, this narrative invites them to consider the implications of relegating pacifism to a matter of individual conscience rather than a church-defining issue. The Assemblies of God was never a historic "peace church," but many within the fellowship considered themselves to have the same witness against war for the same Jesus-based reasons (in 1940 the *Pacifist Handbook* listed the Assemblies of God as the third-largest church in America that opposed war).[2] Perhaps the demise of pacifism in the Assemblies of God can encourage the Historic Peace Churches to be intentional and focused in their peace witness as well as to consider the implications of a move to "individual conscience" regarding theological matters of life and death. Warning signs that pacifism might not last appear throughout this story; peace church members may assess their own faith traditions for similar occurrences.

For the others who journey with us in this Pentecostal story, I hope this is an informative and interesting book that aids careful reflection on the gospel of Jesus Christ, the use of violence, and the Christian citizen's relationship to the nation. In fact, these are relevant issues for all people everywhere. For even though the story we are reading starts about one hundred years ago, the concerns are as old as humanity and will be with us for years to come.

—*Paul Alexander*
  Glendora, California

Notes

1. I even discovered the long hidden secrets that my grandfather (Walter B. Smith, Mt. Pleasant, Texas) and my wife's grandfather (Rev. Charnel Adrian Bird, Hawkins, Texas) had been Assemblies of God conscientious objectors during World War II.

2. Ernest S. Williams, "The Conscientious Objector," *The Pentecostal Evangel*, 15 June 1940, 4.

ACKNOWLEDGMENTS

A host of family, friends, and associates have made this work possible. Deborah, my patient and amazing-in-more-ways-than-I-can-count wife, deserves more praise and appreciation than I could possibly express in this lifetime (but she says that massages really help). She has continually encouraged, challenged, and critiqued me while also being a wonderful mother to our children as this book grew from an idea (1998) to a dissertation (2000) to the hope for a movement (2001) to the volume you know hold in your hand (2009). Together we have struggled with and rolled our eyes at the issues in this book, and we've spent many long nights talking through what it all means. I thank my son Nathan Bird and my daughter Kharese Shalom for the unbelievable joy, fun, education, excitement, and love they have brought to my life. I thank them from the depths of my heart for being who they are.

Daniel McGee first introduced this topic to me and allowed me to pursue my interests while also focusing my energy on a feasible study, to him I will forever be indebted. I sincerely thank Barry Harvey for encouraging me to read Stanley Hauerwas and to take John Howard Yoder's class at Baylor University in June 1997. Bob Patterson and David Hendon served as insightful readers who consistently improved each draft of the dissertation version of this book. Baylor University enabled the initial edition by granting me the Young Christian Scholars Fellowship; special thanks are due to William Bellinger Jr. for recommending me for the award. Don Thorsen, my department chair at Azusa Pacific University, provided me with a teaching schedule and resources that tremendously helped the expeditious completion of the final draft.

Joyce Lee, of the Flower Pentecostal Heritage Center, devoted many hours to locating and copying essential archival material. Dan Shong located and organized chronologically the hundreds of *Evangel* articles that I had to read and evaluate. Brian Pipkin pored over the thousands of names of World War II conscientious objectors to provide the valuable table in Appendix B, and Stephanie Woodcarefully indexed every single page of this book. Marcy Mapes and Eugene Holder helped acquire numerous resources from libraries around the country. The interviewees who provided previously undocumented information helped make this book more complete: Charnal Adrian Bird, Michael Chase, Howard Cummings, Stanford Linzey, William Robertson, Dave Roever, Helen Rosengartner, Evelyn Smith, and Walter B. Smith.

I deeply appreciate the Society for Pentecostal Studies for the work they inspire and the venue they provide for presenting this type of work. I thanks European Pentecostal Charismatic Research Association for the opportunity to make my first academic presentation of this material and Keith Warrington and Neil Hudson of the *Journal of the European Pentecostal Theological Association* for publishing it. Allan Anderson, Jay Beaman, Chaplain Gene Brown (Col., US Army, ret.), Anthea Butler, David Daniels, Murray Dempster, Howard Kenyon, Gary McGee, Mel Robeck, Arlene Sanchez-Walsh, Joel Shuman, Harold Staiti, Jarred Stover, John Wyckoff, Amos Yong, and innumerable others assisted by conversing with me on this topic and encouraging me to finish. I also want to acknowledge the encouragement of Chuck Fager and Ann Riggs who both cheered me on and published a portion of this book in *Quaker Theology*. Albert Meyer and Alan Kreider have also been wonderfully supportive. Glen Stassen first introduced me to just peacemaking theory and has continually been an inspiration for Deborah and me.

There is no way I can ever express the enormity of the gratitude I feel for all of those in Pentecostals and Charismatics for Peace and Justice who have helped keep hope alive for me and Deborah these last several years. Eric Gabourel, Terry Johns, Marlon Millner, and Shelly McMullin shouldered increasingly large burdens of leadership responsibilities to free up more time for me to finally finish this book. Aaron Alexander, Dallas Gingles, Jonathan Jeter, Rob Reid, and Christa Savely have also been instrumental in enabling me to complete this task. The friendship and ministry of Daniel Timmerman, my pastor for many years, created a safe space for my family to worship.

I thank Southwestern Assemblies of God University for shaping me into a person who cares about the issues in this book by instilling in me a passion for sharing Jesus with the whole world, for teaching me to value and practice careful exegesis of Scripture, and for showing me how to seek and trust the empowerment of the Holy Spirit. My undergraduate experience was a life-changing joy because of faculty like Danny and Amy Alexander, LeRoy Bartel, Delmer and Eleanor Guynes, Doyle Jones, Adonna Otwell, Robert Harden, Terry Phipps, and John Wyckoff. They hired me as a twenty-three-year-old with an M.Div., hired me again after I completed my Ph.D. coursework, and gave me a schedule that allowed me time to work on my dissertation. I also sincerely appreciate the encouragement of Dr. James K. Bridges, who was mentored by William Burton McCafferty, when he supported me by affirming the importance of teaching the history of Pentecostal pacifism in Assemblies of God schools.

I especially wish to acknowledge the patience and editorial work of J. Denny Weaver in helping bring this book to life, though the shortcomings that remain are all mine. It is truly an honor to be part of the C. Henry Smith Series.

Finally, but in no way least significantly, I gratefully acknowledge the prayers, support, and unfailing love of my parents, Jerry and Sharon Alexander, and the rest of my family (Harold, Geraldine, Mark, Joy, Breleigh, Judah, Levi, W. B., Evelyn, C. A., Grace, Velma, Rodney, Betty, Ronda, Rick, Cole, Brandon, Marci, Teri, Jason, Jorilyn, and Raegan). Our journey has at times been difficult because of this study, but you have always loved me. Thank you.

peace
toWAR

ONE

PENTECOSTAL PACIFISTS?

This is a story of transformation. It focuses on one significant part of one of the most amazing religious phenomenons in history. This remarkable global movement is Pentecostalism, which started a mere century ago and has grown to include almost six hundred million people in thousands of fellowships found throughout the world. About twenty-five percent of Christians today are some type of Pentecostal or charismatic, the large majority of whom live in the two-thirds world.

Pentecostals believe that all of the New Testament gifts of the Holy Spirit, including healing and speaking in tongues, are for contemporary Christians. Pentecostals also believe in the baptism in the Holy Spirit as a work of grace subsequent to salvation. They teach that Jesus promised to send the Holy Spirit (Acts 1:8) and then empowered the faithful witness of his followers by filling them on the day of Pentecost (Acts 2). Faithful and effective evangelism and discipleship followed and the church grew (Acts 2-28).

The focus of this book is the General Council of the Assemblies of God, the largest of the Pentecostal denominations with close to forty-eight million adherents globally, a little less than three million of whom are in the United States. The Assemblies of God formed April 2, 1914, when some three hundred white ministers and laypeople gathered in Hot Springs, Arkansas, for ten days of preaching and planning. It was not the first Pentecostal denomination, and most of the founding ministers of the Assemblies of God had been ordained in the Church of God in Christ, the Pentecostal denomination founded by Bishop C. H. Mason that has been predominantly African-American since 1914. E. N. Bell called for the organizational conference in the *Apostolic Faith* magazine because he perceived a need for "doctrinal unity, conservation of the work, foreign missions interests, chartering churches under a common name for legal purposes, and the need for a Bible training school."[1] The Assemblies of God adopted their doctrinal statement— the sixteen Fundamental Truths—in 1916, and they remain virtually unchanged to this day.

In 2007 the Assemblies of God had 12,100 churches and nineteen colleges and seminaries in the United States. They claimed 236,022 churches and 1,891 Bible colleges and training centers in 191 other nations. The national leadership consists of the General Superintendent, Assistant General Superintendent, General Secretary, General Treasurer, Director of World Missions, Director of U.S. Missions, and an Executive Presbytery of eleven ministers. There are fifty-eight districts in the United States. These are determined by geography ("North Texas"), ethnicity ("Korean"), or both ("Gulf Latin").

The Assemblies of God comprises about seven percent of global Pentecostalism, and only about six percent of its members are U.S. citizens. Thus the Assemblies of God is only one part of the Pentecostal story, which is only one part of the Christian story. But the story of transformation regarding pacifism is an account worthy of a thorough exposition because, as amazing as it may seem now, the majority of early Pentecostal denominations were officially pacifist.

In the fifty years between 1917 and 1967, the American Assemblies of God changed their official position regarding war from absolute pacifism to authority of the individual conscience.[2] In 1917, during World War I, they humbly stated their adamant stance in the following resolution which was sent to President Woodrow Wilson: "Therefore, we, as a body of Christians, while purposing to fulfill all the obligations of loyal citizenship, are nevertheless constrained to declare we cannot conscientiously participate in war and armed resistance which involves the actual destruction of human life, since this is contrary to our view of the clear teachings of the inspired Word of God, which is the sole basis of our faith."[3] The statement requires a second reading. It represented the Pentecostal movement as a whole, and the Assemblies of God in particular, in the early twentieth century.

In 1967, during the Vietnam War, the Assemblies of God dropped the entire argument for pacifism and replaced it with the following statement: "As a Movement we affirm our loyalty to the government of the United States in war or peace. We shall continue to insist, as we have historically, on the right of each member to choose for himself whether to declare his position as a combatant, a noncombatant, or a conscientious objector."[4]

Even at first blush this change raises several questions. From where did the original statement come? Was it simply borrowed to help a few people get exemption from military service, or did the pacifism reflect a well-reasoned theological position from self-aware Pentecostals who were articulating the beliefs of the majority? Or did it simply reflect the sentiment of most American Christians in 1917? And why did it practically disappear? How did such a distinct change occur? Publicly proclaimed nonviolence in a time of war is about as radical as one can get, especially during World War I, and it is about as far away as one can get from public support for weapons buildup and increased military strength. Yet the Assemblies of God did both in different parts of the twentieth century. How did the original statement stand for fifty years, more than *twenty years* past World War II? How did they justify the new position in 1967? What biblical, theological, or philosophical rationale did they use to remove a statement that had remained since the beginning? And what has happened in the American Assemblies of God since the 1960s?

Drawing out answers to these and other important questions will comprise the essence of this book. I hope to show that the early claim of a nonviolent ethic has historical and theological roots among the predecessors of the Pentecostal movement and that it fit well within first-generation Pentecostalism because its adherents saw Jesus as central. They interpreted Scripture through Jesus' eyes; this meant that Old Testament stories and arguments that seemed to contradict Jesus' teachings were not authoritative.

Pacifism derives its meaning from the Latin for peacemaker. It can be defined broadly as the belief that war, violence, and the taking of human lives are inappropriate. Lisa Cahill's observation about *Christian* pacifism corresponds well to the way the early Assemblies of God formulated their arguments against Christian participation in war.

> Christian pacifism . . . does not begin so much as an ethical reply
> to the violence question (as it is often interpreted to do, especially
> by just war theorists) but as a practical embodiment of a religious
> conversion experience—as a way of life rather than a theory.
> Christian pacifism is essentially a commitment to embody com-
> munally and historically the kingdom of God so fully that mercy,
> forgiveness, and compassion preclude the very contemplation of
> causing physical harm to another person. The moral rule that ab-
> solutely excludes resort to arms is a secondary consequence of the
> pacifist conviction, not its focus or zenith.[5]

Just as there are a variety of reasons for supporting war and taking
human lives, there are a variety of rationales for pacifism. Many argue *for*
war without reference to God (in general), Jesus (in particular), or
Christianity; others try to support Christian participation in war theologically and biblically. People of other religions besides Christianity, including both Muslims and Jews, also believe in the necessity of war.
Most politicians, whether Democratic or Republican, offer secular, political, and philosophical arguments for war. Supporters of warfare include evangelical Christians and atheists, and each offers approval for a
variety of reasons.

Likewise, there are nonreligious/political pacifists, pacifists of other
religions, and Christian pacifists. One could naturally expect their various reasons for opposition to war to appeal to a variety of arguments as
well. Even Christian pacifists do not agree completely on the exact reasons why war is wrong for Christians.[6] As Martin Ceadel has observed,
since the same policy can be advocated by different people for contradictory reasons, we must identify the dynamics at the ideological level.[7]
This book explores the early Assemblies of God worldview that accepted
Christian pacifism so willingly.

A Word on the Terms Pacifism and Crucifism

The word *pacifism* was coined in about 1902. It simply comes from
the Latin *pax*—"peace" and *facere*—"to make," so it means "to make
peace." A "pacifist" is a "peacemaker." Pacifism is an active process seeking to make, create, or build something—peace. It is not related to the
word *passive*, even though the two are often thought to be closely connected. Passive comes from the Latin *passivus,* "capable of feeling or suf-

fering," but by 1477 it had come to mean "not active." Critiques of the words *pacifist* or *pacifism* are often directed toward the inactivity and passivity thought to be inherent in the concept. But a translation of Jesus' words (from Greek) "Blessed are the peacemakers [*eirenopoios*]" could also be "Blessed are the pacifists [not passivists]." My intent is not to defend the word *pacifist* but to clarify that it is not advocating passivity but the making of peace—a practice highly regarded and taught by Jesus. Taking our lead from the formation of the word *pacifist* in Latin, a person who makes war could be called a "bellicist" and the making of war could be called "bellicism" (*bellum*—war, *facere*—to make).

Many early Pentecostals who believed that Christians should not kill did not like the word *pacifist* and actually said they were not "pacifists." I understand this concern, since I could not use the word to describe myself, with a straight face, for years. To me the term still sounds weak and passive; it does not conjure up images of action and change for the better. Nevertheless, even though it is a recent creation, pacifist does serve as an appropriate technical term to describe the early Pentecostals who believed in making peace through the spread of the gospel rather than through war and violence. We will also identify them as conscientious objectors and nonviolent; they called themselves Pentecostal Christians.

The word *crucifism* or *crucifist* was coined even more recently. I first heard it October 2006 from Shane Claiborne at the Pentecostal Charismatic Peace Fellowship conference in Philadelphia, Pennsylvania. Crucifists are Christians who take up their crosses to honor Jesus' teaching that "if anyone would be my disciple, he must deny himself, pick up his cross, and follow me."[8] Crucifism is similar to what Mennonites and Church of the Brethren have traditionally called *discipleship*, and it comes from the word *crucifixion,* which is death on a cross. Discipleship in this context always included rejection of the sword and a willingness to follow Jesus to the death.[9]

The desire to use the word *crucifist* reflects the general dislike of the word *pacifism* and more directly connects to Jesus' specific words to his disciples. Jesus loved, forgave, and died for his enemies and said we should too. Crucifists say there is no Christian justification for laying down one's own cross and putting someone else on it, or slaying with a sword. I will use both words in this book to describe the Christian refusal to kill other people and the willingness to die for the faith.

THREE QUESTIONS

That brings us to the questions that inspired this book. These questions annoyed me when I first stumbled on this history. They also so intrigued me that I had to work on them until I found some satisfactory answers. First, why were Pentecostals, specifically my own fellowship, the Assemblies of God, pacifists in the first place? The 1917 statement declaring the fellowship's opposition to Christian participation in war was clear and absolute in affirming that "we cannot conscientiously participate in war and armed resistance which involves the actual destruction of human life since this is contrary to our view of the clear teachings of the inspired Word of God, which is the sole basis of our faith."[10]

The potential answers to this question vary tremendously, ranging from the accusation that Pentecostals simply reflected the pacifism of the dominant culture to the possibility that they actually did decent biblical and theological work and focused so much on Jesus that they got the nonviolence teaching right. Pacifism served as an authentic aspect of their Pentecostal self-understanding, yet perhaps they simply adopted it from the Historic Peace Churches (Brethren, Mennonites, Quakers) by means of the holiness movement. Or perhaps they were not pacifistic at all—but only claimed to be to protect a small minority. Or perhaps a great number of pacifists lived, taught, and preached the peace witness to the point that it was adopted as official doctrine because the majority believed it to be an integral part of the Pentecostal way of following Jesus. Perhaps they had a Christ centered hermeneutic, they read the Bible through Jesus' eyes, and this led them to view New Testament nonviolence as the culmination of progressive revelation.

The truth lies in some combination of these diverse hypotheses, and twenty-first century Pentecostals who think about pacifism "back then" will continue to have different explanations for it. Since history does not read itself and our perspectives on pacifism or Pentecostalism can influence the way we answer this question, considering the milieu of those years will help show why Pentecostalism and pacifism went together so well, at least for awhile.

But why only for awhile? This is the second perplexing question. Figuring out why they were pacifist is only the beginning of our journey, since the Assemblies of God is quite the opposite today. Its members deleted their pacifist statement in 1967, fifty years after it had been adopted, though perhaps the belief had long since diminished. Certainly the position against Christian participation in war changed, but more than that changed. The Assemblies of God needs to be viewed as part of a larger movement; it is not the only denomination to have abandoned an earlier witness against war.[11] Early pacifism and later support for war has occurred in many Christian renewal movements, including Methodism, Holiness groups, Baptists of various kinds, Churches of Christ, Quakerism—and is even now happening to some degree among the Brethren and Mennonites. Perhaps these Christian movements that start out as pacifistic and then change have elements in common.

Working through why the early Assemblies of God preached pacifism and then why their peace witness eroded leads to a third question. Which way—pacifist or bellicist, peacemaking or warmaking—fits the ethos of Pentecostalism? The answer depends on how one understands Pentecostalism and Christianity, and this book will show that it largely depends on how one focuses on Jesus' teachings and how much one conforms to American and broader religious society. If Pentecostalism is essentially the empowerment of the Holy Spirit to follow Jesus and make disciples of all nations, and Jesus is authoritative on the war/killing question, then nonviolence fits perfectly (as it actually did historically). If Pentecostalism is the empowerment of the Holy Spirit to make disciples of all nations, but the defense of America and the existence of warfare in the Hebrew Scriptures are authoritative on the war/killing question, then warmaking it is (as is currently the case in the American Assemblies of God).

These questions deserve thorough answers, and many Pentecostals have wrestled with them. The arguments of the Assemblies of God itself will serve as the evidence for how varying views of the place of war fit within the witness of Pentecostal believers.

METHODOLOGY

This narrative of Assemblies of God pacifism ambles through the twentieth century and ends up at the cusp of the twenty-first century. Assemblies of God people lived then and now in the context of many layers of overlapping events and as participants in different stories. Chapter two focuses on four contemporaneous stories in the early 1900s—the tales of America, Christianity, Pentecostalism, and pacifism—and these provide the context in which to understand the emergence of the peace witness in the Assemblies of God. It also prepares the way for an understanding of how Assemblies of God folk balanced their identities as Americans, Christians, Pentecostals, and pacifists. Chapter three explores Quaker and Holiness influences on Assemblies of God pacifism and clarifies how Pentecostal theology allowed conscientious objection to fit so well.

But this story concerns more than the Assemblies of God origins as a pacifist fellowship. Their later transformation must be examined. Using a narrative methodology, chapters four through seven explore conscientious objection, American patriotism, the authority of individual conscience, and ministry to the military within sequential chronological slices of Assemblies of God history. Chapter eight introduces Pentecostal scholars (and others) who have explored—and some who seek to reinvigorate—a Pentecostal peace witness. Chapter nine offers a reflective analysis of the dramatic change that occurred by considering the importance of Jesus and the dangers of desiring acceptance and effectiveness.

THE SCOPE OF EARLY ASSEMBLIES OF GOD PACIFISM

Early Pentecostals sometimes disagreed about pacifism and war. These tensions have led scholars to debate the extent of pacifism in the early Assemblies of God. This book joins this discussion. Jay Beaman, Roger Robins, Howard Kenyon, and Dwight Wilson have argued that the majority of the early Assemblies of God held noncombatant views and supported conscientious objection.[12] However, Murray Dempster has suggested that pacifists constituted a prophetic minority in the Assemblies of God, and Grant Wacker has claimed that Assemblies of God pacifism disappeared by the end of World War I.[13]

When viewing the evidence, decisive factors include the weight given to the many official pacifist statements and articles themselves, the longevity of the position—it lasted for twenty-two years after World War II—and the nationalistic and pro-war context in which it arose. In anticipation of the chapters that follow, the basic arguments will be reviewed here. This book will argue that pacifism likely represented the majority stance among a population of Christians who primarily concerned themselves with evangelism rather than war. Arguments for Jesus-centered nonviolence were quite persuasive in that context.

Early Assemblies of God Pacifism as a Majority

Jay Beaman stated that "overwhelming pacifist belief characterized the [early Pentecostal] movement" and the early Assemblies of God had been "largely pacifist."[14] He based the former claim on the fact that sixty-two percent of denominations formed before 1917 and fifty percent of those formed before 1934 had at one time contained a pacifistic statement of some kind.[15] He founded both claims on the "literary witness" which revealed that key leaders in each denomination supported pacifistic views. The earlier the formation of a Pentecostal denomination, the greater the chance that it would declare itself opposed to the destruction of human life in warfare, but even twenty percent of those formed after 1934 contained "pacifist belief."[16] Since the General Council of the Assemblies of God organized in 1914, three years before American participation in World War I, and created its military statement in 1917, its members exemplified an early Pentecostal denomination opposed to killing in war.

Beaman's contention that the majority of early Pentecostals held pacifist beliefs is true if official statements actually reflected the beliefs of the majority of constituents. Beaman blamed the loss of pacifism on the cultural accommodation that the Assemblies of God experienced: "upward mobility . . . may have been the single greatest factor in the change that took place. . . . Religiously and socially, Pentecostals were moving into the mainstream and it seems likely that their values would reflect that move."[17]

Roger Robins agreed with Beaman. Robins argued, "The bulk of literature on the topic in Assemblies of God organs was decidedly pacifistic." Thus, "the resolution represented the majority sentiment."[18] However, Robins recognized that several irregular circumstances surrounding the resolution raised questions regarding the extent of its acceptance. First, the General Council never received the opportunity to vote to accept the resolution when it met in August 1917. It had been approved only by the executive presbytery in April 1917, then forwarded to Washington, D. C. Robins reasoned that this possibly happened because of the lack of uniformity on the topic. In other words, since it might not pass they should not take a chance on a vote.

But the constituency did vote in 1927 and 1947 to keep the resolution in. This meant it was affirmed by the majority of the Assemblies of God—even after World Wars I and II. If pacifism was not the majority position in the early Assemblies of God, the statement would surely have been changed after World War I—but was not. Ample opportunities existed for altering or deleting it after World War II—but this did not happen. This retention of the statement even after World War II points to its majority status in at least the first generation of the Assemblies of God.

Other evidence also points toward the majority status of pacifism. The Assemblies of God did not enforce the statement and added qualifications that allowed members to use their own consciences. At least one leader (E. N. Bell) supported those who wished to fight. However, even Bell printed pacifist articles for the *Pentecostal Evangel*. Therefore, Robins concluded that pacifism "must be viewed as an expression of majority opinion both in the Assemblies of God and in the Pentecostal movement at large . . . [which] was predominantly, though not uniformly, pacifistic in its convictions."[19] Writing to the Assemblies of God in their own literature, Robins told them, "Despite the presence of diversity, pacifism was clearly the predominant view."[20] Robins blamed the loss of pacifism on the neglect of Scripture and "assimilation into mainstream American culture."[21]

Howard Kenyon concurred with Beaman and Robins. He insisted that "pacifism was a popular position throughout the ranks of Pentecostalism" until the end of World War I.[22] However, Kenyon claimed that the cultural assimilation thesis overgeneralized. He argued that the demise of pacifism occurred because the early Assemblies of God held apparently conflicting beliefs that they did not reconcile: authority of conscience, pacifism, loyalty to the government, and evangelism.[23] These four themes are examined in detail in the following chapters.

Dwight Wilson wrote that "the literature of early Pentecostals indicates that they were generally but not universally pacifist" and that before the American entry into World War I "most American Pentecostals were adamantly opposed to war."[24] These scholars, while recognizing diversity and tension, agreed that the majority within the early Assemblies of God believed in abstinence from the violence of warfare. They had differing yet complementary explanations for the demise of pacifism from a majority stance to a practically nonexistent position.

Early Assemblies of God Pacifism as a Minority

Grant Wacker and Murray Dempster argued that pacifism was a minority position in the early Assemblies of God. As a leading historian of Pentecostalism, Wacker states that his own "interpretation runs closer to the older, prerevisionist literature which (for different reasons) minimized the breadth and depth of pacifism in the tradition."[25] Dempster thought that "the loss of pacifism seems almost incredible within such a short time-frame if pacifism was the majority position among Pentecostals."[26] But Assemblies of God pacifism withstood two world wars and persisted even while numerous other denominations changed their position. The following conversation with Dempster and Wacker will provide the core of the argument that the majority in the early Assemblies of God were pacifists. The rest of the book will fill in additional details.

Dempster advocated the minority view for several reasons. First, he noted that the issue was controversial from the outset of the discussion in 1914. Several pastors and the Texas District Council sided with the government rather than the "radical" preachers who opposed the flag in 1918.[27] However, this book will show that entertaining the views of the Texas Council merely reflects the sensitive and intimidating wartime context and the respect of leaders for all views in time of war. Chapter four explains this in much more detail, but note that leaders did not renounce their peace witness; they simply couched it in language respectful of the government. By first stating their loyalty to America, they were able to reject killing and support conscientious objection less abrasively than did preachers such as Frank Bartleman.

Second, Dempster observed that the pacifistic articles in the early years had a persuasive character, as if the authors addressed them to an unconvinced majority.[28] It is certainly correct that many articles reflected the author's desire to persuade, but that rhetorical orientation reflects the ever-widening audience of *The Pentecostal Evangel*. Furthermore, articles about tongues as the initial physical evidence were written in persuasive mode as well—and speaking in tongues was central to the definition of what it meant to be a Pentecostal.

Third, Dempster argued that the 1917 statement emerged from questionable circumstances. He believes that "it was politically necessary to protect those Pentecostals who were pacifists—whatever their number—from military service."[29] He explains that the Assemblies of God responded to pressure from the government by making "demonstrably hyperbolic" claims about their pacifism to qualify for exemption.

However, the Assemblies of God took a huge risk as a fledgling organization to take the stand against war that it did, risking even the publication of the valuable *Pentecostal Evangel*. In the context of wartime America very few, if any, organizations risked themselves for a position that they did not really hold. And most other Pentecostal denominations concurred. The fact that the Assemblies of God adopted and publicly proclaimed a counter-cultural teaching in such a dangerous context seems to show that it was a majority position. Add to this the fact that the Assemblies of God produced a large number of noncombatants during World War II, and we have significant evidence that pacifism was a meaningful part of the ethos of early Pentecostalism.

Fourth, Dempster pointed to the words of pacifists such as Donald Gee and Frank Bartleman who chided the Pentecostals for their pro-war actions during World War I.[30] But Gee and Bartleman actually critiqued the entire church, not just the Pentecostal movement. Gee directed most of his condemnations toward "the nominal churches of Christendom."[31] Since he had been writing about the global church's failure during the war, Bartleman qualified his statement when he addressed Pentecostals. A woman told him that she and her conscientious objector son "suffered equally . . . in insults, scorn and slurring remarks heaped upon [them], *even by many Pentecostal professors*."[32] Both Gee and Bartleman recognized that some Pentecostals had been patriotic and militant during World War I and bemoaned the fact. These observations from Gee and Bartleman provided the basis for Dempster's conclusion that

> the change in the Pentecostal position on military service makes more sense if explained as a loss of a prophetic minority of pacifists. . . . But before they had an opportunity to cultivate a pacifist *tradition* based on shared theology and ethics, history had overtaken them and the patriotic war spirit invaded the house never to leave.[33]

In 1997, Beaman responded to Dempster's conclusion with "serious questions" that argued once again for pacifism as the majority view among the early Assemblies of God.[34] Beaman questioned why the Assemblies of God would have been so inclusive of a minority position and pointed out that the Assemblies of God did not distance themselves from pacifism the way a non-pacifist majority would have.[35] Beaman also argued that the Assemblies of God had to change the way they interpreted the Bible and had to wait for the older generation to "pass from the scene" before they could change the statement. He insisted that these facts show a "deeper affirmation of pacifism than Dempster allows."[36] In other words, even when the later statistics clearly show that pacifism was a minority, the Assemblies of God still respected the biblical basis for the position. Beaman did not believe that the convictions of a pacifist minority would be printed by a majority who disagreed with them.[37] Those opposed to pacifism made up only a small minority.

Finally, Beaman questioned whether early Assemblies of God pacifists did theology differently than nonpacifists. The evidence within this book shows that pacifists relied more heavily on Jesus, the New Testament, and narrative sections of the Bible than did nonpacifists, while militants referred much less often to Jesus and employed the Hebrew Scriptures and Romans 13:1-7 more regularly.

Grant Wacker proposed that the Assemblies of God only "permitted a variety of views in its official publication until 1917, when the United States entered the conflict" and that "after May [1917], no more articles supporting pacifism appeared in official publications."[38] However, the extensive evidence in chapter three of this book shows that the Assemblies of God published articles and encouraged conscientious objection and noncombatant service during American participation in World War I,[39] immediately after the war ended, throughout the 1920s and 1930s, and into the early 1940s.[40] Furthermore, attempts to change the pacifist article in the constitution and bylaws of the Assemblies of God failed in the 1940s; it was not finally eliminated until 1967. This alone suggests that pacifism was a significant part of the tradition and did not disappear during World War I.

During the spring and summer preceding the publication of the pacifist statement, there was the enactment of the Selective Service Act (May 18, 1917), the wide unveiling of the famous "I Want You" posters, and extremely high patriotism and popular support for the war. American flags draped buildings and avenues throughout the United States, yet the executive presbytery of the Assemblies of God could confidently proclaim that "the principles of the General Council were in opposition to war from its very beginning" and that "the General Council meets every requirement of the law relating to religious bodies . . . whose religious principles are opposed to participation in war."[41] This witness by the Assemblies of God in the face of intense nationalism and support for war led the U.S. government to recognize it as a pacifist church, and the anti-combatant articles continued to outnumber significantly the pro-combatant ones.

Wacker also claimed that "no one requested prayers for conscientious objectors. . . . One can only assume that they were either too few to count or that editors screened out such requests, knowing how most readers would react."[42] Yet the April 28, 1917, edition carried exactly such a request and testimony of a Pentecostal conscientious objector.[43] Wacker reasons that published prayer requests for soldiers show the lack of commitment to conscientious objection, yet the very issue he quotes (October 5, 1918) also contained Arthur Sydney Booth-Clibborn's article advocating nonviolence, for "the true conscientious objector is the sort of Christian who is gladly willing to go unarmed among the savage heathen, far beyond the 'protecting' reach of a six inch shell. He is equally willing to dispense with all 'protection' in 'civilized lands.'"

E. N. Bell (1866-1923), General Superintendent of the Assemblies of God in 1914 and from 1920-1923, supported Christian participation in war more than any other leader in the early Assemblies of God. Wacker suggested that "there is no evidence that any elected official within the denomination publicly resisted Bell or his point of view."[44] However, there is ample evidence that at least thirteen different authors wrote articles in the *Evangel* that opposed Bell's view. These included three General Superintendents, two General Secretaries who also served as editors of *The Pentecostal Evangel* for a combined thirty-six years, and a college dean.[45]

In fact, just shortly after Bell's death the "darkening clouds" of war prompted an article by elected leader and editor Stanley Frodsham in which he encouraged constituents not to participate should the occasion arise. He quoted a Quaker resolution passed in Philadelphia that called violence "unchristian" and renounced "for the future all participation in war."[46] He then stated that

> when the editor [Stanley Frodsham] of the paper [*The Pentecostal Evangel*] received a copy and handed the same to the Chairman of the Council [General Superintendent], Brother Welch expressed the warmest sympathy for the sentiments of the Friends. The statement on our Council minutes concerning nonparticipation in war is *somewhat stronger* than the above.[47]

Frodsham confidently and rightly recognized that the Assemblies of God had adopted a stricter stance against war than the Quakers themselves, and this in 1924. Bell might have been vocal about the authority of the Christian's individual conscience to allow him to fight, but those who preceded him and most of those who followed him for the next two decades consistently presented conscientious objection as the Pentecostal path of faithfulness.

Even while Bell was General Superintendent of the Assemblies of God from 1920 to 1923, several articles appeared that promoted pacifism. In 1920 Arthur Sydney Booth-Clibborn claimed that any participation in warfare cheapened both Calvary and Pentecost and was "a disaster of untold magnitude."[48] In 1922 D. M. Panton preached that

> the Church's right attitude to war [is to] at least refuse to participate in war herself, and so make good her profession of peace. In the first two centuries of our era, so swordless was the Church of Christ, that Celsus, the Gnostic, in the first written attack ever made on the Christian Faith, grounds his censure on this very fact, and says: The State receives no help in war from the Christians; and if all men were to follow their example, the Sovereign would be deserted, and the world would fall into the hands of barbarians.[49]

So while some claim that Bell represented the attitude of the Assemblies of God and the pacifists were a minority that quickly disappeared, it seems that Bell was actually almost a lone voice who could not silence the conscientious objectors. Pacifist authors published articles in the primary Assemblies of God publications before, during, and after Bell's time in office. Even World War II, twenty years later, did not convince the Assemblies of God constituency to change their official position of conscientious objection.

In fact, the pacifist voice within the Assemblies of God actually existed right up to World War II. In 1938 the General Superintendent of the Assemblies of God in the United States reprinted the pacifist position statement, wanting to reflect on war "while free from the emotional effects of such events."[50] He desired to "assist the thinking of our youth in the event that they should be called for military service" and he did so by emphasizing the nonviolence to which the Assemblies of God was committed.

Could not such a one [if drafted] serve as a cook, a helper in a hospital, a stretcher carrier, a driver of an ambulance, or of a truck? There are many services which one could fulfill without 'armed resistance which involves the actual destruction of human life.'[51]

In 1939 *The Pentecostal Evangel* published articles that declared, "War does not fit in with the teaching and example of our Lord Jesus Christ. This is in accordance with the Christian teaching of the first three centuries," and "it was usual for a soldier to lay down his sword when he accepted the truth of Christ. The declaration of faith has become historic: 'I am a Christian, and therefore I cannot fight.'"[52] In May 1940, *The Pentecostal Evangel* printed a powerful promotion of conscientious objection by Donald Gee, General Superintendent of the Assemblies of God in Britain.[53] The timing of this article by the American Assemblies of God revealed that they were trying to hold to their peace witness, for one month later the American General Superintendent quoted the *Pacifist Handbook* as listing the Assemblies of God, with 173,349 members, as the third largest church in America that "opposed . . . war."[54] He then said, "The Assemblies of God may well be classified among the 'conscientious objectors.' It is doubtful that it could be classified among the unqualified 'pacifists,' since it is pledged to 'assist the Government in time of war in every way morally possible."[55]

As late as October 1940, *The Pentecostal Evangel* proclaimed that the "*universal* feeling in the ranks of the Assemblies of God [is] that military service is incompatible with the gospel of Jesus Christ, and that a Christian cannot fully follow the teachings of his Lord and Master if he engages in armed conflict."[56] The author exhorted constituents to be sure that they were true conscientious objectors and not just "hid[ing] behind the position of the church to which they belong."[57] He also recommended the *Pacifist Handbook*. His article revealed that the leaders of the Assemblies of God believed, or at least claimed, that the "general belief" of Assemblies of God members in 1940 was that combatant participation in war was wrong.[58] The sincerity of this claim can be doubted, but the fact remains that they continued to teach conscientious objection.

In view of the significant participation of Assemblies of God men in World War II, the 1947 General Council appointed a committee to evaluate the appropriateness of the article on military service. They realized that their actions as a fellowship had not exactly corresponded to their stated position. However, the committee reported that they had not found it necessary to change the position.

> After considerable thought and prayer on this very vital subject, your committee feels that it will be unable to formulate an article on Military Service that will better represent the attitude of the Assemblies of God than that which is now a part of our General Council By-laws.[59]

This report was adopted *without debate*. One can doubt the extent of Assemblies of God pacifism in 1947, but the ministers and elected officials did not take this opportunity to change the pacifist doctrine. Perhaps at this point the fellowship was not ready to overturn the strongly worded Jesus-focused scriptural support for nonviolence, or perhaps so many leaders still agreed with it that they did not want to change it. The fact that perhaps as many as half of Assemblies of God men had chosen noncombatant service also meant that the statement did in fact still represent many Pentecostals. Regardless of the explanation, the Assemblies of God reaffirmed the pacifist doctrine in 1947, and it lasted another twenty years before the Vietnam era constituency finally deleted it.

My interpretation of pacifism within the early Assemblies of God in particular and early Pentecostalism in general supports those scholars who argued that pacifism was the majority position. First-generation Pentecostals wrote about and promoted conscientious objection in official publications quite often, the denominational leaders continued to support the stance publicly until at least 1941, and the constituency reaffirmed it in 1947. Furthermore, "quite a large number"[60] of conscientious objectors and noncombatants in the third-largest peace church in America during World War II are best explained by the interpretation that pacifism was deeply and broadly integrated into the first-generation Pentecostal worldview. Further evidence throughout the rest of this book will support this view.

DEFINING AND RESTORING THE NEW TESTAMENT CHURCH

Much of the impetus for the Pentecostal movement as a whole, from which the Assemblies of God emerged, came from the recognition that the Holy Spirit was empowering both men and women to proclaim to the entire world the gospel of Jesus the Messiah. They believed this was happening just as in Acts, when the Spirit was poured out on the day of Pentecost and the early Christians then preached about Jesus and lived as Jesus wanted them to. Jesus was essential to their way of being in the world. Whether one calls this their theology, ethics, worldview, hermeneutic, ideology, or lifestyle, one thing is clear: Jesus was in the center of their thinking and doing, their words and deeds. Where the New Testament said, "Long ago God spoke to the fathers through the prophets at different times and in different ways, but in these last days he has spoken to us by his Son . . . the exact representation of his character,"[61] Pentecostals said, "Military service is incompatible with the gospel of Jesus Christ."[62] Since Christians were and are followers of the Christ, the teachings and example of Jesus the Christ were central to their understanding of their place in the world.

Though it might seem odd to have to argue for the primacy of Jesus for Christians, he has been an elusive figure in some Christians' discussions of war and peace. This journey through Assemblies of God history will show how seriously the pacifists took Jesus, how they would not separate him from their ethics, and how their enthusiasm to evangelize the world was not divided from their arguments about war and peace. They used Scripture to help them define what the New Testament church looked like (tongues, healings, signs and wonders, love of enemy), and they unashamedly attempted to participate in what they believed was the restoration of God's people in the last days. Though this restorationism may seem quaint, it was a powerfully cohesive motif that provided a clear authority to which to appeal (Jesus and his followers as revealed in Scripture) and a clear path of faithfulness to be walked (crucifism/conscientious objection/nonviolence).

NOTES

1. http://ag.org/top/about/history.cfm (accessed July 17, 2007).

2. The General Council of the Assemblies of God (AG) is referred to both as the General Council and as the Assemblies of God. Within this book, the singular Assembly of God refers to one individual congregation within the denomination.

3. *General Council Combined Minutes 1914-1917* (Springfield, Mo.: Gospel Publishing House, 1917), 11-12. Also in "The Pentecostal Movement and the Conscription Law," *The Weekly Evangel*, 4 August 1917, 6. The full statement makes five references to specific scriptures: Luke 2:14, Hebrews 12:14, Exodus 20:13, Matthew 5:39, and Matthew 5:44.

4. *Minutes of the General Council of the Assemblies of God* (Springfield, Mo.: Gospel Publishing House, 1967), 14.

5. Lisa Sowle Cahill, *Love Your Enemies: Discipleship, Pacifism, and Just War Theory* (Minneapolis: Fortress, 1994), 2.

6. John Howard Yoder has identified nineteen varieties of religious pacifism in *Nevertheless: The Varieties and Shortcomings of Religious Pacifism* (Scottdale, Pa.: Herald Press, 1992).

7. Martin Ceadel, *Thinking About War and Peace* (Oxford: Oxford University Press, 1987), 2.

8. Crucifist is also the name of a "Death Metal" band whose motto is "Skull-Smashing Face-Ripping Death."

9. "First and fundamental in the Anabaptist vision was the conception of the essence of Christianity as discipleship.... Disciples must deny themselves and take up their cross daily and follow Him." Harold Bender, *Anabaptist Vision* (Scottdale, Pa.: Herald Press, 1944), 20, 35.

10. *General Council Minutes 1914-1917* (Springfield, Mo.: Gospel Publishing House, 1917), 11-12.

11. Michael W. Casey, "From Patriotism to Pacifism: The Emergence of Civil Religion in the Church of Christ during World War I," *Mennonite Quarterly Review* 66 (1992): 376-390.

12. Jay Beaman, *Pentecostal Pacifism: The Origin, Development, and Rejection of Pacific Belief Among the Pentecostals.* Forward by John Howard Yoder (Hillsboro, Kan.: Center for Mennonite Brethren Studies, 1989); Roger Robins, "A Chronology of Peace: Attitudes Toward War and Peace in the Assemblies of God: 1914-1918." *Pneuma* 6 (Spring 1984): 3-25; Howard Kenyon, "An Analysis of Ethical Issues in the History of the Assemblies of God." Ph.D. diss., Baylor University, 1988; Dwight J. Wilson, "Pacifism," *Dictionary of Pentecostal and Charismatic Movements*, ed. Stanley M. Burgess and Gary B. McGee (Grand Rapids, Mich.: Zondervan, 1988). Murray W. Dempster, "Reassessing the Moral Rhetoric of Early American Pentecostal Pacifism," *Crux* 26 (March 1990): 23-36.

13. Murray Dempster, "Jay Beaman, *Pentecostal Pacifism: The Origins, Development and Rejection of Pacific Belief among the Pentecostals* (Hillsboro, Kansas: Center for Mennonite Brethren Studies, 1989), 142 pp. $10.00 paper. Reviewed by Murray W. Dempster," *Pneuma* 11, no. 1 (Fall 1989): 60. Murray W. Dempster, "Reassessing the Moral Rhetoric of Early American Pentecostal Pacifism," *Crux* 26, no. 1 (March 1990): 23-36. Murray W. Dempster, "'Crossing Borders:' Arguments Used By Early American Pentecostals in Support of the Global Character of Pacifism," *The Journal of the European Pentecostal Theological Association* 10, no. 2 (1991): 63-80. Pacifism in Pentecostalism: The Case of the Assemblies of God," in *Proclaim Peace: Christian Pacifism from Unexpected Quarters,* ed. Theron F. Schlabach and Richard T. Hughes (Champaign, Ill.: University of Illinois Press, 1997), 31-57. Grant Wacker, *Heaven Below* (Cambridge, Mass.: Harvard University Press, 2001).

14. Jay Beaman, *Pentecostal Pacifism*, 21, 73.

15. Ibid., 29. These statements, including the Assemblies of God's, generally allowed noncombatant service.

16. Ibid., 30.

17. Ibid., 107.

18. Roger Robins, "A Chronology of Peace," 23.

19. Ibid., 24.

20. Robins, "Our Forgotten Heritage," 4.

21. Ibid.

22. Kenyon, "An Analysis," 396.

23. Ibid., 397.

24. Wilson, "Pacifism," 658.

25. Wacker, *Heaven Below*, 347.

26. Dempster, "Crossing Borders," 74.

27. Ibid., 75.

28. Ibid., 74. Dempster, "Jay Beaman," 62-63.

29. Dempster, "Crossing Borders," 75.

30. Ibid.

31. Donald Gee, "War, the Bible, and the Christian," *The Pentecostal Evangel*, 8 November 1930, 6.

32. Frank Bartleman, "War and the Christian," tract, circa 1922, 3. Bold emphasis in the original.

33. Ibid., 75-76. Emphasis in the original.

34. Jay Beaman, "Pacifism Among the Early Pentecostals, Conflicts Within and Without: A Response to Murray W. Dempster and Theodore Kornweibel Jr.," in *Proclaim Peace: Christian Pacifism From Unexpected Quarters*, ed. Theron F. Schlabach and Richard T. Hughes (Champaign, Ill.: University of Illinois Press, 1997), 85.

35. Ibid.

36. Ibid., 86.

37. Ibid., 87.

38. Ibid., 243, 245.

39. The following authors argued for pacifism and conscientious objection in 1917 and 1918, during World War I. These were all printed in *The Weekly Evangel* (which later became *The Pentecostal Evangel*). Baron D'Estournelles de Constant, "The Sinister Education of War," *The Weekly Evangel*, 20 January 1917, 2. "What is War?" *The Weekly Evangel*, 21 April 1917, 2. "The Crisis," *The Weekly Evangel*, 21 April 1917, 7. Samuel H. Booth-Clibborn, "The Christian and War. Is it too Late?," *The Weekly Evangel*, 28 April 1917, 5. "Compulsory Military Service: An English Conscientious Objector's Testimony," *The Weekly Evangel*, 28 April 1917, 7. Samuel H. Booth-Clibborn, "The Christian and War," *The Weekly Evangel*, 19 May 1917, 4. J. W. Welch, "An Explanation," *The Weekly Evangel*, 19 May 1917, 8. "The Pentecostal Movement and the Conscription Law," *The Weekly Evangel*, 4 August 1917, 6. "The Pentecostal Movement and the Conscription Law," *The Weekly Evangel*, 5 January 1918, 5. Oscar Barl, "Reports From the Field: Fort Riley, Kansas," *The Weekly Evangel*, 19 October 1918, 14. A. B. Cox, "In Prison and Out Again," *The Weekly Evangel*, 29 June 1918, 14. Arthur Sydney Booth-Clibborn, "Nigh, Even At The Doors," 7 September 1918, 2.

40. The following authors argued for pacifism and conscientious objection in the years following World War I and during World War II. Lydia Hatfield, "The Law of Christ for Believers," *The Christian Evangel*, 12 July 1919, 3. Arthur Sydney Booth-Clibborn, "European Pentecostal Notes," *The Pentecostal Evangel*, 6 March 1920, 11. D. M. Panton, "Coming War," *The Pentecostal Evangel*, 25 November 1922, 10. Stanley H. Frodsham, "From The Pentecostal Viewpoint," *The Pentecostal Evangel*, 21 June 1924, 4. Donald Gee, "War, the Bible, and the Christian," *The Pentecostal Evangel*, 8 November 1930, 6. Donald Gee, "War, the Bible, and the Christian," *The Pentecostal Evangel*, 15 November 1930, 2. "War Behind the Smoke Screen," *The Pentecostal Evangel*, 6 December 1930, 3. Ernest S. Williams, "In Case of War," *The Pentecostal Evangel*, 19 March 1938, 4. "The Christian and War," *The Pentecostal Evangel*, 29 July 1939, 2. "War and Christianity," *The Pentecostal Evangel*, 23 September 1939, 10. Edmund B. Chaffee, "The Early Church and the Sword," *The Pentecostal Evangel*, 27 January 1940, 3.

41. Ibid., 7.

42. Wacker, *Heaven Below*, 247.

43. "Compulsory Military Service: An English Conscientious Objector's Testimony," *The Weekly Evangel*, 28 April 1917, 7.

44. Wacker, *Heaven Below*, 247.

45. John W. Welch, Earnest S. Williams, and Donald Gee were superintendents and William Burton McCafferty was a college dean and founding member of the Assemblies of God. Stanley Frodsham was elected as General Secretary (1916), Missionary Treasurer (1917), and then editor of all Assemblies of God publications (1921-1949). J. Roswell Flower, also a founding member of the Assemblies of God, served as its first Secretary-Treasurer (1914) and founder and first editor of the *Evangel* (1913-1920). He continued in elected leadership until 1959.

46. Stanley H. Frodsham, "From The Pentecostal Viewpoint," *The Pentecostal Evangel*, 21 June 1924, 4.

47. Ibid. Emphasis added.

48. Arthur Sydney Booth-Clibborn, "European Pentecostal Notes," *The Pentecostal Evangel*, 6 March 1920, 11.

49. D. M. Panton, "Coming War," *The Pentecostal Evangel*, 25 November 1922, 10.

50. Ernest S. Williams, "In Case of War," *The Pentecostal Evangel*, 19 March 1938, 4.

51. Ibid.

52. *The Pentecostal Evangel*, 29 July 1939, 2. *The Pentecostal Evangel*, 23 September 1939, 10.

53. Donald Gee, "Conscientious Objection," *The Pentecostal Evangel*, 4 May 1940, 4.

54. Ernest S. Williams, "The Conscientious Objector," *The Pentecostal Evangel*, 15 June 1940, 4. The two larger ones were the Churches of Christ (433,714) and the Brethren (192,588). The Quakers were listed as having 105,917 members.

55. Ibid.

56. "The Attitude of the General Council Toward Military Service," *The Pente-

costal Evangel, 12 October 1940, 13. Emphasis added. Based upon the context of the other articles that supported noncombatant service, this article probably referred to combatant military service.

57. Ibid.

58. Ibid.

59. General Council Minutes, 1947, 13.

60. J. Roswell Flower, "The Plight of the Christian in the Present World War," The Pentecostal Evangel, 12 June 1943, 6.

61. Hebrews 1.1-3, author's translation.

62. "The Attitude of the General Council Toward Military Service," The Pentecostal Evangel, 12 October 1940, 13.

TWO

AMERICAN, CHRISTIAN, PENTECOSTAL, AND PACIFIST: THE HISTORICAL CONTEXT OF THE FIRST-GENERATION ASSEMBLIES OF GOD

INTRODUCTION

The emergent days of Pentecostalism (1901-1920) occurred within the splendor and power, the pain and suffering, and the expanding wealth of Progressive Era America. Americans, Christians, Pentecostals, and pacifists had as many opinions about war then as they do now, and the location of the Assemblies of God on the spectrum set them apart from many other American Christians, for they were much more opposed to war than the average Christian in the United States. The Assemblies of God distanced itself from political nonreligious pacifists but expressed appreciative kinship with other Christian pacifists, such as the Quakers. But this chapter is not about the American Assemblies of God directly; instead it sketches the contexts in which it emerged to espouse nonviolence as an official denominational position. Understanding these seminal Pentecostals and their contemporaries requires viewing them against a series of issues, contexts, and movements in the early twentieth century: the United States, other Christian denominations, Pentecostalism in general, and other pacifists and peace churches.

Many scholars have investigated and written about the formative years of Pentecostalism.[1] One of the most influential was Robert Mapes Anderson's contribution, *Vision of the Disinherited: The Making of American Pentecostalism*.[2] He developed the thesis that the root source of the Pentecostal movement was social discontent. He claimed that the sociological setting of the early Pentecostals was remarkably similar to that of the early Church.[3] This allowed the early Pentecostals to understand and imitate the "ecstatic millenarianism that permeates the New Testament" when other Christians of higher social status overlooked (or ignored) that element of early Christianity. "The world of the early Pentecostals," reports Mapes,

> was one of share-cropping and tenant-farming, of backwoods cabins and ghetto tenements, of poverty and unemployment, of crime and vice, of racism and discrimination, of grinding, monotonous labor and fatigue, of material squalor and spiritual despair. Encumbered with racial and ethnic characteristics that constituted ineradicable handicaps in American society, faced with near-insuperable social and economic obstacles, restricted by background and opportunity from direct assault on the fundamental sources of their unhappy state, the Pentecostals found in Pentecostalism not only solace, but meaning and purpose for their lives.

Pondering the marginal status of Pentecostals, Mapes memorably observes that

> Rejected by the world, the Pentecostals in turn rejected the world. Lacking the skills and opportunities to improve their fortunes in this world, they renounced worldly success and developed their talents within the limits of the community of the Spirit. Denied the satisfaction of social relationships devoid of prejudice and condescension, they found salvation in a sublime experience of union with the Divine that carried them above their grueling, insipid lives, and in the fantastic contemplation of an imminent reversal of social roles and rewards.[4]

While many scholars disagree that the origins of Pentecostalism can be reduced to socio-economic factors and the deprivation theory, they still recognize the lower socio-economic status of many first-generation Pentecostals.[5] In *Heaven Below,* Grant Wacker perceptively recognizes that "a minority found themselves stuck at the bottom of the class and status ladder" while "a majority occupied the lower-median and median rungs of the social ladder."[6]

Sanchez-Walsh notes that "we can see that Pentecostals were not very different from the rest of American society, and, in fact, some of the early leaders had the financial or educational means or both to seek out a more 'respectable' religion not wedded to poor rural folk."[7] Early issues of *The Pentecostal Evangel* contain evidence that the Assemblies of God constituents were, along with most Americans, from the lower echelons of society. They were encouraged to trust God for train fare when there was a General Council.[8] The uneducated were heralded as the ones who could properly interpret the Bible, whereas only weak Christians succumbed to "German higher criticism."[9] Indeed, the early Pentecostals continually reminded themselves that the apostles were uneducated and poor and were still mightily used by God.[10]

Receiving honor from "the world" was considered a sure sign that one was going down the wrong path,[11] whereas humble and lowly people who experienced hostility from the world were the true followers of Christ.[12] Early Pentecostals referred to the "haves" and "have nots," clearly identifying themselves with the latter[13] while insisting that "Christians normally find themselves on the bottom."[14] Speaking against greedy capitalists, bankers, and manufacturers revealed that they considered themselves to be among the laboring poor, the same poor who were forced to fight wars for the rich.[15]

The early Pentecostals who asserted this crucifist theology did not come from the upper middle or upper socio-economic classes. They were marginalized and poor yet many came from "the stable working class;" they were not members of either the religious or secular establishments but many of them had decent jobs.[16] These radical evangelicals found it appropriate that God chose to begin the great Pentecostal work among "negroes, poor, lowly, ignorant, and despised . . . because there was no room for it in the modern church."[17]

THE UNITED STATES OF AMERICA
IN THE EARLY TWENTIETH CENTURY

The first twenty years of the twentieth century in America was an era of stark contrasts. A brief overview of events reveals the degree to which Americans experienced life differently. There was extreme change, excitement and fear, prosperity and poverty, living improvements for some and the lynching of hundreds of others. Production of steel and oil boomed, ethnic segregation stiffened both in practice and in the courts, women had to struggle valiantly to get the privilege of voting, and children worked by the millions in factories.[18] The first World Series was played in 1903. By 1910 ten million people per week, or eleven percent of the population of eighty-nine million, went to the movies, while one percent of African-American children were receiving an education.[19] Pentecostalism experienced its birth during this time of hope and trepidation. Assemblies of God pacifism reflects the texture of American life during this transitional period, as Pentecostalism flourished among both the materially less fortunate as well as the relatively stable middle class.

AFRICAN-AMERICANS

White American racist attitudes toward blacks have deep roots and the unfortunate legacy of racism is far reaching. The prevalent ideas of the late nineteenth and early twentieth centuries regarding race had notable and distinguished proponents. Abraham Lincoln, explaining the difference between releasing slaves and respecting black people, made his perspective clear in a speech in 1858.

> I am not, nor ever have been in favor of bringing about in any way the social and political equality of white and black races [applause]. I am not nor ever have been in favor of making voters or jurors of Negroes, nor of qualifying them to hold office, nor to intermarry with white people; and I will say in addition to this that there is a physical difference between the white and black races which I believe will forever forbid the two races living together on terms of social and political equality. And inasmuch as they cannot so live, while they do remain together there must be the position of superior and inferior, and I as much as any other man am in favor of having the superior position assigned to the white race. . . . I do not understand that because I do not want a Negro woman for a slave I must necessarily want her for a wife [Cheers and laughter]. So it seems quite possible for us to get along without making either slaves or wives of Negroes. I have never seen to

my knowledge a man, woman or child who was in favor of producing a perfect equality, social and political, between Negroes and white men. . . . I will to the very last stand by the law of this State, which forbids the marrying of white people with Negroes [Laughter and applause]. . . . I am not in favor of Negro citizenship [Renewed applause].[20]

This sheds light on why Reconstruction failed and why the states worked to prevent African-Americans from voting. The 1880s and 1890s saw the proliferation of exclusionary practices, including the nullifying of the Civil Rights Act of 1875, which had outlawed segregation. In 1896 the Supreme Court approved segregation, and by 1900 only five percent of eligible African-Americans voted in the South.[21] This legally sanctioned apartheid contributed to numerous kinds of violence against blacks in the South, where ninety percent of African-Americans resided. Historians recognize that few protested the "color line"; even many progressives who opposed child labor and supported both women's right to vote and labor unions overlooked the oppression of blacks.

Woodrow Wilson, president of the United States from 1912-1920 and the first southerner elected since the Civil War, called the pro-Ku Klux Klan movie *Birth of a Nation* "history written in lightning," imposed Jim Crow segregation in the District of Columbia, and opposed the admission of African-Americans to Princeton. He expressed his belief that blacks were an "inferior and ignorant race but would eventually, probably in two or three centuries, achieve a measure of economic or political, if not social, equality in America."[22] However, the National Association for the Advancement of Colored People (NAACP) was created in 1909 with both black and white leadership.

Within this context of legal segregation, white supremacy, and terrible treatment of American blacks, an amazingly interracial Pentecostal movement came about in 1906 in Los Angeles, California, under the humble leadership of William Seymour, a son of former slaves. The interracial worship and leadership led Frank Bartleman, a white preacher who participated in the Azusa Street revival, to observe with pride that "The color line was washed away in the blood [of Christ]."[23]

White bishops and black workers, men and women, Asians and Mexicans, white professors and black laundry women come together as equals (1906!). "Proud well-dressed preachers came to 'investigate.' Soon their high looks were replaced with wonder, then conviction comes, and very often you will find them in a short time wallowing on the dirty floor, asking God to forgive them and make them little children."[24]

Bishop Charles H. Mason (black) led the Church of God in Christ along with Elder William B. Holt (white) for several years, and many of the founders of the Assemblies of God participated in that fellowship from 1907-1913. Furthermore, it is generally agreed that many Pentecostal groups can trace their heritages to the multi-ethnic Azusa Street mission "where there were no differences in color, races, everybody was somebody, especially as long as you had received the Holy Ghost."[25]

Native Americans

As the nineteenth century ended, the Native American population of millions had been reduced to some fifty thousand people. Social scientists of the time predicted the extinction of the Amerindians due to the genocidal conquest and expansion of America. One commander of the U.S. Army wrote that "we took away their country and their means of support, broke up their mode of living, their habits of life, introduced disease and decay among them and it was for this and against this they made war. Could anyone expect less?"[26] Massacres such as Wounded Knee, South Dakota (1890), the giving of blankets intentionally infested with smallpox, the Dawes Act which forced relocation, and the general history of treatment of Native Americans did not prompt even progressives to address their situations. Instead, most were moved to "reservations" and regarded as inferior. Meanwhile the amount of land devoted to reservations for Native Americans had decreased seventy-four percent between 1880 and 1910.[27]

Women, Children, and Labor

During the early twentieth century, the situation of women, children, and laborers improved somewhat. Women worked for about one-third the wages that men earned, but they also formed the Women's Trade Union League in 1903 and were able to strike their way to better wages as well as unionize some sweatshops in the garment district of

New York City. Since women were excluded from politics, many focused on social reform for the seven to eight million working women who were mostly immigrants, African-Americans, and the rural poor. Not until 1920 did the ratification of the Nineteenth Amendment give women the right to vote in America.

By 1900 about two million children worked in coal mining, textile factories, and other industries, but laws were eventually enacted that began to restrict child labor. Almost ten million immigrants entered the United States between 1900 and 1910, forty percent of whom were illiterate. Injustice and abuse within industries were revealed by what Theodore Roosevelt called "muckrakers." These investigative reporters provided sensational reports of economic, social, and political evils to their readers. "Millions of middle-class people became aware of the many ways the American social reality contradicted the ideal image of America."[28] These muckrakers incrementally contributed to progressive reforms in America during these years. Upton Sinclair's *The Jungle*, published in 1906, revealed the cruel exploitation of workers and the filthy conditions in the meat packing industry and prompted President Roosevelt to investigate. The Meat Inspection Act and the Pure Food and Drug Act of 1906 were passed because of the realistic novel, but Sinclair observed that he "had aimed at their hearts and hit their stomachs."

Industrialization and expansion were thriving during this time, with such notables as J. P. Morgan, William Randolph Hurst, John D. Rockefeller, Henry Ford, and Andrew Carnegie flourishing. Carnegie Steel Company was the world's largest by 1901, and Carnegie himself was worth five hundred million dollars (equivalent to more than twelve billion dollars cash).[29] Economic growth and material acquisition were promoted as excellent ideals. Rockefeller's Standard Oil Trust controlled eighty five percent of America's oil capacity and made him America's first billionaire. By 1900, when the American Telephone and Telegraph Company (AT&T) acquired its monopoly, Americans were using over 800,000 telephones.

FOREIGN POLICY

Particularly relevant for this book is the subject of United States foreign policy. Toward the end of the nineteenth century, the United States became less isolationist and more involved in the affairs of foreign countries. It built a modern navy, expanded overseas trade, fought a war with Spain, and acquired a colonial empire (Samoa, Hawaii, Cuba, the Philippines, Guam, and Puerto Rico). Captain Alfred T. Mahan argued that expanding sea power would help expand commercial ties and strengthen overseas colonial possessions. Rockefeller and Carnegie were able to sell their products (steel, kerosene, etc.) to more markets because "an amalgam of powerful economic, strategic, and ideological forces provided an expansionist dynamic. Together they turned a hitherto inward-looking continental power into an expansionist and international power."[30]

President Theodore Roosevelt declared in 1904 that America must at times operate as "an international police power," and by 1916 the United States had militarily intervened in Cuba, Panama, Nicaragua, the Dominican Republic, Haiti, and Mexico.[31] Although President Woodrow Wilson claimed neutrality when the European War began in 1914, the economic ties to the Allied powers brought wartime prosperity to America. Wilson at first said America would not trade with warring nations so as to help shorten the war, but he soon rescinded his decision. The war trade with the Allies climbed from $753 million in 1914 (sixteen billion in 2006 dollars) to three billion in 1916 (fifty-six billion in 2006 dollars), with American banks making $2.3 billion in loans during the neutrality period.[32] By spring 1917, the "once mighty lords of international banking, the British . . . had mortgaged themselves heavily to American creditors." Trade with Germany dropped and loans from America amounted to 27 million dollars from 1914-1916. Once America entered the war it expended $33.5 billion, two thirds of which was borrowed and most of which was spent in America.

AMERICAN CHRISTIANITY IN THE EARLY TWENTIETH CENTURY

Christianity in the United States experienced both amazing fights and growth during the first twenty years of the 1900s. Evangelical revivalists fragmented over tribulation theories, Pentecostals emerged with disagreements amongst themselves, and fundamentalists battled both modernists and Pentecostals. George Marsden identified four varieties of Christianity and culture circa 1910 that help place Assemblies of God pacifism in the context of the views held by other American Christians during the same era: the premillennial extreme, the central tension, the preservation of Christian civilization, and the postmillennial transforming of culture by the word.[33] Many first-generation Pentecostals could be classified as "the premillennial extreme."

The Premillennial Extreme

Marsden describes a minority of dispensationalists who carried the cultural pessimism of premillennialism to its logical extreme. Their favorite topic was "the signs of the times," and they had a prophetic worldview through which they viewed world events in relation to the second coming of Christ. Famines, earthquakes, and war abounded, civilization had failed, and "so called Christian nations were ready to blow out each other's brains."[34] The wealth and luxury of the entrepreneurs fulfilled biblical prophecies of greed and depravity in the last days. Commercialization and global economic relationships were considered the resurrection of Babylon, "grasping after more, never content, and determined to rule, their wealth is a minister to corruption, an inspiration to official dishonesty, and a menace to the peace and comfort to society."[35]

Some of these extremists viewed progressive reforms as Satan's work; they did not even support the prohibition movement against alcohol. They were anti-socialist and anti-democracy since both were simply failed government systems, which were the weakness of iron mixed with clay revealed in Daniel's vision (Dan. 2). Advancements in science and technology showed the pride of humanity and the increase of knowledge that signaled the end of time. They argued that Christ rejected both the culture and the world, and this sometimes included separation from the "worldly church." Many "premillennial pessimists" withdrew from the established churches for "God's greatest call is separation."[36] None of these examples come from Pentecostals, but the *Pentecostal Evangel* and other Pentecostal publications presented extensively, if not exclusively, this same theology and relation to the world.

The Central Tension

The more typical approach in America during this time, what Marsden calls "central tension," beheld the same signs of the times but was more optimistic about socialism, democracy, and the work of the church. Ministers such as William B. Riley combined revivalism and social reform, working in urban ministries to relieve both sin and suffer ing. Riley believed that Christians should side with the poor against the rich and labor against capital, work for democracy, and elect reformers who would outlaw vices such as liquor.[37]

These dispensationalists in the middle valued evangelism over politics and therefore recognized the international political possibility of "a kind of peace that force can procure; but it will be a lull before the awful storm." They found unity in the Bible Institutes, of which they established almost a dozen by 1910. Moody Bible Institute valued Bible study above all other studies but encouraged one to read "intelligently and widely as time permits, giving the Bible first place always and reading other books through it."[38] However, these conservative Christians did not like the emotions exhibited by the likes of Billy Sunday (1862-1935) and Pentecostals. They forbade Sunday from coming to Moody Bible Institute, saying that he "outrages every accepted canon of religious worship."[39] Regarding social reform, which Marsden called the "most obvious practical test of the degree to which the culture and its welfare was considered a proper Christian concern," these sometimes optimistic premillennialists opposed liquor traffic, gambling, prostitution, and political corruption the same way they would "kick a banana peel off the sidewalk."[40]

The Preservation of Christian Civilization

William Jennings Bryan (1860-1925) typifies Marsden's third type of American Christians, those who desired to "preserve Christian civilization" through moral reform. Bryan was the leader of the Democratic Party from 1896 to 1912, ran for president three times, and served as secretary of state for Woodrow Wilson from 1913 to 1915. He pushed for the Bible and religion to be prominent in American civilization and promoted prohibition and international peace. He attempted to combine Christian piety and American democratic nationalism, believing that common sense could lead all humans toward Christian/American ideals. His optimism was based on a high view of inherent human morality, "a persistent faith in the essential goodness of Man who would respond immediately and wholeheartedly to the truth once he was made to see it and understand it."[41]

These Christians were ecumenical and sought an end to doctrinal exclusiveness, attacked the liquor trade and prostitution, and appealed for more "industrial work" for African-Americans. They also labored to "thoroughly Christianize America" by making Bible teaching mandatory in public schools and devoted days to international peace. The interdenominational Men and Religion Forward Movement, led primarily by conservative evangelicals, mobilized laymen to evangelism and social action.[42]

William Jennings Bryan pragmatically equated the defense of Christianity with the success of Western civilization. Unconcerned with the differences between Methodists, Baptists, and his own Presbyterianism, he preached Christian civilization as the "greatest that the world has ever known because it rests on a conception of life that makes life one unending progress toward higher things, with no limit to human advancement or development."[43] This was the most popular conservative view of Christianity and culture, sounding similar to the premillennialist Presbyterian Billy Sunday. They both presented a "simple do it yourself (with God's grace) Gospel message with the traditional American moral virtues of decency, patriotism, manliness, thrift, sobriety, piety, and hard work . . . a broad, somewhat tolerant, not highly doctrinal, moralistic, patriotic, and often optimistic version of evangelical Protestantism."[44]

Changing Culture With Doctrine

Those Americans who sought to "transform culture by the Word" are the fourth type of Christian in the early twentieth century. They agreed with Bryan and Sunday that Christianity and civilization were intimately connected, they disagreed over how the church's mission should be accomplished. This old school Presbyterian tradition embodied at Princeton Theological Seminary held three basic convictions. First, culture and its achievements were viewed pessimistically because of the pervasive effects of sin in humanity.

Second, separation of church and state meant that the church should fully abstain from involvement or proclamations regarding the running of the nation. Individuals could be political; not the church.

Third, the most important action of the church was to foster right belief from which may come moral action. But faith, as defined by the creeds, came first. Benjamin B. Warfield (1851–1921) represents this postmillennial approach to doctrinal purity as that which would allow Christianity "to reason its way to dominion." He believed the whole world would be won to Christ before his return through the preaching of the gospel. J. Gresham Machen (1881-1937), who also taught at Princeton, believed that evangelism and missions would only yield temporary fruit if not accompanied by the solid intellectual work of the universities, "what today is only a matter of academic speculation begins tomorrow to move armies and pull down empires."[45] Machen disagreed with both liberal and fundamentalist approaches. The former sought to subordinate Christianity to culture and thus change Christianity from what it should be while the latter destroyed or ignored culture to maintain a supposedly pure Christianity. He believed that the crisis was intellectual, so the culture had to be transformed by consecrating it to God, by cultivating the arts and sciences in service to God.

Theological fundamentalists across the board, such as dispensationalist C. I. Scofield (author of the 1909 Scofield Reference Bible), B. B. Warfield, and H. A. Ironside, distanced themselves from Pentecostals by insisting that tongues had ceased in the first century. *Pentecost Rejected*, "Fundamentalism Knows no Relation to 'Pentecostalism,'" and *Holiness, The False and the True* typified the evangelical attack by conservative Christians on the holiness Pentecostal movement.[46] Nevertheless, Pentecostals appreciated the writings of fundamentalists and used them when they contributed to preaching the gospel. First-generation Pentecostals read the writings of all these groups, but as radical evangelicals they fit most comfortably among the "premillennial extremists."

AMERICAN CHRISTIANS DURING WORLD WAR I

Christians in America did not have a distinctive political or social perspective in the early twentieth century, and World War I showed the great diversity present in the evangelical movement. As many reactions to the war were present among conservative Christians as among any other group in America, including crusading super-patriots like Billy Sunday and pacific-ists such as William Jennings Bryan.[47] Bryan resigned from being secretary of state in 1915 rather than help the country move toward war, yet he supported the war once America was involved. However, he was not as blatantly anti-German in his rhetoric as so much of America was during that time.[48]

Both conservative Baptists and conservative Presbyterians were patriotic and pro-war. Billy Sunday did not hesitate to condemn Germans as a "great pack of wolfish Huns whose fangs drip with blood and gore."[49] He preached that if you turned hell over it would have "made in Germany" stamped on the bottom and that Christianity and patriotism were synonymous terms. He would often end his sermons by jumping on the pulpit and waving an American flag. Many Baptists hoped for peace and believed that America should prepare for war. Their conservative journals, like *The Watchman-Examiner,* supported the war, but not wildly the way some Americans did. Presbyterians on the other hand had no qualms about American military power being used by God. Their postmillennial theology led them to believe that the Christian government had to wield the sword, and the church should support the peace that comes by way of force.

In contrast to these postmillennialists, the premillennialists did not trust government and believed that no particular nation should be considered blessed by God. The kingdom of God alone deserved their loyalty. This "anti-worldly" stance often led to a rejection of Christian participation in warfare. Premillennialists rejected peace plans and politics along with military power and war. They were not pacifist for the sake of bringing world peace but because the end was near and efforts to help nations get along were futile.

Premillennialists such as Arno C. Gaebelein disagreed with William Jennings Bryan's peace initiatives and remained interested in World War I only as it related to prophecies being fulfilled and the return of Christ. Even after the war began, some dispensational premillennialists remained solidly opposed to Christian participation, easily dismissing Old Testament examples of warfare that other Protestants used to justify their involvement. Premillennialists obeyed the government when its commands did not conflict with God's and prayed for the nations, since they considered praying more powerful than fighting anyway. Most accepted noncombatant service as legitimate forms of Christian service.[50]

Other premillennialists opposed Christian participation in sacrifices "to the monstrous war god" before 1917. Even when losing friends on the Lusitania, they believed "vengeance belongs to God, not to us . . . our part is to feed our hungry enemy (Rom. 12.20) and to overcome evil with good."[51] These Christians even suggested voting against Teddy Roosevelt as a vote against war and quoted Bertrand Russell's antiwar arguments.

Wartime premillennialist interest in prophecy and lack of support for war alarmed liberal Christians, such as those at the University of Chicago Divinity School, who began to attack premillennialism in 1917.[52] The primary accusation of the liberal Christians was that premillennialism like that espoused at Moody Bible Institute and by Pentecostals "bred a lack of patriotism and hence was a threat to the national security."[53] These modernist liberals based their critique on the belief that Christianity and civilization advanced together and could not be separated.

"Modernism" was the belief that religious principles could be applied to culture and society. This new postmillennialism was best seen in the progress of the cultures of democratic nations such as those in Europe and America. Most of the liberal Christians enthusiastically supported the war as necessary for the advancing of democratic civilization, for it corresponded to their hopes for the kingdom of God. Marsden notes that patriotism was "unrestrained" as those at the University of Chicago Divinity School mocked the premillennial belief that Jesus would come again. They pointed out that millennial expectations surged during wartime and dangerously struck "at the very heart of democratic ideals by denying human responsibility for the reform and betterment of society."[54]

The wartime paranoia affected liberal and conservative Christians alike. Liberals accused premillennialists of being pro-German and of even being supported financially by German sources. *The Biblical World*, by Shailer Mathews, and the liberal *Christian Century* promoted the idealism of the war and attacked premillennialists continually, accusing them of undermining enthusiasm for the war. In "The Premillennial Menace," Case argued that since premillennialism "regards the present world as irremediably bad" it harmed the war effort and contradicted his belief that "the American nation is engaged in a gigantic effort to make the world safe for democracy . . . it would be almost traitorous negligence to ignore the detrimental character of premillennial propaganda."[55] During World War I the postmillennial liberal modernists were the most patriotic and pro-war Christians of all.

Conservative premillennialists quickly responded by accusing liberals of getting their Christianity from Germany, the home of the militarism that caused the wars that were engulfing the world. The premillennialists saw a correlation between higher criticism, rationalism, liberal theology, and an uncritical nationalism that fanned the flames of war fury. Conservative American Christians argued that America was on the same road, with bad theology leading to militarism and demoralization.

However, the vast majority of both liberal and conservative Christians, even many of those premillennialists who had opposed war going into 1917, succumbed to the strong American patriotism of 1918. *The Christian Herald, Our Hope*, and the *Christian Worker's Magazine* had either opposed or moderately supported Christian participation in war. By 1918 all three had arrived at the opinion that the righteous war was God's way of punishing the evil Germans and was "the Christian's duty to serve his government in this conflict even to the taking up of arms . . . [it is] our responsibility to God as executioners of His avenging justice."[56]

The King's Business, a staunch premillennialist antiwar journal, went from encouraging love of even German enemies (1917) to equating the Kaiser to the devil in 1918, claiming that "never did Crusader lift battleaxe in holier war against the Saracen than is waged by our soldiers of the cross against the German."[57] The journal's premillenialists reversed their opinion about the benefits of war because President Wilson called for a day of repentance (May 30, 1918) and Americans had responded to a greater degree than they expected. These previously pessimistic premillennialists concluded "God has done wonderful things for this nation."[58]

William Riley, who soon rose to national prominence as the leader of the World's Christian Fundamentals Association, defended participation in war with appeals to "dual citizenship." He argued that Christians should be loyal both to God and the United States—and that this entailed the duty to defend civilization against barbarism. However, while Riley agreed that America should make the world safe for democracy, he wondered who could make democracy safe for the world. He warned against Christians putting too much hope in democracy rather than in redemption. Nevertheless, he helped move the premillennialists, who traditionally put no trust in nations and were accused of being unpatriotic during the war, toward being "sufficiently patriotic to make the defense of Christian civilization in America one of its major goals."[59]

World War I helped bring many types of Christians, from liberal theologians to fundamentalist premillennialists, together under the

American flag. For most, America had become the issue. But the radical evangelicals in the Pentecostal movement remained unconvinced.

AMERICAN PACIFISTS DURING WORLD WAR I

The Assemblies of God was not the only group that officially declared its objection to shedding human blood during World War I. Although several fellowships had decried war before American entry into it, most Americans eventually went along with President Wilson's decision to ensure an Allied victory. Nevertheless, a few other organizations and individuals continued to voice their nonviolent perspectives despite the enormous pressure from the surrounding American culture. We can divide these pacifists into two categories: nonreligious (political) and religious. The former category was not nearly as significant as the latter, which will be further subdivided into various Christian groups.[60] By examining the nature of each we will be able to see the similarities and differences that existed between the Assemblies of God and others who opposed participation in warfare. That comparison is aided by the fact that Pentecostals sometimes went to the trouble to explain points of similarity and dissimilarity between themselves and other pacifists.

Peter Brock identifies precursors to these early twentieth-century pacifisms. The Christian witness of Anabaptist-Mennonite nonresistance and the Quaker peace testimony provide the backbone of pacifism. Institutional peace societies (whose impulse came from both the evangelical movement and the Enlightenment) and socialist antimilitarists provided the other motivations for objection to war. We will begin by investigating the stance of those most removed from the witness of the early Pentecostals.

Political Pacifists

Although nonreligious pacifists comprised a minority of pacifists historically and were not an influence on the Assemblies of God, nonreligious pacifists provided a significant aspect of the antiwar movement in the 1900s. "Wherever industry developed, there labor eventually strove to exert pressure so as to extract from its rulers better working conditions and a greater say in the affairs of the state."[61] Organized labor found its political voice in the socialist movement, and Brock calls this Socialist Antimilitarism. However, no socialist group ever adopted a completely pacifist stance, since most of them, especially Marxists, believed that violence would be necessary at some point to end capitalism and introduce an egalitarian worker's world. Guy Hershberger states that these objectors to war are not pacifist at all, since they object only to certain wars. He quotes a World War I objector as saying, "I am not a pacifist . . . but regard myself as a patriotic political objector, acting largely from public and social grounds."[62]

Brock observes that many socialist objectors who were interviewed during World War I abstained not because of politics or tactics but as "an act of obedience to a secular version of the Sermon the Mount."[63] Individualistic socialism was their religion, and they believed that the capitalist system hurt the free development of the individual. They opposed war because it destroyed "personal liberty and the spiritual and material welfare of the citizen." As atheists or agnostics, they believed in the sacredness of human life, nonresistance, and the brotherhood of humanity. Some socialists opposed war completely; others thought it could be used against capitalist systems. In 1919 a leading socialist, Dr. Alfred Slater, estimated that two-thirds of socialists would use violence for a socialist revolution. But among the one-third of absolute pacifist socialists some said, "Bolshevism and Militarism are one and the same thing, only differing in the ends for which violence is proposed . . . killing is killing even when you kill a capitalist."[64]

Many socialists experienced disillusionment with the Soviet bureaucracy since democratic decentralization, rather than centralized democracy, was the most common political expression of socialist pacifism. Bertrand Russell opposed both Soviet communism and non-communist states while presenting rational arguments against war and hopes for an international society in which violence would only be used to enforce the rule of law between nations. These pacifistic hopes of world peace were nowhere near what early Pentecostals thought about when they refused to participate in war.

International Peace Societies

Peace societies formed in England and America during the nineteenth century to encourage temperance, further antislavery efforts, reform prisons, work for women's rights, and promote "permanent and universal peace." The London Peace Society was completely opposed to war, but the American Peace Society had pacific-ists as well as pacifists, so it accepted all who wanted to work to remove war from the world.

They wanted to establish ways of preventing international war through arbitration, arbitration clauses in treaties, the codification of international law, and disarmament. Going further, in 1838 William Lloyd Garrison founded the New England Non Resistance Movement that rejected both war and the machinery of government as incompatible with Christianity. However, the moderates continued to work methodically and patiently within the system rather than thinking it should be ignored or overthrown.[65]

Brock claims "the impulse behind this organized peace movement was derived in part . . . from the powerful evangelical movement, which also underlay many of the other reform movements of the age."[66] The rationalists condemned war as inhumane and irrational, as being in total contradiction to their ideal of brotherhood and unity. This led to the secular arguments against war that functioned independently from religion or a doctrine of sin.

Almost three million Americans fought in World War I, while fewer than four thousand were conscientious objectors. Ninety percent of these came from groups of Christians like Mennonites, Quakers, Brethren, and Pentecostals.[67] The first three became known as the "Historic Peace Churches," a term first used at a joint meeting of the three at Newton, Kansas, in 1935.[68]

Anabaptist Nonresistance

The Anabaptists were the radical expression of the Protestant Reformation of the early 1500s in Europe who believed in adult voluntary baptism rather than infant baptism. They also separated from the state and were persecuted by Catholics, Lutherans, and Calvinists. Menno Simons (d. 1561), whose followers were called Mennonites, wanted to restore the fellowship of the first-century church by practicing discipleship as depicted in the New Testament. Since this meant following Christ's command to "love your enemies," Anabaptists served neither in the military nor as magistrates who had to mete out punishment for offenses. They believed that governments were simply the less wicked punishing the more wicked, so they often insisted on being apolitical. The Mennonites who migrated to Holland and Germany integrated with the culture and eventually gave up their nonresistant theology.

Those who lived in Switzerland, Russia, the United States, and Canada continued to live apart from the culture and remained nonviolent.

Mennonites during the American Revolutionary War (1775-1783), who had been consistent voters in the previous decades, refused to fight with the patriots. They told government officials that they would donate their finances and other goods to the poor and to the families of soldiers instead. In attempts to unite citizens for the war, many Americans demanded that all males pledge their allegiance to the revolution and to the bearing of arms. Failure to do so would result in loss of the privilege to vote, hold office, or serve on a jury. Mennonites declined, and the federal and state governments taxed and fined them heavily, jailed some objectors, and even sentenced seven Amish to death.[69] "The great majority of Mennonites pleaded religious scruples against bearing arms," and some received a tarring and feathering from local citizens for their witness.[70] Mennonites also refused to pay for substitutes to fight in their place.

During the American Civil War (1861-1865), the majority of Mennonites in both the north and the south continued to stand by their Christian peace witness. They would not finance cavalry units or arms, but they charitably contributed funds for the care of sick soldiers. However, they did pay fees ranging from $200-$500 for exemption and also hired and raised money among their congregations for substitutes. Confederate general Thomas "Stonewall" Jackson complained that Mennonites forced into battle refused "to take correct aim."[71] One conscripted Mennonite's captain continually sent him into battle with a gun. Each time upon his return the captain would ask if he had shot. He would reply, "No, I didn't see anything to shoot at." The captain would retort, what about "all those Yankees?" And he would respond, "They're people. We don't shoot people."[72] Theron Schlabach, noted historian of Mennonites in America, observed that the Civil War provided them with the opportunity to develop new writings on their Christian peace witness.

Mennonites continued to oppose Christian combat during American involvement in World War I (1917-1918). Although the General Conference Mennonite denominational branch did not issue any statements, the "Old" Mennonite church adopted a comprehensive statement against military service in 1917 at Yellow Creek church in northern Indiana; 181 bishops, ministers, and deacons empowered it with their signatures.[73] According to James Juhnke, "when American Protestants marched off on a military crusade and explained their action with fervent rhetoric, the Mennonites did not produce a single statement to justify war on Christian or biblical grounds."[74]

The Peace Testimony of the Religious Society of Friends (Quakers)

The Society of Friends is a Christian pacifist group originating in the seventeenth century. The Friends benefited from the leadership of George Fox (1624-1691) and William Penn (1644-1718, founder of Pennsylvania) as they worked to revive primitive Christianity. They agreed with Mennonites about nonviolence but differed in their stance toward the state and culture. They were more optimistic about transforming the world and reforming society by Christianizing politics. They believed in being led by the Spirit of Christ, the inner light, and worked to abolish slavery and rejected war.

Quakers often refused to pay a fine to avoid military service, since they believed the state did not have the right to demand money from a person who simply acted according to his or her conscience. They came to believe that magistrates could govern and be pacifists at the same time. "I believe it possible, therefore, to base both private and public life on Matthew V and Romans XII," said William Hull.[75] While Mennonites often rejected participation in the political life of the ruling class, Quakers developed an intense interest in politics, were middle class, and actually ruled Pennsylvania from 1682 to 1756. During the American Revolution seventeen percent of Quaker males were disciplined for fighting in the war, and thirteen percent were disfellowshipped from their meeting.[76]

Quakers defended their rights nonviolently and had a more outward-reaching pacifism that attempted to affect domestic politics and international relations. Quakers even attempted to plan for peace between nations but did not require that all the statesmen involved be Christians. However, many Quaker politicians eventually sacrificed their pacifism for greater political power.[77]

Church of the Brethren

The Brethren trace their origin to 1708 in Switzerland. They were radical pietists who refused to bear arms or take oaths being "completely assured of it through the Scriptures as well as through the inner instruction of the Spirit."[78] Brethren represented the restorationism of both pietism and Anabaptism, believing the early Christian church to be normative for faith and practice. They thought they were restoring and preserving the faith of the apostles, wanting "to return the church to the exact condition in which Jesus had left it."[79] Since they would not fight, many revolutionaries accused them of being traitors during the Revolutionary War. Their desire to stay neutral or support the British crown was based on the support of the "powers that be" found in Romans 13. Those who most supported the revolution were Presbyterian or Anglicans who opposed Brethren political interests.[80] Brethren also refrained from fighting in the Civil War.

Their nonresistance included acceptance of proper authority, and by 1914 a Brethren minister had been elected governor of Pennsylvania. In 1918 the Brethren affirmed nonresistance but allowed that "in a democracy, it is not wrong for Brethren to serve their communities and municipalities to promote efficiency and honesty in social and civic life when the nonresistant principles and the New Testament doctrines are not violated."[81] Durnbaugh notes that the Brethren shifted from consistent nonresistance to "a more activist pacifism" and supported President Wilson's 1915 attempt to discourage war. They encouraged noncombatant service during World War I, and their statement in 1918 strongly resembled the Assemblies of God statement of 1917, "We believe that war or any participation in war is wrong and entirely incompatible with the spirit, example, and teachings of Jesus Christ [and] we can not conscientiously engage in any activity or perform any function, contributing to the destruction of human life."[82] This published statement and their corresponding refusal to bear arms led to severe penalties under the Espionage Law, and Brethren leaders agreed to stop distributing the statement. This corresponds to the actions of E. N. Bell, Assemblies of God editor of the *Pentecostal Evangel* during World War I, who encouraged Pentecostals to take a softer tone regarding their antiwar stance.

Churches of Christ

Members of the Churches of Christ were leading Christian pacifists from the Civil War to World War I but became a politically conservative pro-war denomination by the Vietnam era.[83] They split from the Disciples of Christ in the late nineteenth century (first appearing in the U.S. census in 1906) in order better to restore the New Testament church and follow the pattern found in Scripture. David Lipscomb (1831-1917) represented their theology when he declared that

> the kingdoms of the world are recognized by Christ as the king-doms of the devil. Christ's subjects are in the world but not of it. His kingdom is not of this world; his subjects cannot fight with carnal weapons. Their citizenship is in heaven, the weapons of their warfare are not carnal, but mighty through God to the pulling down of strongholds. His children are pilgrims and strangers in the earthly kingdoms.[84]

Even with the increasing support of war in 1917, most of the Churches of Christ pastors remained pacifists, answering their critics by saying "Jesus was a pacifist."[85] The Espionage Act, which came into effect June 15, 1917, enabled the government to shut down any press that discouraged war participation, and the editors of Churches of Christ periodicals were threatened with arrest. Thus in August 1917 they decided to stop printing anything that might seem to oppose the war. One Church of Christ scholar argued that they began to "equate the political pro-war position with Christianity itself" and that "for the first time in the Churches of Christ the fate of America was intertwined with the fate of Christianity."[86] Pacifists and conscientious objectors became a minority during World War I and were actively attacked by those within the church that supported the war, while the new theology that emerged transformed fallen government into the guarantor of Christianity itself.[87]

The Churches of Christ had used arguments against war that were similar to those used by the Assemblies of God. They both quoted Scripture extensively and referred primarily to the example of Jesus and the New Testament church. Their leaders fit the four criteria of the radical expression of the Reformation: the ideal of a pure church, the attempt to restore early Christianity on the basis of the biblical witness, a heightened sense of eschatology, and separation of church and state.[88] The Churches of Christ also experienced the same transformation that eventually transpired in the Assemblies of God.

Church of God (Anderson, Ind.)

The Church of God came to life during the holiness revivals of the 1880s. They believed in John Wesley's entire sanctification that frees believers from sin and a church that is entered into by profound conversion. In 1898 their official paper, *The Gospel Trumpet*, stated that

> there is no place in the New Testament wherein Christ gave instruction to his followers to take the life of a fellow-man. In older times it was "an eye for an eye and a tooth for a tooth" . . . Jesus says "but I say to you, do good to them that despitefully use you," etc.—Matt. 5:44. "Avenge not yourselves." "If thine enemy hunger, feed him; if he thirst, give him drink"—not shoot him.[89]

As "followers of the Prince of Peace" whose "weapons of warfare are not carnal" they announced their opposition to Christian participation in war at the beginning of World War I.[90] By the end of the war they had retreated from pacifism but soon picked it up again, declaring in 1932 that "we will never again sanction or participate in any war."[91] The Church of God Peace Fellowship formed in the 1930s under the leadership of a former editor of *The Gospel Trumpet*, an administrator on the missionary board and the dean of Anderson College. But during World War II only twenty Church of God men were in conscientious objector camps while the majority supported the war. Strege believes that the Church of God failed to maintain their pacifism because they did not attempt to form the characters of succeeding generations toward nonviolence, for "it is difficult to maintain pacifist commitments in the face of a powerful nationalist ideology."[92] The Church of God eventually endorsed the consciences of both those who killed and those who did not. This familiar outcome parallels the Assemblies of God narrative quite closely.

Church of God in Christ (Pentecostal)

The Church of God in Christ (COGIC) came into being in 1907, after Bishop Mason (1866-1961) returned to Memphis, Tennessee, from the Azusa Street revival in Los Angeles, California. Theodore Kornweibel Jr. claims that the newly formed fellowship might not have garnered a lot of attention had it not been for their Christian pacifism during World War I.[93] COGIC doctrine forbade Christian participation in military combat, because "we believe the shedding of human blood or taking of human life to be contrary to the teaching of our Lord and Savior, and as a body, we are adverse to war in all its various forms."[94] This belief inevitably led the government to investigate COGIC and other pacifist denominations. Kornweibel notes that public opinion associated pacifism with pro-German sentiment and an assistant secretary of war shared his "dislike and distrust of this small minority of Americans professing conscientious objections to warfare."[95] COGIC proclaimed their loyalty to the United States but encouraged their members to seek conscientious objector status.

A Bureau of Investigation (later renamed the Federal Bureau of Investigation, aka FBI) agent charged that C. H. Mason "openly advised against registration and made treasonable and seditious remarks against the United States government."[96] He believed that Mason could be convicted of treason, obstructing the draft, and giving aid and comfort to the enemy. Both the FBI and the War Department opened files on Mason and the Church of God in Christ, and multiple agents interviewed Mason. The *Vicksburg Post* ran an article claiming that Mason's preaching to resist the draft had led the state adjutant general to declare that it was virtually impossible to get blacks in Lexington to respond. The response to this article almost led to the lynching of Bishop Mason, but an FBI agent drove him out of town with a borrowed car.

The FBI also investigated E. R. Driver, a founding minister and the leader of the Church of God in Christ in California, since "this colored minister is supposed to have considerable influence among a number of people of his race and his attitude is very aggressive with reference to this country's entrance into the war."[97] A COGIC pastor in Arkansas was tarred and feathered and lucky to escape with his life in 1918. The *Memphis Commercial Appeal* told the story.

> A pastor of the colored holy roller church . . . was given a coat of tar and feathers last night as a result of alleged seditious remarks for some months concerning the president, the war, and a white man's war. . . . It is said his flock has shown no interest in the war work, while the Negroes of other churches have been most liberal, $2000 having been subscribed by the Methodist and Baptist churches Sunday night. This church is circulating literature which he says was sent to him by a brother preacher in Memphis [C.H. Mason], showing from Bible quotations that it is not right for Christians to fight. The literature is scattered broadcast over the country. [This punishment] will result in great good to

demonstrate to not only blacks but some whites that it is time to get into the war work and quit talking such rot as is attributed to Payne.[98]

Military intelligence and the FBI investigated many more COGIC pastors in Texas, Arkansas, California, Tennessee, and Kentucky for undermining military preparedness. Conscripted black men would appear at the draft board with papers signed by Mason, who was eventually brought before a federal grand jury in Paris, Texas. Although COGIC members have served in the military, official doctrine still opposes Christian participation in war and encourages drafted members to be inducted as conscientious objectors and to refuse "advanced weapons training given to combatant soldiers."[99]

CONCLUSION

Most Americans and most American Christians rallied to the cause during World War I and supported the war almost unanimously. However, most Pentecostals expressed their solidarity with the relatively few Christian pacifists and the Assemblies of God supported conscientious objection despite the counter-cultural and dangerous nature of this witness.

NOTES

1. Anthea Butler, *Women in the Church of God in Christ: Making a Sanctified World* (Chapel Hill, NC: University of North Carolina Press, 2007). Cecil M. Robeck, *The Azusa Street Mission and Revival* (Nashville, Tenn.: Thomas Nelson, 2006). Allan Anderson, *An Introduction to Pentecostalism: Global Charismatic Christianity* (Cambridge, England; New York: Cambridge University Press, 2004). Grant Wacker, *Heaven Below: Early Pentecostals and American Culture* (Cambridge, Mass.: Harvard University Press, 2001). Vinson Synan, *The Holiness-Pentecostal Tradition: Charismatic Movements in the Twentieth Century* (Grand Rapids, Mich.: Eerdmans, 1997). Walter J. Hollenweger, *Pentecostalism: Origins and Developments Worldwide* (Peabody, Mass.: Hendrickson, 1997). Harvey Cox, *Fire From Heaven: The Rise of Pentecostal Spirituality and the Reshaping of Religion in the Twenty First Century* (Reading, MA: Addison-Wesley Publishing, 1995).

2. 1979; reprint (Peabody, Mass.: Hendrickson Publishers), 1992.

3. Ibid., 232.

4. Ibid., 240.

5. Grant Wacker, *Heaven Below* (Cambridge: Harvard, 2001), 197-216. The

chapter entitled "Society" outlines early American Pentecostal social location in great detail. A. G. Miller, "Pentecostalism as a Social Movement: Beyond the Theory of Deprivation," *Toward a Pentecostal Theology*, no. 9 (October 1996): 97-114.

6. Wacker, *Heaven Below*, 199.

7. Arlene Sanchez-Walsh, *Latino Pentecostal Identity: Evangelical Faith, Self, and Society* (New York: Columbia University Press, 2003), 12.

8. E. N. Bell, "Wars and the Missionaries," *The Christian Evangel*, 12 September 1914, 1.

9. "Light on the Present Crisis," *The Weekly Evangel*, 1 July 1916, 6-7, 9.

10. E. N. Bell, "Questions and Answers," *The Christian Evangel*, 7 September 1918, 2; "Two Million Dollars an Hour," *The Christian Evangel*, 31 July 1915, 3.

11. Arthur Sydney Booth-Clibborn, "Gentileism," *The Pentecostal Evangel*, 13 November 1920, 4.

12. Arthur Sydney Booth-Clibborn, "Nigh, Even at the Doors," *The Christian Evangel*, 5 October 1918, 6.

13. D. M. Panton, "Coming War," *The Pentecostal Evangel*, 25 November 1922, 11.

14. Arthur Sydney Booth-Clibborn, "Nigh, Even at the Doors," 1.

15. Frank Bartleman, "What Will the Harvest Be?" *The Weekly Evangel*, 7 August 1915, 1.

16. Wacker, *Heaven Below*, 208.

17. Max Wood Moorhead, in *Cloud of Witnesses to Pentecost to India*, November 1908, 15; cited in Wacker, *Heaven Below*, 198.

18. Eric Foner and John A. Garraty, eds. *The Reader's Companion to American History* (Boston: Houghton Mifflin, 1991). Gary B. Nash, et al. *The American People: Creating a Nation and a Society* (New York: Harper & Row Publishers, 1990). George Brown Tindall, with David E. Shi. *America: A Narrative History* (New York: W. W. Norton and Company, 1992). http://www.archives.gov/education/lessons/hine-photos/.

19. George Donelson Moss, *America in the Twentieth Century* (Upper Saddle River, N.J.: Prentice Hall, 1997), 42-59.

20. Abraham Lincoln, "Fourth Lincoln-Douglas Debate, Charleston, Illinois" September 19, 1858, in *Speeches and Writings 1832-1858* (New York: Library of America, 1989), 636-37. Miscegenation (Euro Americans marrying African Americans) was still illegal in sixteen states in the U.S. when in 1967 the Supreme Court ruled such laws unconstitutional. In 2000 Alabama became the last state to repeal its laws forbidding interracial marriages, forty percent of voters still wanted to keep the law.

21. Moss, *America*, 16.

22. Christopher Booker, *African Americans and the Presidency* (Danburgy, Conn.: Franklin Watts, 2000).

23. Frank Bartleman, *Azusa Street: The Roots of Modern-day Pentecost*. Introduction by Vinson Synan. (Southfield, N.J.: Bridge, 1980), 54. Originally published as *How "Pentecost" Came to Los Angeles – How it Was in the Beginning* (1925).

24. Walter Hollenweger quoting William Seymour in Iain MacRobert, *The Black*

Roots and White Racism of Early Pentecostalism in the USA (London: Macmillan Press, 1988), xiii. William Seymour, *The Apostolic Faith*, Los Angeles, vol. I, no. 1, Sept. 1906, p. 1, col. 1. The first sentence is Hollenweger's; the material in quotation marks is Seymour in 1906. Also see Cecil M. Robeck, *The Azusa Street Mission and Revival* (Nashville: Thomas Nelson, 2006).

25. Lawrence F. Catley, interview by Vinson Synan, Leonard Lovett, and Cecil M. Robeck, Jr. at the Society for Pentecostal Studies Meeting, May 1974. Catley participated in the Azusa Street revival from 1906-1909. Iain MacRobert, *The Black Roots and White Racism of Early Pentecostalism in the USA* (London: Macmillan, 1988), 56.

26. John A. Garraty, *A Short History of the American Nation* (New York: Longman, 1997), 294.

27. *Statistical Abstract of the United States of America: 1910, Thirty Third Number* (Washington, D.C.: Government Printing Office, 1911), 23. By 1934 sixty-two percent of the Native American land provided in the Dawes Act had been acquired by whites.

28. Moss, *America*, 52.

29. Five hundred million dollars in 1901 was in 2006 worth $12,233,009,708.74 using the Consumer Price Index, $10,315,929,203.54 using the Gross Domestic Product (GDP) deflator, $55,479,166,666.67 using the unskilled wage, $76,321,128,058.61 using the nominal GDP per capita, and $294,524,553,571.43 using the relative share of GDP. Lawrence H. Officer and Samuel H. Williamson, "Measures of Worth. 2007" MeasuringWorth.com, 2007 (accessed August 21, 2007). Lawrence H. Officer and Samuel H. Williamson, "Better Measurements of Worth," *Challenge: The Magazine of Economic Affairs*, Vol. 49, No. 4 (July/August 2006), 86-110.

30. Moss, *America*, 26.

31. Theodore Roosevelt, quoted in Henry F. Pringle, *Theodore Roosevelt* (New York: Harcourt, Brace, 1931, 1945), 207.

32. Moss, *America in the Twentieth Century*, 89. MeasuringWorth.com (accessed August 21, 2007).

33. George Marsden, *Fundamentalism and American Culture: The Shaping of Twentieth Century Evangelicalism 1870-1925*, 124-138.

34. Isaac Haldeman, *The Signs of the Times*, 3rd. ed. (New York, 1912), 12, cited in Marsden, *Fundamentalism and American Culture*, 125.

35. Haldeman, *The Signs of the Times*, 21.

36. A. C. Gaebelein, "The Present Day Apostasy," *The Coming of the Kingdom of Christ: A Stenographic Report of the Prophetic Bible Conference Held at the Moody Bible Institute of Chicago Feb. 24-27, 1914* (Chicago, 1914), 154.

37. Marsden, *Fundamentalism and American Culture*, 128.

38. Editorial, *Institute Tie* VIII (August 1908), 884.

39. *The Watchman*, 1907 quoted in William G. McLoughlin Jr., *Modern Day Revivalism* (New York, 1959), 419.

40. Marsden, *Fundamentalism and American Culture*, 131.

41. Lawrence W. Levine, *Defender of the Faith: William Jennings Bryan: The Last*

Decade, 1915-1925 (New York, 1965), 26.

42. Marsden, *Fundamentalism and American Culture*, 133.

43. William Jennings Bryan, "The Old Time Religion," *Winona Echoes 1911*, 50.

44. Marsden, *Fundamentalism and American Culture*, 135.

45. Marsden, *Fundamentalism and American Culture*, 137.

46. A. M. Hills, *Pentecost Rejected: and the Effect on the Churches* (Titusville, Pa.: 1902). H. A. Ironside, *Holiness, The False and the True* (Neptune, N.J.: 1912). "Fundamentalism Knows no Relation to 'Pentecostalism,'" *Christian Fundamentals in School and Church* VIII (Jan-Mar, 1926), 31-35.

47. Martin Ceadel defines pacific-ists as peace oriented non pacifists who consider warfare a conceivable, though unfortunate, necessity. Martin Ceadel, *Thinking About War and Peace* (Oxford: Oxford University Press, 1987), 101.

48. Marsden, *Fundamentalism and American Culture*, 142.

49. Marsden, *Fundamentalism and American Culture*, 142.

50. Marsden, *Fundamentalism and American Culture*, 143.

51. Editorial *King's Business* VII (March 1917), 216. Editorial *King's Business* VI (August 1915), 653. Cited in Marsden, *Fundamentalism and American Culture*, 144.

52. E. N. Bell, the first General Chairman of the Assemblies of God, graduated from the University of Chicago.

53. Marsden, *Fundamentalism and American Culture*, 146.

54. Shailer Matthews, "Will Jesus Come Again?" (Chicago, 1917). Shirley Jackson Case, *The Millennial Hope: A Phase of War Time Thinking* (Chicago, 1918), v-vi. Cited in Marsden, *Fundamentalism and American Culture*, 146.

55. Shirley Jackson Case, "Premillennial Menace," *Biblical World* LII (July 1918), 21, 16-17.

56. Editorial, *Christian Worker's Magazine* XVIII (June 1918), 775.

57. *The King's Business* IX (May 1918), 365-366.

58. Editorial, *The King's Business* IX (December 1918), 1026-27.

59. Marsden, *Fundamentalism and American Culture*, 152.

60. Non-Christian pacifists (Jewish, Buddhist) were such a small segment in America that we need not investigate them in this section.

61. Peter Brock, *Pacifism in the Twentieth Century*, 13-14. Twenty thousand had applied for conscientious objector status, but over sixteen thousand changed their minds after being inducted.

62. Guy Franklin Hershberger, *War, Peace, and Nonresistance* (Scottdale, Pa.: Herald, 1991), 200-01.

63. Peter Brock, *Pacifism in the Twentieth Century*, 35.

64. Aylmer Rose, *The Tribunal*, No. 156 (May 8, 1919), 4.

65. Peter Brock, *Pacifism in the Twentieth Century*, 11.

66. Peter Brock, *Pacifism in the Twentieth Century*, 12.

67. Peter Brock, *Pacifism in the Twentieth Century* (Syracuse, N.Y.: Syracuse University Press, 1999), 34-35.

68. Robert Kreider, "The Historic Peace Churches Meeting in 1935," *Mennonite Life*, June 1976, 21-24; Donald F. Durnbaugh and Charles W. Brockwell, Jr., "The

Historic Peace Churches: From Sectarian Origins to Ecumenical Witness," in *The Church's Peace Witness*, ed. Marlin E. Miller and Barbara Nelson Gingerich (Grand Rapids, Mich.: Eerdmans,1994), 182-195; Donald F. Durnbaugh, ed., *On Earth Peace: Discussion on War/Peace Issues Between Friends, Mennonites, Brethren and European Churches, 1935-1975* (Elgin, Ill.: The Brethren Press, 1978).

69. Richard K. MacMaster, *Land, Piety, Peoplehood: The Establishment of Mennonite Communities in America (1683-1790)*, The Mennonite Experience in America, vol. 1 (Scottdale, Pa.: Herald Press, 1985), 229, 232, 250, 275. They also lost their privilege to vote, hold office, or serve on a jury.

70. MacMaster, *Land, Piety, Peoplehood*, 253, 250.

71. Theron F. Schlabach, *Peace, Faith, Nation: Mennonites and Amish in Nineteenth-Century America*, The Mennonite Experience in America, vol. 2 (Scottdale, Pa.: Herald Press, 1988), 177-178, 186, 191-192.

72. Schlabach, *Peace, Faith, Nation*, 190.

73. James C. Juhnke, *Vision, Doctrine, War: Mennonite Identity and Organization in America (1890-1930)*, The Mennonite Experience in America, vol. 3 (Scottdale, Pa.: Herald Press, 1989), 215, 228.

74. James C. Juhnke, *Vision, Doctrine, War*, 216.

75. Letter from William I. Hull to Walter C. Woodward, April 5, 1937. Cited in Hershberger, *War, Peace, and Nonresistance*, 178.

76. MacMaster, *Land, Piety, Peoplehood*, 276.

77. Peter Brock, *Pacifism in the Twentieth Century*, 7-9.

78. Donald F. Durnbaugh, "The Brethren Peace Witness in Ecumenical Perspective" in *The Fragmentation of the Church and Its Unity in Peacemaking* ed. Jeffrey Gros and John Rempel (Grand Rapids: Eerdmans, 2001), 60.

79. Carl F. Bowman, *Brethren Society: The Cultural Transformation of a 'Peculiar People'* (Baltimore: Johns Hopkins University Press, 1995), 26.

80. Durnbaugh, "The Brethren Peace Witness," 70.

81. L. W. Schultz, *Minutes of the Annual Conference of the Church of the Brethren on War and Peace* (Elgin, Ill.: Board of Christian Education, Church of the Brethren, 1935), 26.

82. Schultz, *Minutes*, 17-25.

83. Michael W. Casey, "From Pacifism to Patriotism: The Emergence of Civil Religion in the Churches of Christ During World War I," *The Mennonite Quarterly Review*: 376-390.

84. David Lipscomb, *Civil Government: Its Origins, Mission, and Destiny* (Nashville, Tenn.: Gospel Advocate Company, 1889). Cited in Casey, "From Pacifism to Patriotism," 377.

85. Casey, "From Pacifism to Patriotism," 379.

86. Casey, "From Pacifism to Patriotism," 382, 384.

87. Casey, "From Pacifism to Patriotism," 385.

88. Thomas H. Olbricht, "The Peace Heritage of the Churches of Christ," in *The Fragmentation of the Church and Its Unity in Peacemaking*, ed. Jeffrey Gros and John Rempel (Grand Rapids: Eerdmans, 2001), 203.

89. "Should We Go To War?" *The Gospel Trumpet* (April 14, 1898), 4. Cited in

Merle D. Strege, "An Uncertain Voice for Peace: The Church of God (Anderson) and Pacifism" in *Proclaim Peace: Christian Pacifism From Unexpected Quarters*, ed. Theron Schlabach and Richard Hughes (Chicago: University of Illinois Press, 1997), 115.

90. "Our Attitude toward War," *The Gospel Trumpet* (April 26, 1917), 12.

91. *Minutes of the General Ministerial Assembly of the Church of God* (June 23, 1932), cited in Merle D. Strege, "An Uncertain Voice for Peace: The Church of God (Anderson) and Pacifism" in *Proclaim Peace: Christian Pacifism From Unexpected Quarters*, ed. Theron Schlabach and Richard Hughes (Chicago: University of Illinois Press, 1997), 116.

92. Strege, "An Uncertain Voice for Peace," 117.

93. Theodore Kornweibel Jr., "Race and Conscientious Objection in World War I: The Story of the Church of God in Christ," in *Proclaim Peace: Christian Pacifism From Unexpected Quarters*, ed. Theron Schlabach and Richard Hughes (Chicago: University of Illinois Press, 1997), 59.

94. Kornweibel, "Race and Conscientious Objection," 61-62.

95. Kornweibel, "Race and Conscientious Objection," 61.

96. Agent M. M. Schaumburger to Bureau of Investigation, September 24, 1917, Old German case file 144128, Record Group 65, Investigation Case Files of the Bureau of Investigation, National Archives.

97. Kornweibel, "Race and Conscientious Objection," 61.

98. "Negro Preacher Tarred," *Memphis Commercial Appeal*, April 18, 1918, 11.

99. Kornweibel, "Race and Conscientious Objection," 75. Also see David A. Hall Sr., "What the Church Teaches About War: A COGIC Conscientious Objection Principle," in *Essays to the Next Generation: Issues Vital to Life, Salvation, and Spirituality of the Church of God in Christ* (Memphis, Tenn.: David A. Hall Sr. Publishing, 2004). Dr. Hall is pastor of Mason Temple Church of God in Christ in Memphis, Tennessee (Bishop C. H. Mason's church) and CEO of the COGIC publishing house.

THREE

FRIENDS, HOLINESS, AND THE FULL GOSPEL: THE THEOLOGICAL CONTEXT OF FIRST GENERATION ASSEMBLIES OF GOD PACIFISM

THE RELIGIOUS SOCIETY OF FRIENDS (QUAKERS)

The Assemblies of God explained its pacifism by referring to Quakerism in the opening sentence of the introductory paragraph of the article explaining their military service resolution.

> From the very beginning the movement has been characterized by Quaker principles. The laws of the kingdom, laid down by our elder brother, Jesus Christ in His Sermon on the Mount, have been unqualifiedly adopted, consequently the movement has found itself opposed to the spilling of the blood of any man, or of offering resistance to any aggression. Every branch of the movement, whether in the United States, Canada, Great Britain or Germany, has held to this principle.[1]

Since referring to Quakers was a common way of communicating clearly that one was opposed to war, the Assemblies of God may have merely used conventional language to express their pacifism. But the great similarities between the Pentecostal movement and the Friends had already been noted by B. F. Lawrence in his 1916 history of the Pentecostal movement.[2] He observed that both Friends and Pentecostals encouraged women to preach and lead equally with men, spoke in tongues frequently, and experienced regular persecution.[3] One year later the Assemblies of God cited their Quaker principles in explanation of their nonviolence.

An examination of the pacifists within the Assemblies of God reveals that several of them were Quakers who had become Pentecostals. The Quakerism of Arthur Sidney Booth-Clibborn (a Pentecostal minister with a 250-year Quaker family heritage) and his children (some of whom were founders and ministers in the Assemblies of God) helped the Assemblies of God appreciate pacifism as an integral part of early Christianity.[4] Each of these was influenced by a Quaker heritage and each had a significant impact on Pentecostal pacifism by way of the holiness movement. The most direct evidence of this impact was the Assemblies of God appreciation of Booth-Clibborn's book, *Blood Against Blood*.[5] The Assemblies of God highly recommended it because it presented strong biblical and theological arguments against war and violence.[6]

Early Pentecostal pacifism contained many parallels to the early Quaker peace testimony. These parallels reveal why an Assemblies of God mention of Quaker principles was both appropriate and deliberate. A few Pentecostal historians, theologians, and ethicists have noted the influence of Quakerism upon the movement,[7] and some Assemblies of God scholars have investigated the Quaker influence as well.[8] They focused upon the similar emphases on the Holy Spirit and *glossolalia* while most did not discuss pacifism in detail.[9]

This minimal mention of pacifist parallels is seen clearly in the article "Quakers (Society of Friends)" in the *Dictionary of Pentecostal and Charismatic Movements*.[10] In the article Burgess highlighted the fact that the Quakers emphasized the "experience of the Holy Spirit" and that they believed "Scripture corroborates and interprets one's prior spiritual experience." He also referred to "visions, healings, prophecies, and a power from God that they likened to first-century Pentecost. There is even evidence of tongues-speech. . . ." The reference to a relationship between the Quaker peace ethic and Pentecostal pacifism appeared in the final sentence of the eight-paragraph article: "Quakers even provided arguments for early Pentecostals who tended to be strongly pacifistic." This was probably a reference to Booth-Clibborn's book and shows that Burgess recognized the significant strength of early Pentecostal pacifism.

The early Assemblies of God leaders thought it helpful to refer to the Quaker principles that characterized the Pentecostal movement.[11] The constituency of the Assemblies of God accepted this relationship with Quakerism without quarrel, which signified that Assemblies of God members must have agreed with the claim that their movement was defined by Quaker principles "from the very beginning." The claim and widespread acceptance of Quaker influence invites an investigation to discover the nature of the relationships between historic Quakerism and early Pentecostalism.

Friends Who Influenced the Early Assemblies of God

Arthur Sidney Booth-Clibborn (1855-1939) served as the clearest and strongest link between Quakerism and the Assemblies of God. This section will elucidate Booth-Clibborn's Quaker heritage, his arguments in favor of Christian pacifism, and the impact he had on the early Assemblies of God.

"The Society of Friends," wrote Donald Green, "has produced so far only two systematic thinkers . . . Robert Barclay and Joseph John Gurney."[12] Both of these authors, who wrote the most widely read and best known explanations and defenses of Quakerism, were ancestors of Arthur Sidney Booth-Clibborn. Robert Barclay penned *An Apology for the True Christian Divinity as the Same is Held Forth and Preached by the People, in Scorn, Called Quakers* in 1678, and Joseph John Gurney wrote *Observations on the Religious Peculiarities of the Society of Friends* in 1824. Voltaire lauded the former,[13] and the latter went through ten editions in England and America.[14] When Booth-Clibborn stated that "ancestral examples . . . affected both my views and duties in this question of the two opposite kinds of war,"[15] his readers could be assured that he had been influenced by some of the greatest examples of Quakerism.

Booth-Clibborn's Quaker heritage began in the mid-1650s, when John Clibborn tried to burn down a Quaker meetinghouse that had been erected on his land in Moate, Ireland. Instead, he converted to Quakerism because of the preaching of Thomas Lowe—who also influenced William Penn to adopt Quaker peace principles. John Clibborn resigned his military position under Oliver Cromwell and harbored refugees during the wars that followed. "His life was attempted three times" because he was a Quaker, but he would not testify against his enemies because "he bore them no ill-will."[16]

During that same decade, Colonel David Barclay, who was at one time the military governor over the majority of Scotland, "experience[ed] the new birth," renounced war as anti-Christian, and was accused of succumbing to "the scandalous errours [sic] of Quaquarism [sic]."[17] John Greenleaf Whittier noted in both poetry and prose the persecutions suffered by David Barclay.[18] His son Robert Barclay became the influential theologian and traveled with both George Fox and William Penn. Joseph John Gurney also descended from David Barclay and persuasively argued for the relevance and importance of Quakerism on a broad scale through public speaking and publishing.

Booth-Clibborn touted his female Quaker ancestors as wonderful examples of nonviolence and "prominent women ministers in the Society."[19] He claimed that women in ministry encouraged peace, provided good role models, and that "the restoration of women's ministry to its normal place in the public service of Christ [would show] the unlawfulness of war for the Christian."[20]

Arthur Sidney Booth-Clibborn valued his rich Quaker heritage, and he had no intention of distancing himself from it. His acceptance of the holiness movement and the Pentecostal message did not detract from his pacifism. He considered himself a Quaker and wrote his book, *Blood Against Blood*, from the perspective of a Quaker missionary. He was "recorded" as a Quaker minister at an "unusually early age" and never drifted from those Quaker truths even while working with the Salvation Army, which he joined in 1881 at the age of twenty-six.[21] In fact, twenty years later he left the Salvation Army over the issues of pacifism, healing, and premillennialism. This was after General William Booth (founder of the Salvation Army) rejected his requests to preach the "full plain Gospel of the Sermon on the Mount."[22] Dubbed the "apostle of abandonment," Booth-Clibborn spent time in jail in Switzerland and lived "under the sentence of death from the anarchists of five continental lands for over ten years."[23] While he was street preaching in 1905, an angry mob attacked him and pierced his leg with an iron bar. The resulting blood poisoning turned to gangrene and required four surgeries to save his life. He never completely recovered.

Blood Against Blood was the first of two systematic presentations of Christian pacifism by Quaker Pentecostals.[24] In it Booth-Clibborn encapsulated the Quaker arguments against war that were eventually adopted by the Assemblies of God. He insisted that absolute nonparticipation in war should be a Christian ethic, not just a Quaker one.[25] He presented the two-fold premise of his book in the title. First, the blood of carnal warfare was opposite the blood of Christ, and the two were "mutually excluding and never reconcilable."[26] Second, the blood of Christ was the only power by which the blood of warfare could be overcome and conquered. "Christianity is the *only* remedy to war. Not a bloodless gospel on the one hand, not an adulterated evangelicalism on the other. It must be Blood against blood."[27]

Booth-Clibborn did not support antiwar movements or arguments that were not Christian. He believed that "moralists" who placed their hopes "in the social effort of man to save his own world on material lines" were doomed for failure.[28] He declared that the nonresistance of Tolstoy and those who followed "Tolstoyism" was "purely a negative force" even though it attempted to follow the example of the Sermon on the Mount.[29] Booth-Clibborn's reasoning was based on his understanding that Tolstoy denied both the divinity and the resurrection of Jesus of Nazareth. Thus nonviolence in itself was not the goal. He described the life of a faithful Christian and participation in war was simply not an option for a disciple of Jesus.

John Howard Yoder described Booth-Clibborn's kind of pacifism as that of "the virtuous minority" or "vocational pacifism."[30] Christians were to live according to a different ethic than that which could be required of the rest of the world. This approach calls "into doubt this axiom that the same ethics are for everybody . . . all are invited to live on this level, but not all are expected or required to do so."[31] This minority morality allowed the church to function according to its prophetic vocation without demanding that everybody else live the same way. Booth-Clibborn did not espouse Ceadel's optimistic pacifism that hoped to change the world for good, but a pessimistic pacifism that witnessed to truth in the painful and sinful interim.

Booth-Clibborn was a faithful Quaker, but he also appreciated, supported, and participated in the Pentecostal movement. His and and his wife's "sympathies were with the Outpouring, even from the beginning. How could it be otherwise when nine of their children had received their Pentecost."[32] Indeed, Arthur Booth-Clibborn himself received the baptism in the Holy Spirit under the ministry of a Quaker minister.[33] His public endorsement of the Pentecostal movement provided it with more respectability than it otherwise would have had, and he shared that Pentecostalism "reminds me of the days of early Quakerism, and of what one has known of the days of closest fellowship with the Crucified One."[34] He even argued that the combination of Pentecostalism and pacifism formed an unbelievably powerful spiritual force. James Robinson noted that he maintained a "strong belief that acceptance of the pacifist and Pentecostal message by the [Salvation] Army would have returned it to its roots, to the time it was a spiritual force in the nation. . . ."[35]

Arthur Booth-Clibborn's influence on the early Assemblies of God came primarily from his book and numerous articles in *The Pentecostal Evangel*, but his children also had an impact. William Booth-Clibborn (d. 1969), the fifth child of Arthur Booth-Clibborn, was a charter member of the Assemblies of God in 1914 and wrote many books of his own.[36] His 1936 work entitled *The Baptism in the Holy Spirit: A Personal Testimony* illustrates the close connection his family, especially his pacifist father, had with the beginning of the Pentecostal movement. William Booth-Clibborn related several statements his father made about the Pentecostal revival and experience. In reference to a woman at a mission hall, Arthur wrote that "She is speaking by the Spirit and Power of God in a language unfamiliar to her. This is the unknown tongue you read about in Scripture. Is it not wonderful that God should be again baptizing with the Holy Ghost like He did in the early days of the Christian Church."[37] Arthur Booth-Clibborn also "proclaimed to one and all that this [Pentecostal] revival was destined to sweep the world."[38]

William Booth-Clibborn even claimed that "unless my parents had stepped out on questions of conscience and the advocacy of advanced truths such as . . . the anti-Christian character of all carnal warfare, we would never have been ready as a family to experience Pentecost in our home."[39] This significant statement revealed the connection between Quaker pacifism and early Pentecostalism in the mind of at least this one founder of the Assemblies of God. It also revealed the connection between the baptism in the Holy Spirit and pacifism. For although pacifism preceded the baptism in the Holy Spirit as preparation through holiness, the Booth-Clibborns explained that the Holy Spirit provided the power to be nonviolent even in the face of hatred.

Three sons and two daughters of Arthur Booth-Clibborn also related to the Assemblies of God. Eric Booth-Clibborn was an Assemblies of God missionary who died shortly after reaching the French African Sudan.[40] He wrote five articles for *The Pentecostal Evangel,* and his wife wrote one as well.[41] Samuel Herbert Booth-Clibborn wrote two articles against war that were published in 1917 in *The Weekly Evangel.*[42] They reflected the arguments presented by his father in *Blood Against Blood* and were absolutely pacifistic. He also penned a book modeled after his father's that declared the same unquestionable ethic for Christians.[43]

The early Assemblies of God leaders had great respect for Booth-Clibborn and his family. In 1915, *The Weekly Evangel* strongly recommended *Blood Against Blood* to all of its readers when E. N. Bell and J. R. Flower served as editors.

> A most striking, realistic and forceful book by Arthur Sidney Booth-Clibborn, an English Pentecostal Evangelist and Elder who has put into words the principles burning in the hearts of all the Pentecostal saints on the subject of whether a Christian should go to war or not. This book presents war from a Christian standpoint and is not intended for those out of Christ. Should the United States go to war with Germany, or any other nation, what shall be the attitude of the Pentecostal people. Send for a copy of this wonderful book and then make a decision. Price 55 cts. Postpaid. The Gospel Publishing House. . . .[44]

Another advertisement lauded it by stating that "The Gospel Publishing House is in possession of a powerful book" and encouraged Pentecostals to "purchase it and become imbued with the spirit of its contents, in a complete opposition and protest against war and the shedding of blood."[45] They were selling an edition replete with Quaker references, quotes, and an impressive account of Booth-Clibborn's Quaker heritage. It had clearly already made an impact on the leadership of the Assemblies of God, because that same issue of *The Weekly Evangel* contained a reference to Quakerism: "The Pentecostal people . . . are uncompromisingly opposed to war, having much the same spirit as the early Quakers, who would rather be shot themselves than that they should shed the blood of their fellow men."[46]

Great Britain banned *Blood Against Blood* after introducing conscription in 1916,[47] but in 1917 the American Assemblies of God still advertised it in *The Weekly Evangel* by reproducing fourteen powerful antiwar lines. They quoted such eminent Christians as George Fox, "I cannot fight for the spirit of war is slain within me" and Tertullian, "Our religion teaches us that it is better to be killed than to kill."[48] Arthur Booth-Clibborn inspired many "young conscientious objectors in their personal turmoil, and by his advocacy of an ethic with elements of social radicalism" he challenged the conservatism of established denominations. "I have realized that the more the Salvation Army comes into favour [sic] with the unconverted wealthy, and with statesmen and politicians, the conservatism which this entails makes it very difficult if not impossible for it to preach the whole Gospel."[49]

The Booth-Clibborn family had an impact on the early Assemblies of God through the numerous articles printed in *The Pentecostal Evangel*. Arthur Booth-Clibborn authored thirteen from 1918-1922, while William penned six articles from 1915-1926 and Eric published five before his death in 1924. Theodore, Lucile, and Genevieve each had one article printed.[50]

Quaker Pacifism

Quaker pacifism did not appear *ex nihilo* to become the defining testimony of the Society of Friends. The roots of Quaker pacifism can be found in the Lollards (followers of John Wyclif) of the fourteenth and fifteenth centuries and English Anabaptists and Baptists of the sixteenth and seventeenth centuries. The Lollards told the English parliament in 1395 that "Christ . . . taught for to love and to have mercy on his enemies and not for to slay them."[51] They also tacked their statement to the doors of Westminster Abbey and St. Paul's Cathedral so that the entire city would know they were against war. However, like many Christian pacifist groups that followed them, not all within their ranks agreed with the ethic of nonviolence. One of the Lollard leaders exhibited his militant tendencies by rebelling against the government in 1414.[52]

The English Anabaptists were "mostly obscure weavers or petty traders and craftsmen."[53] Their marginalized and low socio-economic status was a familiar situation for Christian pacifists and seems to provide a context from which an Anabaptist in 1575 testified, "Christ is the true expounder of the law, and saith, resist not, and gave us an example to follow his steps."[54] However, this same man evidenced within his own thought the tensions between loyalty to government and a consistent peace testimony. He assured the government that he was not against their ability to use the sword against evildoers and that their authority was ordained by God.[55] This recognition of divine authority for governing powers to kill evildoers as well as enemies of the state is what troubled the Assemblies of God so many years later and eventually led to their choice of war over pacifism. It also sounded almost exactly like the initial proclamation of pacifism by the Assemblies of God, stressing loyalty to the government first but then insisting, nevertheless, that they could not participate in the destruction of human life.[56]

Another similarity between English Anabaptism and the early Pentecostals is the fact that both were separatists who severed ties with the established churches. The Anabaptists served as the foundation for the first free churches in England—the Congregationalist and Baptist denominations. The early Pentecostal movement consisted of people from many different denominations who had distanced themselves from their previous associations. These twentieth-century separatists eventually formed thousands of Pentecostal and charismatic denominations.[57]

In 1609 a pacifist founded the first English Baptist church. John Smyth, who had left the Church of England and subsequently joined the Mennonites,[58] evidenced several themes that characterized the early Assemblies of God. First, he desired to be like the "primitive church, which was completely perfect [and] did not acknowledge the magistracy in its midst." This reference to the primitive church revealed hints of a restorationist motif that was so prevalent in early Pentecostalism. He carried it further by stating that members of the "the church of the new testament" led "unarmed and unweaponed li[ves]."[59] His pacifism was rooted in being like the New Testament church and this nonviolence was accompanied by recognition that the government was "a necessary ordinance of God . . . for the punishing of the evil."[60] This loyalty to the existing government accompanied by restorationist and perfectionist pacifism reveals early roots of the Assemblies of God position, and the tension between discipleship and political "responsibility."[61]

Early Quakerism Compared with the Early Assemblies of God

When such a prominent Quaker Pentecostal as Arthur Booth-Clibborn observes that first generation Pentecostalism resembled his understanding of early Quakerism, this calls for an elaboration of the similarities.

RADICAL

Similar revolutionary impulses existed in the emergent days of both Quakerism and Pentecostalism. Both were radical movements that broke away from the established and powerful churches in attempts to be more like the primitive church. Quakers have been likened to "radical Puritans"[62] and labeled as "far more radical than some historians would still admit."[63] It may be possible to consider early Pentecostals "radical Evangelicals"[64] or even radical Fundamentalists who "merely carried biblical literalism—the bedrock of Fundamentalism—to its logical conclusion."[65]

The problem with this latter assessment is that Pentecostals only appeared to be biblical literalists at first glance. Their hermeneutic was actually more Christ- and Spirit-centered, and they believed in the discontinuation of many practices literally taught in Scripture (animal sacrifices, circumcision, head coverings for women, etc.). "They believed that the whole of Scripture was inspired, but they 'rightly divided' it, giving the New Testament, and particularly Acts (their hermeneutical key), *de facto* supremacy."[66] Their antiestablishment attitude allowed them to view war from the perspective of outsiders. They attacked America's treatment of the native Americans and the "wrong to the black people."[67] As a minority within both Christianity and the world, they could proclaim a radical message of Christian discipleship to both the religious and secular establishments. Being against the established powers meant that a superior way, the way of Jesus, needed to be restored.

RESTORATIONISM

The early Quakers had a fanatical desire to restore New Testament Christianity after "a thousand years of Catholic apostasy" with their "intensely transforming religious awakening."[68] Compare this to the advertisement appearing in the 1908 magazine *The Pentecost*, "LOST— Somewhere between the days of Pentecost and Present time: real Bible salvation. Search yourself and see if you have it."[69] The Quaker and Pentecostal views of history were quite similar. The Quakers considered themselves a renewal movement that would bring new life to the kingdom of God because they were returning to the New Testament way. Joseph John Gurney titled his book *Primitive Christianity* and wrote an entire essay "On the Discipline of the Primitive Christians and on that of the Society of Friends" in which he sought to show that the Quakers were the most like New Testament Christians.[70] An Assemblies of God historian titled his book *Suddenly . . . From Heaven: A History of the Assemblies of God*[71] which encapsulated the view that "the church ended in Acts 28, went underground for 1900 years and then reemerged at Azusa Street."[72]

DEFENDERS OF THE POOR

Both early Quakers and early Pentecostals were "socially disreputable" and represented the outcasts. Quakers "spoke out on behalf of the poorer sections of the population."[73] William Penn wrote that

> the sweat and tedious labor of the husbandman, early and late, cold and hot, wet and dry [is] converted into the pleasure, ease and pastime of a small number of men; severity [is] laid upon nineteen parts of the land to feed the inordinate lusts and delicious appetites of the twentieth . . . the very trimming of the vain world would clothe all the naked one[s].[74]

Early Pentecostals proclaimed that war created situations in which "the poor must live on half rations. The sick must die. We cannot buy new clothes. We cannot buy good food. We cannot travel. Rent prices are criminally high."[75] They also declared that "the rich man's dog gets more meat than the poor man's family."[76] Frank Bartleman attacked "Wall Street interests, Pork Barrel administration," "human leeches," and "Dollar patriotism." The Quaker testimonies of simplicity and equality were heard when he said, "Think of Charlie Chaplin, the popular Movie Actor, getting around half million dollars and over, for one year's salary, while millions are starving."[77] Carl Brumback claimed that the Assemblies of God helped correct the problem of rich churches that neglected the poor and caused them to "get out of the race and join the ranks of the unchurched. A mute cry went up to the throne of God from the hearts of these 'common people' for a church where they could feel 'at home.'"[78] Both the Quakers and the early Assemblies of God accepted the rejected ones of society and trumpeted their causes. Prophetic discernment of the evils of classism and materialism rang clear.

EVANGELIZATION

Quakers desired to evangelize everyone in the world, from the soldiers in the military to the peoples across the seas. From their earliest days Quakers proselytized among the soldiers and "found a sympathetic hearing and valuable support among both the army officers and rank and file."[79] This eventually resulted in the authorities being "alarm[ed] at the spread of Quakerism among the soldiers."[80] The Assemblies of God confirmed their desire to "Work Amongst the Soldiers" at the General Council in 1917.

> Bro. Raymond Richey was asked to speak about the work the Lord has laid upon his heart among the soldier boys, and in a very enthusiastic way he told how wonderfully the Lord had opened up the way for him, giving him favor in the eyes of the authorities, and how signally his efforts had been blessed so far.[81]

This resulted in the adoption of a resolution that encouraged the Assemblies of God to "adopt every available means consistent with scriptural teaching and example to co-operate with every approved agency for revivals among the soldiers."[82]

Early Quaker evangelism efforts compelled them to rent halls so they could spread their message to the masses. They also prophesied in the streets, "Early Quaker prophetic messages of judgment and confrontation were often given in a marketplace. . . ."[83] Some Quakers wanted to go to America in the 1670s so they could "convert Indians."[84] The twentieth-century Pentecostal movement began in a rented hall on Azusa Street in Los Angeles, and Pentecostals were generally ready to preach on any street corner if an audience could be found. Missionary zeal was an integral aspect of the early Assemblies of God and related directly to why they claimed to be a pacifist church. The first reason provided to the Assemblies of God constituency as an explanation of the pacifist resolution in 1917 was that "from its very inception, the Pentecostal Movement has been a movement of *evangelism*, studiously avoiding any principles or actions which would thwart it in its great purpose."[85] They understood killing to be a hindrance to missions and evangelism was certainly more important than war.[86]

WOMEN MINISTERS

Another remarkable similarity between early Quakerism and the early Assemblies of God was their attitude toward women. Quakers allowed God to speak through any person who was willing and "the equality in ministry of all Friends, rich and poor, young and old, educated and unschooled, and especially women and men, was noticed by everyone in the 1650s."[87] Margaret Fell wrote a tract in 1666 entitled "Women's Speaking" which was a breakthrough and showed that the Quaker women wrote as well as preached. In fact, Quaker women served as heads of households, supervised business meetings, and publicly conveyed "the most revolutionary message that all daily life was equally part of God's direct Call to each of his 'saints.'"[88]

Robert Barclay, in his 1678 *An Apology for the True Christian Divinity*, insisted "that every good Christian (not only men, but even women also) is a preacher."[89] Joseph John Gurney penned an entire chapter entitled "On the Ministry of Women" in which he declared that "Friends believe it right, freely and *equally*, to allow the ministry of both sexes."[90] This excellent chapter expounded on the manifold reasons why women have been and always will be used by the Spirit to speak words of exhortation and instruction to the church. He dealt with Paul's prohibitions by showing that the apostle was talking about speech that was not "prompted by the immediate impulses of the Holy Spirit."[91]

Many early Pentecostals also approved of women in ministry. In the first year of the Assemblies of God (1914), nearly one-third of ordained ministers were women.[92] They cited Peter in Acts 2 as he quoted from Joel, "your sons and your *daughters* will prophesy." They used this to show that women "could communicate religious truth under divine inspiration."[93] It is traditionally claimed that the first person to be baptized in the Holy Spirit with the evidence of speaking in tongues in the twentieth century was Agnes Ozman, and many of the pioneers of Pentecostalism were women.[94] Women frequently wrote articles in *The Pentecostal Evangel* in which they exhorted and encouraged the constituency. An example is "Daily Portion From the King's Bounty" by Mrs. A. R. Flower, who inspired women in ministry with poetry, "So her life was full of sunshine, for in toiling for the Lord, She had found the hidden sweetness that in common things lied stored."[95]

Both Quakers and the early Assemblies of God recognized to a greater degree than other religious groups that the Spirit empowered women for ministry. Both renewal movements broke with tradition and society as they elevated the status of the women in their assemblies.[96] Promoting women in ministry and nonviolence were related endeavors. Arthur Sidney Booth-Clibborn believed that allowing women to minister would help the "unlawfulness of war for the Christian [to] become ever more evident."[97]

LOYALTY TO GOVERNMENT

Early Quakers and the early Assemblies of God held similar views toward government. Despite their disestablishment actions and speech in many areas, each group also contained members who supported their governments. Both groups experienced tension because of these competing emphases. Some wanted to be loyal to their vision of the radical Christ; others also felt the need be faithful to the government. Their qualified cooperation with the state must be viewed in light of the proclamation of their peace testimony. Both groups dealt with their governments in similar manners: drafting resolutions, sending letters to those in authority, and declaring their loyalty to the earthly institutions. They both limited this allegiance with the qualification of nonviolence, but the qualification only lasted fifty years in the Assemblies of God.

George Fox and other early Quakers were emotionally involved in the Commonwealth government. Peter Brock commented that "their past tied them to the parliamentary cause in countless ways that made it extremely hard to separate decisively from it."[98] This is why Fox supported Cromwell's army and encouraged the government to use military force against the papacy. He hoped for swift victory when his side was fighting and told Cromwell, "let thy soldiers go forth with a free willing heart."[99] Fox held strong loyalties to his government and believed that it was ordained of God.

Fox supported the use of force when the government was upholding peace and ridding the world of evil, even though he believed that it was neither Christian nor something in which he himself could participate.

> Here the outward swordmen have not learned yet to beat their swords and spears into ploughshares and pruning hooks. Yet ye that are in that seed, see that ye accuse no man falsely, that hath the sword of justice, which is to keep the peace, and is a terror to the evil-doers, and to keep down the transgressors, and for the praise of them that do well.[100]

The early leaders of the Assemblies of God emphasized their loyalty to the United States government too. In 1917 the General Council prefaced their pacifist resolution with "While recognizing Human Government as of Divine ordination and affirming our unswerving loyalty to the Government of the United States. . . ."[101]

That same Council showed that they supported basic respect for the government when it condemned "insulting the flag."[102]

Bro. E. L. Banta spoke on the importance of our loyalty to the powers that be, since they are ordained of God; and told of some so-called Pentecostal preachers who thought they were doing honor to God by insulting the flag and of the humiliation to them that followed. Bro. A. P. Collins followed and said we were on Bible grounds in honoring the government, and said that the flag stood not only for civil freedom but also for religious liberty; and that at the Texas District Council they had purposed to cancel the credentials of any preacher who spoke against the government. This body also agreed that such radicals do not represent the General Council.[103]

A. P. Collins, a member of the General Presbytery, considered civil freedom and religious liberty qualities worthy of respect during World War I. Yet even the Texas Pentecostals did *not* disagree with the ethic of conscientious objection to war. Both Quakers and Pentecostals expressed loyalty to their own governments during war time.

Brock argued that at first Fox did not require, or even think it necessary, that all Quakers agree with him regarding his noncombatant position. Since Cromwell (in their view) was seeking justice, there was tension between the two ideals of peace and security. The achievement of security, even through violent means, was important enough for Fox to "enthusiastically support the government."[104] Thus the early Quakers differed from the Anabaptist-Mennonite tradition and accepted at least the police functions of civil government.[105]

The early leader of Quakerism, George Fox, wavered on pacifism and expressed a strong loyalty to his government until it looked as if his cause (the parliamentary system) would be defeated by the restoration of the monarchy. Once his side lost, he decided to disapprove fighting. By the end of 1659, he had confirmed his position for Christians and proclaimed, "All that pretend to fight for Christ, are deceived; for his kingdom is not of this world, therefore his servants do not fight. Therefore fighters are not of Christ's kingdom, but without Christ's kingdom."[106]

Even as they passed the pacifist resolution and declared themselves conscientiously opposed to war, early Assemblies of God leaders allowed room for those among them who wanted to fight for America. When the Assemblies of God explained the pacifist position to the constituency in May 1917, the second paragraph of the article began with the following qualification: "It is not intended to hinder anyone from taking up arms who may feel free to do so. . . ."[107] J. W. Welch, the chairman of the executive presbytery and author of the article, also stated his own opinion:

> Personally I should deplore the necessity for our young men to bear arms against others, but would be pleased to see many of them serve in a capacity that would afford them an opportunity to save life and to point men to Christ who may be facing death in the trenches.[108]

Thus the Assemblies of God was like the Quakers in choosing not, at the beginning, to forbid members to participate in war even though the leaders of the group favored a noncombatant stance.

Before Fox's pacifist decision, Quaker leader John Lilburne, a former Leveller,[109] quit the military and renounced violence.[110] He was only one of several Quakers who became pacifists in the 1650s. Thomas Lurting was a "fighting Quaker" who served in the English Navy until he developed "some scruple of conscience" during an attack on Barcelona. The reality of war seems to have convinced him that war was in every way opposed to the character of Christ. His firsthand experiences convinced him that he both had to be a pacifist and to convince as many of his Quaker brothers as possible of his perspective.[111] Arthur Booth-Clibborn's experience is similar in that his intense antiwar activism and writing was prompted by his firsthand experiences in the Anglo-Boer War (1899-1902). His famous book *Blood Against Blood* was penned shortly after he witnessed the violence of that war firsthand.

Quaker pacifism became an official principle of the Society of Friends in 1660. This took place after the restoration of the monarchy in England destroyed "the utopian millenarian hopes" of early Quakers. Fox then began to hold an uncompromising position that forbade any Quaker to serve in the military, because "it was contrary to our principles, for our weapons are spiritual and not carnal."[112] This was quite different from the way that the Assemblies of God developed. The Americans were on the winning side of World Wars I and II, and the American Pentecostals continued to stress their loyalty to government and to allow each Christian to choose whether or not to fight.

SUMMARY

This survey of evidence should render Assemblies of God references to a Quaker heritage less mysterious than they once were. Quaker pacifism and the twentieth-century Pentecostal movement were linked together historically by several Quaker Pentecostals. The early Assemblies of God leaders read, published, and recommended the pacifistic and inspirational literature of Quakers. They also shared many theological perspectives with Quakers and were founded in part by descendants of Quakers. Both early Quakers and early Pentecostals were radical, restorationist, defenders of the poor who allowed women to minister while evangelizing the masses and remaining loyal to their governments.

THE HOLINESS INFLUENCE ON
EARLY ASSEMBLIES OF GOD PACIFISM

The nineteenth-century Holiness movement developed as a response to the perceived "lack of sanctification" in Methodism,[113] and it served as an inspiration for the twentieth century Pentecostal movement.[114] Holiness believers wanted to return to John Wesley's original emphasis on perfect love and sanctification, and the resulting prominence of Christian perfection (holiness) was complementary to pacifism. This eventually influenced the first members of the General Council of the Assemblies of God. An investigation of the Holiness impact on Assemblies of God pacifism must begin with a description of the perfectionist and almost pacifistic theology of John Wesley and early Methodism.

John Wesley and War

John Wesley's strong emphasis upon perfect love contributed to a pacifistic interpretation of his writings. He believed that war was absurd and decidedly anti-Christian. He denounced war and even sympathized with Quaker arguments against war.[115] Love of humanity was at the forefront of Wesley's teaching and preaching. He preached that Christian love "suffers all the malice and wickedness of the children of the world. And it suffers all this, not only for a time, for a short season, but to the end; still feeding our enemy when he hungers; if he thirst, still giving him drink."[116] Furthermore, "the lover of mankind has no eye at all to his own temporal advantage . . . he desires nothing but the salvation of their souls."[117] In the same paragraph that he condemns wars and violence among Christians and compares them to Babylon, "the mother of harlots," Wesley encourages Christians to have so much love in their heart for "every soul, that thou mayest be ready to lay down thy life for his sake!"[118] Wesley denounced wars and told his followers that they should love their enemies enough to die for them. This willingness to die for others was a result of perfect love and seems to serve as evidence that he was a pacifist.

Wesley's exposition of the Christian as a peacemaker revealed his belief that Christians should be "lovers of God and man, who utterly detest and abhor all strife and debate, all variance and contention; and accordingly labor with all their might . . . to prevent this fire of hell from being kindled. . . ."[119] He described the peacemaker as one who,

> being filled with the love of God and of all mankind, cannot confine the expressions of it to his own family, or friends, or acquaintance, or party, or to those of his own opinions,—no, nor to those who are partakers of like precious faith; but steps over all these narrow bounds, that he may do good to every man, that he may, some way or other, manifest his love to neighbors and strangers, friends and enemies.[120]

Wesley's pursuit of perfect Christian love led him to see that "war [proves that] the very foundations of all things . . . are utterly out of course in the Christian . . . world."[121] He explained that one could never reconcile war with any attempt to "walk also as [Jesus] walked." War, a "horrid reproach to the Christian name," defied reason, virtue, and humanity.[122] Wesley argued that trying to solve international disputes by means of war was foolishness.

Wesley's practicality led him to recommend impartial arbitration as a remedy for war; however, he did not go so far as to demand nonviolence as a test of perfect love.[123] In fact, the opposite is true, despite his teachings to love the enemy and his denunciations of war. He claimed that it was lawful to bear arms "because there is no command against it in the New Testament."[124] Thus his interpretation of Romans 13 led him to support King George against the American Revolution. Wesley attacked as false the claim that the American Revolution was about freedom from slavery. He quoted an American tract and then repudiated it.

> The writer asserts twenty times, "He that is taxed without his own consent, that is, without being represented, is a slave." I answer, No; I have no representative in Parliament; but I am taxed; yet I am no slave. Yea, nine in ten throughout England have no representative, no vote; yet they are no slaves; they enjoy both

civil and religious liberty to the utmost extent. . . . "Who then is a slave?" Look into America, and you may easily see. See that Negro, fainting under the load, bleeding under the lash! He is a slave. And is there "no difference" between him and his master? Yes; the one is screaming, "Murder! Slavery!" the other silently bleeds and dies. But wherein then consists the difference between liberty and slavery? Herein: You and I, and the English in general, go where we will, and enjoy the fruit of our labors: This is liberty. The Negro does not: This is slavery. Is not then all this outcry about liberty and slavery mere rant, and playing upon words?[125]

This Wesleyan critique of the American Revolution deserves wider recognition in Christian circles, for his support of war highlights the fact that pro-war Christianity does not mean that Christians necessarily fight together. In evaluating Wesley's permissive attitude toward war, H. Richard Niebuhr observed that "he was much more concerned about swearing in soldier's camps than about the ethical problem of war and the useless sacrifice of soldiers' lives."[126] Wesley had expressed disgust for war but also believed loyalty to government sometimes justified the use of violence. Nevertheless, one can comprehend how many of his followers eventually understood his teaching on perfection to exclude any participation in warfare.

Methodism and War

Methodists in America at first expanded John Wesley's concerns about war and violence but then lapsed into a less critical nationalism that resorted to arms. Many Methodists refused to fight for either side in the Revolutionary War in America, but their testimony changed dramatically during the Civil War.

Donald and Lucille Dayton have claimed that the "major witness left by American Methodists during the Revolutionary War was one of conscientious objection."[127] This pacifism could be seen in the lives of such early Methodists as Francis Asbury (1745-1816), Jesse Lee, and Freeborn Garrettson. Francis Asbury, the first superintendent of the Methodist Episcopal Church in the USA, refused to sign Maryland's oath of loyalty because he believed that "he as a minister should not bear arms."[128] Jesse Lee (b. 1758) refused to serve in the militia and stated, "As a Christian and as a preacher of the gospel I could not fight. I could not reconcile it to myself to bear arms, or to kill one of my fellow creatures."[129] Freeborn Garrettson (1752–1827) explained his antipathy toward war by declaring, "From reading, my own reflection, and the teachings of the good Spirit, I was quite drawn away from a belief in the lawfulness of shedding human blood under the gospel dispensation. . . ."[130] These early Methodists served as examples of the link between Wesley and the Wesleyan Methodists that affected the American Holiness Movement.

The Civil War in America was a difficult time. The Methodist church had split over the issue of slavery; both sides were willing to fight and kill to defend their position. Some churches armed themselves, and Methodist itinerant ministers carried weapons on their circuits.[131] The Methodist churches recruited soldiers, and William Sweet estimated that fifteen percent of the Union Army were Methodists.[132] Perhaps Abraham Lincoln best revealed the Methodist attitude toward war during that time: "It is no fault in others that the Methodist Church sends more soldiers to the field, more nurses to the hospitals, and more prayers to heaven than any. God bless the Methodist Church!"[133] The Methodists went from broad nonresistance to broad combatant participation in and support of war in about one hundred years. This shift constitutes one of the reasons the American Holiness Movement emerged—as a reaction to the loss of "holiness" within American Methodism.

The American Holiness Movement and War

The American holiness movement originated from Wesley's perfectionism and Methodism. In 1839 Timothy Merritt, a Methodist minister, published the *Guide to Christian Perfection* so that John Wesley's teachings on sanctification and perfection would become a reality in nineteenth-century America.[134] This specialization of holiness, combined with revivalism and historic pietism, led to "as widespread a popular quest for the beatific vision as the world has known."[135] They had a desire for practical holiness in this life and believed that a second work of grace, sanctification, followed conversion. Christians expected to live significantly different lives following this second crisis experience. They believed God would restore the church to its primitive power through Christian perfection. Included in this quest for perfection was a concern for the proper Christian attitude toward involvement in warfare.

Wesleyan Methodists

Anti-slavery congregations withdrew from the Methodist Episcopal Church in 1841 to form the Wesleyan Methodist Church.[136] They became a predominant promoter of the holiness revival and from the beginning they preached nonviolence. They emphasized sanctification and perfection and adopted an article in 1844 that revealed the pacifist theology of their organization. "We believe the gospel of Christ to be every way opposed to the practice of war in all its forms; and those customs which tend to foster and perpetuate the war spirit, to be inconsistent with the benevolent designs of the Christian Religion."[137]

This aligned them with the Christian peace churches, and they published many "articles, letters, and editorials" expressing strong pacifist arguments in *The True Wesleyan*.[138] "We profess to believe all war anti-Christian, and have published our sentiments to the world. . . . Are we not under special obligation at a time like this [Mexican War, 1846-1848] to exert ourselves in the spread of peace principles, through the press, by the pulpit, and every other means within our reach?"[139] They applauded Quaker nonresistance and hoped that "no Wesleyan be found either spilling the lifeblood of his brother or giving encouragement to others to do so."[140] In 1847 they adopted two strongly worded resolutions that communicated the intensity with which they adhered to their Christian theology of nonviolence.

#1) That the spirit of the gospel, which is the spirit of Christ: "Love which worketh no ill to his neighbor," and the precepts of the gospel, which require us to "render good for evil;" to love, bless, and pray for our enemies; are so inconsistent with the spirit and practice of war, that both can no more be engaged at the same time than heaven and hell; and can be no more reconciled than Christ and Belial can be united; and that whoever is the advocate and friend of one is necessarily the enemy of the other. . . .

#4) The man who claims to be a Christian and most of all a public teacher, and knowingly gives his influence, ecclesiastically or politically, to perpetuate the system of either war or slavery, is a most arrant hypocrite, and no more worthy of Christian fellowship than a mahamattan [sic], infidel, or the midnight assassin.[141]

Wesleyan Methodists also taught that "it was not until Christianity became corrupt that the Christians became soldiers." Frank Bartleman, an early Pentecostal who had been an ordained minister with the Wesleyan Methodists, reiterated this language several years later in *The Pentecostal Evangel*. The Wesleyan Methodists even required pacifism as a prerequisite for membership in their denomination.[142] However, they did eventually "make participation in war a matter of individual conscience instead of denominational directive."[143]

Thomas Upham

Thomas Upham was a prolific author and influential holiness leader. He wrote the *Manual of Peace* to demonstrate to "the humble Christian . . . who makes Christ his great example and truly desires to be animated by the same Spirit" that war was "utterly wrong and sinful."[144] His wide-ranging book addressed the "evils and remedies of war" and its influence on domestic life, the morals of soldiers, national prosperity, the progress of civilization, and missions. He examined war in the light of nature, the Old Testament, and the principles of the gospel. Upham drew objections to war from the New Testament and the testimony and practice of early Christians, and related participation in war with the millennium. He made extensive observations and suggestions regarding the development of international law, blockades, free shipping, private property, fisheries, military chaplaincy, capital punishment, and the slave trade. A comparison with the Bible shows his prominence in the holiness movement: "Not Wesley, not Fletcher, not Finney, not Mahan, not Upham, but the Bible, the Holy Bible, is the first and last, and in the midst always."[145] He penned many articles on holiness themes that were widely read; it can be safely asserted that his pacifist views were absorbed into the holiness movement.

National Camp Meeting Association for the Promotion of Christian Holiness

The formation of the National Camp Meeting Association for the Promotion of Christian Holiness in 1867 marked the separation of the holiness movement from the Methodist church. This new organization became the primary voice of the holiness movement and used camp meetings, traveling preachers, holiness associations, missions, and numerous publications.[146] Both their radical holiness and their association with historic peace churches assisted the new holiness churches in forming a pacifist witness.[147] Quakers and Mennonites were drawn to the holiness movement and brought their peace testimonies with them. The Pentecostal movement grew out of this late nineteenth-century holiness phenomenon, and many of the founders and molders of the Assemblies of God were holiness preachers.[148]

Holiness Pacifists Who Influenced the Assemblies of God

The Assemblies of God experienced a direct impact from several holiness pacifists who became Pentecostals. The two most prominent ones were Frank Bartleman and Charles H. Mason.

FRANK BARTLEMAN (1871-1935)

Frank Bartleman is best known for his involvement in and chronicling of the Azusa Street revival in Los Angeles, California (1906-1909). However, he was also a vocal holiness Pentecostal pacifist who published numerous articles chastising Christian participation in war.[149] It has been surmised that he inherited his pacifism from his Quaker mother,[150] but this fails to correspond to his upbringing. He described his father as a fierce, patriotic, backslidden, hard-working, profane, violent man whom he greatly feared. His mother was "a very good, patient woman," but she never joined the church, "could not help her boys to really find God," and was not a believer.[151] Bartleman related that he "grew up with no personal knowledge of God" and considered himself a "heathen."[152] He experienced his conversion in a storefront mission at the age of twenty-two, joined a Baptist church, and read the Bible "from Genesis to Revelation."[153]

He worked in the slums, preached revivals, studied his Bible, and participated in D. L. Moody's camp meetings. He claimed to have met Moody personally for the first time in 1896 and subsequently sold his books.[154] D. L. Moody was a conscientious objector in the Civil War and had stated that "there has never been a time in my life when I felt I could take a gun and shoot down a fellow being. In this respect I am a Quaker."[155] Bartleman read Moody's biography, so he was certainly exposed to his pacifism.[156]

Bartleman traveled throughout the South as a holiness evangelist, attended "colored" churches, and concluded that black Christians were more dependable than white Christians.[157] These experiences probably prepared him to follow William Seymour's leadership at Azusa Street a few years later.[158] He carried a gun "for dogs" during this time but declared "you could not hire me to sleep with a loaded gun in the house."[159] It seemed important to Bartleman that he qualify the carrying of a firearm as being for dogs, not for protection against humans. This reveals his aversion to violence even at this early stage in his Christianity.

Bartleman pastored a Wesleyan Methodist church and participated in the Wesleyan conferences. This denomination still advocated a peace witness when Bartleman was a member. They modified their statement somewhat after the Civil War, but they still declared that they believed "the gospel of Christ to be intended to extirpate the practice of war and hence we cannot but deprecate those customs which needlessly foster and perpetuate the war spirit."[160] Bartleman also read the works of John Wesley during this time and quoted him extensively in his books.[161] In reference to a tent meeting he attended a few years later he stated, "they were Wesleyan Methodists, so that put me right at home."[162] The Wesleyan Methodists offered him parishes until he moved to California in 1904.[163]

Bartleman did most of his work with the Holiness Associations. He joined the State Holiness Association of Colorado, attended and preached at holiness camp meetings, and served as the pastor of a "Holiness Band" in Greeley, Colorado.[164] He was proud of the radical nature of his faith and considered it godly to have "an utter recklessness concerning men's opinions and other consequences. . . ."[165]

Bartleman's account of the Azusa Street mission revealed the merging of holiness "perfect love" into Pentecostal pacifism. It also reveals a connection between the fruit of the Spirit and the realities of life; their primitivist impulses were to be translated into a life of love in actual practice.

> Divine love was wonderfully manifest in the meetings. They would not even allow an unkind word said against their opposers, or the churches. The message was the love of God. It was a sort of "first love" of the early church returned. The "baptism" as we received it in the beginning did not allow us to think, speak, or hear evil of any man. . . . The Lord fought our battles for us in those days. We committed ourselves to His judgment fully in all matters, never seeking to even defend the work or ourselves.[166]

The participants of this early twentieth-century Pentecostal revival were mostly holiness Christians who had been rejected by their churches. They were ridiculed in the press, threatened, and harassed continually—yet did not retaliate.[167] They attributed this ability to withstand attacks to the power of the Holy Spirit in their lives. Bartleman related a specific example of this attitude when his own life was endangered by a mob led by "a very wicked atheist." He felt that he was going to die at their hands but "had to be willing to face martyrdom." Even though they were after him with clubs he felt no fear because "the fire of God seemed to encircle and possess me."[168] His nonviolence in this instance corresponded with the articles he wrote several years later against Christian participation in warfare.

Frank Bartleman had a significant effect on the early Pentecostal movement as a whole and the Assemblies of God in particular. His books, articles, and tracts were distributed by the hundreds of thousands; almost every Pentecostal magazine that existed in the early twentieth century published his work.[169]

Charles H. Mason (1866-1961)

Bishop Charles H. Mason was a Pentecostal pacifist who influenced the Assemblies of God through the denomination he founded, the Church of God in Christ. Mason had been a Baptist but left that association when he accepted holiness teachings and experienced his own "sanctification." He "was not satisfied with a faith that brought no fruit, or else fruit of so poor a quality, spiritually, and a religion that had none of the signs spoken of in Scriptures. . . ."[170] He and a fellow black holiness preacher, C. P. Jones, formed the Church of God in Christ as a holiness denomination in 1897. Their emphasis on sanctification caused them to be persecuted by other churches in the area; they even experienced rounds from a shotgun being fired into their building.[171]

Bishop Mason went to William Seymour's Azusa Street Revival in 1906 and was baptized in the Holy Spirit and spoke in tongues. The Church of God in Christ then became one of the first and eventually one of the largest Pentecostal denominations in existence.[172] Many white Pentecostals (among them the majority of the future founders of the Assemblies of God)[173] received their ordination through the Church of God in Christ so that they could receive reduced rail fares and be recognized by the United States government as ministers.

Bishop Mason was arrested and jailed during World War I because of his pacifism. He was also accused of being a German sympathizer and responded by saying, "I cannot understand, after preaching the gospel for twenty years and exhorting men to peace and righteousness, how I could be accused of fellowshipping with the anti-Christ of the Kaiser."[174] He recalled the persecutions he endured during World War I.

> The Holy Ghost through me was teaching men to look to God, for he is their only help. I told them not to trust in the power of the United States, England, France or Germany, but trust in God. The enemy (the devil) tried to hinder me from preaching the unadulterated word of God. He plotted against me and had the white people to arrest me and put me in jail for several days. I thank my God for the persecution. "For all that live godly must suffer persecution." 2 Tim. 3:12. . . . The presiding officers talked with me, after which they told me that I was backed up by the Scripture, and would not be hurt by them. . . . If God be for you, who can be against you![175]

The General Council of the Assemblies of God has been considered an "offspring" of the black Church of God in Christ.[176] Bishop Mason allowed a group of white Pentecostals to affiliate with and borrow the name of his group from 1910 to 1914. This white group held annual conventions in 1912 and 1913 as the Church of God in Christ but formed the General Council of the Assemblies of God in 1914.[177]

A survey of *The Pentecostal Evangel* seems to indicate that Mason had little influence on the Assemblies of God. Not a single article by him or about him was published until his death was reported six months after the fact in "Bishop Mason with the Lord."[178] Thirty-six years later a Church of God in Christ graduate student at the Assemblies of God Theological Seminary wrote an article that discussed Bishop Mason.[179] "Our Colored Brethren" and "No Smoking or Drinking," both of which were published in 1950, were about the Church of God in Christ.[180] Other than these four articles, nothing in the volumes of *The Pentecostal Evangel* would indicate any affiliation between the Assemblies of God and the Church of God in Christ.

Nevertheless, the Church of God in Christ was the wellspring from which the Assemblies of God grew. Mason's followers were aware of his pacifism and a significant number emulated it. The historiography of the white Pentecostals has traditionally minimalized the black influence; however, Mason's pacifism is part of the inheritance initially accepted in the Assemblies of God but later rejected.

Summary

Assemblies of God pacifism emerged from its holiness and Quaker heritage. Holiness and Quaker preachers united their quest for perfection with the power of the Holy Spirit to form a Pentecostal peace witness based on prioritizing the life and teachings of Jesus of Nazareth. Their crucifism reflected the Jesus centered and biblically justified Quaker arguments against war as well as their desire for sanctification. These influences were accompanied by several theological emphases within early Pentecostalism that encouraged a nonviolent ethic.

THE PENTECOSTAL FULL GOSPEL AND ASSEMBLIES OF GOD PACIFISM

Many early Pentecostals named their denominations "Full Gospel" and considered themselves preachers of the Full Gospel. They did not want to leave anything out, regardless of the consequences. The Assemblies of God agreed and emblazoned "All the gospel," another version of this sentiment, on their official seal. However, "All the gospel" also had a nice ring to it—both it and "Assemblies of God" could be shortened to AG. Their attempts to believe and teach all of the full gospel correlated with several theological emphases conducive to pacifism. These formed a cohesive message, of which nonparticipation in war was an integral part.

When Pentecostals read the Bible they took it seriously and prioritized Jesus and the Spirit-empowered church in the New Testament over the Hebrew Scriptures. They tried to interpret its teachings well even when doing so brought controversy. This led them to an apocalyptic eschatology; they expected the imminent return of Jesus Christ. Accompanying this idea was the belief that the Pentecostal movement would restore the church to her former glory in preparation for Christ's return. Therefore the Pentecostals wanted to do everything, as much as possible, like the first-century Christians. This restoration was possible because of the baptism in the Holy Spirit, which empowered Christians to live holy lives and fulfill their mission by witnessing to the world about Jesus. Each of these emphases contributed to the view that Christians, especially Spirit-baptized Pentecostal Christians, were to be nonviolent.

The Significance of Jesus and Scripture

The early Pentecostals tried to take the Bible so seriously and follow Jesus so well that they believed and accepted teachings even when they went against the grain of conventional Christianity. They were aware of both the continuity and discontinuity between the Old and New Testaments and gave priority to the fulfillment of the old covenant in the new. Much evidence for this assertion exists, but a few examples will suffice. Their attitude toward the Bible could be seen clearly in the following exhortation entitled "Live By the Word:"

> Jesus told Satan not by bread alone, but by EVERY WORD that proceedeth out of the mouth of God man shall live. Again it is said, "No WORD OF GOD shall be void of power." Jesus says too, "The WORDS that I speak unto you, they are spirit and they are life." This ought to be enough to cause every one to devour and live on the word of God. . . . Unless we hold firmly to God's word, we shall in some way, be swept from our moorings. Therefore, KNOW THE WORD. PREACH THE WORD.[181]

A 1915 Gospel Publishing House advertisement showed the degree to which they valued the Bible: "Protect Your Children. The Bible and the truths it teaches will be a talisman of protection and strength to them all the days of their life."[182]

The early Pentecostals exhorted their members to tithe because Jesus reiterated it. "In Malachi 3:8 the Lord asks, 'Will a man rob God?' And He then declares, 'Ye have robbed me—in tithes and offerings . . .' for He says we 'are cursed with a curse' if we rob Him of His tithes. Jesus says in Matthew 23:23 that we ought to pay tithes and not to omit judgment, mercy and faith."[183]

They claimed that they would not accept a teaching if it could not be backed up the Bible.[184] They rejected the use of wine in the eucharist because "wine is not once mentioned in connection with the Lord's Supper. Read the different accounts in the four Gospels, then read 1 Cor. 10:16, and 1 Cor. 11:23-25. It is strikingly apparent that Jesus shunned the use of the word 'Wine.' In each case he speaks of the fruit of the vine or else the simple words, 'the cup.'"[185] Early Pentecostals also interpreted literally 1 Peter 2:24, "By his stripes we were healed." Consequently, they believed that God could and would heal them.

The early Pentecostals devoted themselves to the belief that Scripture was of supreme significance, even if the results seemed foolish or harmed them. One leader proclaimed, "I propose to stick with the Word, though the heavens fall; though it comes in contact with all the man-made creeds in the world."[186] Their straightforward reading allowed them to speak in languages they had not learned, experience visions, hope for healings and miracles, be used in all the gifts of the Holy Spirit, and anticipate the impending end of all things.[187] Each of these beliefs is still held by the Assemblies of God. But they did not just naively do everything in the Bible—they started with Jesus and let him help them read the rest. Pentecostals did not sacrifice sheep, forbid eating pork, stone adulterers, or enforce circumcision—even though all these things are commanded in the Bible.

This serious and Christ-centered approach to Scripture provided a framework within which early Pentecostals could apply Jesus' teachings about nonviolence. If Jesus said "love your enemies," then they had no choice but to do as Jesus had instructed. As an early Pentecostal missionary reported, "The Scripture referred to reads as follows: 'Hereby perceive we the love of God, because He laid down His life for us: and WE OUGHT TO LAY DOWN OUR LIVES FOR THE BRETHREN."[188] There is much more evidence that they took Scripture seriously regarding ethics of warfare; Pentecostals wanted "to interpret as clearly as possible what the Scriptures teach upon the subject, as we have from the beginning declared the Bible to be our only rule of faith and practice."[189] "It is not what we think about it, but we are pledged already as Christians to obey Christ and the teachings of the New Testament. If we are fully on the Lord's side on this question, we will have to say what the Lord says about it."[190]

The Bible, especially the New Testament, was quoted, interpreted, and taken seriously whenever conscientious objection or nonparticipation in war arose. Arguments for war from the Old Testament sounded to them like arguments for animal sacrifices, circumcision, and food taboos. They were not concerned with explaining away the difficult concept of dying for what they believed. They already believed so many other ideas strange to the twentieth-century person that the absurdity of enemy love actually had a peculiar sort of attraction for them. Since it was taught by Jesus and lived by the early church, they simply adopted it as a truthful and acceptable manifestation of the "full Gospel."[191]

Premillennial Eschatology

The second coming of Jesus Christ has been called the "central concern of the initial Pentecostal message."[192] Equipped with a hermeneutic that encouraged them to take the Bible seriously, the early Pentecostals found much within its pages to increase their apocalyptic expectations. Their writings were filled with eschatological references and terminology, for they believed they were preaching the final word to the world and to the church. The bridegroom was coming for his bride, the latter rain was falling, and the end times were upon them for they were "the church of the end."[193]

The early Pentecostals were convinced that the events through which they were living were signs that the end was near. They were aware of the turmoil in the world; this confirmed their suspicions that the prophecies in the Bible were about to be fulfilled. J. Roswell Flower stated this clearly:

> We are watching every development of the crisis in Europe with the greatest of interest, with our newspapers in one hand and the Bible in the other, checking off each prophecy as it is being fulfilled, knowing of a surety that the coming of the Lord cannot be long delayed.[194]

They saw the end coming and were amazed that others did not have their clarity of insight. "All things that Christ prophesied are coming to pass so quickly I wonder more people do not realize it. Some of us will live to see the terror. . . ."[195] One early Pentecostal even interpreted Daniel's vision of the gold, silver, brass, and iron-clay statue to mean that the dawn of democracy heralded the end.

> There would be four great empires of man from that time . . . that the last phase would be democratic; and that the fifth would be Divine. The accurate and startling fulfillment of all but the Apocalypse brings us today to the very threshold of the End.[196]

Their apocalyptic eschatology had a direct influence on the way they viewed wars and military involvement. They outlined this relationship in the following statement:

> One of the principle reasons that we as Pentecostal people are interested in the present war, raging in Europe and Asia, is that it is closely connected with the return of the Jews to their beloved

land, Palestine; and the final adjustment of the nations and the return of the Lord Jesus Christ, the Jewish Messiah and the Christian's hope. . . . [197]

Wars served as accompaniments to cries for peace which would usher in the end. "Wars . . . show the political condition of the world, leading up to the one final conflict, preceeding which there is to be declarations of universal peace."[198] However, Pentecostals placed no hope in the peace summits of their day. "The world is not growing better, and Peace Conferences will never usher in a glad millennium, for evil men and seducers are waxing worse and worse."[199] The combination of biblical seriousness, apocalyptic eschatology, and war can be seen in the following declaration by Pentecostal evangelist L. C. Hall in 1913:

> The arms factories are running to the limit, powder mills are busy, army and naval academies are full of students, learning the arts of war, which is only legalized killing. (God says, "Thou shalt not kill") The air has a new occupant, the war air ship, (foretold by the prophet Habakkuk in Chap. 1 verse 8) . . . What does it mean? Ah! *The Great Crisis is at Hand!* . . . heaven shall be shaken, and they shall see the Son of man coming in a cloud with power and great glory, and when these things begin to come to pass, THEN LOOK UP AND LIFT YOUR HEADS FOR YOUR REDEMPTION DRAWETH NIGH. HALLELUJAH! Luke 21:23-28.[200]

Because of their belief that the world was not going to last much longer, the early Pentecostals had little motivation to fight to defend their nations, which brought condemnation from liberal postmillennialists. Jesus was coming back for his pure bride, not for a bloodied soldier who had been fighting for worldly interests. "Is any child of God going to side with these belligerent kings? Will he not rather side with the Prince of Peace under whose banner of love he has chosen to serve?"[201]

A major element of this type of eschatology is the rejection of many social institutions, especially the government, since they are part of a decaying order. The early Pentecostals did in fact reject secular and "human" attempts at making the world a better place to live. Samuel H. Booth-Clibborn even rejected the Red Cross and noncombatant military service because they helped send men back to war.[202]

It is a challenge to know what to reject and what to cooperate with, to know with how many fallen powers the faithful church should work. To believe the end is truly near complicates Christian action and hope for improvement—not participating in sin while also working for a better world takes careful and critical thought. Instead of participating in the institutions of this world, the early Pentecostals chose to focus on what they believed to be their great commission: the restoration of the New Testament church and the evangelization of the world.

Restorationism

Early Pentecostals wanted to be like the New Testament church. Grant Wacker identifies this primitivism as the "determination to return to first things, guided solely by God's Spirit in every aspect of their lives, however great or small. . . . [It is] a downward or even backward quest for the infinitely pure and powerful fount of being itself."[203] They believed that the church had fallen from its original power and that the Pentecostal movement was God's plan to restore it. B. F. Lawrence explained:

> And now perhaps you are asking, "In what particulars are you so earnestly striving to revert to primitive Christianity?" The answer is of course, "In every way . . ." we desire a return to New Testament power and custom along all those lines of activity which made evident beyond controversy that the church was the living body of a living Christ.[204]

The quest to be like the church described in Acts was necessary because Christianity had strayed from its origins. Bartleman wrote in 1915 that "Nine years ago [a reference to the beginning of the Azusa Street Revival in 1906] the Holy Spirit began to lead us into the Book of Acts and show us the meaning of that Word that had been hidden since the backsliding of the church in the early centuries."[205] Restoration included believing in healing, signs and wonders, *glossolalia* (speaking in unknown tongues), all the gifts of the Spirit,[206] and the "gift ministries" of apostles, prophets, evangelists, pastors, and teachers. If the church was again to be holy and powerful like the first-century church, then the Pentecostals had to live as the first-century Christians did. They wanted simplicity and were anti-denominational because they saw the primitive church as being exactly that. They cried "Back to Pentecost" and hoped that they could experience the "old time religion."[207]

Nonparticipation in war was an integral aspect of restoring primitive Christianity. Some early Pentecostals viewed the Roman emperor Constantine's conversion in the fourth century as the beginning of militarism in the church and a prominent contributor to the apostasy they tried to correct. In fact, Arthur Booth-Clibborn claimed that "wherever there is a revival of the spirit of Apostolic Christianity, there also appears a revival of the conviction and the testimony that war is anti-Christian."[208] The restoration of primitive Christianity necessarily included the restoration of a peace testimony that foreshadowed God's ultimate peaceful kingdom. However, the restoration of a holy church was only part of the plan for the end times. The world needed to be evangelized, and that mission also conflicted with combatant participation in warfare.

Missions

The desire to evangelize like the New Testament Christians, accompanied by the belief in the imminent end of all things, motivated the early Pentecostals to zealous mission endeavors, leading them to urge hasting "to the ends of the earth with the glad news of salvation before it is too late."[209] They believed they had to accomplish this immediately and certainly had no time to acquire an education or learn the necessary languages.

> If Jesus tarries until we have to learn all the languages of the world in colleges, He will not come soon, for not one hundredth part of the languages of the world is known or taught in our high schools and colleges. It is daring mockery to say this world will be evangelized through the channel of education. . . . The gift of languages of the world by the Holy Spirit is of more importance.[210]

Reports from mission fields in both America and around the world filled early Pentecostal monthly and weekly papers. A sampling from any issue of the *Word and Witness* would yield messages from missionaries in such locales as Egypt, Persia, South Africa, China, West Africa, Japan, India, South America, and Washington, D.C.[211] They devoted several pages in each issue to reporting "News from the Foreign Fields." The concept of killing human beings when one was supposed to be sharing the gospel with them seemed a ludicrous idea to many Pentecostals. They were also keenly aware of the irony of a Christian from one nation killing a Christian from another nation. "Converting men by the power of the gospel, and later killing these same converts, across some imaginary boundary line is unthinkable."[212] They also employed the Jews as an example of the inappropriateness of those actions.

> Never before in all their unhappy history have the Jews suffered as during the last year [1914]. All have been loyal to the country to which they owe allegiance, although realizing that they were fighting men of their own racial and religious aspirations . . . particularly embarrassing has this been in Germany, Russia and Austrian Poland, being virtually civil war.[213]

Booth-Clibborn argued that crucifists make the best missionaries because they are willing to lay down their lives like Christ did. Like a soldier who rushes into close contact with his enemy even if it kills him,

> the same is true of the apostolic Christian. He gets in closest contact with the "enemy," because he is determined to save even should he get killed in the attempt . . . are not out-and-out, what-care-I Christians the only sort who can win to Christ the desperate anarchist, or lead to repentance the Parisian Apache or the Yorkshire rough. . . ? Christ gave himself for us. We give ourselves for humanity. We do exactly what the worldly soldiers do in their wars. We sacrifice our lives if need be; but we kill no one. All complications disappear once this point is made plain. It seems so simple that it appears childish to say it. In this it resembles the whole plan of salvation by grace.[214]

The mission of the Pentecostal Christian to convert the sinner to the prince of peace rather than kill him for a transient nation inextricably linked evangelization and pacifism. However, Pentecostals also believed that this radical approach to missions was not for the faint of heart and could not be followed by ordinary Christians. Only the power of the Holy Spirit made it possible.

Baptism in the Holy Spirit

Christians who had been baptized in the Holy Spirit would accomplish the restoration of the New Testament church and the evangelization of the world. This work of grace, which they viewed as being subsequent to salvation, empowered the believer to preach and live the gospel. *Glossolalia* (speaking in an unknown language) accompanied and evidenced this baptism. Initially, the early Pentecostals believed that they would speak in known languages and proclaim the glorious works of God to unbelieving foreigners (*xenolalia*).[215] Eventually this idea faded away and was replaced by the belief in glossolalia.

Speaking in tongues, however, was only one aspect of the baptism in the Holy Spirit. The main purpose of the baptism in the Holy Spirit was to provide boldness to Christians so that they could be used by God to perform signs and wonders by healing the sick, speaking powerfully about Jesus, being reconciled, suffering, or even dying if necessary. These signs pointed to Jesus Christ as the Savior of the world and authenticated the message. Early Pentecostals related the power of the baptism in the Holy Spirit with the power to be a cross-carrying, enemy-loving, Jesus-following crucifist.

Samuel H. Booth-Clibborn explained why Jesus and his followers could overcome evil with nonviolence. He attributed Jesus' ability to drive out the entire crowd in the temple to the fact that he was filled with the Holy Spirit.

> Spiritual power—not carnal brute force—is the weighty fact we must grasp here. . . . A poor, humble, practically unknown man of the laboring class suddenly enters the outer Temple court, just as business is humming; and promptly creates havoc! . . . They all stand transfixed and helpless! Why? Ah, beloved, here's the secret, and may God help us to learn it! . . . It was simply God's Holy Ghost power.[216]

Booth-Clibborn dealt with the Christian response to war and presented a Spirit-filled Jesus as the model for his Pentecostal readers. His father, Arthur S. Booth-Clibborn, also linked the power of Pentecost with separating "from all association with the world in its war and its peace programmes." He knew that in so doing the Christian would have to live his or her "Christianity as tragically and as triumphantly as those to whom, in the early days, conversion to Christ meant being thrown to the lions, singly or in families." Thus, the proper order for the true Christian experience was "a bloody Calvary, a Pentecost of fire, and the hostility of an entire world [conversion, Holy Spirit baptism, faithful witness]."[217]

Arthur Booth-Clibborn elaborated on the link between the baptism in the Holy Spirit and pacifism in 1920 when he warned that killing in warfare cheapened Pentecost, for the latter clearly negated the former.

The shadow of war has by no means left the world yet. Worse things may be coming. During this pause believers who have been in any uncertainty as to the relationship between war and the Christianity of Christ might do well to study the matter carefully and to fully make up their minds. This Pentecostal movement is a most sacred deposit and trust wherever it has been received by an individual or an assembly. Truly it is a case of "taking the shoes from off our feet." Any cheapening of the price of Pentecost would be a disaster of untold magnitude. The company in the upper room upon whom Pentecost fell, had paid for it the highest price. In this they approached as near as possible to him who had paid the supreme price to send it.[218]

Booth-Clibborn argued that Pentecost had arrived by way of sacrifice; any selfish fighting for national interests directly contradicted it. The many Pentecostal Christians who had lived "the Christianity of Christ" before them understood that "the purity and fullness of the individual Pentecost [empowered witness of Christ] must depend upon the completeness of the individual Calvary [refusal of violence/willingness to die/crucifism]."[219]

Acts, especially Acts 1:8, became a central focus, since it related Jesus' desire for his disciples to be filled with the Holy Spirit, empowered, and then spread the witness to the ends of the earth. The original invitation to the first "General Convention of Pentecostal Saints and Churches of God in Christ" (out of which came the Assemblies of God) was "only for saints who believe in the baptism with the Holy Ghost with the signs following."[220] The emphasis on "signs following" revealed that the early Pentecostals were concerned with the results of being baptized in the Holy Spirit. Numerous articles expounded on this theme, but one entitled "Sane and Insane Practices . . . The Pentecostal Baptism in the Holy Ghost Gives Power to Evangelize" placed the baptism in the Holy Spirit in proper perspective.

> It is manifestly more important to get souls saved than to have people healed or filled with the Holy Ghost. [We should not] put a premium upon the baptism in the Spirit which the Scriptures do not. The purpose of the baptism is clearly stated in Jesus' own words "Ye shall receive power after that the Holy Ghost is come upon you, and ye shall be witnesses of Me." This experience qual-

ifies the child of God for service . . . let us put first things first, and not get the cart before the horse.[221]

That service involved loving one's enemies even when the results were painful. Early Pentecostals did not necessarily expect every Christian to understand or to be able to lay down his or her life for others. But some believed nonviolence was a necessary aspect of following Jesus as an "Apostolic" and "Spirit-filled" Christian. That ultimate sacrifice was made possible by the example of Jesus and the empowerment of the Holy Spirit.

Summary

Assemblies of God pacifism, nonviolence, and conscientious objection received theological encouragement from the witness of Friends and Holiness Christians, and a few Pentecostal emphases helped it find a comfortable home. Most first-generation Pentecostals accepted the crucifist teaching of Jesus and expected the imminent end of history while attempting to restore New Testament Christianity and evangelize the world because of their special empowerment by the Holy Spirit. They refused to be sidetracked by participation in the wars of this world, since killing clearly contradicted "seeking first the kingdom of God." Pacifism reinforced the reality of their Full Gospel and served as a concrete realization of the truths they professed. Nonviolence was an ethical component of their radical—down to the roots—theology.

The disestablishmentarian tendencies of the Assemblies of God contributed to their pacifism, but the fact that some supported the government to the point of fighting led to a tension that eventually did away with the pacifist position. The Assemblies of God had many similarities with early Quakerism, published numerous articles by Quakers, and included at least one Quaker among its founders. The Assemblies of God also benefited from the influence of both black and white holiness pacifists. The early Assemblies of God pacifists had peaceful heritages upon which they could rely and a Christ-centered interpretation of Scripture that supported their convictions. Their interpretation of world events informed them that they did not have time to waste, while their interpretation of the Bible instructed them to save men rather than kill them. Their history and their theology allowed crucifism to fit perfectly into their worldview.

NOTES

1. "The Pentecostal Movement and the Conscription Law," *The Weekly Evangel*, 4 August 1917, 6. Notice the inclusion of both Allied and enemy nations as having Pentecostals who are nonresistant.

2. B. F. Lawrence, "The Apostolic Faith Restored," in *Three Early Pentecostal Tracts*, ed. Donald W. Dayton (New York: Garland Publishing, 1985).

3. Ibid., 35-36.

4. Although Frank Bartleman's mother was a Quaker, he explained that his parents did not influence him religiously. Frank Bartleman, *From Plow to Pulpit, From Maine to California* (Los Angeles: by the author, 1924), 6, 31; reprinted in *The Higher Christian Life: Sources for the Study of the Holiness, Pentecostal, and Keswick Movements*, ed. Donald W. Dayton, no. 5 *Witness to Pentecost: The Life of Frank Bartleman*, with a preface by Cecil M. Robeck, Jr. (New York: Garland Publishing, 1985). Charles Parham's minimal Quaker associations had little effect upon the development of Assemblies of God attitudes toward war. He had been ostracized from the infant Pentecostal movement in 1907 because of sodomy charges, and nothing he wrote ever appeared in *The Pentecostal Evangel*.

5. Arthur Sidney Booth-Clibborn, *Blood Against Blood* (1901; reprint New York: Charles Cook, 1914).

6. It was recommended in at least three editions of the *Word and Witness* in 1915 (a predecessor to the *Pentecostal Evangel* which was edited by the Assemblies of God founders E. N. Bell and J. R. Flower) as well as in *The Christian Evangel*. *Word and Witness*, June 1915, 2; July 1915, 2; August 1915, 4. *The Christian Evangel*, 19 June 1915, 1.

7. Roger Robins recognized the relationship between the Assemblies of God and Quakerism because of "shared values and beliefs" but stated "the Quaker connection should not be pressed." He was more concerned with demonstrating the pacifism of the early Assemblies of God than showing any direct Quaker influence. "Our Forgotten Heritage: A Look at Early Pentecostal Pacifism," *Assemblies of God Heritage* (Winter: 1986-87), 3-5. He claimed that "the Quaker influence among Pentecostals was not small" but did not elaborate in "A Chronology of Peace: Attitudes Toward War and Peace in the Assemblies of God: 1914-1918" *Pneuma* (Spring: 1984), 19. It should also be noted that the Quaker peace witness preceded Pentecostalism about two hundred and fifty years.

8. Edith Blumhofer mentioned that Samuel Herbert Booth-Clibborn's father, Arthur Sidney Booth-Clibborn, was a Quaker by birth and that *The Pentecostal Evangel* recommended his strongly pacifistic book, *Blood Against Blood*. Blumhofer also noted that Maria Woodworth-Etter (1844-1924), an early Pentecostal evangelist, was supported by Quakers and that Assemblies of God education was modeled after Quaker principles, "Friends conceded that the Bible was authoritative and then talked about the Spirit." *The Assemblies of God*, vol. 1 (Springfield, Mo.: Gospel Publishing House, 1989), 351, 34, 314. William Menzies did not reference Quakerism in his presentation of Assemblies of God attitudes toward military service, *Anointed to Serve: The Story of the Assemblies of God* (Springfield, Mo.: Gospel Publishing House, 1971). Stanley H. Frodsham also did not mention Quaker ideals or pacifism

in *With Signs Following: The Story of the Pentecostal Revival in the Twentieth Century* (Springfield, Mo.: Gospel Publishing House, 1946). Carl Brumback related the story of a "Quakeress" and Quaker minister (not named) who prayed for the healing of Alice Reynolds Flower's mother in 1872 but did not mention pacifism, *Suddenly . . . from Heaven: A History of the Assemblies of God* (Springfield, Mo.: Gospel Publishing House, 1961), 11.

9. Leonard Lovett noted that Quakers experienced glossolalia, "Black Origins of the Pentecostal Movement" in *Aspects of the Pentecostal-Charismatic Origins*, ed. Vinson Synan (Plainfield, N.J.: Logos, 1975), 126. Martin Marty briefly mentioned Quakers in a lineage from Montanists to Pentecostals, "Pentecostalism in American Piety and Practice" in *Aspects of the Pentecostal-Charismatic Origins*, 205. Nils Bloch-Hoell noted Quaker glossolalia, screaming, convulsions, baptism in the Holy Spirit, and entire sanctification, *The Pentecostal Movement* (New York: Humanities Press, 1964), 16, 139. But he decided there was "no direct historical or genetic connection between the above-mentioned movements [Quakers, Shakers, Mormons] and the Pentecostal Movement." Walter Hollenweger praised the early pacifism of the Pentecostals and referred to Arthur S. Booth-Clibborn's *Blood Against Blood* but did not mention he was a Quaker, *Pentecostalism* (Peabody, Mass.: Hendrickson, 1997), 187. Hollenweger also noted that there was a group called the Quaker Pentecostals of the USA but did not elucidate, *The Pentecostals* (Minneapolis, Minn.: Augsberg, 1972), 72. Donald Dayton linked Quakerism and Pentecostalism as "the more radically, pneumatically oriented movements" and credited Quakerism/Pietism with influencing Pentecostal thought regarding divine healing, *Theological Roots of Pentecostalism* (Peabody, Mass.: Hendrickson, 1987), 42, 117. John Thomas Nichol included the glossolalia of Shakers and the unique pacifist position of the International Pentecostal Assemblies which "differentiate[d] the IPA from the other Pentecostals" but said nothing about Quakers, *Pentecostalism* (New York: Harper & Row, 1966), 22, 144.

10. Stanley M. Burgess, "Quakers (Society of Friends)" in *Dictionary of Pentecostal and Charismatic Movements*, ed. Stanley M. Burgess, Gary B. McGee, and Patrick H. Alexander (Grand Rapids, Mich.: Zondervan, 1988), 752.

11. The men who comprised the 1917 Executive Presbytery of the Assemblies of God that wrote this resolution were J.W. Welch, Stanley H. Frodsham, J. Roswell Flower, D. W. Kerr, and D. B. Rickard. *The Weekly Evangel*, 19 May 1917, 8.

12. Donald Green, introduction to *A Peculiar People: The Rediscovery of Primitive Christianity*, by Joseph John Gurney (1824; reprint Richmond, Ind.: Friends United Press, 1979), v.

13. Arthur Booth-Clibborn, *Blood Against Blood*, 170.

14. Green, *Peculiar People*, iv.

15. Arthur Booth-Clibborn, *Blood Against Blood*, 172.

16. Arthur Booth-Clibborn, *Blood Against Blood*, 169.

17. Arthur Booth-Clibborn, *Blood Against Blood*, 169.

18. Arthur Booth-Clibborn, *Blood Against Blood*, 170.

19. Arthur Booth-Clibborn, *Blood Against Blood*, 172.

20. Arthur Booth-Clibborn, *Blood Against Blood*, 175.

21. Ibid. He and his wife, Catherine Booth (daughter of General William Booth, founder of the Salvation Army), were prominent founders and leaders of the Salvation Army in France, Switzerland, Holland, and Belgium.

22. James Robinson, "Arthur Booth-Clibborn: Pentecostal Patriarch," *The Journal of the European Pentecostal Theological Association* 11 (2001): 75.

23. Handwritten note in the *Booth-Clibborn Collection,* "held by Mrs. Ann Booth-Clibborn in Edinburgh whose husband, Stanley Booth-Clibborn, was formerly Bishop of Manchester and a grandson of Arthur Booth-Clibborn," cited in Robinson, "Arthur Booth-Clibborn," *JEPTA*, 76.

24. His son authored the other one. Samuel H. Booth-Clibborn, *Should a Christian Fight? An Appeal to Christian Young Men of All Nations* (Swengel, Pa.: Bible Truth Depot, n.d.). Internal evidence indicates that the book was written in either 1917 or 1918 during American participation in World War I.

25. Arthur Sydney Booth-Clibborn, *Blood Against Blood*, 29.

26. Arthur Sydney Booth-Clibborn, *Blood Against Blood*, 44.

27. Arthur Sydney Booth-Clibborn, *Blood Against Blood*, 45. Emphasis in the original.

28. Arthur Sydney Booth-Clibborn, *Blood Against Blood*, 50-51.

29. Arthur Sydney Booth-Clibborn, *Blood Against Blood*, 59.

30. John Howard Yoder, *Nevertheless: Varieties and Shortcomings of Religious Pacifism* (Scottdale, Pa.: Herald Press, 1971), 77-83.

31. Ibid., 78.

32. William Booth-Clibborn, *The Baptism in the Holy Spirit: A Personal Testimony*, 4th. ed. (1936; reprint Dallas, TX: Voice of Healing Publishing, 1962), 74.

33. Arthur Sidney Booth-Clibborn, 21. It should be noted that he did not call this a "Pentecostal" experience at that time.

34. Letter (dated April 7 1908 from Brixton) published in the magazine *Cloud of Witnesses* to *Pentecost in India,* (No. 6, 1908) ed. Max Moorhead; cited in Robinson, "Arthur Booth-Clibborn," *JEPTA*, 81.

35. Robinson, "Arthur Booth-Clibborn," *JEPTA*, 88.

36. *General Council Minutes*, 1914, 13. He wrote twenty-one books by 1968, *Saved by Sight: The Vision Without Which We Perish* (Northridge, Calif.: Voice Christian Publications, 1968), 10.

37. William Booth-Clibborn, *The Baptism in the Holy Spirit: A Personal Testimony* (Portland, Ore: Booth-Clibborn Book Concern, 1936), 19.

38. Ibid., 47.

39. Ibid., 10.

40. Brumback, 339. William Booth-Clibborn, *The Baptism in the Holy Spirit: A Personal Testimony* (1936), 28.

41. Mrs. Eric Booth-Clibborn, "Obedient Unto Death," *The Weekly Evangel*, 2 January 1926, 12. See bibliography for complete listing.

42. "The Christian and War: Is It Too Late?" *The Weekly Evangel*, 28 April 1917, 5. "The Christian and War. Article 2. Christ Cleansing the Temple." *The Weekly Evangel*, 19 May 1917, 4. The content of these articles is examined in chapter two.

43. Samuel H. Booth-Clibborn, *Should A Christian Fight: An Appeal to Christian*

Young Men of All Nations. It contained much of the same material that appeared in his articles in *The Weekly Evangel.*

44. "Blood Against Blood. Should Christians Go to War?" *The Weekly Evangel,* 10 July 1915, 3.

45. *The Weekly Evangel,* 19 June 1915, 1.

46. "Pentecostal Saints Opposed to War," *Weekly Evangel,* 19 June 1915, 1.

47. Robinson, "Arthur Booth-Clibborn," *JEPTA,* 86.

48. "What is War?" *The Weekly Evangel,* 21 April 1917, 2.

49. Robinson, "Arthur Booth-Clibborn," *JEPTA,* 88.

50. See bibliography for a complete listing.

51. H. S. Cronin, ed., "The Twelve Conclusions of the Lollards," *The English Historical Review* 22:2 (April 1907): 302-303; quoted in Peter Brock, *The Quaker Peace Testimony 1660 to 1914* (York, England: Sessions Book Trust, 1990), 1.

52. Brock, *The Quaker Peace Testimony,* 2.

53. Ibid., 3.

54. Albert Peel, ed., "A Conscientious Objector of 1576," *Transactions of the Baptist Historical Society* 7:1/2 (1920): 123; quoted in Peter Brock, *The Quaker Peace Testimony 1660 to 1914* (York, England: Sessions Book Trust, 1990), 4.

55. Brock, *The Quaker Peace Testimony,* 3.

56. This is similar to the "Nonpacifist Nonresistance of the Mennonite 'Second Wind'" described by Yoder in *Nevertheless,* 108-111. For Anabaptists this stance is often traced to the Schleitheim Confession (1527). Also see Gerald Biesecker-Mast, *Separation and the Sword in Anabaptist Persuasion,* C. Henry Smith Series vol. 6 (Telford, Pa.: Cascadia Publishing House, 2006), 97-132.

57. In 1988 there were more than eleven thousand Pentecostal denominations and three thousand independent charismatic denominations. Pentecostals/charismatics "are found within all 150 traditional non-Pentecostal ecclesiastical confessions, families, and traditions . . . are found in 8,000 ethnolinguistic cultures, speaking 7,000 languages, covering 95 percent of the world's total population." Twenty-eight percent (562,526,000) of Christians are Pentecostals/charismatics, i.e. one-twelfth of the world. D. B. Barret, "Statistics, Global," *Dictionary of Pentecostal and Charismatic Movements,* 811, 813.

58. Brock, *The Quaker Peace Testimony,* 5.

59. Timothy George, "Between Pacifism and Coercion: The English Baptist Doctrine of Religious Toleration," *The Mennonite Quarterly Review* 58:1 (January 1984): 38.

60. Ibid., 34.

61. See John Howard Yoder, *Discipleship as Political Responsibility* (Scottdale, Pa.: Herald Press, 2003).

62. Hugh Barbour and J. William Frost, *The Quakers,* Denominations in America (Westport, Conn.: Greenwood Press, 1988), 5.

63. Barry Reay, *The Quakers and the English Revolution* (London, 1985), 3.

64. Gary B. McGee, "The Debate over Missionary Tongues Among Radical Evangelicals, 1881-1897," in *Toward Healing Our Divisions: Reflecting on Pentecostal Diversity and Common Witness, The 28th. Annual Meeting of the Society for Pentecostal*

Studies Held in Springfield, Missouri 11-13 March 1999 (Society for Pentecostal Studies, 1999), 6.

65. Robert Mapes Anderson, *Vision of the Disinherited: The Making of American Pentecostalism* (Peabody, Mass.: Hendrickson, 1992), 6. Anderson stated "Pentecostals stood in somewhat the same relationship to other Fundamentalists as the Quakers did to other Puritans." There is debate regarding the extent to which Pentecostals should have been considered Fundamentalists, since they were so open to the Spirit and were consistently rejected by the established Fundamentalists of the day.

66. Bracy V. Hill III, "A Search for a Scriptural Hermeneutic in Early Pentecostal Pacifism," unpublished paper written for Ph.D. seminar at Baylor University, 2005.

67. Frank Bartleman, "What Will the Harvest Be?" *The Pentecostal Evangel*, 7 August 1915, 2.

68. Barbour and Frost, *The Quakers*, 11.

69. *The Pentecost* 1 (November 1908): 7.

70. Joseph John Gurney, *A Peculiar People: The Rediscovery of Primitive Christianity* (1824; reprint, Richmond, Ind.: Friends United Press, 1979), 454-492.

71. In the forward to this work J. Roswell Flower asks the rhetorical question, "Is it possible for the church of the twentieth century to revert to the principles of the church of the first century, and to expect that the miraculous leadership of the Holy Spirit, so explicitly recorded in the Acts of the Apostles, may be realized in the church today?" Carl Brumback, *Suddenly . . . from Heaven: A History of the Assemblies of God*, 6.

72. Murray Dempster, "Reassessing the Moral Rhetoric of Early American Pentecostal Pacifism," *Crux* 26 (March 1990): 26.

73. Brock, *The Quaker Peace Testimony*, 10.

74. William Penn, *No Cross, No Crown*, 1, Ch. 18, 10; quoted in Barbour and Frost, 44.

75. Frank Bartleman, "War and the Christian," tract, 4.

76. Frank Bartleman, "In the Last Days," *Word and Work*, September 1916, 393.

77. Frank Bartleman, "Christian Preparedness," *Work and Work*, c. 1916, 114.

78. Brumback, *Suddenly . . . from Heaven*, 6.

79. Brock, *The Quaker Peace Testimony*, 11.

80. Ibid.

81. *General Council Combined Minutes*, 1914-1917, 16.

82. Ibid.

83. Barbour and Frost, *The Quakers*, 39.

84. Ibid., 73.

85. "The Pentecostal Movement and the Conscription Law," *The Weekly Evangel*, 4 August 1917, 6. Emphasis added.

86. Ironically, evangelizing the military eventually helped reverse the early Assemblies of God attitudes toward war. It became a reason to support both the soldiers and the wars they fought.

87. Barbour and Frost, *The Quakers*, 43.

88. Ibid. See also Hugh Barbour, "Quaker Prophetesses," in *Seeking the Light*, ed. J. William Frost and John M. Moore (Wallingford and Haverford, Pa.: 1986), 41-

60; Mary Maples Dunn, "Women of Light," in *Women of America: A History*, ed. Carol Ruth Berkin and Mary Beth Norton (Boston: 1979), 114-138.

89. Barclay, *An Apology for the True Christian Divinity*, 203.

90. Gurney, 261, *A Peculiar People: The Rediscovery of Primitive Christianity*. Emphasis in the original.

91. Ibid., 265.

92. *General Council Combined Minutes*, 1914, 13-15. One hundred fifty-two out of five hundred thirty-one ministers were women. In the Assemblies of God women were allowed to serve as evangelists and missionaries. However, the first General Council in 1914 decided (by male voters) that women could not pastor or hold administrative offices. This contrast with Quakerism parallels the loss of pacifism predicted by Booth-Clibborn when he related women in ministry to pacifism.

93. A. J. Gordon, "The Ministry of Women," *The Alliance Weekly*, 1 May 1948, 277; quoted in Kenyon, 190. This article was printed over fifty years after Gordon's death in 1895.

94. See Mary Jackson, "The Role of Women in Ministry in the Assemblies of God," Ph.D. diss., The University of Texas at Arlington, 1997. Also see Anthea D. Butler, *Women in the Church of God in Christ: Making a Sanctified World* (Chapel Hill, N.C.: University of North Carolina Press, 2007). "Women, Role of," *Dictionary of Pentecostal and Charismatic Movements*, 893-899.

95. Mrs. A. R. Flower, "Daily Portion From the King's Bounty," *The Weekly Evangel*, 4 August 1917, 7. Mrs. H. J. Johns, "Camp Fremont, California," *The Christian Evangel*, 7 September 1918, 7. Mrs. Belle Price, "Praying for the Soldiers," *The Weekly Evangel*, 7 July 1917, 11.

96. However, in the early Assemblies of God the same man who limited their pacifism also limited women in ministry. E.N. Bell, a Southern Baptist minister who became a Pentecostal, disapproved of women in authority and also approved combatant participation in war. He had neither a holiness nor a Quaker background. This is evaluated further in chapter four.

97. Arthur Sidney Booth-Clibborn, *Blood Against Blood*, 175.

98. Brock, *The Quaker Peace Testimony*, 17.

99. Quoted in Hugh Barbour, *The Quakers in Puritan England* (London, 1964), 196.

100. Fox, *Epistles*, no. 188 (1659); quoted in Brock, 16. This is a clear reference to Romans 13, which is the primary New Testament passage employed to justify the use of violence to maintain civil peace.

101. *General Council Minutes*, 1917, 11-12.

102. *General Council Minutes*, 1917, 17.

103. *General Council Minutes*, 1917, 17.

104. Brock, *The Quaker Peace Testimony*, 18.

105. Ibid.

106. Fox, *Journal*, 357; quoted in Brock, 23.

107. J. W. Welch, "An Explanation," *The Weekly Evangel*, 19 May 1917, 8. This is a significant concession that is evaluated in chapter two.

108. Welch, "An Explanation," *The Weekly Evangel*, 19 May 1917, 8. Welch ex-

pressed a cultic law pacifism that allowed noncombatant military service, i.e. he was an alternativist pacifist rather than an absolute pacifist. Yoder, *Nevertheless*, 97. Brock and Young, *Pacifism in the Twentieth Century*, 42.

109. Levellers were a seventeenth-century religious group that "demanded that no man be ruled by another against his will, and called for absolute social and political equality." Bacon, 10.

110. Brock, *Quaker Peace Testimony*, 18.

111. Brock, *Quaker Peace Testimony*, 19.

112. George Fox, *Journal*, 357; quoted in Brock, 23.

113. D. William Faupel, *The Everlasting Gospel: The Significance of Eschatology in the Development of Pentecostal Theology* (Sheffield, England: Sheffield Academic Press, 1996), 54-76.

114. Donald W. Dayton, *Theological Roots of Pentecostalism*, 35-113; Donald W. Dayton, "From Christian Perfection to the 'Baptism in the Holy Ghost,'" in *Aspects of Pentecostal-Charismatic Origins*, ed. Vinson Synan (Plainfield, N.J.: Logos, 1975), 39-54; Melvin E. Dieter, "Wesleyan-Holiness Aspects of Pentecostal Origins: As Mediated Through the Nineteenth-Century Holiness Revival," in *Aspects of Pentecostal-Charismatic Origins*, ed. Vinson Synan (Plainfield, N.J.: Logos, 1975), 55-80. Charles Edwin Jones, "Holiness Movement" in *Dictionary of Pentecostal and Charismatic Movements*, 406-409.

115. Wesley read the works of Quaker author Anthony Benezet and was impressed by his anti-slavery work. Wesley established a relationship by correspondence with Benezet, who encouraged Wesley to write against the slave trade. Wesley took Benezet's book recommendations seriously and it is quite possible that he was influenced by his Quaker pacifism. Warren Thomas Smith, *John Wesley and Slavery* (Nashville, Tenn.: Abingdon, 1986), 76-89. It should also be noted that Wesley developed his theology of grace upon St. Augustine's definition of sin as perverted love, thus St. Augustine possibly influenced Wesley's views on warfare. See Mildred Bangs Wynkoop, *A Theology of Love: The Dynamic of Wesleyanism* (Kansas City, Mo.: Beacon Hill Press, 1972), 49, 155. For more about St. Augustine's influence on Wesley see Roland H. Bainton, *Christianity* (Boston, Mass.: Houghton Mifflin Company, 1987).

116. John Wesley, *The Works of the Rev. John Wesley, A.M.* vol.1 *Sermons* (New York: Eaton and Mains, 1910), 193.

117. Wesley, *The Works of the Rev. John Wesley, A.M.* vol.1 *Sermons*, 194.

118. Wesley, *The Works of the Rev. John Wesley, A.M.* vol.1 *Sermons*, 198.

119. Wesley, *The Works of the Rev. John Wesley, A.M.* vol.1 *Sermons*, 203.

120. Wesley, *The Works of the Rev. John Wesley, A.M.* vol.1 *Sermons*, 203.

121. John Wesley, "The Moral State of Mankind" in *The Doctrine of Original Sin*; quoted in James H. Potts, *Living Quotes of John Wesley* (New York: Hunt and Eaton, 1891), 78.

122. Ibid.

123. John Alfred Faulkner, *Wesley as Sociologist, Theologian, Churchman* (New York: The Methodist Book Concern, 1918), 19-21. Manfred Marquardt notes that Wesley evangelized among the soldiers but did not require that they leave the mili-

tary, *John Wesley's Social Ethics: Praxis and Principles*, trans. John E. Steely and W. Stephen Gunter (Nashville, Tenn.: Abindgon, 1992), 128.

124. "Bennett Minutes of the First Conference (1744)," quoted in Richard Cameron, *Methodism and Society in Historical Perspective* (New York: Abingdon, 1961), Volume I of "Methodism and Society."

125. John Wesley, "A Calm Address to Our American Colonies (1775)," in *The Works of John Wesley, vols. 11-12: Thoughts, Addresses, Prayers, and Letters* (Grand Rapids: Baker, 1996), 81.

126. H. Richard Niebuhr, *The Social Source of Denominationalism* (New York: Henry Holt, 1929), 68; quoted in Donald W. and Lucille S. Dayton, "An Historical Survey of Attitudes Toward War and Peace Within the American Holiness Movement," Seminar on Christian Holiness and the Issues of War and Peace (June 7-9, 1973), 3. This paper also appears with the same title as chapter 8 in *Perfect Love and War: Dialogue on Christian Holiness and the Issues of War and Peace*, ed. Paul Hostetler (Nappanee, Ind.: Evangel Press, 1974), 132-152.

127. Dayton and Dayton, "An Historical Survey," 6.

128. Richard Cameron, *Methodism and Society in Historical Perspective* (New York: Abingdon, 1961), 89.

129. Minton Thrift, *Memoir of the Rev. Jesse Lee* (New York: Bangs and Mason, 1823; reprint, Arno Press, 1969), 26. Jesse Lee, *A Short History of the Methodists in the United States of America* (Baltimore, Md.: Magill and Clime, 1910).

130. Nathan Bangs, *The Life of the Rev. Freeborn Garrettson* (New York: Mason & Lane, 1838), 57.

131. Sweet, *Methodism in American History*, 282-283.

132. Sweet, *Methodism in American History*, 286. This calculates to 300,000 Methodists serving in the Union military during the four years of the Civil War. It has also been estimated that an even higher percentage of the Southern military were Methodists.

133. Abraham Lincoln, "Letter to the General Conference of 1864," quoted in Sweet, *Methodism in American History*, 299.

134. Dieter, *The Holiness Revival of the Nineteenth Century*, 1. It is not within the scope of this book to detail the origins of the American Holiness Movement. See Jones, *Perfectionist Persuasion: The Holiness Movement and American Methodism, 1867-1936* (Metuchen, N.J.: The Scarecrow Press, 1974).

135. Dieter, *The Holiness Revival of the Nineteenth Century*, 3.

136. Daniel R. Chamberlain, "First Pure, Then Peaceable: The Position of the Wesleyan Methodist Church on War and Peace from its Founding to the Civil War," *Within the Perfection of Christ: Essays on Peace and the Nature of the Church*, ed. Terry L. Brensinger and E. Morris Sider (Nappanee, Ind. and Grantham, Pa.: Evangel Press and Brethren in Christ Historical Society), 217.

137. *Discipline of the Wesleyan Methodist Connection*, 1844, 93; quoted in Dayton and Dayton, *An Historical Survey*, 7.

138. Daniel R. Chamberlain, "First Pure, Then Peaceable: The Position of the Wesleyan Methodist Church on War and Peace from its Founding to the Civil War," *Within the Perfection of Christ*, ed. Terry L. Brensinger and E. Morris Sider, 219.

139. R. S. Ensign of Zanesville, Ohio, "War," *The True Wesleyan*, July 10 1847, 109. Quoted in Daniel R. Chamberlain, "First Pure, Then Peaceable: The Position of the Wesleyan Methodist Church on War and Peace from its Founding to the Civil War," *Within the Perfection of Christ*, ed. Terry L. Brensinger and E. Morris Sider, 220.

140. R. S. Ensign of Zanesville, Ohio, "War," *The True Wesleyan*, July 10, 1847, 109; quoted in Daniel R. Chamberlain, "First Pure, Then Peaceable: The Position of the Wesleyan Methodist Church on War and Peace from its Founding to the Civil War," *Within the Perfection of Christ*, ed. Terry L. Brensinger and E. Morris Sider, 220.

141. St. Lawrence Annual Conference, Watertown, N.Y., 1847; quoted in Dayton and Dayton, *An Historical Survey*, 7.

142. St. Lawrence Annual Conference, Watertown, N.Y., 1847; quoted in Dayton and Dayton, *An Historical Survey*, 7.

143. Daniel R. Chamberlain, "First Pure, Then Peaceable: The Position of the Wesleyan Methodist Church on War and Peace from its Founding to the Civil War," *Within the Perfection of Chris*, ed. Terry L. Brensinger and E. Morris Sider, 228.

144. Thomas Upham, *Manual of Peace* (New York: Leavitt, Lord, and Company, 1836), 98, 112.

145. The original source of this is not certain. The Daytons note that it is attributed to the *Guide to Holiness* and a "Congregational paper," Dayton and Dayton, "An Historical Survey," 8. The earliest appearance is George Hughs, *Fragrant Memories of the Tuesday Meeting and the Guide to Holiness* (New York: Palmer and Hughes, 1886), 38.

146. Dayton and Dayton, "An Historical Survey," 14. They note that by 1883, fifty-two national camp meetings had been held.

147. Dayton and Dayton, "An Historical Survey," 14. The Daytons note three factors that contributed to the holiness peace testimony: radical legalism, separation from Methodism (which removed the holiness movement from the establishment), and the influx of peace church traditions.

148. C. E. Jones, "Holiness Movement," *Dictionary of Pentecostal and Charismatic Movements*, 406-409.

149. Bartleman claimed to have written over 550 articles. He also published 250,000 copies of 58 tracts he wrote in a two-year period. Frank Bartleman, *How Pentecost Came to Los Angeles: As It Was In The Beginning* (Los Angeles: by the author, 1925), 93, 127; reprinted in *The Higher Christian Life: Sources for the Study of the Holiness, Pentecostal, and Keswick Movements,* ed. Donald W. Dayton, no. 5, *Witness to Pentecost: The Life of Frank Bartleman*, with a preface by Cecil M. Robeck, Jr. (New York: Garland Publishing, 1985).

150. Beaman, *Pentecostal Pacifism*, 54.

151. Frank Bartleman, *From Plow to Pulpit, From Maine to California* (Los Angeles: by the author, 1924), 6, 31; reprinted in *The Higher Christian Life: Sources for the Study of the Holiness, Pentecostal, and Keswick Movements*, ed. Donald W. Dayton, no. 5, *Witness to Pentecost: The Life of Frank Bartleman*.

152. Bartleman, *From Plow to Pulpit,* 6, 9.

153. Bartleman, *From Plow to Pulpit*, 22.

154. Bartleman, *From Plow to Pulpit*, 28.

155. William Moody, *The Life of Dwight L. Moody* (New York: Revell, 1900), 82.

156. Bartleman, *From Plow to Pulpit*, 95.

157. Bartleman, *From Plow to Pulpit*, 46.

158. Seymour was an African-American.

159. Bartleman, *From Plow to Pulpit*, 58.

160. Chamberlain, "First Pure, Then Peaceable," 228.

161. Bartleman, *From Plow to Pulpit*, 85. Frank Bartleman, *How Pentecost Came to Los Angeles: As It Was In The Beginning*, 5, 18, 46, 53, 74, 88, 97.

162. Bartleman, *From Plow to Pulpit*, 98.

163. Bartleman, *From Plow to Pulpit*, 109. Once in California he applied for a Wesleyan Methodist parish in Oregon but nothing came of it.

164. Bartleman, *From Plow to Pulpit*, 99.

165. Frank Bartleman, *How Pentecost Came to Los Angeles: As It Was In The Beginning*, 47

166. Bartleman, *How Pentecost Came to Los Angeles*, 54-55.

167. The *Los Angeles Times* regularly ran articles about the "weird babble of tongues" and "wild scenes" in "derogatory tones." C. M. Robeck, Jr., "Azusa Street Revival," *Dictionary of Pentecostal and Charismatic Movements*, 32.

168. Robeck, "Azusa Street Revival," 95-96.

169. *The Pentecostal Evangel* printed three articles by Bartleman and published at least one of his tracts.

170. Elsie W. Mason, "Bishop C. H. Mason, Church of God in Christ," in Milton C. Sernett, ed. *Afro-American Religious History: A Documentary Witness* (Durham, NC: Duke University Press, 1985), 286. The source for this article is *The Man, Charles Harrison Mason (1866-1961)*, (Memphis, Tenn.: Church of God in Christ, 1979), 10-20.

171. Elsie W. Mason, "Bishop C. H. Mason," 288. The fact that they were African-Americans may have contributed to the harassment; however, they reported no such attacks when they were Baptists.

172. In 2001 they had over 5.5 million members. C. E. Jones, "Church of God in Christ," *Dictionary of Pentecostal and Charismatic Movements*, 205.

173. At least 352 white Pentecostals were ordained in the Church of God in Christ between 1907 and 1913. Most of them went on to form the Assemblies of God in 1914. Wayne E. Warner, "Church of God in Christ (White)," *Dictionary of Pentecostal and Charismatic Movements*, 203.

174. C. H. Mason, "The Kaiser in the Light of the Scriptures," sermon of 23 June 1918, 4; quoted in Kenyon, 64.

175. Mason quoted in German R. Ross, *History and Formative Years of the Church of God in Christ* (Memphis, Tenn.: Church of God in Christ, 1969), 23-24.

176. Ithiel Clemmons, "Insidious Racism in American Religious Statistics," *The Whole Truth*, February 1983, 3.

177. For a detailed account of the relationship see Kenyon, 60-77.

178. "Bishop Mason With the Lord," *The Pentecostal Evangel*, 13 May 1962, 27.

179. Elijah H. Hankerson III, "The Church of God in Christ," *The Pentecostal Evangel*, 31 May 1998, 9.

180. "Our Colored Brethren," *The Pentecostal Evangel*, 8 July 1950, 12. "No Smoking or Drinking," *The Pentecostal Evangel*, 9 September 1950, 7.

181. *Word and Witness*, 20 March 1913, 2. Emphasis in the original.

182. *Word and Witness*, September 1915, 8. Gospel Publishing House was the official publisher for the General Council of the Assemblies of God.

183. H. A. Goss, "Shall We Pay Tithes? If So, To Whom?" *Word and Witness*, 20 May 1913, 2.

184. Regarding the argument that manual labor was evidence of a lack of faith, the editor of the *Word and Witness* asked "where is the chapter and verse that teaches this? Nobody can find it." *Word and Witness*, 20 March 1913, 2. This was the normal method of presenting and rejecting doctrinal and ethical ideas.

185. J. Roswell Flower, "The Lord's Supper," *Word and Witness*, August 1915, 5. Flower also notes that Jesus and Paul use the word *wine* in many other situations that are not related to the eucharist.

186. George F. Taylor, *The Spirit and the Bride* (Dunn, N.C.: the author, 1907), 114; quoted in Faupel, *The Everlasting Gospel*, 27.

187. It remained consistently true that the pacifists took the New Testament more seriously than the Old Testament but both were believed to convey literal events, even though the instructions in the Old Testament had been fulfilled by Jesus (i.e. kill anyone who does not worship Yahweh, Exodus 22.20). The nonpacifists consistently referred to the Old Testament, avoided Jesus, and quoted Romans 13. The evidence for this is provided throughout chapters two, three, and four.

188. Daniel C. O. Opperman, "Who is to Blame," *Word and Witness*, 20 March 1913, 2. Emphasis in the original. "The 'Pentecostal' believer, above all others, will insist upon a Scriptural basis for whatever stand he may take." Donald Gee, "War, the Bible, and the Christian," *The Pentecostal Evangel*, 8 November 1930, 6.

189. J. W. Welch, "An Explanation," *The Weekly Evangel*, 19 May 1917, 8.

190. Lydia Hatfield, "The Law of Christ for Believers," *The Christian Evangel*, 12 July 1919, 3.

191. This term refers to the idea that the Pentecostals were finally preaching and living according to all the gospel, since they were not omitting any of it. In fact, "All the Gospel" has served as an alternate meaning for the "AG" which designates the Assemblies of God. "The Whole Gospel for the Whole Man in the Whole World" was also a motto for the *Word and Witness* and its successor, *The Pentecostal Evangel*, since 1915.

192. Faupel, *The Everlasting Gospel*, 20. Faupel's text is an excellent contribution toward understanding the prominent role of eschatology in early Pentecostalism.

193. Frank Bartleman, "War and the Christian," *Word and Work*, (circa 1915), 83.

194. J. Roswell Flower, "The Need of the Hour," *Word and Witness*, August 1914, 1. Also in "Rumors of Wars," *The Christian Evangel*, 14 August 1914, 2.

195. Archer P. Collins, "Signs of Our Times," *Word and Witness*, 20 October 1913, 1. Collins was a member of the Executive Presbytery of the Assemblies of

God.

196. D. M. Panton, "Democracy and the End," *Word and Witness*, May 1915, 5. Furthermore, "Colossal Man has thus been tested in every part: absolutism, oligarchy, militarism, democracy—all ranks and classes have received, and grossly mishandled, world-power." Significantly, some early Pentecostals did not view democracy as God's only way to work in the world. This allowed them to be free from the obligation to kill people in order to defend it. Democracy was just one of the human attempts to operate the world.

197. "Preparations for the Return to Palestine," *Word and Witness*, August 1915, 2.

198. Archer P. Collins, "Signs of Our Times," 1.

199. C. W. Doney, "The Gospel of the Kingdom," *Word and Witness*, 20 March 1914, 2.

200. L. C. Hall, "The Great Crisis Near at Hand," *Word and Witness*, 20 November 1913, 1.

201. Stanley H. Frodsham, "Our Heavenly Citizenship," *Word and Witness*, October 1915, 3.

202. Samuel H. Booth-Clibborn, *Should a Christian Fight?*, 84.

203. Grant Wacker, *Heaven Below* (Cambridge, Mass.: Harvard University Press, 2001), 12.

204. Bennett F. Lawrence, *The Apostolic Faith Restored*, with a forward by John W. Welch (St. Louis, Mo.: Gospel Publishing House, 1916), 12-13. John Welch was the pacifist chairman of the Assemblies of God at the time.

205. Frank Bartleman, "Present Day Conditions" *Weekly Evangel*, 5 June 1915, 3.

206. Those mentioned in 1 Corinthians 12 are the word of wisdom, the word of knowledge, faith, the gift of healing, the working of miracles, prophecy, discerning of spirits, tongues, and interpretation of tongues.

207. Lawrence, *The Apostolic Faith Restored*, 12.

208. Arthur S. Booth-Clibborn, *Blood Against Blood*, 146.

209. "The Latter Days," *Word and Work*, 29 September 1907, 23.

210. E. A. Sexton, "College vs. Gifts of the Spirit," *The Bridegroom's Messenger*, 1 October 1907, 1. Here also is a reference to the enabling power of the Holy Spirit to help carry out the mission of evangelizing the world.

211. *Word and Witness*, August 1915, 5-7. *The Christian Evangel, Word and Work,* and *Bridegroom's Messenger* contained the same emphasis on mission work.

212. Frank Bartleman, "Christian Citizenship," tract (circa 1922), 2; quoted in Dempster, "Crossing Borders," 72.

213. "Preparations for the Return to Palestine," *Word and Witness*, August 1915, 2. This section was a quotation of an article that appeared in the *St. Louis Globe-Democrat*.

214. Booth-Clibborn, *Blood Against Blood*, 97. Note the restorationism and appeal to Christ's example in Booth-Clibborn's theology.

215. R. P. Spittler, "Glossolalia," *Dictionary of Pentecostal and Charismatic Movements*, 335-341.

216. Samuel H. Booth-Clibborn, "The Christian and War," 4. Emphasis in the original.

217. Arthur S. Booth-Clibborn, "Nigh, Even at the Doors!" *The Christian Evangel,* 5 October 1918, 6.

218. Arthur S. Booth-Clibborn, "European Pentecostal Notes," *The Christian Evangel,* 6 March 1920, 11.

219. Arthur S. Booth-Clibborn, "European Pentecostal Notes." "Crucifism" means that taking up one's cross shapes one's life of faithfulness to Jesus.

220. "General Convention of Pentecostal Saints and Churches of God in Christ. Hot Springs, Arkansas, April 2 to 12, 1914," *Word and Witness,* 20 December 1913, 1.

221. E. Armstrong, "Sane and Insane Practices," *Word and Witness,* July 1915, 5.

FOUR

WAR IS NOT CONSISTENT WITH THE DOCTRINES OF CHRIST: THE ASSEMBLIES OF GOD PEACE WITNESS FROM 1914-1940

INTRODUCTION

In 1917 the Assemblies of God professed to the United States Government that they were a pacifist fellowship. This organization of around 8,500 Christians defended their declaration with appeals to Jesus, Scripture, their heritage, and the evangelistic nature of the worldwide Pentecostal movement.[1] The first members of the Assemblies of God held a variety of perspectives regarding Christian participation in warfare, and the word *pacifism* itself has been controversial.[2] For purposes of clarification, the first generation Assemblies of God views will be classified according to the following terminology. First, absolute pacifists believed that Christians should not participate in war either as combatants or as noncombatants.[3]

Second, noncombatant pacifists would not kill in warfare but would serve in the military in other capacities.[4] This is a complex category, since some Assemblies of God folk identified themselves as conscientious objectors when they served as noncombatants in the military, and they did not like thinking of themselves as "pacifists." It may sound strange to Mennonites and other historic peace church members to hear noncombatants referred to as conscientious objectors, but the Christians who conscientiously opposed killing in war yet served as medics, cooks, and barbers did consider themselves objectors.

Third, a minority believed that Christians should let their consciences guide them toward absolute pacifism, noncombatant pacifism, or combatant military service. This last group is described as those in favor of the authority of individual conscience regarding military service. This by default ends up being a pro-combatant position.[5]

Between 1914 and 1940, four themes revealed the official and unofficial positions of the Assemblies of God regarding war: nonviolence, ministry to the military, patriotism, and the authority of individual conscience. Both loyalty to the government and the authority of conscience to participate in war, either as a combatant or a noncombatant, were ideas exhibited by a minority in the Assemblies of God even in the early years. The occurrence of such concepts was infrequent for the most part before 1941 but did appear during American participation in World War I (1917-1918) amid the patriotic fervor that swept the country. However, the theology and practice of not shedding blood, either as an absolute pacifist or a noncombatant, and the desire to minister to soldiers were emphasized repeatedly from 1914-1940. The pre-World War II Assemblies of God had pacifism and ministry to the military in the foreground while patriotism and the choice to fight remained in the background.

American Censorship and Suppression of Pacifists During World War I

Assemblies of God pacifism emerged during World War I, "one of the most intolerant periods for free speech and expression of religion in American history."[6] President Wilson established the Committee on Public Information in April 1917 to persuade Americans that the war was holy and the enemy was evil.[7] Two months later, the Espionage Act passed to empower the suppression of any dissent or critique of the war effort. The Bureau of Investigation (renamed the Federal Bureau of Investigation in 1935) investigated over one million persons, organizations, and publications. The Department of Justice even sued Mennonites who signed a Christian statement encouraging nonviolence.[8]

President Wilson empowered the Postmaster General, Albert Burleson, to confiscate and revoke mailing privileges from any periodicals or mail that he deemed a hindrance to the draft or the war effort.[9] Burleson expanded the order and told all the American postmasters to keep "a close watch on unsealed matter, newspapers, etc. containing matter which is calculated to . . . embarrass or hamper the Government in conducting the war."[10] Within the first month he declared fifteen major publications nonmailable.[11] Many more magazines, journals, and newspapers, including Christian ones, were shut down without court approval. The Church of Christ *Gospel Advocate* presented a Christian pacifist stance toward the war, so the district attorney in Tennessee threatened the editor with arrest "if such publications did not cease."[12] The *Gospel Advocate* complied and did not publish any more pacifist articles throughout the war.

In another case, a Bureau of Investigation officer and the local postmaster in Lometa, Texas, seized three thousand copies of a Church of Christ preacher's pamphlet that encouraged conscientious objection. They also took his list of addresses with the names of all the preachers he mailed the pamphlet to. They did this because he appeared "drunk with the faith of his religion to such an extent that he placed the good of his country secondary to his religion."[13] This action silenced him as well.

The editor of the pacifist *Gospel Herald*, fearing he would be shut down, apologized for an article after the local postmaster sent a copy of one of his articles to the solicitor of the Post Office Department in Washington. The solicitor told the postmaster that he "should not have allowed the paper containing the objectionable matter to have passed through the mails," that other editions should be nonmailable, and that the Bureau of Investigation had been contacted regarding the Espionage Act violation. The editor explained that "the doctrine of nonresistance has been a cherished doctrine of the Church from the beginning" but that the article did unfortunately contain "some very radical statements to which the management of the paper does not subscribe."[14] In addition to the loss of mailing privileges, the Department of Justice also threatened and actually arrested numerous pacifists for expressing views that opposed the war. These arrests often made front-page news.[15]

Private and government-sanctioned groups such as the National, State, and County Councils of Defense; the National Security League; and the American Protective League encouraged citizens to turn in their neighbors if they suspected them of disloyalty. They also pressured Mennonites, Pentecostals, Quakers, and others with threats of violence if they did not buy Liberty Bonds and donate to the Red Cross and the YMCA. Newspapers listed the names of donors so that those who did not give could be intimidated into donating.[16] Regular tactics of coercion included tarring and feathering, beatings, painting the pacifists as well as their houses and churches yellow, forcing conscientious objectors to kiss the American flag and sign checks, and mandating the use of only the English language in church services.

Zealous patriots burned to the ground Mennonite churches in Michigan and Oklahoma, and in Kansas the main building at Tabor College (Mennonite Brethren) as well as a Lutheran church went up in flames.[17] Earlier in the evening, local citizens had forced the Lutheran pastor to ring the church bells in a victory celebration, then they burned the church. Near Lawrence, Kansas, the locals tarred another Lutheran preacher for not preaching in support of the Liberty bond drives.[18] A coal miner who refused to buy a Liberty bond "was thrown by other miners into the reservoir at mine No. 18 of the Western Coal and Mining Company near Pittsburg [Kansas], hanged for a few seconds, then dumped into a barrel of grease. He was jailed at Girard with a broken nose and other injuries."[19] Lynchings increased steadily throughout the war and reached their highest levels in summer 1918.[20]

Cordell (Okla.) Christian College taught the view of its sponsoring denomination, the Churches of Christ, that "it is wrong for Christians to take part in warfare." Michael Casey tells the tragic story of how the Washita County Council of Defense, in an "atmosphere where beatings, economic coercion, and the threat of vigilante violence occurred with frightening regularity," forced the actual closure of the university in summer 1918.[21] The Council held hearings and declared that because the faculty and administration taught nonviolence and did not support the war effort, the school should "be so re-organized as will unreservedly conform to all military policies and requirements of the government in the present war. . . . All doctrines and teachings . . . must comply strictly and to the fullest extent with the military policy of the government."[22] The Council demanded an administration and faculty that would stand for "constituted authority in all its dignity and power."

The board of regents resisted. So a mob of fifty men gathered and their leader declared that they should "close the school and leave town at once or mob violence would prevail." When the board chair refused and said they would submit to their persecution, he was told that "instead of fifty men, there will be *five hundred men* here to attend to you if you do not clear out at once." The leadership of the college, after continual threats of violence, decided to close the school. The Oklahoma State Council of Defense vindicated the Washita County Council with the decision that they "had arrived at the proper results." No recrimination ever came for the citizens who forced the closure.[23]

More than 2.8 million men served in the military during World War I; only 3,989 claimed exemption as conscientious objectors. Public antagonism toward COs led one organizer of an enthusiastic crowd in Ohio to teach that citizens should handle objectors with "an axe, a shovel, and a halter. . . . Use the axe to kill the man, and the shovel to bury him, and . . . the halter to lead one of his cows to market. Then you'll have money to buy bonds."[24]

The army court-martialed more than five hundred of the COs and sentences ranged from ten years to life in prison.[25] COs in prison and in the military barracks were regularly tortured. They were beaten, denied food, handcuffed for days in body stretching positions that resulted in blood bursting from open wounds, and subjected to "scrubbing and tubbing." They were stripped of their clothes, put in cold showers, and raked with brooms until their skin was removed and they "looked like a piece of raw meat."[26]

At least two Christian COs, Joseph and Michael Hofer, died at Fort Leavenworth, Kansas, because of mistreatment they received there and at Alcatraz in San Francisco, California. The army sentenced them to thirty-seven years in prison for refusing to wear a military uniform, so they were put in an Alcatraz dungeon with no clothing except the uniforms they refused to wear. After being starved for days, with no blankets or clothes, and told they would die there if they did not cooperate, they were chained to iron bars and beaten with sticks.

After four months of this treatment, diseased with eczema and scurvy and with arms swollen by insect bites, they were shipped to Fort Leavenworth. Arriving in the middle of the night, they were driven through the streets "like pigs" by soldiers with open bayonets. They were stripped again in the freezing cold. In the days that followed they were forced to stand nine hours per day chained to the bars of their cell with only bread and water to sustain them.

Another CO sent word to their wives in Washington, who left immediately by train for Kansas. They arrived the night Joseph died, November 28, 1918. The commanding officer ordered that Joseph be dressed in the military uniform he had refused to wear, and this is how his wife found him as he lay in his coffin. Michael died a few days later on December 2. Only then, on December 6, did the Secretary of War issue an order "prohibiting handcuffing, chaining, and the otherwise brutal punishment of military prisoners."[27] Three months later 260 religious COs still remained at Fort Leavenworth, at least nineteen of whom were Pentecostals.[28]

Refusing military service, "to fight for God, nation, and flag," incensed the American public more than any other issue during World War I. Society called conscientious objectors "cowards, slackers, parasites, scoundrels, traitors, and individuals not worthy of holding American citizenship."[29] In 1918 Dave Allen, a twenty-six year old Pentecostal in Alabama, was beaten and shot to death by two police officers in his home, in front of his wife, because he would not fight in World War I. The report of his murder was printed in a Pentecostal magazine. It started by quoting the letter from Sister Allen, his widow. "They asked him to hold up his hands; he did that also. They then proceeded to handcuff him. He asked them not to do it as he would go without it. They then began beating him almost to death, they shot him and left him dead in the floor."

J. B. Ellis, the Church of God (Cleveland, Tenn.) overseer of Alabama who had himself served time in jail for refusing to buy war bonds, traveled down to investigate and get all the details.

> I talked to many who were present immediately after the killing and they all said that the circumstances surrounding the murder corroborate with the testimony of Sister Allen. Evidently they had knocked him over on the bed and beaten him almost to death there. A great pool of blood was on the bed. From the sign on the floor, as well as the statement of his wife, he got up off the bed and was beaten across the room, through the door and about three or four feet into another room where they shot him twice. Both balls entered his breast ranging downward, indicating that he was on his knees when they shot him. Sister Allen said that he kept his hands above his head all the time trying to ward off the blows and protect his head. His hands, head and neck were beaten almost to

a pulp. The Dr. who held the inquest said he would hardly have recovered from the blows if they had not shot him. . . . Brother Allen was in the second draft and was called for in October. Knowing that his Bible church opposed war, he felt he could not kill. . . . He carried his Bible with him everywhere he went. . . . We feel he might be classed among the martyrs. We extend to his wife and parents our heartfelt sympathy. God's grace will be sufficient. Keep pressing on. . . . I am looking for the time to come when many will have to seal our testimony with our blood.[30]

In this context of "the most strenuous nationalism and the most pervasive nativism that the United States had ever known"[31] the Assemblies of God argued for and tried to embody Christian nonviolence.

THE ASSEMBLIES OF GOD DEFENSE OF PACIFISM AND CONSCIENTIOUS OBJECTION, 1914-1940

One might argue that the lower socio-economic context of early Pentecostals, as pointed out in the previous chapter, might encourage their participation in violence and war. Nationalism and a willingness to do violence are common among those suffering at the bottom of society as well as those at the top. For instance, the Central Intelligence Agency and the U.S. State Department recognize that terrorists are more easily recruited in areas where employment is low and poverty is high.[32] "Marginalized, powerless, and poor" people are not more naturally nonviolent. In fact, there may be an increased willingness among the marginalized to do violence on behalf of the state. When there are not other jobs for them to have, serving in the military provides a needed income. And since the state values and makes heroes of those who kill on its behalf, killing for the state is a way for the marginalized to be recognized and gain status within the state.[33] So while their social setting seems to be conducive to violence, the Assemblies of God proclaimed a nonviolent revolution that critiqued nationalism, civil religion, and war. There was more to the Pentecostal love of enemy theology than their socio-economic condition.[34]

The manner in which most in the early Assemblies of God preached and wrote against war stood in stark contrast to the support exhibited by their fellow Christian citizens. The earliest period (1914-1916) contained volatile sentiments vehemently opposed to nationalism or any manner of participation in warfare. An intense concern for the eschatological implications of war accompanied these ideas. World War I marked a slight decrease in antiwar rhetoric because of the intense social pressure to silence pacifists, but this is also when the official pacifist resolution passed and the arguments against war were summarized. The evidence from the period between the World Wars (1919-1940) revealed that pacifistic writings were common and quite powerful.

Some scholars have claimed that pacifism ceased to exist around World War I and that the Assemblies of God only "permitted a variety of views in its official publication until 1917, when the United States entered the conflict" and that "after May [1917], no more articles supporting pacifism appeared in official publications."[35] The primary publication being referred to, *The Weekly Evangel* (which later became *The Pentecostal Evangel*), actually carried numerous pacifistic articles and encouraged conscientious objection and noncombatant service during American participation in World War I,[36] immediately after the war ended, throughout the 1920s and 1930s, and into the early 1940s.[37] Furthermore, attempts to change the pacifist article in the constitution and bylaws of the Assemblies of God failed in the 1940s, and it was not finally eliminated until 1967.

Throughout this entire time (1914-1940), the concern for war as it related to missions remained prominent. Missions included foreign missionaries and their struggles in war zones as well as the concern for ministering to soldiers. In fact, there were more articles about missions and war than about participation and nonparticipation in war combined.[38] This is significant because evangelism (missions) is the first reason mentioned for pacifism in the explanation of the 1917 resolution.[39] Although some Assemblies of God people were pro-choice even from the earliest days, many others consistently testified against the place of war in the life of a believer.

1914-1916

The first article in *The Christian Evangel* that dealt with war considered its relationship to the end of the world. The author proclaimed that the rapture of the saints might well occur at the height of the war, because "we are not mistaken and the Lord is coming soon, sooner than we realize."[40] The author did not specifically articulate a position regarding participation, but his "final word" does not leave much room for fighting.

If these things be so, what manner of persons ought we to be in all manner of holy conversation and godliness. . . . Will you be ready to meet him? Will He find you ready and watching, your loins girt about and your staff in your hand? Be ready, for in such an hour as ye think not, the son of man cometh. Don't be too much absorbed in watching the daily papers for war news, but keep looking up with enraptured gaze for the return of the Lord![41]

If he opposed the distraction of reading about the war in the paper, he would surely have opposed participating in the actual war itself. Every month and practically every issue in the latter part of 1914 contained articles that interpreted the European war in its relationship to the second coming of Jesus Christ.[42] Using Ceadel's categories we see this as evidence that some early Pentecostals were pessimistic pacifists—they understood their nonviolence to be an expression of their faithfulness to Jesus rather than an effective political strategy.

An English Pentecostal expressed a sentiment directly opposite what one in favor of fighting would express. He hoped that the defeats experienced in battle and the hardships brought about by war would be interpreted as the judgments of God so that the churches would be full and "the inhabitants of the world will learn righteousness."[43]

William Burton McCafferty (1889-1963), who eventually served as a professor and Academic Dean of Southwestern Bible Institute (now Southwestern Assemblies of God University) in Waxahachie, Texas, from 1931-1963, was a charter member of the Assemblies of God. A conscientious objector from Texas, he influenced first- and second-generation Pentecostalism in the south. In 1915 he penned an uncompromising article that adamantly opposed combatant participation in warfare, and he reiterated this theological position throughout his life.

At the time he was responding to the one article in the *Evangel* that had supported Christian participation.[44] The authors of the previous article had argued rationally that the Christian was obligated to defend the weak and innocent with violence. The only Scriptures they used were references that supported obedience and subservience to the state (Rom. 13.1-7; 1 Tim. 2.1-2; 1 Pet. 2.12-17). McCafferty based his entire argument on the exegesis of Scripture passages that supported nonviolence, spiritual warfare, and heavenly citizenship.

McCafferty rejected the option of fighting to defend the weak against the "bully" because the disciples wanted to do the same thing but were taught that it was wrong.

> In Luke 22:49, the disciples asked Jesus, "Lord, shall we smite with the sword?" They prayed, but, instead of waiting for an answer, one immediately drew the sword and went to battle. . . . Let us wait for an answer from God. Let us not begin to reason from the natural point of view. . . . What was the answer of Christ to the disciples (Christians) to this question? (Matth. 26:51) "Put up again thy sword into his place." This is what God is saying to the Christians of today, "Ye followers of the Prince of Peace, disarm yourselves" for "the weapons of our warfare are not carnal." (the musket, sword, siege gun or cannon). 2 Cor. 10:4.[45]

McCafferty did not allow human reason to dissuade him from the serious application of the words of Jesus. Although it was "natural" to defend oneself, the follower of Jesus was supposed to do what Jesus himself did—live supernaturally by the power of the Holy Spirit.

> The argument that we must go to war in behalf of the weaker nation because of its being in the right, is not consistent with the doctrines of Christ. It is also against the teaching of Christ to fight in self-defense. "For even hereunto were we called, because Christ also suffered leaving us an example that we should follow His steps, who did no sin (violence, Isa. 53:9) who, when he was reviled, reviled not again. . . ."[46]

He also argued that Christians were not citizens of their earthly nations so they should not defend them with violence.

> John 17:16. Our citizenship is not of this world, our citizenship is in heaven. Phil. 3:20. We belong to the kingdom of God and the kingdom of God and the kingdoms of this world are not allied. . . . Christians are separate from the world and are subjects of God's kingdom, a kingdom of peace. . . .[47]

McCafferty employed fourteen Scripture verses, all of which were from the New Testament with the exception of one reference to Isaiah 53 (which he used to equate sin with violence). He concerned himself with finding and presenting the attitude that Jesus and his disciples took regarding war. Any other argument, regardless of how "natural" it seemed, had to be measured against the direct teachings and lives of Jesus and the New Testament Christians. This is the first article in the

Evangel that systematically presented a pacifist argument, and it revealed a method followed by subsequent Pentecostal conscientious objectors and the Assemblies of God itself.

Both the July 3 and July 10, 1915, issues of *Weekly Evangels* presented advertisements for Arthur Sydney Booth-Clibborn's strongly worded pacifist book, *Blood Against Blood*.[48] Booth-Clibborn employed a multitude of Scriptures and illustrations to prove that a Christian had no place in the bloodshed of war. The editors of *The Weekly Evangel*, E. N. Bell and J. R. Flower, heartily recommended it.

> A most striking, realistic and forceful book by Arthur Sydney Booth-Clibborn, an English Pentecostal Evangelist and Elder who has put into words the principles burning in the hearts of all the Pentecostal saints on the subject of whether a Christian should go to war or not. This book presents war from a Christian standpoint and is not intended for those out of Christ. Should the United States go to war with Germany what will be the attitude of the Pentecostal people. Send for a copy of this wonderful book and make a decision.[49]

High praises for a text about pacifism being the Christian view of war reveals that the early leaders of the Assemblies of God thought this was who they were and the direction the fellowship was going. Consider the words they used to describe Christian pacifism, nonviolence, and conscientious objection—"realistic," "wonderful," "principles" on the "hearts of all Pentecostals." *Blood Against Blood* provided articulate biblical and theological arguments for Christian nonviolence that first-generation Pentecostals found compelling and persuasive.[50] They still asked the question, "What will be the attitude of the Pentecostal people?" but the preponderance of articles between 1914 and 1916 recommended abstinence from killing.[51]

An unnamed author in 1915 provided evidence that American Pentecostals were more concerned about promoting peace than supporting or preparing for war.

> The nations [should have] . . . spread the gospel of Peace and made known the rule of Jesus . . . "the King of Peace" instead of obeying the "traditions of men" and preparing big guns, air craft, rapid firers [sic], submarines, a big navy, and bigger army for the destruction of human life.[52]

This Pentecostal suggested that the nations could do positive actions such as spreading the gospel of peace. In different words this would be a call to peacemaking and a critique of militarization and arms build-up.

The following week witnessed the first article by Frank Bartleman in *The Weekly Evangel*. He voiced the concerns of the marginalized in society and condemned war in no uncertain terms. His first paragraph proclaimed that only hypocrites pray for peace while helping the war to continue. He asserted that America's claim of neutrality was a lie because America made the European war possible by selling arms to all the participants. "The nation, the voters, the church members, could stop this if they would insist upon it . . . [but] we are willing to receive these millions of blood money. We had better pluck out the stars from our flag and instate dollar marks in their place."[53]

Amid this critique we hear a note of hope in the church and even in democracy and America. Even the pessimistic Bartleman thought it could be stopped if people would repent of their greedy ways. He does not say he thinks it will happen, only that it "could" happen. He continues by contrasting the symbols of the nations, "wild beasts and birds of prey," with the human heart (representing peace) that Nebuchadnezzar had taken away from him. His concern for the poor manifests itself repeatedly.

> The poor people must spill their blood to save the rulers fortunes. . . . The servant class must be emancipated. The lords must turn their great "preserves" into potato patches to feed the starving thousands of the common people. . . . [Soldiers are] blinded by sin, blinded by ignorance, blinded and controlled by their leaders.[54]

Bartleman did not condemn soldiers. He blamed sin—which could be remedied by salvation; ignorance—which could be remedied by discipleship; and the control of the politicians—which could perhaps be remedied by voting them out of office. By targeting sin, ignorance, and the corruption of greedy rulers he could view the soldiers as victims.

He also predicted terrible after-effects of the war.

> We will have nations of murderers after this war. A generation with their hands stained with the blood of other human beings. . . . Whole nations will be fired with hatred in heart and mind

against one another for coming generations. Not only men but the women and the children. Unborn generations are thus cursed.[55]

He presented the selfish motives and horrific results of war in such ways that made it completely incompatible with Christianity. He condemned specific sins of every nation, from England and America to Germany, Russia, Italy, France, and Japan, declaring that "We speak without fear or favor. . . . We favor no country."[56] Lest anyone question his lack of loyalty to the government, he provided his attitude toward too much national fidelity. "Patriotism has been fanned into a flame. The religious passion has been invoked, and the national gods called upon for defence in each case. What blasphemy!"[57] In this manner the answering of the war question seemed to be taking definite shape in the Assemblies of God.

Bartleman contributed an article to *The Weekly Evangel* one month later. In it he continued his tirade against the greedy nations and nationalism, his defense of the outcasts, his condemnation of war, and he added a call to repentance.

> It is not worth while for Christians to wax warm in patriotism over this world's situation. There is little justice or mercy in the fallen nations. . . . Our American press has been controlled by English capital. . . . Before the reports in our press can be believed we must first search out the motive. And that is impossible to do. Men are paid to write to bias the public. There is no effort for justice. In fact the whole game is played for selfish conquest. American capitalists, leaders and manufacturers are as deep in the mud as the others. . . . We are a nation of grafters. . . . [Germans] are in the wrong sometimes also, and they are likely to stand by their country, right or wrong. England will do that also. America will do the same thing. There is not principle enough in any of these countries to overcome that.[58]

By August 1915, Germany had declared war on Russia, France, and Belgium and had invaded the latter two. Great Britain had declared war on Germany, Austria-Hungary, and Turkey. The United States did not declare war on Germany for another eight months (April 6, 1917).[59] Bartleman appealed to principle as a reason to abstain and blamed "nominal Christianity" (the opposite of radical Pentecostal Christianity) for the disastrous wars. Discussing the evils of war caused him to re-member the other evils in which America had participated, and he thus revealed more of his social conscience and political awareness.

> A fortune in war supplies and provisions awaits our merchants, manufacturers and capitalists. They are willing to plunge our nation even into war to get this. Our rulers dare not say no to them if they hope to retain office. . . . What prosperity we are experiencing as a nation today is being derived from furnishing shot and shell to the Allies across the water to kill Germans. I supposed this is a righteous business with God? We have killed off about all of our American Indians. What we have not killed outright we have starved through some big grafter at Washington diverting the appropriations of the Government for their support to his own pocket. And we have fed our soldiers in our recent campaign against Spain with rotten canned goods to enrich the same big grafters. . . . Will not God deal in judgment with such a nation as this? Most assuredly! We have stolen the land from the North American Indians. . . . Our wrong to the black people was avenged in blood. What will the next be? We are living on blood money today and trying to wash our hands in innocency in the matter. But it will not come off.[60]

While many pointed to the errors of others, Bartleman named two of the most unchristian, challenging, and controversial issues in American history—genocide and slavery.

Bartleman condemned participation in the European war, but there is one sentence in this article that could be construed as approval of bearing arms. A look at the context will help with interpretation.

> Hence we need a call at this time as a nation to repentance. I suppose it will be always possible for our nation to hire men to slay others. But the spirit of patriotism is not going to burn very bright in a people who are ruled by grafters.[61] The game is not worth the candle.[62] Especially when it is for mere love for some other nation. A foreign invasion would be a different thing altogether.[63]

This statement seems to imply that if America were invaded he would have supported fighting to defend it. But that sentiment would have contradicted his opinions in his other writings and even the theology of this article. He could not fight even for a righteous nation, much less an evil one, and he had already decided that "there is no righteous nation in the earth today."[64] In the above paragraph, Bartleman was writing about Americans (not Christians) and how they would support American involvement in the war. He believed that they would not be very patriotic, since their politicians were "rotten" and "greedy," i.e. making rich men richer is not worth the battle. This was especially true when the poorest Americans were fighting for the safety of nations other than their own.

Bartleman then observed that Americans would certainly fight if America itself were invaded, despite the corruption of their leaders. His recognition of the fact that Americans would fight to defend their country was not intended as an approval of Christian participation. Bartleman's antiwar and antinationalism message was consistent, but his failure to condemn the Germans in harsher language than he condemned the Americans elicited a rebuke in the next issue.

J. Roswell Flower penned an article and printed a letter from a reader who condemned Bartleman as "a German first and a Christian afterwards—so personally interested in the war as to have lost sight of the impartial view of a Christian."[65] Flower agreed and admitted that Bartleman's article was "too strongly worded and that it should not have appeared except in a greatly modified form."[66] E. N. Bell's absence during this time served as one of the primary reasons it did appear, "as Brother Bell was still away from the office and we could not advise with him, we allowed the article to go in the paper."[67] Even though Flower apologized for the "mistake" of printing the article he supported its nonpatriotic stance and even affirmed nonparticipation in war.

> We are not citizens of this world, but citizens of a better country and our interests are all for that country to which we all hope to go. In this office there is a Canadian, a Dutchman, an Englishman, and for a time a German. We have no arguments about the war as we are only interested in it from a Christian standpoint and its effect on the coming of the Lord. God's people must all get to this place, where national prejudices must die and where the glory of God only will be sought.[68]

Flower wanted every member of the Assemblies of God to mature to the point where they felt loyalty only for God and not for their nation.

Flower showed the premillennial nonconformity of first-generation Pentecostalism by encouraging the death of national prejudices. This "heavenly citizenship" perspective corresponds with the theology of Christian pacifism, and Stanley Frodsham developed it more fully the following month.

To agree with Bartleman, develop Flower's thoughts, and keep the critique of war and nationalism going, Frodsham argued that "an attitude of strict neutrality to the warring nations" needed to be expanded to include actual rejection.[69] The timing of this article shows that even after a reprimand of Bartleman, the Assemblies of God was still committed to a peace witness.

> When one comes into that higher kingdom and becomes a citizen of that "holy nation" (1 Pet. 2:9), the things that pertain to earth should forever lose their hold, even that natural love for the nation where one happened to be born, and loyalty to the new King should swallow up all other loyalties.[70]

This absolute loyalty to God made all the affairs of the earth appear completely different. There was no room for pride, and the removal of pride brought the removal of hatred and war. Pentecostals believed that if Jesus himself did not need his followers to kill for him, then how could a Christian kill for a lesser cause, nation, or leader?

> National pride, like every other form of pride, is abomination in the sight of God. And pride of race must be one of the all things that pass away when one becomes a new creature in Christ Jesus. . . . When seen from the heavenly viewpoint, how the present conflict is illumined. The policy of our God is plainly declared in the Word, "Peace on earth, good will toward men."[71]

Frodsham employed the New Testament to prove that Christians should not be racists, nationalists, or participants in the wars of this world. He set the kingdoms of this world in direct opposition to the kingdom of God and forced a choice upon his audience: "Is any child of God going to side with these belligerent kings? Will he not rather side with the Prince of Peace under whose banner of love he has chosen to serve?"[72]

Choosing to follow peace rather than war meant rejection by the world, but Frodsham knew what really mattered, "The world, especially the religious world, has no use for the children of God, but the Lord taketh pleasure in his people. . . . It is important for the saint of God to remember that his citizenship is in heaven."[73] He willingly spoke against uncritical loyalty to the government, against the related participation in war, and against seeking approval from other Christians. He employed strong words and numerous scriptural arguments to inspire the Assemblies of God to follow God rather than America.

In 1916 a poem entitled "War Profits" announced that God's love would turn to anger when he faced warriors and killers. "His Spirit not always doth strive With those so desirous of blood; And the love you now spurn will to anger be turned In that day when you stand before God."[74] A few months later a pacifist from England sent his testimony to *The Weekly Evangel* for publication. The editors introduced it by saying, "God answers the prayers of those who plead with Him for exemption."[75] These desires for exemption set the stage for the military service resolution of 1917.

1917-1918

Even though they allowed their members to bear arms, the Assemblies of God maintained and codified their antiwar position during the last two years of World War I. As following sections explain, this antiwar position was accompanied by statements of respect for the government and with discourse on the authority of conscience, which some might see as the beginning of erosion of antiwar beliefs. Nonetheless, the pacifist theology assumed official form by means of a resolution that was incorporated into the constitution and bylaws of the General Council in 1917. This section examines the Assemblies of God pacifistic and conscientious objection writings that emerged amid the Great War.[76]

Early Pentecostals spoke against war not just because the killing itself was immoral but also because of the effects it had on its participants. They sometimes expressed their perspective regarding the intrinsic evil of war by quoting other writers, since they read about war in magazines and journals outside their own religious persuasion.

> I see the best, the most gentle men coming back transformed. I will not say that they have actually become wicked; but it is something much worse; they have grown accustomed to do evil unconsciously, to give the lie to all their lives, all that they believed, all that they desired, hitherto. To kill has become their duty, their sole object and purpose of life. . . . Their hearts are hardened.[77]

It is no coincidence that many unequivocal antiwar citations appeared just two weeks after the U.S. declared war on Germany and one week before the Assemblies of God informed the United States government that they were conscientiously and theologically opposed to war. These statements presented a clear message about the incompatibility of Christianity and war, and this message was contrary to the attitude of most American Christians at this time.

One direct quote came from Booth-Clibborn's *Blood Against Blood*. Under the title "What is War?," it also served as yet another advertisement for the book.

> General Sherman: "War is hell. . . ." George Fox, when offered a captaincy: "I cannot fight, for the spirit of war is slain within me." Sydney Smith: "God is forgotten in war: every principle of Christianity is trampled upon." Tertullian: "Our religion teaches us that it is better to be killed than to kill." John Wesley: "Shall Christians help the Prince of Hell, who was a murderer from the beginning, by telling the world of the benefit or need of war?"[78]

That same issue carried an article that listed Scriptures that opposed war. The author attempted to address "The Crisis" of whether or not a Christian could go to war by asking "what saith the Scriptures concerning this all important matter?"[79] He then catalogued several quotations of Jesus himself to make his point.

> He said of disciples on another occasion, "They are not of this world, even as I am not of the world. . . ." "Our citizenship is in heaven." (Phil.3:15 R.V.). . . . Let us be loyal to Him. . . . "Blessed are the peacemakers: for they will be called children of God." It is not those who delight in war, but those who are so permeated by the Spirit of the Prince of peace, and who seek to bring others into a blessed condition of peace with God and with their fellow man that inherit the blessing of the Master. . . . "But I say to you, That ye resist not evil. . . . Love your enemies, bless them that curse you, do good to them that hate you. . . ."[80]

The column right next to this one, written by Mrs. A. R. Flower, explained that war called patriots to the aid of their country. In contrast, the child of God needed to answer the call to "deeper consecration, unceasing prayer, and earnest endeavor for souls."[81] This was the only part that the Pentecostals were to take.

Just one week later, the son of Arthur Booth-Clibborn tackled the war question. Samuel Booth-Clibborn forcefully echoed the sentiments of his father and employed a Scripture-laden approach to show the absolute nature of Christian nonviolence. He separated Christians from "Pacifists" who used mere politics and "Socialists" who, although their "zeal for peace" was admired, worshipped materialism.[82] Even though early writers in the Assemblies of God expressed pacifist theology, they scorned the term itself because of its connection with non-Christian "human" efforts to establish world peace. The Assemblies of God pacifists were quick to contrast themselves with nonreligious and socialist antimilitarists who thought that pacifism was an effective defense policy, which Ceadel would call optimistic pacifism. Booth-Clibborn addressed his message only to Christians. "Yes, us Christians, who have been preaching this Gospel of LOVE, JOY, and PEACE so loud and so long. Now that it has come to practicing what we preach, now the fiery test will be applied—are we willing to go through for Jesus?"[83] He was an evangelical political radical who based his nonviolence in his Christology and ecclesiology, not in its supposed effectiveness at ending war.

He discounted Old Testament accounts of warfare because they "liv[ed] in the age of Law and Judgment; whilst we dwell in the Dispensation of Grace and Mercy." He disallowed any use of the Old Testament to justify killing in warfare as "thick ignorance . . . resulting in this everlasting muddling up of O. T. and N. T. teaching, of Law and Grace, of Judgment and Mercy, of War and Peace. . . ."[84] He established his entire position on Jesus and the new covenant that fulfilled the old covenant.

> Find me in the New Testament where Christ ever sent His followers on such a mission? On the contrary He sent them out to save men—not to butcher them like cattle. . . . No! as far as the Christian is concerned, the "eye for an eye" system has given place to the "Turn to him the other cheek also" of Matt. 5:39-44.[85]

When challenged with the question of self-defense, Booth-Clibborn responded with a four-point answer. First, he argued that a "murderous individual" employs his free will while wars are fought by "poor harmless people . . . driven like cattle and quite against their will by godless governments into butchering each other."[86] Note that he was not "anti-soldier"; he viewed soldiers as victims of the system of war just like those they killed. He then claimed that God often protected his children "according to their faith; for they put their trust in Him rather than the police." As a Pentecostal, he trusted in God to provide a miracle. But he knew this would not always happen. His belief in the miraculous did not lead to a naiveté that expected a miracle to happen every time. For should the "brute" actually break in and threaten one's life, "if it should come to actual violence—Matthew 5 and Romans 12 would still remain true, and God's Word would still have to be obeyed." If no miracle of deliverance came from God, the Christians should not then take matters into their own hands with violence—they still live faithfully as Jesus did. Thus, even when it seemed like Booth-Clibborn might justify self-defense because it seemed to differ from war, he did not.

He then made his fourth point.

> Many religious persecutions which down the ages have been the inevitable accompaniment of every new and powerful movement; and yet these very persecutions have set the seal of God's approval in the most striking way on the doctrine of Christian nonresistance. Those same early non-resisters, mind you, were the same martyrs, of whom, in recent days of inherited religion, the boast is so often heard, that 'their blood was the seed of the church!'[87]

Samuel H. Booth-Clibborn lauded the faithfulness of early Christians and radical movements who did not fight and who did not succumb to patriotism. This statement revealed that Booth-Clibborn wanted the Assemblies of God to stay true to its restorationist, Spirit-empowered, missions-focused origins. Pacifism provided the integral avenue for this to be accomplished.

An English conscientious objector told his story only two pages after Booth-Clibborn's article.

> I stuck to the Scriptures and gave my objection from a scriptural standpoint. . . . They told me that they did not want me to preach to them but to simply answer questions. . . . At last one of them asked what I would do if an enemy came to my home and was about to kill my mother. I told him I would pray.[88]

This conscientious objector appealed to the authority of Scripture to defend his nonparticipation and then served in a noncombatant role because he did not receive full exemption. He told his readers that he "could not see any other stand to take as a Christian who is measuring his walk by the Word of God . . . it is quite wrong for a Christian to fight." The letter filled almost a full page, and the editor concluded it by saying, "We publish it, believing it will help many of our young men in the stand they will take at this time."[89] In 1917, at the beginning of American involvement in World War I, the Assemblies of God assumed that the majority of its members would take a stand as conscientious objectors.

When America had been at war for six weeks, the *Weekly Evangel* presented two pieces that addressed the Assemblies of God perspective on killing. Samuel H. Booth-Clibborn provided the first with the second installment of his previous article. He started by encouraging spiritual formation and discipleship as necessary preparation for these difficult conversations.

> It is also essential that we bring unprejudiced, humble, and earnest minds and hearts to bear on this matter, as I've found ninety per cent of militaristic Christians to be lacking in the above kind of "Preparedness,"—as is evidenced by a biased, feverish state of mind, fatal to clear spiritual thinking.[90]

He believed that the majority of defencist or crusading Christians were biased toward their own nation and overly emotional; he hoped for Christians instead to be unprejudiced, humble, and careful thinkers. He reiterated the belief that "it was simply God's Holy Ghost power!" enabled one to accomplish amazing things for God as a nonviolent person.[91] He also implemented one of the most unique arguments against participation in war that occurred in the early Assemblies of God.

> But there is another way in which the temple can be destroyed, viz., by dragging into it the present horrible hatred, pride, and bloody butchery! "Know ye not that ye are the temple of God and that the Spirit of God dwelleth in you? If any man destroy (R. V.) the temple of God, Him shall God destroy!" (And "all they that take the sword shall perish by the sword.")[92]

Pentecostals commonly quote this classic passage about the "temple of God" to prohibit drinking alcohol or smoking, but Booth-Clibborn appealed to the concept to show that Christians must not desecrate themselves by hating and killing. He argued that Christians could choose but one position regarding this question, especially since they were filled with the "Spirit."

This same week J. W. Welch, the chairman of the executive presbytery of the General Council of the Assemblies of God from 1915-1920 and 1923-1925, penned an article that related their opinion regarding military service. He introduced it by stating that the purpose was "to interpret as clearly as possible what the Scriptures teach upon the subject, as we have from the beginning declared the Bible to be our only rule of faith and practice."[93] The scriptural foundation allowed them to "hope to secure the privilege of exemption from such military service as will necessitate the taking of life for all who are real conscientious objectors and who are associated with the General Council."

Welch claimed that they were not saying anything new but merely stating "the position always held by this company of believers" because the imminence of conscription meant that the time had now arrived that necessitated this position. He told the constituency that they should be willing to serve in any capacity that did not require killing and that he himself was appalled at the idea of Assemblies of God men bearing arms. He concluded by warning against joining the Assemblies of God just to get out of combatant military service. The executive presbytery decided not to publish the actual resolution in May; they waited until August to provide it to their constituents and readership.

The lay reader of *The Weekly Evangel* read the military service resolution for the first time in the August 4, 1917, edition.[94] The executive presbytery (probably J. W. Welch) wrote a three-paragraph introduction to the resolution, then related the chronology of the events that had transpired since April. Significantly, missions served as the first justification for the resolution. The early Assemblies of God concerned itself primarily with spreading the good news of Jesus Christ and they did not want to adopt any stance that would work against their evangelistic efforts. If any person had never read anything up until this point about the Assemblies of God and the military, the introduction to the topic, as introduced by the executives of the Assemblies of God, would have been in the context of evangelism.

> From its very inception, the Pentecostal Movement has been a movement of evangelism, studiously avoiding any principles or actions which would thwart it in its great purpose. All the wings of the movement, which have grown out of the work that originated in the Southwestern States and the Pacific Coast are a unit in this respect.[95]

To accomplish this goal they realized that they could not participate in warfare because the goals of the two conflicted. They believed that telling the story of Jesus and then killing that same person served as a blatantly hypocritical contradiction. For early Pentecostals, a person was either a missionary or a mission field, and missionaries were not supposed to kill mission fields. Another way of saying this is that the Pentecostals had the mission of God as their highest priority. Only later did the mission of America become important enough to justify Christians killing unbelievers. The move from pacifism to defencism or crusading can be seen as a change in their understanding of mission. The author then recalled the Quaker heritage of the Assemblies of God and appealed to their serious approach to the words of Scripture to explain their position.

> From the very beginning, the movement has been characterized by Quaker principles. The laws of the kingdom, laid down by our elder brother, Jesus Christ, in His Sermon on the Mount, have been *unqualifiedly* adopted, consequently the movement has found itself opposed to the spilling of the blood of *any* man, or of offering resistance to *any* aggression. *Every* branch of the movement, whether in the United States, Canada, Great Britain or Germany, has held to this principle.[96]

The leaders of the Assemblies of God claimed to speak for the entire Pentecostal movement and gave the impression that there were no dissenters among their ranks. The wording of the paragraph above would have led one to believe that every Assemblies of God person in the world, even the German and British ones, was opposed to participation in warfare. Since the antiwarfare, pacifistic, and conscientious objection articles in the *Evangel* up to this point outnumbered the combatant participation articles by more than ten to one, the above statement seems to reflect a sentiment within the Assemblies of God that was much stronger than the procombatant position.[97]

The author then explained that previously there had been no reason to state the position of the Assemblies of God. Now that "war clouds gathered and actual war was declared" they found it necessary to commit to writing "the established principles or creed of all sections of the Pentecostal Movement, and especially that part represented by the General Council."[98] They claimed that the entire Pentecostal movement be-

lieved killing in war was wrong. Jay Beaman found that sixty-two percent of Pentecostal denominations formed before 1932 had official
pacifist articles.[99] The full Assemblies of God resolution, with its title,
read as follows:

> Resolution Concerning the Attitude of the General Council of
> the Assemblies of God Toward any Military Service which In-
> volves the Actual Participation in the Destruction of Human
> Life.
>
> While recognizing Human Government as of Divine ordina-
> tion and affirming our unswerving loyalty to the Government of
> the United States, nevertheless we are constrained to define our
> position with reference to the taking of human life.
>
> WHEREAS, in the Constitutional Resolution adopted at
> the Hot Springs General Council, April 1-10, 1914, we plainly
> declare the Holy Inspired Scriptures to be the all-sufficient rule of
> faith and practice, and
>
> WHEREAS the Scriptures deal plainly with the obligations
> and relations of humanity, setting forth the principles of "Peace
> on earth, good will toward men" (Luke 2:14); and
>
> WHEREAS we, as followers of the Lord Jesus Christ, the
> Prince of Peace, believe in implicit obedience to the Divine com-
> mands and precepts which instruct us to "Follow peace with all
> men" (Heb. 12:14); "Thou shalt not kill" (Exod. 20:13); "Resist
> not evil" (Matt. 5:39); "Love your enemies" (Matt. 5:44); etc.,
> and
>
> WHEREAS these and other Scriptures have always been ac-
> cepted and interpreted by our churches as prohibiting Christians
> from shedding blood or taking human life;
>
> THEREFORE we, as a body of Christians, while purposing
> to fulfill all the obligations of loyal citizenship, are nevertheless
> constrained to declare we cannot conscientiously participate in
> war and armed resistance which involves the actual destruction of
> human life, since this is contrary to our view of the clear teachings
> of the inspired Word of God, which is the sole basis of our
> faith.[100]

The first "whereas" stated that Scripture served as the only determi-
nant of doctrine and ethics. Beliefs needed to be defended only with
scriptural support since it was "all-sufficient." Furthermore, they argued

that their sole authority, the Bible, "plainly" provided one unequivocal position about their "obligations" regarding participation in warfare. They expressed this single principle by quoting five Scriptures, four from the New Testament and one from the Old Testament. The fourth and final whereas declared that many more Scriptures than they had even listed had "always" been interpreted by Pentecostals to forbid killing. It is quite significant that all four "whereas" paragraphs refer to Scripture to justify their conclusion. They did not appeal to reason or any philosophical principles. They appealed only to Scripture.

The final paragraph of the resolution recognized that it did not support absolutely loyal American citizenship by incorporating the word *nevertheless*. But it also could have been interpreted to allow noncombatant service since it did not involve "the actual destruction of human life."[101] The presbytery then once again defended their principle of conscientious opposition to war and killing by mentioning the "clear teachings" of the Bible as the "sole basis" of their faith. The multiple references to Scripture revealed the manner by which the early Assemblies of God justified and defended their nonparticipation. This had already been clear in the *Evangel* articles and it continued consistently in this bylaw. They introduced their resolution by referring to evangelism, Quaker principles, and Jesus Christ.[102] They loaded their resolution with praises for Scripture, descriptions of Scripture, and Scriptures themselves: "Holy," "Inspired," "all-sufficient," "rule," "obligations," "principles," "Divine commands," "precepts," and "sole basis."[103] This early method stands in stark contrast to the manner in which the Assemblies of God justified their military service resolution fifty years later.[104]

With the above resolution in hand, the executive presbytery could confidently proclaim that "the principles of the General Council were in opposition to war from its very beginning" and that "the General Council meets every requirement of the law relating to religious bodies . . . whose religious principles are opposed to participation in war."[105] The intensity and claims of the Assemblies of God position served to support the idea that it was an organization containing conscientious objectors. The government officially recognized it as a peace church, and the anticombatant articles in the *Evangel* revealed that many Pentecostals did in fact oppose Christian participation in war and killing. These protests were accompanied by the voices of a few Assemblies of God members who supported the right of Christians to fight. Both themes continued together, but the noncombatant position remained the more prominent of the two until 1941.

The year 1918 was one of nationalism, war hysteria, and FBI investigations of Christians who opposed war. Nevertheless, the Assemblies of God continued to witness publicly that it opposed Christian participation in war. They were polite, respectful, and kind about it, but they did not discontinue their countercultural witness. The editors republished the military service resolution in its entirety on January 5, 1918.[106] They did this to help those seeking exemption from the draft. A few months later, an Assemblies of God missionary to the soldiers reported that twelve Pentecostals were in a noncombatant unit in San Antonio, Texas.[107] A Pentecostal conscientious objector reported that there were three Assemblies of God conscientious objectors with him in Fort Riley, Kansas.[108] Another Assemblies of God man refused to pledge "for the war fund" and was put in jail.[109] All of these potentially treasonous reports came even while E. N. Bell was delicately trying to present the Assemblies of God as a respectful denomination.

Three articles and a poem by Arthur Sydney Booth-Clibborn appeared in 1918. He rejected "anti-Bible 'pacifism' advocated by large sections of the Labor Party in Great Britain and the United States of America."[110] Instead, he believed the Christian should have a "'conscientious objection' to war based, so to speak, on a previous engagement with Christ in a truly missionary, a truly witnessing or martyr spirit."[111] His article revealed the close relationship between missions and Pentecostal conscientious objection, "The true conscientious objector is the sort of Christian who is gladly willing to go unarmed among savage heathen, far beyond the 'protecting' reach of a six inch shell. He is equally ready to dispense with all 'protection' in 'civilized' lands."[112] Booth-Clibborn based this idea on the fact that early Christians had died because of their faith and love and end-time Christians must do the same. "A bloody Calvary, a Pentecost of fire, and the hostility of an entire world" both required and enabled complete rejection of any participation in war.

> All this being so, the intensely practical character of that "hope," as the "purifying" hope of 1 Jno 3:3 [sic], became ever more fully unveiled. It was seen to be absolutely essential to the separating of the church from all association with the world in its war and its

peace programmes, its "new age" programmes, its unregenerate humanism, its regeneration-denying "reformation" schemes, and the "social work" it prescribes to the Church as a condition of the favor and support of its press.[113]

During the last two years of World War I, the Assemblies of God promoted conscientious objection and witnessed several of their own claim exemption. Jacob D. Mininger (1879-1941), the superintendent of the Mennonite Gospel Mission in Kansas City, Kansas, found at least three Assemblies of God conscientious objectors imprisoned at Fort Leavenworth, Kansas in 1919.[114] Eddie Clemens, an African-American from New York City, had been sent from Ft. Jay on Governers Island in New York. Reingold Sass from Milwaukee, Wisconsin, came from Camp Greenleaf in Georgia, Tennessee, and Virgil J. Stauffer hailed from Wakarusa, Indiana. Another who self identified as "Pentecostal Assembly" may have been Assemblies of God—William Schulz from St. Joseph, Michigan, sent from Fort Custer.

Pentecostals represented 7.3 percent of the conscientious objectors at Fort Leavenworth, a disproportionately high amount given Pentecostalism's still relatively low numbers.[115] Pentecostalism did not come close to approaching 7.3 percent of the American population of 103,208,000 of 1918—that would have required over seven million Pentecostals.[116] In 1916 the Assemblies of God reportedly had only 118 churches and 6,703 members, less than .001 percent of the 101,961,000 Americans.[117] Yet the Assemblies of God provided about 1.5 percent of the conscientious objectors at Fort Leavenworth. So World War I ended with Pentecostals having provided more than their proportionate share of the conscientious objectors. In the years between World Wars I and II support for conscientious objection continued.

1919-1940

The *Evangel* printed pacifist articles on a regular basis between 1919 and 1940, and brief samples indicate the mood of the times. The Assemblies of God, as indeed the world, was also very concerned about the next war and the terrible effects it would have. During this time many articles were devoted to that topic as well.[118] In fact, the Assemblies of God noted as early as 1922,[119] and more definitely by 1924,[120] that the policies put in effect against the Germans after World War I could well lead to another even more terrible war.

In 1919 a female author quoted fourteen Scripture references as a way of proving that combatant participation in warfare was absolutely not Christian. Thirteen were from the New Testament and one was from the Old Testament (Isa. 9.16). She then concluded,

> I don't believe in the face of all these Scriptures Christians should believe it to be right to engage in fights or kill one another. It is not what we think about it, but we are pledged already as Christians to obey Christ and the teachings of the New Testament. If we are fully on the Lord's side on this question, we will have to say what the Lord says about it.[121]

In 1920 Arthur Sydney Booth-Clibborn claimed that any participation in warfare cheapened both Calvary and Pentecost and was "a disaster of untold magnitude."[122] He reasoned that the depth and maturity of one's Pentecostal experience was directly proportional to one's willingness to die (his or her Calvary). Christology and pneumatology (Jesus and the Holy Spirit) worked harmoniously together to enable the Pentecostal conscientious objector. Booth-Clibborn thought that if one is truly filled with the Spirit of Christ, then taking up one's cross as commanded by Christ would only make sense.

A strongly worded article appeared in 1922 that criticized the church for condoning wars and argued for nonviolence. The author quoted prominent church leaders of his day who were speaking against war. He then questioned why they did not speak so forcefully during the war. "What a bitter commentary on the Church it is that after nineteen centuries every Church in the Great War supported its own Government, its policy, methods and aims."[123] The author also condemned "political pacifists" who blame "human organization" rather than "human nature." He saw war as a "battle between the 'haves' and the 'have-nots.'" Therefore, the human heart had to be changed and that could be accomplished only through conversion to Christ. "The Gospel of Christ is the world's only hope—the sole promise of peace."

> The Church's right attitude to war [is to] at least refuse to participate in war herself, and so make good her profession of peace. In the first two centuries of our era, so swordless was the Church of Christ, that Celsus, the Gnostic, in the first written attack ever made on the Christian Faith, grounds his censure on this very fact, and says: The State receives no help in war from the Chris-

tians; and if all men were to follow their example, the Sovereign would be deserted, and the world would fall into the hands of barbarians. Origin gave an answer profoundly in the spirit of James: The question is—what would happen if the Romans should be persuaded to adopt the principles of the Christians? This is my answer—We say that if two of us shall agree on earth . . . it shall be done of them by the Father who is in heaven . . . they would pray to the Word, who of old said to the Hebrews, when pursued by the Egyptians, "The Lord shall fight for you, and you shall hold your peace." No mortal knows what could be got, by man or class or nation or world, by substituting prayer for war. . . .[124]

By 1924 the "darkening clouds" of war prompted an article by Stanley Frodsham, the editor of *The Pentecostal Evangel*, in which he encouraged Pentecostals never to participate should the occasion arise. He titled it "From the Pentecostal Viewpoint" and placed the lengthy article right under the statement "*The Pentecostal Evangel* is the official organ of the General Council of the Assemblies of God." This article is significant, because it shows that Pentecostals were engaged politically and aware of global trends. Frodsham reports of an American who traveled through Europe and came back with startling news.

After visiting nearly every country in Europe, talking with politicians, industrialists, labor leaders, and the man in the street, he states the question is not, "Will there be another war?" but "When and where will the next war be?" After telling of the grievances he found in almost every country, grievances that have been a direct result of the Versailles treaty, for each country which received territory thought it got less than its due . . . this writer states, " (1) There are today more men under arms in Europe than in 1914, and at least eight countries are on a war footing. (2) There are more active causes for war, and these are being more actively agitated than at any time within the past fifty years. (3) . . . The dread of war does not exist. The people think war preferable to the way they are now living. . . . These people are thinking of war largely because they have precious little to think about. They are hungry, they are desperate, and they are armed. The big war did not teach them the futility of war. They mostly think that the war stopped too soon and that they were juggled out of their rights by the peace. This applies equally to the victors and the vanquished."[125]

Although Frodsham believed that Christians were better served by reading the Bible rather than the newspaper, he was certain that the Assemblies of God needed to know the state of the world. He did not focus this article on the second coming of Jesus Christ; he instead provided analysis of the international political situation and gave a theological rationale for pacifism. The seriousness of the situation, five and half years after World War I, is related by Frodsham with an extended quote from Brigadier General John Morgan.

> Germany found herself by the treaty of Versailles a captive giant in the hands of Europe . . . an object of derision to some, of contempt to others. . . . Now in the temple of European society there are two pillars upon which the whole of that temple rests—one is the pillar of credit, the other is the pillar of law. . . . Germany, in her agony . . . has breathed a prayer. . . . If she is to go down into the abyss, she is determined to drag all Europe down with her. . . . What a field you have left for exploitation by some great German blood, who . . . will appeal to sixty millions of German people so desperate that they have nothing left to lose, and sweep like an avalanche across the West.

In response to this dire forecast, Frodsham quoted in its entirety a Quaker statement passed in Philadelphia that called violence "unchristian" and that renounced "for the future all participation in war."[126] He then stated that

> When the editor of the paper [*The Pentecostal Evangel*] received a copy and handed the same to the Chairman of the Council, Brother Welch expressed the warmest sympathy for the sentiments of the Friends. The statement on our Council minutes concerning nonparticipation in war is *somewhat stronger* than the above.[127]

Frodsham was undoubtedly encouraged and strengthened by the peace witness of the Friends, since he talked about it with the General superintendent and shared it with the entire Assemblies of God. He also believed that the Assemblies of God had adopted a stricter stance against war than the Quakers themselves, and the Quaker statement was quite clear. Furthermore, he declared that Christians needed to denounce war during war rather than only during times of peace. "In the hour of man's greatest agony the Christian churches in every land brought no gift of healing, but held the clothes of those who stoned humanity."[128]

He also reminded his readers that the early church rejected warfare, that warfare was the result of lust, and that

> "the Master says the last word on the subject: 'Ye have heard that it hath been said, Thou shalt love they neighbor, and hate thine enemy. But I say unto you, Love your enemies, bless them that curse you, do good to them that hate you. . . . He further stated, 'They that take the sword shall perish by the sword.' The Father gave witness to the . . . Lord Jesus with a very definite command, 'This is my beloved Son, hear ye him. . . .'"[129]

Frodsham's unequivocal presentation of biblically based Pentecostal conscientious objection to war represented the movement well and continued to be the view of Pentecostals for many more years.

Donald Gee (1891-1966), a prominent Assemblies of God leader in England who served both as vice-chairman (1934-44) and chairman (1945-48) of the British Assemblies of God, penned an uncompromisingly pacifistic article in 1930. He desired to consider the situation during the "relative calm" of peace so that scriptural principles would prevail when war arrived. He began by asserting that

> However passionately patriotism may overwhelm everything else in time of war, the world certainly expects the Christian church to take a stand against war, and it is deeply disappointed at heart when that stand is not taken, however much it may persecute for the time the "conscientious objector."[130]

He then turned to an exposition of Scripture because "The 'Pentecostal' believer, above all others, will insist upon a scriptural basis for whatever stand he may take."[131] He discounted the Old Testament as an example for Christians since they were "times of ignorance" that were "temporary." He employed the teaching of Jesus as primary but said that it "is almost too familiar to need restating. . . . He consistently teaches forgiveness of enemies and . . . makes no attempt at self-defense at any time. . . . It is commonly admitted that the attitude of Jesus Christ toward war left no uncertainty."[132]

Gee then considered the attitude of the New Testament church. He argued that they did not fight in physical wars even though "military metaphors are freely used, but the warfare is strictly spiritual and the weapons are 'not carnal.'"[133] Jesus healed the centurion's daughter because he was the "friend of publicans and sinners," not because he approved of the soldier's occupation. Gee believed that a converted soldier would leave the military if he was properly discipled. Then, as if prophesying about the future of the Assemblies of God, he lamented that "there have doubtless been many men in military service who have never seen, or only dimly realized, how opposed such an occupation with all it involves must ever be to the spirit and teaching of Jesus Christ."[134] He concluded by stating that even though Christians were to be loyal to their government,

> a situation may arise at any time when a human government legislates along a line directly opposed to the revealed will of God contained in Scriptures. . . . When the clash is between the law of God and the law of man, then the only answer for the Christian is contained in the immortal words of Peter, "We ought to obey God rather than men." Acts 5:29. Conscientious objection then becomes the only possible course, however serious the consequences.[135]

Gee stressed heavenly citizenship and allegiance to God and lamented the fact that "patriotism is unfortunately allowed to run wild in so many believers."[136] He considered fanatical patriotism to be anti-Pentecostal.

> More than all else we must be delivered from that unthinking patriotism which says, "My country, right or wrong." The writer has observed as a solemn fact that those of our Pentecostal brethren who took a strongly patriotic attitude in the last war have mostly gone backward in spiritual power and influence ever since, while those who put Christ and his Word before all have advanced by divine grace to positions of spiritual leadership.[137]

Although Gee was convinced that complete nonparticipation was the best path for a follower of Jesus Christ, he allowed for conscience to determine the extent of one's objection. "The extent to which a believer feels called to maintain a conscientious objection to military service must always remain a personal matter."[138] Gee thought that Christians could choose among various noncombatant options but combatant participation was not an option. One Christian might have been content to serve in an ambulance corps, since they were not killing, but another Christian might consider even that not to be acceptable.

He concluded his commentary with the hope for a world without war that could only be brought about by Christian pacifism and conscientious objection to war, "There can be no doubt whatever of the ultimate result, if Christians all over the world refused to participate in war and bloodshed."[139] The General Council published Gee's pointed opinions and did not bother to balance them with any procombatant writings during the entire decade of the 1930s. However, they continued to print articles that promoted conscientious objection.

A book review in 1930 revealed the pacifism of the Assemblies of God leadership. *War Behind the Smoke Screen,* by William G. Allen, received a very favorable review by the editors of *The Pentecostal Evangel,* and it was sold by the Gospel Publishing House. Allen argued that war stood in "true contrast to the teachings of Jesus Christ."[140] He showed how the United States deceived the public during the first world war and how the church failed in its peace witness. The reviewer was most amazed at the fact that the New Testament had been censored during the war.

> So severe and horrible was the war spirit in the United States even, that the New Testament was subjected to censorship because the teachings of Jesus regarding love for enemies and forgiveness were seen by military authorities to be contrary to their attempt to create the necessary hatred in the hearts of the people which would make them fighters. . . . "When [some] desired to have the Sermon on the Mount printed for free distribution . . . [they] were advised by federal authorities not to do so, on the ground it might be considered pro-German."[141]

The Assemblies of God had been talking about the real possibility of another world war for over a decade. But by 1938 Hitler had been in power in Germany for five years and had introduced conscription. Germany had quit the league of nations and was occupying the Rhineland, Mussolini had taken Ethiopia, and Spain was in a civil war. Ernest S. Williams (1885-1981), the General Superintendent of the American Assemblies of God from 1929-1949, reminded the members of their official position and encouraged them to consider their options in case of war. He stated that he wanted to do this "while free from the emotional effects of such events." He also complimented the U.S. government because it "had been kind in the past in that it has recognized genuine 'conscientious objectors' and has provided for them 'noncombatant' service. It is our hope that it will be as kind in the future."[142] He then printed the complete military service resolution as it had been revised in 1927 since they had "as a Church gone on record . . . relative to military service."[143] Williams clearly did not want Pentecostals to fight, but he did make suggestions that he thought were in line with their official conscientious objector stance.

> Could not such a one serve as a cook, a helper in a hospital, a stretcher carrier, a driver of an ambulance, or of a truck? There are many services which one could fulfill without "armed resistance which involves the actual destruction of human life."[144]

Williams interpreted the military service resolution as allowing noncombatant service. He did not claim to speak for the General Council but wrote as "an individual" to "assist the thinking our youth in the event that they should be called for military service." Nevertheless, he still wrote as the General Superintendent of the Assemblies of God and he recommended the noncombatant route rather than the combatant.

During 1939 two absolutely pacifistic articles appeared in the pages of *The Pentecostal Evangel*. Both quoted the early church fathers and other Christian examples of pacifism. "The Christian and War" began as follows.

> War does not fit in with the teaching and example of our Lord Jesus Christ. This is in accordance with the Christian teaching of the first three centuries, as shown in the writings of Justin Martyr, Irenaeus, Tertullian, Origen, Athanasius, Lactantius and Basil.[145]

"War and Christianity" proclaimed the same message. "The refusal of the Christians to bear arms lasted for the first two or three centuries. It was usual for a soldier to lay down his sword when he accepted the truth of Christ. The declaration of their faith has become historic: 'I am a Christian, and therefore I cannot fight.'"[146]

The appeal to the early history of the church continued in 1940, when Edmund B. Chaffee reminded the Assemblies of God that "the Church Fathers are almost a unit in condemning war for the Christian."[147] He blamed Constantine for the loss of the peace testimony and even cited Adolf Von Harnack to support his position.

The early Christians from the days of the first disciples up until the time of Constantine in A. D. 325 condemned war. It was not until the Roman Empire took over Christianity and made it a part of the State that Christians ceased to bear constant testimony against war. The great German historian Harnack declares that no Christian became a soldier of his own will before the time of Marcus Aurelius, that is, until the latter part of the second century.[148]

As the war intensified Donald Gee again contributed some advice regarding nonparticipation. He proposed that producing military equipment and armaments was inconsistent with true conscientious objection. By doing so he continued the critique of structural problems. The Pentecostal conscientious objectors did not just teach an ethic of nonviolence, they saw that their peace witness should include critiques of manufacturing military equipment and profiting from war. He also insisted that a true conscientious objector would reveal his conscience in other areas of life besides war.

> Have we ever voluntarily lost a job for conscience sake, because we felt it was not morally clean and involved the handling of goods, or the using of methods, inconsistent with Christian principles? . . . All will agree that there is something suspicious about a conscience that only comes to life when a war breaks out and military service is demanded.[149]

Gee demanded that the conscientious objector disagree with all wars, not just certain ones because of political reasons. Gee clearly was not a political pacifist. Furthermore, he thought that a conscientious objector should have moral courage, be willing to suffer and die, and be very tolerant of other's views. The timing of his article shows that the Assemblies of God was concerned about their members being able to take the appropriate stand when the occasion arose, and Gee's courageous and biblically informed presentation represented them well in 1940.

One month later, Ernest S. Williams penned another article about conscientious objection. He implemented suggestions and arguments contained in the *Pacifist Handbook*. It listed the Assemblies of God, with 173,349 members, as the third largest church in America that "opposed . . . war."[150] However, Williams emphasized the fact that the Assemblies of God was not really a pacifist church but rather a church with conscientious objectors.

A full-fledged pacifist takes a position which is beyond what the
writer would feel free to take were our nation called to war. . . .
The Assemblies of God may well be classified among the "conscientious objectors." It is doubtful that it could be classified among
the unqualified "pacifists," since it is pledged to "assist the Government in time of war in every way morally possible."[151]

His interpretation of the article certainly allowed for military service in noncombatant positions but did not encourage combatant service
in any way. He also printed the military service article from the Constitution and Bylaws and encouraged his readers to look for "opportunities
for helpful Christian service" as conscientious objectors.[152]

The final year before American involvement in World War II closed
with a one-sided article about the Assemblies of God and military service. As late as October, 1940, *The Pentecostal Evangel* proclaimed that
the "*universal* feeling in the ranks of the Assemblies of God [is] that military service is incompatible with the gospel of Jesus Christ, and that a
Christian cannot fully follow the teachings of his Lord and Master if he
engages in armed conflict."[153] The author exhorted the constituency to
be sure that they were true conscientious objectors and not just
"hid[ing] behind the position of the church to which they belong."[154]
He also recommended the *Pacifist Handbook*. His three-paragraph article revealed that the editors of *The Pentecostal Evangel* still believed that
the "general belief" of Assemblies of God members in 1940 was that
combatant participation in war was wrong.[155]

My interpretation of pacifism within the early Assemblies of God in
particular and early Pentecostalism in general differs from that of those
who say it was a small minority that ceased to have their voices heard
after World War I. Given the amount and quality of primary literature
on the subject, I believe I can safely suggest that the early Pentecostal
peace witness was much deeper and broader than they estimate. The primary reason is that there was much writing about and promoting of
conscientious objection in official publications, and denominational
leaders continued to support it until at least 1941. Their support was
not always presented to persuade; it was presented to educate and help
Pentecostals live out what their church taught.

Furthermore, "quite a large number" of conscientious objectors in
the third largest peace church in America during World War II is best explained by the interpretation that pacifism was deeply and broadly inte-

grated into the first-generation Pentecostal worldview. This corresponds to the fact that when the Assemblies of God contemplated changing the pacifist article, even after World War II there was not yet enough support among the leadership, ministers, or constituency to do so.

However, there were some within the ranks of the Assemblies of God who countered the radical nature of pacifism by supporting the authority of the individual conscience as determinative for combatant loyalty to the United States. They emphasized this idea most during the latter part of World War I, after the Assemblies of God declaration against Christians killing in war. The development of the authority of conscience ideal needs to be examined in contrast to the declarations of pacifism. The earliest references to national loyalty and the authority of individual conscience appear in the Assemblies of God official magazine, *The Pentecostal Evangel*.[156]

NOTES

1. In 1916 the Assemblies of God numbered their membership at 6,703 and did not report another count until 1925 when it reached 50,386. That's a steady growth rate of about 25% and places the 1917 membership at around 8,378. *General Council Statistics 1914-1975*, available from the Office of the General Secretary of the Assemblies of God.

2. John Howard Yoder, *Nevertheless*, 108.

3. Assemblies of God pacifists tended to be vocational pacifists, i.e. they believed that Christians should not kill or participate in war because the role of the Church was to live and speak as a virtuous and prophetic minority. But one single category could not possibly encompass their thought. Another one of Yoder's categories, "the pacifism of the eschatological parenthesis," also described the early Assemblies of God pacifists, i.e. pacifism is appropriate in this dispensation, but was not in the previous one (Old Testament), and God is about to destroy his enemies and bring ultimate peace. Ibid., 115-116.

4. This is what John Howard Yoder calls "pacifism of cultic law." "One can . . . refuse to kill with one's own hands and yet be willing to participate in the military enterprise, since it is only the act of oneself doing the killing which is forbidden." Ibid., 97. Furthermore, "They do not . . . condemn those who take part in war." Ibid., 96.

5. To assist the interpretation of the change in the Assemblies of God, I will occasionally reference Martin Ceadel's four approaches to peace and war in *Thinking About War and Peace* (Oxford: Oxford University Press, 1987). Ceadel identifies crusading (the belief that a state should have "a willingness under favorable circumstances to use aggressive war to promote either order or justice, as it conceives it, and thereby help to prevent or abolish war in the long term"), defencism ("defense is always right and that the maintenance of strong defenses offers the best chance of pre-

venting war"), pacific-ism (peace-oriented non-pacifists who consider warfare a conceivable, though unfortunate, necessity), and pacifism (all participation in or support of war is wrong). This book will show that the Assemblies of God moved from pacifism to crusading.

6. James C. Juhnke, *Vision, Doctrine, War: Mennonite Identity and Organization in America, 1890-1890-1930*, The Mennonite Experience in America, vol. 3 (Scottdale, Pa.: 1989), 218.

7. The Secretaries of State, War, and Navy served on this committee.

8. Michael W. Casey and Michael A. Jordan, "Free Speech in Time of War: Government Surveillance of the Churches of Christ in World War I," *Free Speech Yearbook* 34 (1996): 108. Juhnke, *Vision, Doctrine, War*, 228.

9. Donald Johnson, "Wilson, Burleson, and Censorship in the First World War," *The Journal of Southern History* vol. 28, no. 1 (1962): 46-58.

10. Burleson to Postmasters of the First, Second, and Third Classes, June 16, 1917, in Post Office Department Files (National Archives). Quoted in Johnson, "Wilson, Burleson, and Censorship in the First World War," 48.

11. Donald Johnson, "Wilson, Burleson, and Censorship in the First World War," 48.

12. Casey and Jordan, "Free Speech in Time of War," 105.

13. Casey and Jordan, "Free Speech in Time of War," 106.

14. Michael W. Casey, "The Closing of Cordell Christian College: A Microcosm of American Intolerance during World War I," *Chronicles of Oklahoma* 76 (Spring 1998): 25-27.

15. Herbert Pankratz, "The Suppression of Alleged Disloyalty in Kansas During World War I," *Kansas Historical Quarterly* 1976 42 (3): 280.

16. Herbert Pankratz, "The Suppression of Alleged Disloyalty in Kansas During World War I," *Kansas Historical Quarterly* 1976 42 (3): 277-307.

17. Juhnke, *Vision, Doctrine, War*, 218. Pankratz, "The Suppression of Alleged Disloyalty in Kansas During World War I," 286.

18. Pankratz, "The Suppression of Alleged Disloyalty in Kansas During World War I," 286.

19. Wichita *Beacon*, April 26, 1918. Quoted in Pankratz, "The Suppression of Alleged Disloyalty in Kansas During World War I," 298.

20. Pankratz, "The Suppression of Alleged Disloyalty in Kansas During World War I," 303.

21. Casey, "The Closing of Cordell Christian College," 20.

22. Casey, "The Closing of Cordell Christian College," 29.

23. Casey, "The Closing of Cordell Christian College," 30-35.

24. Juhnke, *Vision, Doctrine, War*, 222.

25. Juhnke, *Vision, Doctrine, War*, 237.

26. Juhnke, *Vision, Doctrine, War*, 208-209.

27. Daniel Hallock, "Persecution in the Land of the Free," excerpt from *Hell, Healing, and Resistance: Veterans Speak* (Rifton, N.Y.: Plough Publishing House, 1998). http://www.plough.com/articles/persecutionintheland.html (accessed August 9, 2007). John C. Wenger, "The Martyrdom of Joseph and Michael Hofer,

1918," *The Gospel Herald*, 25 July 1978.

28. J. D. Mininger, *Religious C.O.'s Imprisoned at the U.S. Disciplinary Barracks, Ft. Leavenworth, Kansas* (Published by J. D. Mininger, 200 South Seventh St., Kansas City, Kansas, March 10, 1919). Hist. Mss. 1-11-2, J. D. Mininger 22/14 Conscientious objectors, Mennonite Church USA Archives, Goshen, Ind.

29. Gerlof D. Homan, *American Mennonites and the Great War: 1914-1918* (Scottdale, Pa.: Herald Press, 1994), 59.

30. J. B. Ellis, "The Murder of Brother Dave Allen," *[Church of God] Evangel*, 27 April 1918, 4.

31. John Hingham, *Strangers in the Land: Patterns of American Nativism, 1860-1925* (New Brunswick, N.J.: 1988), 195; cited in Homan, *American Mennonites*, 57.

32. "We continue to diminish underlying conditions that terrorists exploit to operate and recruit. Poverty, corruption, religious conflict, ethnic strife, and suppressing democratic expression 'breeds frustration, hopelessness and resentment—and ideological entrepreneurs know how to turn those emotions into either support for terrorism or acquiescence to it' (Secretary Powell)." William P. Pope (Principal Deputy Coordinator for Counterterrorism, U.S. Department of State) in *Strategic Asia and the War on Terrorism*, speech delivered September 22, 2004, http://www.state.gov/s/ct/rls/rm/ 2004/37410.htm, accessed February 19, 2007.

33. I owe this insight to J. Denny Weaver.

34. Peter Brock and Nigel Young observed that the Jehovah's Witnesses, who were also pacifists during World War I, were "derive[d] almost exclusively from the economically and educationally underprivileged: factory workers, artisans and petty shopkeepers, and agricultural laborers." They, like early Pentecostals, also emphasized the imminent cataclysmic end of the world. These themes were common among Biblically oriented conscientious objectors. *Pacifism in the Twentieth Century* (Toronto, Ont.: University of Toronto Press Incorporated, 1999), 9-10.

35. Wacker, *Heaven Below*, 243, 245.

36. The following authors argued for pacifism and conscientious objection in 1917 and 1918, during World War I. These were all printed in *The Weekly Evangel* (which later became *The Pentecostal Evangel*). Baron D'Estournelles de Constant, "The Sinister Education of War," *The Weekly Evangel*, 20 January 1917, 2. "What is War?" *The Weekly Evangel*, 21 April 1917, 2. "The Crisis," *The Weekly Evangel*, 21 April 1917, 7. Samuel H. Booth-Clibborn, "The Christian and War. Is it too Late?," *The Weekly Evangel*, 28 April 1917, 5. "Compulsory Military Service: An English Conscientious Objector's Testimony," *The Weekly Evangel*, 28 April 1917, 7. Samuel H. Booth-Clibborn, "The Christian and War," *The Weekly Evangel*, 19 May 1917, 4. J. W. Welch, "An Explanation," *The Weekly Evangel*, 19 May 1917, 8. "The Pentecostal Movement and the Conscription Law," *The Weekly Evangel*, 4 August 1917, 6. "The Pentecostal Movement and the Conscription Law," *The Weekly Evangel*, 5 January 1918, 5. Oscar Barl, "Reports From the Field: Fort Riley, Kansas," *The Weekly Evangel*, 19 October 1918, 14. A. B. Cox, "In Prison and Out Again," *The Weekly Evangel*, 29 June 1918, 14. Arthur Sydney Booth-Clibborn, "Nigh, Even At The Doors," 7 September 1918, 2.

170 / Peace to War

37. The following authors argued for pacifism and conscientious objection in the years following World War I and during World War II. Lydia Hatfield, "The Law of Christ for Believers," *The Christian Evangel*, 12 July 1919, 3. Arthur Sydney Booth-Clibborn, "European Pentecostal Notes," *The Pentecostal Evangel*, 6 March 1920, 11. D. M. Panton, "Coming War," *The Pentecostal Evangel*, 25 November 1922, 10. Stanley H. Frodsham, "From The Pentecostal Viewpoint," *The Pentecostal Evangel*, 21 June 1924, 4. Donald Gee, "War, the Bible, and the Christian," *The Pentecostal Evangel*, 8 November 1930, 6. Donald Gee, "War, the Bible, and the Christian," *The Pentecostal Evangel*, 15 November 1930, 2. "War Behind the Smoke Screen," *The Pentecostal Evangel*, 6 December 1930, 3. Ernest S. Williams, "In Case of War," *The Pentecostal Evangel*, 19 March 1938, 4. "The Christian and War," *The Pentecostal Evangel*, 29 July 1939, 2. "War and Christianity," *The Pentecostal Evangel*, 23 September 1939, 10. Edmund B. Chaffee, "The Early Church and the Sword," *The Pentecostal Evangel*, 27 January 1940, 3.

38. There were at least eighty articles about missions and war while there were approximately forty-six articles dealing with combatant participation or conscientious objection. See bibliography for a complete listing.

39. J. W. Welch, "The Pentecostal Movement and the Conscription Law," *The Weekly Evangel*, 4 August 1917, 6.

40. "War! War! War!" *The Christian Evangel*, 15 August 1914, 1.

41. Ibid.

42. L. V. Roberts, "Prophetic War Horses Sent Out," *The Christian Evangel*, 29 August 1914, 1. "Take Warning," *The Christian Evangel*, 5 September 1914, 1. George Carlyle, "The Great Tribulation," 5 September 1914, 1. James A. Gray, "A Voice From England," *The Christian Evangel*, 3 October 1914, 1. "He is Coming," *The Christian Evangel*, 3 October 1914, 1. J. Roswell Flower, "War-A Fulfillment of Prophecy," *The Christian Evangel*, 31 October 1914, 1. J. Roswell Flower, "The Kings of the East," *The Christian Evangel*, 7 November 1914, 1. "Is European War Justifiable?," *The Christian Evangel*, 12 December 1914, 1-2.

43. James A. Gray, "A Voice From England," *The Christian Evangel*, 3 October 1914, 1.

44. "Is European War Justifiable?," *The Christian Evangel*, 12 December 1914, 1-2. This was the only article that supported Christian participation in warfare between 1914 and 1916.

45. Burt McCafferty, "Should Christians Go To War?" *The Christian Evangel*, 16 January 1915, 1.

46. Ibid. McCafferty appealed to the life of Jesus as an example to be followed. In so doing, he aligned with the type of pacifism Yoder called "the imitation of Jesus." "Its content is not abstract commands but rather the life and word of Jesus. His command and example are to be followed without calculation of social possibilities. . . . It does not expect widespread acceptance, but neither does it acquiesce in the world's noncompliance with Jesus' norm." Yoder, *Nevertheless*, 120.

47. McCafferty, "Should Christians Go To War?" 1.

48. Arthur Sydney Booth-Clibborn, *Blood Against Blood* (1901; reprint New York: Charles C. Cook, 1914).

49. "Blood Against Blood," *The Weekly Evangel*, 3 July 1915, 3. "Blood Against Blood," *The Weekly Evangel*, 10 July 1915, 3.

50. Since this book made an impact on me during my research for the book in hand, I can easily understand how first-generation Pentecostals found Booth-Clibborn's arguments persuasive.

51. The ratio was at least 10:1 in favor of nonparticipation. However, war remained a minor concern compared to missions, revivals, and doctrinal debates.

52. "Tithes and Free Will Offerings," *The Weekly Evangel*, 3 July 1915, 3.

53. Frank Bartleman, "The European War," *The Weekly Evangel*, 10 July 1915, 3.

54. Ibid.

55. Ibid.

56. Ibid.

57. Ibid.

58. Frank Bartleman, "What Will the Harvest Be?" *The Weekly Evangel*, 7 August 1915, 1. He also stated, "This war is not a holy war. . . . The whole thing is a game of chess, with the nations as the players. Kings and leaders, capitalists, are the chess men. They play their nations as the stake. Rulers for their private purse, bankers and financiers of the world for gain, munition manufacturers and provision merchants, all work together in this game. Flesh and blood of the common people, soldiers, are either forced or hired to do the fighting. The souls of men are the material used in the scrabble."

59. Twelve countries were at war in August, 1915.

60. Ibid., 2.

61. Graft in this context is "the acquisition of money, gain, or advantage by dishonest, unfair, or illegal means, esp. through the abuse of one's position or influence in politics, business, etc." grafter. Dictionary.com. *Dictionary.com Unabridged (v 1.0.1)*, Based on the Random House Unabridged Dictionary, © Random House, Inc. 2006. http://dictionary.reference.com/browse/grafter (accessed: November 03, 2006).

62. "The game is not worth the candle" means "what we would get from this undertaking is not worth the effort we would have to put into it. The saying alludes to a game of cards in which the stakes are smaller than the cost of burning a candle for light by which to play." E.D. Hirsch, The New Dictionary of Cultural Literacy, ed. E. D. Hirsch, Jr., Joseph F. Kett, James Trefil (Boston: Houghton Mifflin Company, 2002).

63. Ibid.

64. Ibid., 1.

65. J. Roswell Flower, "What Will the Harvest Be? Article in Last Week's *Evangel* Receiving Just Criticism," *The Weekly Evangel*, 14 August 1915, 2.

66. Ibid.

67. Ibid.

68. Ibid.

69. Stanley H. Frodsham, "Our Heavenly Citizenship," *The Weekly Evangel*, 11 September 1915, 3.

70. Ibid.

71. Ibid.

72. Ibid.

73. Ibid. Frodsham recognized that the Assemblies of God was outside the religious establishment and was continually attacked by fundamentalists and liberals alike.

74. George T. Sisler, "War 'Profits,'" *The Weekly Evangel*, 29 April 1916, 7.

75. "War's Dread Realities," *The Weekly Evangel*, 16 December 1916, 2.

76. E. N. Bell was editor of *The Weekly Evangel* during this time.

77. Baron D'Estournelles de Constant, "The Sinister Education of War," *The Weekly Evangel*, 20 January 1917, 2.

78. "What is War?" *The Weekly Evangel*, 21 April 1917, 2.

79. "The Crisis," *The Weekly Evangel*, 21 April 1917, 7.

80. Ibid.

81. Mrs. A. R. Flower, "Daily Portion From the King's Bounty," *The Weekly Evangel*, 21 April 1917, 7.

82. Samuel H. Booth-Clibborn, "The Christian and War. Is it too Late?," *The Weekly Evangel*, 28 April 1917, 5. Booth-Clibborn rejected pragmatic conscientious objection and revealed that he was a pacifist who appealed to the example of Jesus and completely rejected any form of noncombatant military service. "A truly enlightened Christian will have the spiritual perception to see that this so-called 'noncombatant service' is only a part and parcel of the whole machine. Men and women thus employed are every bit as guilty in the Supreme Court of Heaven of the murder of their fellow-men, as are those in the trenches." Samuel H. Booth-Clibborn, *Should A Christian Fight? An Appeal to Christian Young Men of All Nations* (Swengel, Pa.: Bible Truth Depot, n.d.), 83.

83. Ibid.

84. Again note the use of the term "ignorance." Pentecostals truly believed they were interpreting Scripture well regarding participation in war.

85. Ibid.

86. Ibid. Emphasis in the original.

87. Ibid. Emphasis in the original.

88. "Compulsory Military Service: An English Conscientious Objector's Testimony," *The Weekly Evangel*, 28 April 1917, 7. For other Christian answers to this type of question see John Howard Yoder, *What Would You Do?* (Scottdale, Pa.: Herald Press, 1992).

89. Ibid. Emphasis added.

90. Samuel H. Booth-Clibborn, "The Christian and War," *The Weekly Evangel*, 19 May 1917, 4. Emphasis in the original. Note the designation "militaristic Christians" he employed as he addressed the Assemblies of God, he did not want his audience to be so defined.

91. Ibid. Emphasis in the original.

92. Ibid. Emphasis in the original.

93. J. W. Welch, "An Explanation," *The Weekly Evangel*, 19 May 1917, 8.

94. The resolution had been mailed to all Assemblies of God ministers in May.

95. "The Pentecostal Movement and the Conscription Law," *The Weekly Evan-*

gel, 4 August 1917, 6.

96. Ibid. Emphasis added.

97. Evidence exists that shows that the noncombatant and pacifistic positions were not unanimous. Cf. *Authority to Fight, 1914-1940* above.

98. "The Pentecostal Movement and the Conscription Law," *The Weekly Evangel*, 4 August 1917, 6.

99. Jay Beaman, *Pentecostal Pacifism* (Newton, Kan.: Mennonite Brethren Press, 1989).

100. Ibid. Emphasis in the original.

101. At the least, they did not explicitly forbid noncombatant military service and it did explicitly state their desire to be loyal citizens.

102. These were arguments employed by the Booth-Clibborns and Bartleman.

103. "The Pentecostal Movement and the Conscription Law," *The Weekly Evangel*, 4 August 1917, 6.

104. The Assemblies of God made not one reference to scripture in the 1967 article on military service that officially deferred to the authority of the individual's conscience. *General Council Minutes*, 1967, 35.

105. Ibid., 7.

106. "The Pentecostal Movement and the Conscription Law," *The Weekly Evangel*, 5 January 1918, 5.

107. "Amongst the Soldier Boys," *The Weekly Evangel*, 29 June 1918, 14. However, there were seventy-five Pentecostal soldiers at this same camp.

108. Oscar Barl, "Reports From the Field: Fort Riley, Kansas," *The Weekly Evangel*, 19 October 1918, 14.

109. A. B. Cox, "In Prison and Out Again," *The Weekly Evangel*, 29 June 1918, 14.

110. Arthur Sydney Booth-Clibborn, "Nigh, Even At The Doors," 7 September 1918, 2.

111. Ibid. Emphasis in the original. This is evidence of Booth-Clibborn's vocational pacifism.

112. Arthur Sydney Booth-Clibborn, "Nigh, Even At The Doors," 5 October 1918, 6. It was possible that Booth-Clibborn purposely contradicted E. N. Bell's earlier appeal to American forces for the protection of Pentecostal missionaries. E. N. Bell, "Wars and the Missionaries," *The Christian Evangel*, 12 September 1914, 1.

113. Ibid.

114. Ruth M. Brackbill, "Mininger, Jacob D. (1879-1941)." *Global Anabaptist Mennonite Encyclopedia Online*. 1957. Global Anabaptist Mennonite Encyclopedia Online. Accessed September 1 2007 http://www.gameo.org/encyclopedia/contents/ M56134.html.

115. J.D. Mininger, *Religious C.O.'s Imprisoned at the U.S. Disciplinary Barracks, Ft. Leavenworth, Kansas* (Published by J. D. Mininger, 200 South Seventh St., Kansas City, Kansas, March 10, 1919). Hist. Mss. 1-11-2, J.D. Mininger 22/14 Conscientious objectors, Mennonite Church USA Archives, Goshen, Ind. See Appendix A for the complete list of Pentecostal conscientious objectors.

116. *Statistical Abstract of the United States* (U.S. Census Bureau),

http://www.census.gov/statab/hist/HS-01.pdf. Accessed September 1, 2007. The Assemblies of God comprised only .009% of the American population in 2007 (2.8 million adherents of 302 million). *Assemblies of God Biennial Report, 2005-2007.* Springfield, Mo.: Gospel Publishing House, 2007. Also available at http://www.ag.org/biennialreport. The Assemblies of God has 1,627,932 members but counts 2,836,174 adherents who "consider an Assembly of God their regular church home."

117. *General Council Statistics 1914-1975.* Available from the Statistician's Office at the General Council of the Assemblies of God, http://www.ag.org/top/about/statistics/ index.cfm. Church and member statistics are not available for 1914-1915 and 1917-1923.

118. A. G. B., "The Impending Conflict," *The Pentecostal Evangel*, 2 October 1926, 4-5. "What Future Wars Will Be Like," *The Pentecostal Evangel*, 18 June 1927, 3. "The Next War," *The Pentecostal Evangel*, 25 June 1927, 8.

119. "The Prime Minister regards everything as trivial and incidental compared with the urgent and even terrorizing problem of a world in acute danger. . . . He has seen things in peace which are clearly filling him with dread. There is fear in his mind . . . he knows the mind of Europe as few have had the chance to know and he sees rising the scepter of war. . . . The War has not ended war; rather has it let loose a flood of implacable enmity, and opened a long vista of irremediable strife, making the thought of the future a hideous nightmare." "Coming War," *The Pentecostal Evangel*, 25 November 1922, 10.

120. Stanley Frodsham, "From the Pentecostal Viewpoint," *The Pentecostal Evangel*, 21 June 1924, 4-5.

121. Lydia Hatfield, "The Law of Christ for Believers," *The Christian Evangel*, 12 July 1919, 3.

122. Arthur Sydney Booth-Clibborn, "European Pentecostal Notes," *The Pentecostal Evangel*, 6 March 1920, 11.

123. D. M. Panton, "Coming War," *The Pentecostal Evangel*, 25 November 1922, 10. E. N. Bell was General Superintendent of the Assemblies of God when this article was published. The article also says, "If the Churches of Christ throughout Europe and America allow this thing [the next war] to happen, they had better close their doors. For the next war, if ever it comes, will be a war on civilization itself. . . . Christian leaders from twenty-five nations agreed that 'to the mind of Christ war is an abomination, and His followers should, step by step, take action to make it impossible.'"

124. Ibid., 11. The article continues, "Without regeneration peace can come neither within or without; disarmament, even if practicable, is no solution to the problem. The world is only an ordinary man multiplied by sixteen hundred million; and it is useless to take arms out of men's hands, unless we take the passions out of their hearts; disarm the quarrelsome, and they will fight without arms; on the contrary, those who have been cured of the will to war may be cased in armor from head to foot, but they will not fight."

125. Stanley H. Frodsham, "From The Pentecostal Viewpoint," *The Pentecostal Evangel*, 21 June 1924, 4. Frodsham heard about this report in the April 12, 1924,

"Dearborn Independent" newspaper.

126. Ibid. The Quaker minute stated, "This meeting desires to reaffirm the primary loyalty of all Christians is due God, our Father, and all His human family. We believe that the whole system of determining right by violence and destruction rather than by friendly conference and negotiation is fundamentally wrong, inefficient and unchristian. We call upon Christian people of whatever sect or creed to join in renouncing for the future all participation in war, and to seek through our national representatives such international organization as will supply peaceful methods of dealing with all international differences. We also urge upon Christians consideration of inter-class and inter-racial problems and an effort to solve them through good will and understanding."

127. Ibid. Emphasis added. Frodsham expressed the absolute pacifism of the Booth-Clibborns and Frank Bartleman; furthermore, his position was quite opposite the authority of individual conscience presented by E. N. Bell, who had died the previous year (1923).

128. Ibid.

129. Ibid. "We reject absolutely that false teaching that the words of Christ are 'law and not grace,' and that the sermon on the mount is 'neither the privilege nor the duty of the church.'"

130. Donald Gee, "War, the Bible, and the Christian," *The Pentecostal Evangel*, 8 November 1930, 6. Gee viewed the role of the church as that of a virtuous minority who emulated Jesus by nonviolently standing for what was right regardless of the consequences. This outspoken pacifist was elected chairman even after World War II.

131. Ibid.

132. Ibid.

133. Donald Gee, "War, the Bible, and the Christian," 2.

134. Ibid.

135. Ibid.

136. Ibid.

137. Ibid., 3.

138. Ibid.

139. Ibid.

140. "War Behind the Smoke Screen," *The Pentecostal Evangel*, 6 December 1930, 3.

141. Ibid.

142. Ernest S. Williams, "In Case of War," *The Pentecostal Evangel*, 19 March 1938, 4. Williams also taught at Central Bible College in Springfield, Missouri and served as its dean.

143. Ibid.

144. Ibid.

145. *The Pentecostal Evangel*, 29 July 1939, 2.

146. *The Pentecostal Evangel*, 23 September 1939, 10.

147. "The Early Church and the Sword," *The Pentecostal Evangel*, 27 January 1940, 3.

148. Ibid.

149. Donald Gee, "Conscientious Objection," *The Pentecostal Evangel*, 4 May 1940, 4.

150. Ernest S. Williams, "The Conscientious Objector," *The Pentecostal Evangel*, 15 June 1940, 4. The two larger ones were the Churches of Christ (433, 714) and the Brethren (192, 588). The Quakers were listed as having 105,917 members.

151. Ibid.

152. Ibid. He printed the revised version from 1927.

153. "The Attitude of the General Council Toward Military Service," *The Pentecostal Evangel*, 12 October 1940, 13. Emphasis added. Based upon the context of the other articles that supported noncombatant service, this article probably referred to combatant military service.

154. Ibid.

155. Ibid.

156. This publication experienced several name changes. It was *The Christian Evangel* from July 1913–February 1915; *The Weekly Evangel* from March 1915-March 1917; *The Christian Evangel* from April 1917–September 1919; and *The Pentecostal Evangel* from October 1919 to the present.

FIVE

UNSWERVING LOYALTY TO THE GOVERNMENT: THE SEEDS OF NATIONALISM AND MILITARISM FROM 1914-1940

INTRODUCTION

The word *patriot* comes from the Greek *pater,* which means "father," and *patriotes,* which means "of one's fathers." A patriot is one who "loves, supports, or defends one's own country" and "supports its authority and interests."[1] The word *nation* derives from the Greek *ethnos* which means "people, nation"[2] or "people of the same race or nationality who share a distinctive culture." It comes from the Latin *nationem,* which originally meant "nation, stock, race." So nationalism is "devotion to the interests or culture of a particular nation [*ethnos*]."[3] Since the words *race* and *ethnicity* also derive from ethnos, nationalism and racism ("the notion that one's own ethnic stock [ethnos] is superior,")[4] are closely connected both etymologically and theologically.[5]

First-generation Assemblies of God people were moderately patriotic, but not fervently. For the most part they maintained a healthy critique of America as a sinful nation but viewed it as one in which they lived and for which they prayed. They withheld their support for its wars but spoke of loyalty and respect for the government as long as American interests did not conflict with good theology and the interests of the kingdom of God. If there was a scale of patriotism, with fervent nationalism rating a ten, then most American Christians ranked in the eight-ten range during World War I. However, the Assemblies of God would have ranked no higher than a two-three.

As discussed in the previous chapter, early Assemblies of God writers described nationalism as ungodly while others, during World War I at least, understandably suggested that patriotic language was desirable. The critique of uncritical national allegiance was much stronger among first-generation Pentecostals and far outweighed patriotic rhetoric. Rather than a competing ideal that contradicted Christian pacifism, promotion of respect for the government actually expressed a biblically based respect for the powers that be while also maintaining God's kingship and moral imperatives as supreme. The clearest presentation of patriotic language occurred from 1917-1918, during the height of American involvement in the war and following the Espionage Act and Sedition Act, which limited free speech and increased government pressure on war resisters. Until that time they barely mentioned it, and after World War I it faded away almost entirely until 1941.

SUPPORTING THE NATION, 1914-1940

Before the Great War, 1914-1916

The earliest reference to any appreciation for the United States government came from J. Roswell Flower in August 1915. He presented the sentiments of an anonymous Pentecostal reader who had written a letter supporting the selling of weapons by America to Britain and its allies as well as to the Germans. The article served as Roswell's partial apology for publishing certain parts of Frank Bartleman's antiwar article[6] one week earlier and provided the opposite perspective by publishing the letter. The constituent supported the United States government and declared that

> The article [Bartleman's] is a gross injustice to our own government at a critical time when it is honestly striving to DO RIGHT and in my humble judgment IS doing right to be impartial and offer to sell to ALL alike, being in NO WISE responsible for the fact that the Germans cannot buy war materials. . . .[7]

Although Flower printed this pro-American letter, he followed it with his own admonition to "lose [your] national preferences and prejudices [because] . . . national prejudices must die."[8] By emphasizing heavenly citizenship, Flower revealed that the Assemblies of God leadership wanted to prioritize the international kingdom of God. The person who wrote the letter to *The Weekly Evangel* had no qualms about supporting his government's sale of arms to both sides of a war, even though other Pentecostals were denouncing it.

In 1916 an unnamed contributor to the *Evangel* wrote an article that attempted to show that the European War did not disprove the truth of Christianity. He viewed the war as a contest between "world powers" and that "those true Christians who are engaged in it are simply doing their duty in that state of life in which God has called them."[9] This duty of loyalty to the nations in which they happened to be born was an opinion not widely expressed in the pages of the *Evangel* or in the *General Council Minutes* during these years. In fact, only these two articles promoted loyalty to the government between 1914 and 1916, while at least ten articles challenged such loyalty by espousing nonparticipation.[10] The period 1917-1918 produced a noticeable shift toward national fidelity, but never to the degree represented by other Christian groups in America.

World War I, 1917-1918

The Assemblies of God declared both their pacifism and their "unswerving loyalty" to the United States government during 1917 and 1918. They conscientiously opposed war only after making it clear that they supported their nation as much as morally possible. Peace churches for hundreds of years and amid numerous wars had prefaced their nonviolence with honorable and respectful language for their governments. The Great War created conditions that made resisting the government difficult even for many radical Pentecostals. Even prominent Mennonites, whose members made up the majority of conscientious objectors during the war, tempered their language. The president of Goshen (Ind.) College suggested in 1918 that "in these days of patriotism, it is best that we do not say much about our position but quietly live it."[11] And an article in *The Mennonite* suggested that an "active propagation of peace doctrines in the face of military rule [the American situation during the war] would injure the cause just now."[12]

The realistic awareness of possible retaliation and the desire to honor appropriately the establishment were evident during the year and a half of American involvement in the war. Nine articles in the *Evangel* and four resolutions in the *General Council Minutes* mentioned loyalty to government, while seven articles and two resolutions defended conscientious objection. This is a significant amount of Assemblies of God witness against war, considering many Christian periodicals and denominations reversed their pacifism completely under the intense government pressure during World War I. One of many remarkable about faces came from the American Peace Society, which declared in 1916 "that Jesus Christ was a pacifist." But in May 1917, the society agreed "that war was unavoidable" and backed the administration.[13]

The first Assemblies of God mention of support during this period occurred in the May 19, 1917 article that informed the constituency of the declaration of conscientious objection to killing in warfare. John W. Welch (1858-1939), chairman of the General Council, stated that "We are not opposed to the Government and not unwilling to serve in any capacity that will not require the destruction of life."[14] Welch found it necessary to clarify the fact that the Assemblies of God was loyal to America even though he himself, and the rest of the executive presbytery, deplored the thought of Pentecostal men bearing arms. This first official statement about conscientious objection contained this disclaimer because leaders and members of any group that did oppose the government could be jailed and have their publications banned. The Postmaster General of the United States had declared that he would ban any publication saying:

> That this Government got in the war wrong, that it is in it for the wrong purposes, or anything that will impugn the motives of the Government for going into the war. They can not say that this Government is the tool of Wall Street or the munitions-makers. That kind of thing makes for insubordination in the Army and Navy and breeds a spirit of disloyalty through the country. It is a false statement, a lie, and it will not be permitted. . . . There can be nothing said to hamper and obstruct the Government in the prosecution of the war.[15]

So presenting the tremendously contentious principle of conscientious objection with words such as "we are not opposed to the Government" was simple common sense amid a world war. It was a wise rhetorical strategy designed to keep their organization alive. Their noncompliant actions were countercultural enough; the leaders knew better than to present their peace witness harshly.

Less than three months later, the leaders of the Assemblies of God decided to publish their resolution regarding military service and several other pertinent documents regarding the process of becoming a recognized peace church. These documents revealed their awareness that they needed to be clearly in support of the United States as emotionally charged patriotism swept the country. They introduced the resolution with a statement of national loyalty, "While recognizing Human Government as of Divine ordination and affirming our unswerving loyalty to the Government of the United States, nevertheless we are constrained to define our position with reference to the taking of human life."[16] The executive presbytery employed the word *unswerving* to define their loyalty even though they swerved in one way: the taking of human life. It seems that they used the word to soften the impact of objecting to war, controversial as it was, even often considered treasonous. As Brock and Young noted, it was "little wonder if the ordinary patriotic citizen should equate pacifism with treason and feel sometimes that the place for opponents of war was swinging from a lamp-post."[17]

The fact that the resolution concluded with the same language of national fidelity seems to bolster this idea. The final paragraph of the resolution began with "THEREFORE we, as a body of Christians, while purposing to fulfill all the obligations of loyal citizenship, are nevertheless constrained to declare we cannot conscientiously participate in war and armed resistance. . . ."[18] This loyalty bracket that encompassed the four "whereas" paragraphs shows that loyalty to the government was quite a concern. They wrote to the War Department, so they certainly did not want to communicate in a disrespectful manner, but their language revealed their recognition of their dual allegiance present at this early date. However, since other Christians also struggled with the tension of dual allegiance, the Assemblies of God was not alone.

The letter to President Woodrow Wilson that accompanied the resolution contained the same sentiments.

> We desire to express to your Excellency our loyal support at this time of national crisis and to assure you that we will do all in our power to uphold your hands. . . . It is not the purpose of this Resolution to weaken the hands of the Executive. . . . We want fur-

ther to assure your Excellency that any service of a non-military character . . . will be gladly rendered.[19]

The expressions of loyalty in this letter were clear, but the Assemblies of God simply stated exactly what needed to be said to not have their publications banned. Obstructing conscription or the war could result in treason charges, so they needed to clearly say they were not "weakening the hands" of the president. Since most Americans agreed that conscientious objectors helped the Germans, the Assemblies of God had to say that was not their intention. Both the resolution and the letter were concerned with expressing loyalty to the United States and its "Excellency" as they presented their pacifism, but nonparticipation in war remained the purpose of these publications and the power and significance of this witness amid war should not be underestimated. Even so, loyalty to the government within half a century advanced completely to the forefront in the American Assemblies of God and the origins of that adjustment can be seen here.

The *General Council Minutes* of September 1917 contained an exhortation admonishing ministers not to be anti-government in their opposition to war. It came at a time when the Bureau of Investigation and the War Department investigated and prosecuted over a million activities that were allegedly anti-American.

> Bro. E. L. Banta spoke on the importance of our loyalty to the powers that be, since they are ordained of God; and told of some so-called Pentecostal preachers who thought they were doing honor to God by insulting the flag and of the humiliation to them that followed. Bro. A. P. Collins followed and said that we were on Bible grounds in honoring the government, and said that the flag stood not only for civil freedom but also for religious liberty; and that at the Texas District Council they had purposed to cancel the credentials of any preacher who spoke against the government. This body also agreed that such radicals do not represent this General Council.[20]

A. P. Collins himself viewed war as unchristian and sinful. So the "radical" was the one who did not speak respectfully about the government even while supporting conscientious objection. These "radicals" who spoke against the government or the flag were deemed not to be representative of the Assemblies of God during World War I, but nothing in this statement supports fighting or killing. The Assemblies of God leaders and members had previously published and promoted ideas that would have at that time, during the war, been considered seditious. Now that the United States had been in the war for a few months, it was time to curtail some of the rhetoric. Realizing that A. P. Collins was a pacifist helps the reader see that this is not zealous patriotism but a promotion of respectful disobedience and honorable opposition to the war.

The October 27, 1917 *Weekly Evangel* contained an article that argued hell was real for unsaved soldiers even if they died serving their country. The author wanted to show that they needed to be saved and anyone saying otherwise was a heretic. He defended both hell and loyalty to the government.

> We love our country and the freedom guaranteed by the Stars and Stripes. Every Christian will and must do everything consistent with his faith in Christ to uphold our country amid its present great struggle. . . . We must make it possible for our country to win out for right and freedom. . . . We cannot throw our Bibles to the winds because we are loyal to our country or because we love our soldier boys.[21]

Throwing the Bible "to the winds" meant preaching that soldiers automatically go to heaven. This issue arose because popular American sentiment, inspired by government rhetoric, considered the Great War a holy war.[22] Consistency with faith in Christ was the point of the article. "Love," "uphold," "win," and "loyal" were all applied to the United States of America, but the author claimed that "pre-war theology" was still right. Again, we see challenging and radical beliefs being couched in loyalty language.

A call to repentance in November 1917 lauded national patriotism, "giving fullest value to the splendid patriotism, self-sacrifice, and energy to which the nation has risen. . . ."[23] The author declared that prayers "for victory, for the protection of our loved ones, and for the favorable ordering of the course of battle" needed to be accompanied by prayers of repentance for such evils as "the drink curse."[24]

In 1918 "'a wave of terror' began in the United States where county and state councils of defense, patriotic societies, and mobs began to attack pacifists."[25] In this context E. N. Bell decided to print a column that would help Assemblies of God ministers, some of whom "are not trained in wartime laws," avoid landing "in a Federal Penitentiary, or up before a shooting squad for Treason to the Country."[26] The title "Preachers Warned" introduced his article. Bell warned them "not to do anything *rash*" like the "half dozen preachers [who had] been arrested and put in jail by U.S. Marshals for opposing this war, failing to register in the draft, and such things."[27] These were not paranoid fears but represented actual, regular, and widespread events during World War I in America. Many Pentecostals and other conscientious objectors were brought before firing squads, told to recant, and after refusing they were shot—with empty guns.[28] Many were court-martialed, imprisoned, tarred and feathered, and run out of town. Bell had to lead a denomination of conscientious objectors through a war in which they were being harassed and persecuted. He did so by encouraging them to be respectful and obey the laws, even while maintaining their peace witness.

> The General Council has always stood for law and order. So at our last Council Meeting [September 1917] we took a strong stand for Loyalty to our Government and the President and to the Flag. Let all note this and be duly warned. . . . Many utterances allowable in times of peace may be Treasonable in Time of War, such as the present. Hence all preachers should be careful to *be* and *act* in loyalty to our Country in the Great Crisis, and not to say a word in opposition to the Authorities or to the work of the Government in war matters.[29]

Bell knew the Assemblies of God peace witness could result in arrests and time in jail, and opposing the war could get the *Evangel* shut down. So he hoped to curtail any Assemblies of God people who thought God was leading them to speak against the government or the war. He wanted the pacifist Assemblies of God to be viewed as a good and supportive church rather than one that challenged the status quo.

> It is one thing to be in our own faith opposed personally to taking human life, even in war, but quite another thing to preach against our Government going to war. It is unlawful to do so. It is none of our business to push our faith as to war on others or on the Government.[30]

Bell was right that preaching against war could be illegal due to the severe restrictions on freedom of speech. But he also called opposition to war "our own faith" and included himself. He recognized that nonparticipation in war was a dangerous message to present to others amid the nationalism and broad support for the war they were living through in 1918. Many considered it treasonous, and Bell thought it was not worth going to prison or getting killed. "It is no time or place for Slackers toward our country or our God. Preachers who are excused from war, old or young [should] . . . show their gratitude to God and the Flag . . . and prove this by extra service and sacrifices to the good of mankind, to the Government, and to God."[31] Bell's position seemed to be that even though the Assemblies of God was a church of conscientious objectors they did not have to be mean about it.

The front page of the April 6, 1918, *Evangel* broadcast the words of President Woodrow Wilson. The *Evangel* editors placed the quote in the center of the page, boxed so it would immediately capture the reader's attention. Wilson encouraged people to read their Bibles because doing so would show them "what things are worth while . . .—loyalty, right dealings, speaking the truth, readiness to give everything for what they think their duty. . . ."[32] This message from the president and the Bible about loyalty and duty on the front page during war helped the Assemblies of God ameliorate accusations that they were anti-American.

The ever-increasing violence and jingoism in America paved the way for a resolution at the General Council of 1918 entitled "Expression of Loyalty to the Government."

> Resolved, That the General Council hereby declares its unswerving loyalty to our Government and to its Chief Executive, President Wilson, and that we hereby restate our fixed purpose to help with every way morally possible, consistent with our faith, in bringing the present "World War" to a successful conclusion.[33]

This statement is like those of many other American Christian denominations with one notable exception—"morally possible, consistent with our faith" meant they would not kill. By September 1918 the Assemblies of God decided that it was desirable to go on record as hoping that the United States would win the war. As a pacifist fellowship, they hoped they could help in ways that did not include killing. This 1918 resolution followed a number of articles in the *Evangel* that approved both patriotism and national loyalty.

The Assemblies of God presented their respect for their government during the two years of American involvement in World War I. But the end of the war brought about a sharp decline in loyalty language; there were only two references from 1919-1940. This alone reveals the impetus for the war-time rhetoric, especially since the Assemblies of God support was miniscule and tremendously reserved compared to the rest of the country and the vast majority of American Christians. They were still pessimistic pacifists and still radical evangelicals, they just toned downed their preaching under the cautious and politically conservative leadership of E. N. Bell.

The Interwar Years, 1919-1940

This period saw a resurgence of pacifistic writing in the Assemblies of God and a corresponding decrease in patriotic articles. However, Robert McClay, a World War I Assemblies of God conscientious objector, believed Christians who opposed war still needed to respect the government and its officers. He described to *Evangel* readers the contrast between the attitudes of his fellow pacifists and his own. "Many of those in the guard house [where conscientious objectors lived] were so radical and lopsided they would not even salute the General when he passed, but I said we ought to render to Caesar the things that are Caesar's."[34] McClay chose the exact Scripture reference to defend his action that others might use to question it, but as late as 1932 he was still testifying that he had maintained a peace witness while respecting America. By respectfully saluting the general while refusing to fight for him, he embodied the reality of dual allegiance and still gave priority to Christ. Considering that 4,734,991 Americans served in World War I and that only about 2,000 absolute conscientious objectors were placed in camps such as the one McClay was in, his pacifism reveals more than his salute.

The General Council of 1927 made a significant decision regarding the wording of the article on military service. The resolution originally concluded, "Resolved . . . we cannot conscientiously participate in war and armed resistance which involves the actual destruction of human life. . . ." It followed logically from the "Whereas" paragraphs that contained the scriptural reasons why the Assemblies of God opposed war. In 1927 the antiwar resolution paragraph was introduced with a "Whereas" and the "Expression of Loyalty to the Government" article was amended slightly and added as the new resolution. This resulted in a very illogical article; the entire effect of which cannot be appreciated unless viewed in full.

Whereas, recognizing Human Government as of Divine ordination and affirming our unswerving loyalty to the Government of the United States, nevertheless we are constrained to define our position with reference to the taking of human life.

Whereas, We as followers of the Lord Jesus Christ, the Prince of Peace, believe in implicit obedience to the Divine commands and precepts which instruct us to "Follow peace with all men" (Heb. 12:14), "Thou shalt not kill" (Ex. 20:13), "Resist not evil" (Matt. 5:39), "Love your enemies" (Matt. 4:44), etc., and

Whereas, These and other Scriptures have always been accepted and interpreted by our churches as prohibiting Christians from shedding blood or taking human life;

Whereas, We, as a body of Christians, while purposing to fulfill all the obligations of loyal citizenship, are nevertheless constrained to declare we can not conscientiously participate in war and armed resistance which involves the actual destruction of human life, since this is contrary to our view of the clear teachings of the inspired Word of God, which is the sole basis for our faith. Therefore, be it

Resolved, That the General Council hereby declares its unswerving loyalty to our government and to its Chief Executive, and that we hereby restate our fixed purpose to help with every way morally possible, consistent with our faith.[35]

This combination of two previously separate articles makes "unswerving loyalty" to the government the chief focus. Even though the first paragraph states the intention was to define the position about taking life, the conclusion is about fidelity to America. They actually structured the article so that conscientious objection served as a reason why the Assemblies of God was loyal to America. Either Article XV had lost its focus or pacifism was such an accepted part of the Assemblies of God that it could become a "whereas" rather than the "therefore."

In 1938 General Superintendent Ernest S. Williams reprinted the Assemblies of God Article XV (as it had been changed in 1927) regarding military service and accompanied it with his opinions. He hoped that the constituents would serve in noncombatant roles, if the need should arise, so that "our national peace may be preserved."[36] American Pentecostals needed to support their government, but each person's "individual conscience" could decide the degree to which they would be patriotic. The Assemblies of God said little about loyalty to government before and after World War I but emphasized it greatly during the war. The same pattern reveals itself when the option to fight is considered.

THE AUTHORITY OF THE INDIVIDUAL
CONSCIENCE TO CHOOSE TO FIGHT, 1914-1940

During American participation in World War I (1917-1918), six articles in the *Evangel* allowed for the possibility that an Assemblies of God Christian could choose to kill other humans in defense of his country. Previous to this, there had been one article supporting the idea that Pentecostals should fight for their nations. It had been a compilation of editorials written by various European Christians, and they were all in favor of defeating the aggressors. They viewed war as "inevitable" and believed it was "worse to stand by and make no effort to protect the weak."[37] The "only possible way to peace" was through war and any Christian who thought otherwise operated with "too limited an area of thought and fact."[38] These authors argued for what Ceadel would call a defencist position, and the Assemblies of God leaders considered it a good idea to publish their brethren's thoughts for the American audience. Immediately after publication of that pro-choice article, many articles opposing Christian participation in war were printed in the *Evangel* in the next three years (at least ten between 1914 and 1916). But the authority to choose to fight was defended again during the Great War.

The Assemblies of God knew that their publications could be confiscated and declared nonmailable if any postmaster or government official thought they obstructed the war. So even as they made the dangerous declaration that they conscientiously and theologically opposed combatant participation, they cautiously made allowances for those who wished to fight. The relatively few *Pentecostal Evangel* articles supporting soldiering during World War I must be viewed in light of the intense threats and violence perpetrated against pacifists during those two years, especially since pro-combatant articles ceased as soon as the war ended and conscientious objection remained the official position of the church.

The second paragraph of the article by J. W. Welch explaining the pacifist resolution clarified the fact that the Assemblies of God did not prohibit members from fighting.

It is not intended to hinder anyone from taking up arms who may feel free to do so, but we hope to secure the privilege of exemption from such military service as will necessitate the taking of life for all who are real conscientious objectors and who are associated with the General Council.[39]

This approach reflected the way other Christian pacifists also couched their language, especially after the Espionage and Sedition Acts. They had to make it clear that they did not "hinder" or "obstruct" the war effort through their conscientious objection. Welch also published a letter from the War Department acknowledging that not all members of the Assemblies of God were conscientious objectors: "The President desires to acknowledge receipt of your Resolution by which *certain members* of your church claim exemption from military service."[40] This letter refers to the fact that they mailed the resolution with a cover letter informing the president that the Assemblies of God would not dissuade its members from joining the military. "It is not the purpose of this Resolution . . . to discourage enlistment of any, even of our own people, whose conscientious principles are not involved."[41]

They allowed fighting, but it did not reflect the consensus of the constituency; the Assemblies of God claimed that the combatant was the rare exception while the conscientious objector was the norm.

Every branch of the [Pentecostal] movement, whether in the United States, Canada, Great Britain or Germany, has held to this principle. When the war first broke out in August 1914, our Pentecostal brethren in Germany found themselves in a peculiar position. Some of those who were called to the colors responded, but many were court-marshaled and shot because they heartily subscribed to the principles of nonresistance.[42]

They claimed that a few fought but the majority did not and even sacrificed their lives for their faith. Frodsham wisely mentioned Pentecostal martyrs in Germany who would not fight for the Kaiser. By doing so he bolstered both the conviction and practice of pacifism, argued that most German Pentecostals would not be fighting against the United States, and hinted that American Pentecostals would not want to kill German Pentecostals.

This exception quite possibly means that the Assemblies of God should never have qualified as a pacifist church and that Assemblies of

God ministers could not claim conscientious objector status. The official qualification for exemption required that one be "a member of any well-organized religious sect or organization organized and existent May 18, 1917, and whose then existing creed or principles *forbade* its members to participate in war in any form. . . ."[43] The Assemblies of God adopted their military service resolution April 28, 1917, less than three weeks before the deadline. Possibly because of their haste to comply with the government time requirements they overlooked the fact they were supposed to *forbid* their constituency from participating in war. They did not do so. Instead, they stated that the overwhelming Pentecostal opinion had "always" been that taking human life for any reason was wrong.

Nevertheless, they admitted that some Pentecostals would probably fight and that if they did they would not be in danger of losing their standing with the Assemblies of God. This contrasted with the nonparticipation of peace churches (such as the Quakers) because they would disown their members who participated in war. Since the Quakers had "an unequivocal testimony against all war" they had "the right to remove from their membership, either by dissociation or disownment . . . members who make little or no profession with Friends. . . ."[44]

An *Evangel* article in October 1917 assumed that soldiers who became Christians could still serve in the military. "No boys will need the consolations of Christ's love in their hearts, of the sweet assurance of heaven in their souls, [more] than our soldier boys amid the awful boom of the death dealing cannon in the trenches,"[45] the authors affirmed. Furthermore, these Christian soldiers made it possible "for our country to win out for right and freedom."[46] The author also hinted that being a soldier may not be consistent with faith in Christ, but in the fall of 1917, with popular support for the war being drummed up around the country, it was overshadowed by the support for the ones who fought and served.

At least seventy-five Pentecostals took the option to serve in the military, whether as combatants or noncombatants we do not know. In one of the common "Amongst the Soldier Boys" articles, Pentecostal military men were reportedly admired by their superiors.

> We have about fifty Pentecostal boys in the training camps about here [San Antonio, Texas], while probably twenty-five have already gone abroad. It has been proven beyond a doubt that it is

possible to live a Christian life in the army. And in most cases the
boys have won the respect and confidence of their officers by
their consistent Christian conduct.[47]

A little over one year after the Assemblies of God declared that they
were against participation in war, their official periodical reported that
consistent Christian conduct did not conflict with military service. In
fact, one's Christianity made him a better soldier in whom an officer
could trust.

One of the most conspicuous declarations of the choice that an Assemblies of God person had regarding fighting for his country occurred
October 19, 1918. E. N. Bell answered a reader's question about participation in war with approval of the authority of the individual conscience.

**Would it be murder for a child of God to go to war and shoot
men as do other soldiers?**

Ans. Our faith leaves this with the conscience of each man. We
have never opposed the going to war of our members whose conscience allowed them to go. But every one must keep personal hatred out of his heart.[48]

Bell was correct in that the initial letter to the United States government stated that the Assemblies of God neither forbade nor dissuaded
its members from serving in the military, but again the context and timing must be considered. It seems Bell is giving the best answer he can
during a war while Pentecostals are being investigated and prosecuted
for antiwar preaching. However, the previous chapter provided extensive evidence that many members and leaders of the Assemblies of God
did indeed try to persuade Pentecostals not to participate in war even
though here Bell claims otherwise. Nevertheless, the official Assemblies
of God position on military service was never a matter over which one
would lose his or her credentials or standing.

Furthermore, Bell favored allowing combatant military service and
promoted the ideal of the authority of one's own conscience.[49] Those
against participation in war appealed to Jesus and Scripture as their authority; Bell appealed to conscience. The very next request in Bell's October 19, 1918 column also adressed war.

526. Explain Luke 3:14 and 1 John 3:15 as they relate to war.

Ans. Luke 3:14 refers to soldiers doing police duty in a conquered country. They were not to take advantage of their position to rob people by violence, and were not to trump up a false charge against any one. The Huns are doing both, and God is against it. 1 John 3:15 forbids personal hatred of men.[50]

His first answer implied that God would want his followers to stop "the Huns" from breaking John's instructions found in Luke 3, but he did not actually say Christians should kill Germans even though God is against their actions. He did not take advantage of this opportunity, possibly because it did not occur to him, to employ this verse as New Testament evidence that John the Baptist did not instruct soldiers to leave their profession. Bell did not clarify the second reference as it related to war, perhaps because hatred and killing are synonymous or because it is possible for Christians to eliminate the "hate" which eliminates the murder and the resulting motives were considered pure.

This same *Evangel* contained a letter from an Assemblies of God soldier who requested prayer and had decided that he could serve God in the military. He thought it was going to be impossible but "soon decided that a fellow could live right anywhere if he had Christ and his power."[51] During the war the leadership of the Assemblies of God employed logic to defend conscientious participation and Jesus to defend conscientious objection. The amount of support for combatant participation declined notably during the interwar years (1919-1940).

The 1920s and 1930s found the Assemblies of God concern for war related mostly to the nature of the next global war and the effects of current wars on missionaries. Rarely did someone reveal that the Assemblies of God allowed its members to fight. In 1927 a Marine wrote a letter to *The Pentecostal Evangel* thanking the Assemblies of God for their support of ministry to military personnel. He did not reveal whether or not he was Assemblies of God, but it was certainly possible.[52]

In 1938 Ernest S. Williams, in light of the impending war, reiterated the fact that "The Assemblies of God as a Christian organization does not claim control over individual conscience."[53] Nevertheless, he went on to state that the Assemblies of God was on record as being opposed to combatant participation in war. He focused his article on helping Assemblies of God youth decide what to do should they be drafted.

He clearly preferred and recommended noncombatant service, but he recognized the option of combatant service.

By 1940 many nations were embroiled in conflict and the possibility of American involvement was growing. One unnamed author in the Assemblies of God responded to this by restating in strong terms that "military service is incompatible with the gospel of Jesus Christ."[54] However, this vocal pacifist also recognized that some Pentecostals might not really be conscientiously opposed to war. He admonished his Assemblies of God audience as follows: "Those who intend to claim exemption on conscientious grounds, therefore, should be sure they are true conscientious objectors and are not trying to hide behind the position of the church to which they belong."[55]

Even as he promoted conscientious objection (he recommended the *Pacifist Handbook*), this author did acknowledge that some of his fellow Pentecostals might not share his perspective. However, it is significant that even at this late date, October 1940, it was still customary and acceptable to refer to conscientious objection "the position of the church."

Two November 1940 letters revealed that some Assemblies of God men were willing to fight for America. Both originated from people concerned about ministering to soldiers. The first expressed a desire "to contact as many boys in the service as possible who are Christians, especially those who are Pentecostal or who come from Pentecostal homes."[56] The second was from a pastor in Georgia: "Will be glad to hear from Pentecostal parents whose boys have been conscripted and sent to Fort Benning, Ga., so I can contact them for Pentecost."[57] These authors assumed that Assemblies of God members would be serving in the military in some capacity.

During World War I the General Council of the Assemblies of God expressed respect for their government, just like other peace churches did, while still declaring that they believed Christians should not kill. A few supported the authority of individual conscience to choose whether fighting for the country was appropriate. However, amid a world war they also determined to classify themselves as a peace church that had always been and continued to be full of conscientious objectors.

WAR AND MISSIONS, 1914-1940

Although the Assemblies of God concerned itself with the ethical issues related to participation in warfare, they were just as interested in the effects of war upon their missionary endeavors and their efforts to evangelize the troops. From 1914 to 1940 these two topics provided the subject matter for over one hundred articles.[58]

Scores of pages were devoted to reporting the situations of missionaries in war zones around the world. These articles appeared under such titles as "Wars and the Missionaries,"[59] "Missionaries in Peril,"[60] "Victories despite War,"[61] "The Horrors of War and Famine,"[62] and "In the War Zone."[63] They contained appeals for prayer, finances, and compassion as well as good reports when a missionary was saved from a deadly event or was able to preach the gospel despite war.

> The war has been raging in this province for the last two months.
> . . . With all this we have found the Lord's grace sufficient and He
> has supplied us with wonderful peace. I am sure we couldn't enjoy
> any more peace if we were right home in America. . . . There have
> been some very blessed conversions. . . . Please keep on praying
> for us and the work and those who have been lately saved.[64]

In 1940 *The Pentecostal Evangel* was filled with articles entitled "War and Missions." These updates related the situations of missionaries in Egypt, Palestine, Syria, Iraq, Hong Kong, Scandinavia, Great Britain, Greece, Macedonia, West Africa, China, and India.[65] Each of these places contained Assemblies of God missionaries and the status of their safety was related to the Assemblies of God constituency.

The concern for ministry to the military began in the earliest days of the Assemblies of God. The last two years of World War I, 1917-1918, produced twenty-one *Evangel* articles written about evangelizing soldiers. Most were titled "Amongst the Soldier Boys" or "Work Amongst the Soldiers" and related details about military ministry. Assemblies of God ministers were very concerned with providing New Testaments and the gospel message to those who were about to die while fighting for their country. The Gospel Publishing House even sold "'Active Service' Testaments, bound in Khaki keratol, with the Stars and Stripes stamped on the cover."[66] The cover of the February 16, 1918, *Weekly Evangel* featured a three-by-five inch photograph of soldiers in a chapel service with the headline "Preaching to the Soldier Boys."[67]

This significant concern for military personnel eventually developed into the organization of a Chaplaincy Department in the Assemblies of God. During this era the interest in evangelizing the military revealed that the editors of *The Pentecostal Evangel* considered it to be completely compatible with a conscientious objection stance. Preaching the gospel to those who were about to die was paramount, "The need is for funds to carry the expenses of placing in the hands of the soldiers the printed page, so that those who will have the Word of God in the true fashion, and our skirts be clean of their blood, even though they fail to accept salvation."[68] Regardless of whether it could be an occupation for Pentecostal Christians, it was certainly a mission field for them.

The sheer number of articles about evangelization in, around, and to soldiers substantiates the idea that a primary reason the Assemblies of God promoted pacifism was because they were extremely missions oriented. Not only did they not ignore warfare, they considered it a great opportunity for evangelization.

Summary

The first era of Assemblies of God history, 1914-1940, contained a pro-life, anti-killing ethic which manifested itself in both absolute pacifism and approval of noncombatant service. They consistently ministered to military personnel and never expressed concern that this conflicted with any of their views of war, since evangelization overshadowed other concerns. Their nonviolent ethic was accompanied by respect for the United States government and allowance of conscientious combatant participation in war that gained slight favor only during the intense patriotic fervor of actual American warfare. They referenced Jesus and used the Bible more from 1914-1940 to support their attitudes toward war than at any time afterward (see chapters six and seven).

Enough members, ministers, editors, and elected leaders valued conscientious objection to enable it to be adopted and presented as the main denominational stance even through the end of 1940. This changed almost completely when America entered the second world war in 1941 and the Assemblies of God officially became part of the religious establishment by joining the National Association of Evangelicals in 1942. Conscientious objectors eventually became an embarrassment, since they objected to defending with violence the government with which the Assemblies of God increasingly allied itself.

NOTES

1. Patriot. Dictionary.com. *Dictionary.com Unabridged (v 1.0.1)*, Based on the Random House Unabridged Dictionary, © Random House, Inc. 2006. http://dictionary.reference.com/browse/patriot (accessed: November 06, 2006).

2. Horst Balz and Gerhard Schneider, *Exegetical Dictionary of the New Testament* (Grand Rapids: Eerdmans, 1990), 381-383.

3. *American Heritage Dictionary* (Boston: Houghton Mifflin, 1985).

4. *American Heritage Dictionary* (Boston: Houghton Mifflin, 1985).

5. See Paul Alexander, "Speaking in the Tongues of Nonviolence: American Pentecostals, Nationalism, and Pacifism" *Evangelical Review of Society and Politics* Vol. 1 No. 2 (October 2007).

6. Frank Bartleman, "What Will the Harvest Be?" *The Weekly Evangel*, 7 August 1915, 1-2.

7. J. Roswell Flower, "What Will the Harvest Be? Article in Last Week's Evangel Receiving Just Criticism," *The Weekly Evangel*, 14 August 1915, 2.

8. Ibid.

9. "Light on the Present Crisis," *The Weekly Evangel*, 1 July 1916, 6.

10. The pacifistic articles are examined in a later section of this chapter.

11. J. S. Hartzler to Jason O. Miller, September 20, 1918; cited in Gerlof D. Homan, *American Mennonites and the Great War: 1914-1918* (Scottdale, Pa.: Herald Press, 1994), 60.

12. *The Mennonite*, September 26, 1918; cited in Homan, *American Mennonites*, 60.

13. Peter Brock and Nigel Young, *Pacifism in the Twentieth Century* (Syracuse, N.Y.: Syracuse University Press, 1999), 31.

14. J. W. Welch, "An Explanation," *The Weekly Evangel*, 19 May 1917, 8.

15. Quoted in *Literary Digest*, LV (October 6, 1917), 12. Cited in Donald O. Johnson, "Wilson, Burleson, and Censorship in the First World War," *The Journal of Southern History* Vol. 28 No. 1 (1962): 51-52.

16. "The Pentecostal Movement and the Conscription Law," *The Weekly Evangel*, 4 August 1917, 6.

17. Brock and Young, *Pacifism in the Twentieth Century*, 29.

18. Ibid.

19. Ibid.

20. "Loyalty to the Government," *General Council Minutes*, 1917, 17-18.

21. "Pre-War Theology Right," *The Weekly Evangel*, 27 October 1917, 9.

22. Herbert Pankratz, "The Suppression of Alleged Disloyalty in Kansas During World War I," *Kansas Historical Quarterly* 1976 42 (3): 277-307.

23. "Behold, These Three Years," *The Weekly Evangel*, 10 November 1917, 6.

24. Ibid., 7.

25. Michael W. Casey and Michael A. Jordan, "Free Speech in Time of War: Government Surveillance of the Churches of Christ in World War I," *Free Speech Yearbook* 34 (1996): 106.

26. Bell's respected educational and denominational background perhaps contributed to his desire to mold the Assemblies of God into a respectable denomination. In this article he related his concern that the Assemblies of God have a good public image. This would help them move into the mainstream of American Christianity and away from radical pacifism.

27. E. N. Bell, "Preachers Warned," *The Weekly Evangel*, 5 January 1918, 4. Emphasis added.

28. Eugene Holder. Interview by the author. November 1, 2006.

29. Bell, "Preachers Warned," 5 January 1918, 4.

30. Ibid. This is explicit evidence of the existence of the vocational pacifism that Bell allowed, "The church government appreciates and prays for the government. It also gives to the government a clear testimony as its own convictions on war; but there is no attempt to control the government, and no demand that it follow a given course with respect to specific points of foreign policy. Its only demands are those which the New Testament directs to Christians themselves as regenerated members of the kingdom of God." Guy F. Hershberger, *War, Peace, and Nonresistance* (Scottdale, Pa.: Herald Press, 1969); quoted in Yoder, *Nevertheless*, 77. Yoder used this as a definition of vocational pacifism.

31. Bell, "Preachers Warned," *The Weekly Evangel*, 5 January 1918, 4.

32. "President Wilson's Own Words," *The Weekly Evangel*, 6 April 1918, 1.

33. "Expression of Loyalty to the Government," *General Council Minutes*, 1918, 9.

34. Robert McClay, "Standing True to Scriptural Principles," *The Pentecostal Evangel*, 6 February 1932, 8.

35. *General Council Minutes*, 1927, 28-29.

36. Ernest S. Williams, "…In Case of War…," *The Pentecostal Evangel*, 19 March 1938, 4.

37. "Is European War Justifiable?" *The Christian Evangel*, 12 December 1914, 1.

38. Ibid.

39. J. W. Welch, "An Explanation," *The Pentecostal Evangel*, 19 May 1917, 8.

40. Ibid. Emphasis added. Reproduction of letter to the Assemblies of God from D. L. Roscoe, Captain of Cavalry, United States Army.

41. "The Pentecostal Movement and the Conscription Law," *The Pentecostal Evangel*, 4 August 1917, 6. Reproduction of the letter of April 28, 1917 to President Wilson signed by Stanley H. Frodsham, Secretary of the Assemblies of God.

42. Ibid.

43. Ibid. Emphasis added. Furthermore, "any form" of participation was supposed to be forbidden. This would have included noncombatant service, which the Assemblies of God also allowed.

44. Margaret E. Hirst, *The Quakers in Peace and War* (London: The Swarthmore Press, Ltd., 1923), 504-505. Hirst noted that they sometimes postponed disciplinary action until after the war because the offending members were not present.

45. "Pre-War Theology Right," *The Weekly Evangel*, 27 October 1917, 9.

46. Ibid.

47. "Amongst the Soldier Boys," *The Christian Evangel*, 29 June 1918, 14. This same article reports that about twelve Pentecostal conscientious objectors lived in a noncombatant unit in San Antonio.

48. E. N. Bell, "Questions and Answers," *The Christian Evangel*, 19 October 1918, 5.

49. Bell even promoted authority of conscience regarding doctrinal issues. He was rebaptized in the name of Jesus only (rather than with the trinitarian formula) in August 1915. He desired to stay in the Assemblies of God and wanted the fellowship to allow both positions. "I did not mean to sit in judgment on the consciences of my brothers and sisters in Christ. I grant all, without strife or condemnation from me, the privilege of being baptized with any formula found in the New Testament on baptism. I ask only the same privilege for myself without condemnation from the brethren. Those who want liberty but will not grant it to others, those who simply contend for their own way and try to force it on others, will have to be loved and endured, taught and prayed for until Jesus comes." E. N. Bell, "There is Safety in Counsel," *Word and Witness*, October 1915, 1.

50. Bell, "Questions and Answers," 5. "Hun" was a derogatory nickname used primarily by the British and Americans to describe the German Army. The term was widely used by Allied propaganda to suggest the worst kind of conduct from the German 'Huns', crushing neutral nations and imposing brutal rule upon conquered peoples.

51. Claude Clary, "A Few Lines From Our Soldier Boys," *The Christian Evangel*, 19 October 1918, 14. The letter is from a Pentecostal conscientious objector who mentions three Assemblies of God objectors who are with him in his camp.

52. William I. Berry, "A Note of Appreciation," *The Pentecostal Evangel*, 22 October 1927, 11.

53. Ernest S. Williams, "In Case of War," *The Pentecostal Evangel*, 19 March 1938, 4.

54. "The Attitude of the General Council Toward Military Service," *The Pentecostal Evangel*, 12 October 1940, 13.

55. Ibid.

56. Roy D. Woodall, "Pentecost Afloat," *The Pentecostal Evangel*, 23 November 1940, 11.

57. Jimmie Mayo, "Pentecostal Conscripts," *The Pentecostal Evangel*, 23 November 1940, 11.

58. See bibliography for a complete listing.

59. E. N. Bell, "Wars and the Missionaries," *The Christian Evangel*, 12 September 1914, 1.

60. "Missionaries in Peril: South China in Throes of Civil War, Threatens the Lives of Our Missionaries in the Affected Area," *The Pentecostal Evangel*, 11 December 1920, 12.

61. "Victories in Spite of War," *The Pentecostal Evangel*, 4 August 1923, 12.

62. "The Horrors of War and Famine: China," *The Pentecostal Evangel*, 4 May

1929, 10.

63. Marie Stephany, "In the War Zone," *The Pentecostal Evangel*, 21 January 1928, 7.

64. Ibid.

65. Noel Perkin, "War and Missions," *The Pentecostal Evangel*, 20 July 1940, 8; 31 August 1940, 6; 28 September 1940, 9; 2 November 1940, 6; 7 December 1940, 6.

66. "Testaments for the Soldiers," *The Weekly Evangel*, 29 September 1917, 3.

67. "Preaching to the Soldier Boys," *The Weekly Evangel*, 16 February 1918, 1.

68. "Amongst the Soldier Boys," *The Weekly Evangel*, 16 February 1918, 7.

 SIX

FIGHTING THE BATTLE AGAINST CONSCIENCE WITH REALISM: ASSEMBLIES OF GOD ATTITUDES TOWARD WAR FROM 1941-1967

INTRODUCTION

The ethic of nonviolence among members and ministers in the General Council of the Assemblies of God experienced a transformation during and after World War II. A significant number of leaders and members of the Assemblies of God supported conscientious objection before the bombing of the U.S. naval base at Pearl Harbor on December 7, 1941, but once the United States became involved in the war, their sentiment and actions began to change. Indeed, the preponderance of articles in *The Pentecostal Evangel* on this subject during World War II supported combatant participation in the Allied war efforts.[1] In 1947, the General Council deleted some scriptural support for conscientious objection from the 1917 statement on military service and promoted civil defense in 1957.[2] The transformation culminated at the 1967 General Council with the complete removal of any form of the original 1917 statement against war.

This chapter examines the decline of the peace witness and the dramatic increase of patriotism and promotion of combatant participation in the military. Integral to this study is the investigation of the growth of military evangelism in the Assemblies of God. Ministry to the "soldier boys" became a priority during and after World War II, and this emphasis effectively replaced any previous concern with the ethics of combatant participation for Christians.[3] Inherent in the patriotism, combat, and ministry to the military was the shift from a disenfranchised and marginalized social position to mainstream civil religion. The Assemblies of God increasingly identified with American evangelicals and American exceptionalism.[4] They expressed their ownership of America and American ideals by consistently referring to wars, soldiers, and the flag as "ours." They also greatly reduced their appeals to the example of Jesus regarding nonviolence and warfare, instead preferring the Old Testament to address these topics.

THE DECLINE OF CONSCIENTIOUS OBJECTION, 1941-1967

About thirty-five Assemblies of God men were classified as conscientious objectors during World War II[5] while as many as sixty-five thousand Assemblies of God members served in the military either as combatants or noncombatants.[6] One of those conscientious objectors was Stanley Horton (b. 1916), the now eminent Assemblies of God theologian and scholar. He attended Gordon-Conwell Theological Seminary (M.Div., 1944) and Harvard (S.T.M., 1945) during the war because, as a Pentecostal follower of Jesus, he had applied for and received an exemption from the military just like the *Pentecostal Evangel* had been encouraging its young men to do.[7] Horton has served in the Assemblies of God continually since then and "his firm commitment to the entire trustworthiness of Scripture, concern for evangelism, Pentecostal pneumatology, and nondispensational premillennialism have had a profound influence on the course of AG theology. . . ."[8] But Horton did not travel the route most often chosen by Assemblies of God men in World War II.

Even though "no figures are available"[9] for the number of Assemblies of God men who served in the military as noncombatants, Carl Brumback claimed that "the great majority" of Assemblies of God servicemen during World War II were in fact noncombatants—that would put the number at several thousand, according to his estimate just fifteen years after the war.[10] However, J. R. Flower noted in 1943, two years before the war ended, that even though there were many more noncombatants than conscientious objectors, the combatants outnumbered the noncombatants. Flower's estimate in 1943 is lower than Brumback's estimate in 1961, but both agree that there were large numbers of Assemblies of God noncombatants and a few conscientious objectors. I have located two additional Assemblies of God men who served as noncombatants during World War II precisely because they were Pentecostal Christians,[11] but this does not help us resolve the issue regarding whose estimate is more accurate. We have to examine as much evidence as we can from that time period itself.

PACIFISM AND CONSCIENTIOUS OBJECTION DURING WORLD WAR II

World War II (September 1, 1939-September 2, 1945) involved over seventy nations and about sixty-two million people died. The United States declared war on Japan on December 8, 1941 and Germany declared war on the U.S. on December 11, 1941. Sixteen million Americans served in the U.S. military; perhaps sixty-five thousand of whom were Assemblies of God (.004 percent). Twelve thousand conscientious objectors classified as IV-Es performed "civilian work of national importance" in 152 Civilian Public Service camps throughout the United States and Puerto Rico. Other conscientious objectors like Stanley Horton went to school with the classification of IV-D—"ministers of religion or divinity students."[12] These men who refused all military work, including noncombatant service, represented .00075 percent of all draftees and military personnel (less than one-hundredth of one percent). "Conscientious objectors eligible for military service in noncombatant role" received the I-A-O classification and participated in boot camps and served in the military in a variety of nonviolent roles such as medics, barbers, and clerks.[13] About 22,000 Americans chose this classification. It is understandable that in the context of World War II the Assemblies of God downplayed their pacifist heritage and the numbers of conscientious objectors and noncombatants in their midst; it is amazing that they admitted it at all.

Conscientious objection did not enjoy a staunch defense in Assemblies of God publications or meetings during World War II. Nevertheless, a few authors did reference it and some provided support. However, nothing like Donald Gee's powerful promotion of conscientious objection in May 1940 ever occurred again in the pages of *The Pentecostal Evangel*. Any mention of nonparticipation in war was accompanied by an emphasis on the authority of one's own conscience and loyalty to America. Any other possibly nonviolent tendencies had to be gleaned from between the lines of unrelated articles.

The first occurred in April 1941. An unnamed author argued that the wars in Europe, Asia, and Africa were brought about by demons. He stated that Christ "is not come to destroy men's lives, but to save them" and that Paul said "the weapons of our warfare are not carnal."[14] He concluded that Christian warfare did not include fighting other humans.

> But it is not a warfare against other earthen vessels. Large numbers think they have been equipped for that purpose. No. No. No. The saints are equipped with heavenly armor, and armed with heavenly weapons to fight spiritual wickednesses in the heavenly places.[15]

Although this sounds like the author would not approve Christian participation in warfare, he encouraged the saints to pray for their political leadership so that they could stop "these hosts of evil spirits that purpose the destruction of millions." Therefore, he may have been arguing for a vocational pacifism and exhorted Christians to pray so that the battles could be won in both the spiritual and physical realms.

The Pentecostal Evangel did not publish any other articles that could be interpreted as opposed to combatant participation in 1941, and the General Council in Minneapolis (Sept. 5-11) had no discussion about the issue. However, Stanley Frodsham, the editor of *The Pentecostal Evangel* during this time, responded privately to a letter and revealed that he believed that Assemblies of God youth should enlist as noncombatants.[16] Nevertheless, he also stated in the letter that a distinction existed between murder and defending one's family in time of war. He reiterated the official Assemblies of God pacifist position in another private letter one month later.[17] Frodsham did not at this time recommend the position of absolute pacifism, i.e. the rejection of any kind of service, but encouraged noncombatant service instead. He simultaneously held the view that killing in war was not murder, so he would have approved Christian combatant roles, though he did not encourage them.

In January 1942 a missionary to Hawaii (which did not become an American state until 1959) reported that, "The Hilo people are very calm over this war trouble, believing that Jesus is coming soon. If He allows them to be taken by bombs, they are ready to meet Him. Pray they may be used to bring others to this realization."[18] At least this one Assemblies of God missionary was teaching her converts not to support military action, even in defense of the islands that received Japan's first attack against American forces less than two months before she wrote this letter.

Watson Argue described Jesus as the one "who holds the key to real peace" and who "never marshaled an army, nor drafted a soldier, nor fired a gun, and yet no leader ever had so many volunteers who under His orders, have made so many rebels stack arms and surrender without a shot being fired."[19] This sounds as if Argue was presenting a rationale for nonparticipation, but he was doing the opposite. He stated that "God is a Man of war" and that God had been helping the Allies defeat the Germans and would continue to do so because He always defended the Jews: "the apple of His eye."[20] Somehow the one who "came to heal the brokenhearted" also "causeth His wind to blow" so that it "changed direction and carried the poison gas directly back over the German army killing thousands of German soldiers."[21] Argue's description of a nonviolent Jesus did not affect his view of Christian participation in warfare. Only by taking Argue's comments out of context could they be interpreted as promoting nonviolence.

In January 1942 a professor at Central Bible Institute wrote that ministers should accept their "permanent deferment from physical military service" so that they could "engage in the spiritual aspect of this conflict."[22] Nevertheless, he supported "the brave men of our armed forces" who were "needed" to "go and give themselves to this fight."[23] His nonparticipation ethic extended only as far as ministers, and that was precisely because they were to intercede "in the heavenly realms where spiritual forces are battling" so that the earthly war could be won. Ministry again served as a reason not to fight, but this time the ministry focused on "our" military. Previously, missions had served as a reason not to kill. Now abstinence allowed more prayer for victory and more encouragement for the Allied soldiers.

J. Roswell Flower penned the articles that revealed what little peace witness remained in the Assemblies of God during World War II. In June and July 1943 he submitted two pieces that reiterated the official Assemblies of God stance against combatant service while at the same time justifying combatant participation. He wrote with conviction and condemned neither the noncombatants nor the combatants, although he did refer to the "not more than twenty" Assemblies of God pacifists as an "extreme" and "minute" company.[24] Flower recognized the ethical struggle of a Christian contemplating warfare—especially one who took Jesus' teachings and example seriously.

> His conception of his divine calling, his *training as a follower of Christ*, his convictions and his feelings are all *out of harmony with the war spirit*, and it is with difficulty he is able to adjust himself to the necessities and demands of the hour. He has been taught to believe that as a follower of Christ he is commissioned to save lives and not to destroy them. It is therefore with abhorrence he contemplates the prospect of being required to deprive men of life in armed conflict. It was because of these convictions the resolution was passed by the General Council many years ago, which expressed the unwillingness of the members of the Assemblies of God, as *followers of Christ*, to participate in armed conflict which involves the actual taking of human life. Caught between a sincere desire to be loyal to the country of his birth and at the same time to be *faithful to the teachings of his Saviour and Lord*, the Christian is beset with perplexities which are exceedingly disturbing to his spirit.[25]

Flowers contrasts discipleship with war, and Jesus with "necessities," "demands," and what is "required." He acknowledges that the Assemblies of God had been teaching its constituents that participating in combat was wrong; Flower himself certainly had been. Nevertheless, the Christian could now contemplate the possibility of killing because of the terribleness of the hour. He related that the Assemblies of God had been caught between loyalty to their country and loyalty to the teachings of their "Savior and Lord." These were, admittedly, at odds with each other.

Flower considered it fortunate that the United States allowed them to abstain if, "because of belief or training," they believed it was wrong. In fact, Flower told his readers that "quite a large number of our young men have appealed for and obtained classification as noncombatants, and have been inducted into the armed forces to serve in units devoted to necessary services which can be classified as noncombatants."[26] It is unfortunate that we do not have exact statistics regarding these noncombatants, but we do have Flower's comparison to Assemblies of God combatants. "By far the larger number of the young men who are members of the Assemblies of God have permitted themselves to be inducted, waiving all claims for exemption on the grounds of conscience."[27]

According to Flower, the "large number" of noncombatants was smaller than the "far . . . larger number" of combatants, yet it was greater than the "minute company" of "extreme" pacifists who objected "to all participation in the war." His use of the comparative adjective makes it impossible to decipher the exact number. However, it is clear that he estimated that the large majority chose combatant service.

He devoted the majority of the article to presenting why a Christian could participate with a clear conscience.[28] He mentioned some of the reasons Christians might not fight ("God does not send us forth to destroy lives but to save them." "Jesus taught nonresistance to his disciples. . . .") but then responded to each one with reasons why fighting was allowable.[29] He summed up the justification for military service by noting that "many of the men who have entered the armed forces have weighed these matters carefully and have fought the battle with their conscience with realism."[30]

Flower's contribution three weeks later granted respect to the conscientious objector and requested financial support for them from the constituency. Conscientious objectors were "standing for the right of conscience and therefore should be given consideration and protection in a land which is fighting for freedom of conscience and liberty."[31] Nevertheless, he continued to suggest noncombatant service to those opposed to killing "instead of taking the extreme conscientious objector position."[32] Flower's concern for the conscientious objector was congruent with the position that the General Council adopted in 1943 regarding compulsory military training in the United States. The Assemblies of God went on record as being against mandatory military service and determined to inform Congress of their decision.[33]

The final reference to nonparticipation during World War II came from Flower when he again asked for financial support for Assemblies of God pacifists serving in Civilian Public Service camps. The pacifists were required both to work without pay and pay for their room and board. Therefore, they needed to be assisted by friends outside the confines of a CPS camp. Flower had compassion on them and also felt responsible for their care. He encouraged his readers to send money and raised over $16,000 by August 1945 for the "number of our young men [who] refused all military service on the grounds of conscience."[34] This amount of financial support for conscientious objectors revealed that there was at least some support for their position among the constituents. In contrast, the Assemblies of God constituency gave over $450,000 for the publication of *Reveille* during the same time period, and the Mennonites contributed a total of three million dollars to help conscientious objectors in CPS camps.[35]

The Assemblies of God conscientious objectors who served in Civilian Public Service camps came from all over America and from many walks of life. They were between nineteen and thirty-seven years old and averaged twenty-six years in age. They included a brick mason from Ohio, loggers, lumberjacks, and welders from California, an auto mechanic from Montana, farmers and machinists from Texas, a tool grinder from Michigan, and farmers from Colorado, Wisconsin, and Arizona. There were also several "laborers," a clerk, and a student.[36] The Assemblies of God men who served in CPS camps farmed and labored in many ways, even fighting forest fires started by military training exercises in the mountains of Virginia.[37]

Pacifism and Conscientious Objection, 1946-1967

After World War II references to noncombatant service, conscientious objection, or the ethics of warfare. were extremely rare. They consisted mostly of allusions to the possibility that some people might object to military service. While promoting continued ministry to the military, E. S. Williams stated that "whatever our opinions concerning war may be, military evangelism will continue to be an important part of our youth program."[38] Williams remembered that the official stance was different than what the majority of Assemblies of God persons believed and practiced, yet he subordinated attitudes toward war under military evangelism in one sentence.

By 1947 the recognition of these facts prompted the General Council to appoint a committee to investigate the adequacy of the statement on military service. The committee reported that the existing pacifist statement sufficiently represented the constituency. "Your committee feels that it will be unable to formulate an article on Military Service that will better represent the attitude of the Assemblies of God."[39] They made this statement two years after the General Council had boasted about the 65,000 Assemblies of God servicemen.[40] They were not yet ready to delete the strongly worded rationale for pacifism based on the example of Jesus and the "inspired Word of God." The fact that the statement survived World War II shows that pacifism was ingrained in the Assemblies of God consciousness. In fact, E. S. Williams later expressed regret after the pacifist position was deleted in 1967.[41]

However, they did amend the statement without comment or vote at that time. The reference to "Thou shalt not kill (Exod. 20:13)" was removed. It had been present in every publication of the *Constitution and Bylaws* since 1917 but was removed in the 1947, 1949, and 1951 publications—until it was finally officially removed in 1953.[42] The change more accurately reflected previous Pentecostal arguments against war, since they had relied mostly on the New Testament and rarely employed Exodus 20:13. In fact, the reference to the commandment provided an easier way for a pro-combatant Christian to argue against the practice of conscientious objection.[43] This was evident in *Called To Serve,* written in 1967 by an Assemblies of God chaplain who justified military service by interpreting Exodus 20:13 as "murder" (which was personal and wrong) rather than "killing" (which is for the nation and right).

In January 1950 *The Pentecostal Evangel* mentioned conscientious objectors but did not make any reference to the possibility that there were any in the Assemblies of God. The page that related news of interest to the readers, "The Passing and the Permanent," told of a bill before Congress that would allow the wartime wages earned by conscientious objectors ($1,327,641.76) to be allocated "to a relief agency to be used to furnish books and equipment for libraries and educational institutions abroad."[44] A different article on the same page stated that "as of July 15, 1949, a total of 6,439 men were deferred as conscientious objectors under the 1948 Draft Act."[45] Robert C. Cunningham, the editor of *The Pentecostal Evangel* from 1949-1984, did not evaluate the information as good or bad and did not make any mention of the fact that the Assemblies of God had a history of conscientious objection. This was significant because Cunningham commented on other news items when he thought his contribution was important.[46] Conscientious objection to war had become news about other people.

This was manifested in 1951, when the "Passing and the Permanent" (now defined as "News Briefs from the Christian Perspective") reported that the House of Representatives in Montana had passed a bill outlawing conscientious objection. The State Senate was reviewing the bill that had been suggested by a draft board because the Hutterites and Mennonites refused military service. "If the bill becomes law, it will make conscientious objectors in Montana subject to a stiff fine or a prison term of one to five years."[47] Rather than opposing the bill as other church leaders were doing, the Assemblies of God reporter took the opportunity to oppose conscientious objectors and defend war. "But war may be God's judgment which objectors cannot stop. 'The people of Hiroshima have accepted the atomic bomb as God's judgment upon them.'"[48] By 1951 the Assemblies of God was more establishmentarian than other American churches that openly opposed the bill. They had been in the highly nationalistic National Association of Evangelicals for nine years and were transitioning from radical to conservative politics.

A few months later, "News Briefs from the Christian Perspective" had another opportunity to critique conscientious objectors. After reporting that "the American Government has always made provision for sincere Christians to be exempt from bearing arms if they cannot conscientiously do so" the editor pointed out their inconsistencies.

> But "conscientious objectors" are expected to be conscientious. Aaron K. Yoder, of Jerome, Mich., has been convicted of draft evasion because his conscience concerning war did not seem to carry over into other matters. A member of the Amish Mennonite sect, he claimed military exemption as a pacifist. But contrary to other teachings of his church he smoked cigarettes, attended movies, and dressed in flashy clothes. When it was shown in court that he had strayed from other teachings of his church, he was convicted of draft evasion.[49]

There was no mention of any Assemblies of God affiliation with this option. Public commentary was moving away from advocacy for conscientious objection.

An article published in October 1951 seemed to support non-nationalism and peace rather than war. The author, Bob Evans, related "How a Nazi War Criminal Found Christ." The Nazi, whose name was Wolfgang, "had participated as one of a special force of SS troops in the massacre of American prisoners at Malmedy, Belgium, during the Battle of the Bulge." He challenged Evans attempt to witness to him, "After what I know of Americans, I cannot understand how you can preach to Germans! Your own country is anything but Christian, and your soldiers were brutal to me."[50]

Evan's response revealed that he did not give Christian approval to World War II: "'I am not here to deny or affirm what you say,' I answered. 'In every country there are people whose actions are shameful. But why do those people do such things? Because they do not know Christ. Because they are sinners. . . .'"[51] Evans then told Wolfgang that he did not hate him. Instead, he and the other Christians with him, even the one from France, loved the former Nazi. "Our people are traditional enemies, but I am a Christian. And as a child of God, I can love [you] and desire [your] salvation."

In this article heavenly citizenship stood preeminent over earthly nationalism. Evans distanced himself enough from his earthly citizenship to be able to agree with the German's assessment yet still introduce him to a kingdom of God distinct from America. It hearkened back to earlier days of the Pentecostal movement, but by this time the message was an oddity. Nevertheless, it did occur again six years later.

"The Editorial Viewpoint" in January 1957 encouraged Christians to work toward world peace by preaching the gospel. Any other method would fail because "the world is destined to suffer the scourge of war as long as men persist in sin."[52] However, the gospel alone could "turn Americans and Russians, Arabs and Jews, Africans and Asiatics into friends of God and friends of one another."[53] Promoting love between Americans and Russians during the Cold War was a bold step and one that recognized the superiority of Christian unity. This optimistic hope was anchored in Pentecost and missions.

> In that company of converts there were Parthians and Medes, Romans and Judeans, Egyptians and Asiatics, Mesopotamians and Arabians. They were so moved by the Holy Spirit that they all became fellow penitents, fellow Christians, fellow citizens of Christ's kingdom. They became spiritual brothers, children of God, who could love each other and live together in unity and peace. Our missionaries are seeing the Holy Spirit perform similar miracles throughout the earth today.[54]

This multiethnic and multinational interpretation of Pentecost reflected the theology of early Pentecostal pacifists. Although the actual topic of Christian participation in war was not mentioned in this article, war and sin were considered synonymous and found to be contradictory to the gospel.

Following the publication of a "Servicemen's Issue" of the *Evangel*, which had a picture of attacking paratroopers on the cover, an Assemblies of God pastor wrote a letter to the editor questioning its appropriateness.

> This cover picture, however, did not seem to be in keeping with our aims or teachings. . . . It would seem to put us in the position of condoning and even glorifying war and bloodshed. . . . Let us not be guilty of promoting or even seeming to promote it in any way. . . . Let us be careful lest we be charged with aligning ourselves with those who promote war and bloodshed. . . .[55]

Douglas opposed what he felt to be a gratuitous endorsement of warfare, but he also recognized its necessity: "War seems to be a necessary evil, a matter of self-defense on our part. . . . I was a serviceman myself." The clearest statement against the promotion of war in the 1950s came from a former soldier.

Ernest S. Williams mentioned the historical Assemblies of God perspective in 1959 and said that "the Assemblies of God has never taken the position of absolute conscientious objection [pacifism]. . . . Its position is that nonmilitary [noncombatant] service, a service which exempts from bearing arms, is consistent with our beliefs."[56] He wrote this in response to a question from a reader, "Is it the will of God for any soldier of the cross to take up arms against his fellow men?" The fact that this query was presented revealed that there was at least some concern over the issue among the constituency. It also showed that they were unclear about the issue. However, Williams immediately insisted that many "exemplary" Christians "do not seem to feel that they grieved the Lord through accepting military service."[57] Williams left the matter with each individual conscience.

A few months later, Williams responded to a similar question by avoiding the issue altogether. The inquirer who wrote to *The Pentecostal Evangel* disclosed that he himself was a pacifist. "I was speaking against going to war and a man replied that God is a man of war. Is that in the Bible?"[58] The phraseology of this question seems to indicate that the person believed that he was adhering to a position also held by the Assemblies of God. The "I was speaking against going to war" was written as nonchalantly as "I was preaching the gospel." Williams did not address the issue of Christian participation in warfare but spiritualized both the scriptural reference and the application. "He is a 'man of war' for us, fighting in our behalf against all 'the fiery darts of the wicked.' May we learn better to let God fight our battles rather than for us to try to defeat the foe in our own strength."[59] The issue came up again in August 1961, and Williams provided another noncommittal response, "Without discussing the rightness or wrongness of Christians taking up arms in war, I do not believe Matthew 5:21 has any reference to war."[60] Williams again sidestepped a direct question about participation, "Does 'Thou shalt not kill' in Matthew 5:21 mean that Christians should not have any part in war?"

Perhaps because Williams had received what he felt to be too many questions about the topic, the executive presbyters unanimously rejected an article on conscientious objection in 1961. They thought that it "would not be desirable to air this issue" in *The Pentecostal Evangel.*[61] Williams' sidestepping became the official approach, and nothing else appeared regarding conscientious objection until 1967, when Williams practically apologized for the Assemblies of God peace witness. But before that momentous year there was one last possible reference to the pacifist heritage.

Paul Lowenberg, the Kansas District Superintendent in 1964, alluded to vocational pacifism in his baccalaureate address at Central Bible Institute in Springfield, Missouri. "While our country is armed with an astounding plurality of weapons for both defense and offense, you are limited to just one: the Word of God, which is the sword of the Spirit."[62] He praised both martyrdom and the "better land where men learn war no more." Since he addressed only ministers (Central Bible Institute did not have any non-ministerial degree programs), it is possible that he believed they alone should not participate in earthly wars. But his intention was not to discourage all military service but to encourage the use of the "sword of the Spirit."[63]

The next reference in *The Pentecostal Evangel* regarding conscientious objection or nonparticipation occurred in October 1967, when it was reported that the military service article had been replaced by one that "reflects more accurately the current attitude of the fellowship as a whole."[64] The former statement was deemed inadequate and inappropriate because it "actually committed the entire fellowship to a noncombatant or conscientious objector status." This action is evaluated further in a later section after the escalation of patriotism and the promotion of combatant participation are considered.

Defense of conscientious objection decreased dramatically after 1941. References to pacifism, conscientious objection, or noncombatants almost always occurred with qualifications. Nobody wrote or published articles against Christian participation in warfare. In fact, the opposite was true. During and after World War II, the Assemblies of God began to promote loyalty to the government and military service in ways they never had. Scores of articles appeared supporting military action and defending the right and duty of Christians to defend America with violence.

THE PROMOTION OF LOYALTY
TO THE GOVERNMENT, 1941-1967

During and after World War II, the General Council encouraged allegiance to the United States and defended it with appeals to Scripture and the example set by Jesus himself. America and the Allies were on God's side and fighting the "forces of evil."[65] *The Pentecostal Evangel* contained numerous depictions of the American flag and the Statue of Liberty. These were often accompanied by a Bible, a cross, or people saluting.[66]

Instead of using Jesus as an example of nonviolence, they referred to him as the model patriot. A speaker at the General Council of 1941 declared that "Jesus was absolutely loyal to the powers then governing" and that Americans should follow his loyal example.[67] Assemblies of God ministers preached the gospel while "flags, bunting, and pennants of red, white and blue decorated the 'Army Gospel Tent' in a truly patriotic style which befitted its name."[68] This equating of patriotism and the good news allowed missionaries to the Philippines to hope that "the Stars and Stripes would [always] fly over" their country of ministry.[69]

In January 1942 the editors of *The Pentecostal Evangel* published "The Battle Hymn of the Republic," accompanied by a sketch of soldiers in the Revolutionary War with the American flag clearly displayed. By 1942 American flags were regular occurrences in *The Pentecostal Evangel* and cartoons were being published which depicted "Christ" pulling Uncle Sam toward "Victory" by means of "Intercession."[70] The caption read, "Let's Give Uncle Sam a Hand!"

Wesley Steelberg proclaimed at a youth conference that "we are gathered here in the presence of the Lord to express our loyalty to our God and to our country."[71] He also declared that "as Americans we are proud of our flag. We salute it, and we pledge allegiance to it. We raise it as an ensign of liberty, and we rejoice in what it represents." They believed that since their America represented Christianity to the world, it logically followed that their America must be preserved by whatever means necessary.

> The very liberties we enjoy in the United States of America were bought by the blood of our forefathers. . . . The present war is a conflict between Christ and paganism. . . . Should the forces arrayed against us be triumphant, it would mean . . . the suppression of all evangelical Christianity in all the world, including America. To prevent this calamity, [we] believe, is a cause worth dying for.[72]

It was also a cause worth killing for. The Gospel Publishing House advertised a painting on the next page to help Pentecostals remember these important truths. The painting portrayed an open Bible on a table, an American flag prominently hanging to its left (from the top of the painting to the bottom), and a small cross floating in the distant sky.

> The Stars and Stripes, "Old Glory," is acclaimed the world's most beautiful flag. We hope it shall never be replaced by another. That hope is based upon the unchanging Word of God, the cross and the unending stream of life. This careless generation must learn to appreciate America and the Christian principles upon which she was founded; otherwise our servicemen will die in vain. Let us begin now to more fully appreciate the meaning of Christian democracy. . . . This picture should be upon the walls of every American school, home, office, study and Sunday school auditorium.[73]

In June 1944 one of the Assemblies of God chaplains wrote, "We belong to Uncle Sam. Twenty-four hours a day we are in the service of our country. But Uncle Sam says to serve him first, our personal ambitions are to be considered last."[74] This loyalty to the government of the United States meant that the "religious problem" confronting soldiers consisted of "Where can I pray? When can I pray? When can I read the Bible?"[75] It was no longer a problem of "How can I kill another human being?"[76] for the Assemblies of God servicemen belonged to and served the government.

Assemblies of God loyalty only intensified after World War II. After promoting the American cause for several years, they were ready to support the development of jets that could deliver atomic weapons. "America no doubt will prepare rather than perish. The general feeling is that this nation needs to remain strong in military power."[77] An Assemblies of God seaman was "honored for American Spirit" in 1955 because he displayed "outstanding qualities of leadership best expressing American spirit—honor, initiative, loyalty, and high example to comrades in arms."[78]

In July 1959, Ernest S. Williams answered three questions in his column that allowed him to present a uniform message regarding the relationship between the Assemblies of God and their government. The first question was about Romans 13:1, and Williams stated, "the civil powers are appointed by God and therefore ought to be honored and supported."[79] The second inquiry regarded the possible idolatry of saluting the flag and Williams declared, "It is not [idolatry]. . . . We honor and appreciate the American flag as a symbol of our great country. . . . Our first allegiance is to God, but this does not hinder our allegiance to our country."[80] The final query on this topic was about Christian participation in warfare. Williams took the opportunity to insist that "The General Council of the Assemblies of God . . . has never refused to support the Government in any way in time of national emergency."[81] Three different questions evoked three very patriotic answers.

Allegiance to both God and country were necessary because "God has founded this great nation."[82] This sentiment allowed the editors of *The Pentecostal Evangel* to print a cartoon that portrayed a family saluting (with hands over hearts) both the American and Christian flags. The flags appeared at equal heights under the title, "Loyal to Both."[83] Luke 20:25, "render therefore to Caesar the things which be Caesar's, and unto God the things which be God's," served as a caption and theological justification.

The article which accompanied this print proclaimed "Jesus taught that . . . the Christian should be more conscientious than all in obedience to civil authority, and in helping to make his nation's government truly a 'government of the people, by the people, and for the people.'"[84] By placing words from the American Declaration of Independence in the mouth of Jesus, the author revealed the confusion that existed regarding the distinction between Americanism and Christianity. Following Jesus now required patriotism.

Assemblies of God Navy Chaplain David Plank wrote a book in 1967 that equated godliness with patriotism.[85] The Gospel Publishing House printed, distributed, and promoted the book and its message of loyal combatant service to America. A cross and an American flag appeared on the cover of the book. Plank filled *Called to Serve* with patriotic language and repeatedly appealed to "duty to God and country" as reason to serve.[86] He argued that government had been commissioned by God and that Christians could kill because they "act on behalf of the United States government."[87] He argued that "the American way of life" must be preserved and that Christians should love their country more than themselves.[88] Loyalty to government was no longer considered a possible sin; rather, the absence of patriotism meant that one's Christianity was questionable and decaying.[89] Plank even quoted Thomas Jefferson, "Love your neighbor as yourself, and your country more than yourself." The American Assemblies of God had completely aligned itself with its country.

THE PROMOTION OF COMBATANT PARTICIPATION IN WAR, 1941-1967

This era in Assemblies of God history witnessed the development of widespread support for military service. The General Council did not view it as a concession but as an honor and regularly boasted of their extensive involvement. They viewed combatant military service as honorable, brave, noble, and Christian.[90] The evidence reveals that during World War II, the Assemblies of God proudly and zealously joined in the campaign against the Axis powers. This support for the military solidified and increased during the Cold War (1947-1989), the Korean War (1950-1953), and the Vietnam War (1956-1973).

Combatant Participation in War During World War II

The first reference to the appropriateness of Christian participation in the military during World War II came one month before the American entrance into the war. A district superintendent reported that some soldiers who were "real Christians" helped their churches by assisting in both the youth and adult services.[91] Military personnel ministering to civilians foreshadowed the prominent place that military service would quickly assume in the Assemblies of God.

Three weeks later, Ernest S. Williams set the tone for the direction this topic developed. In response to the question, "Do you believe that killing in war is the same as murder?" Williams plainly declared, "Personally I do not think so. In Old Testament times the same God who said, 'Thou shalt not kill,' referring to murder, at times authorized going to war."[92] Two weeks before the bombing of Pearl Harbor, the General Superintendent of the Assemblies of God gave his blessing to participation in war as a combatant.

The Christ's Ambassador's Herald, an Assemblies of God publication for youth, dedicated its January 1942 edition to "the defenders of America on the fighting front."[93] Assemblies of God ministers who converted soldiers to Christianity did not encourage them to resign from the military. They instead reported how they were serving God wonderfully in the military.[94] The cover of the February 1942 *Pentecostal Evangel* had the silhouettes of marching soldiers carrying rifles with bayonets. The lead story concerned saving souls rather than the ethics of the war.[95] The Assemblies of God leadership repeatedly encouraged their constituency to pray for victory for "our defenders in uniform."[96]

Thus it should be no surprise that an Assemblies of God pastor wrote to *The Pentecostal Evangel* in 1942 that he taught all the young men in his church that it was their duty to serve in the military. He disagreed with the one man in his congregation who refused to serve and declared that he could never advise "any one to be an extreme consciention scrupler [sic]."[97]

A few months later Watson Argue declared that "God is a Man of War" and "what we need in this present war more than anything else is the help of God!"[98] He then presented several Scripture references and illustrations to show that God helped the Allies kill the Germans. God sent a storm so that "199 German submarines, with 3,000 of their crew, were captured or destroyed."[99] God also "sent a fog so that [the Germans] could not see the ships" as they evacuated the soldiers from Dunkirk, France. Argue exhorted his readers to have peace in their hearts as they and God defeated Hitler, the possible antichrist.[100]

In June 1943 J. Roswell Flower, while recognizing the presence of conscientious objectors and noncombatants in the Assemblies of God, provided numerous reasons why a Christian could fight in war with a clear conscience. First, "upon induction into the armed forces personal responsibility ceases" because "government is ordained of God (Rom. 13:1) [with] the responsibility of inflicting the supreme penalty of death upon the murderer."[101] Loyalty to government took precedence over any ethic of nonviolence.

Second, "Thou shalt not kill" referred to murder, whereas killing for the nation is "the prerogative of the State" and approved by God. God condemned Saul for not killing and approved Samuel and Elijah when they killed Agag and the prophets of Baal.[102] This meant Assemblies of God Christians could kill the enemies of America and not be guilty. Indeed, they should have felt proud that they were killing for God.

Third, "While the Lord Jesus taught nonresistance to His disciples it is conceded this was purely a personal matter."[103] Furthermore, Jesus paid taxes that he knew supported military action.[104]

Fourth, John the Baptist did not condemn soldiers.

Fifth, Cornelius was a soldier and a man of God.

Sixth, "every liberty now enjoyed by man has been bought at the price of blood."[105]

These reasons together formed an argument that allowed the majority of Assemblies of God youth to fight "the battle with their conscience with realism."[106] Concern for the defense of the American way won, and thousands fought for the Allies.

Within nine months, at least fifty thousand Assemblies of God men were serving in the military.[107] These "twofold warriors"[108] were defeating Hitlerism with bombs[109] and sin with prayer. Hitlerism was "against God and his Christ" and "God cannot lose, and those who are on His side are on the winning side."[110] The Assemblies of God was proud of their Christian soldiers and referred to them as missionaries, ministers, and witnesses for Christ.[111] They published pictures of smiling soldiers, praying soldiers, armed soldiers, and soldiers reading their Bibles.[112] By the last year of the war, some in the Assemblies of God considered war a positive way of spreading the gospel. The limits of American influence had been extended to the ends of the earth, and since "warfare is God's own illustration," Christians must invade the world like the military did and preach the gospel.[113]

The Assemblies of God provided great support for the military in the final year of World War II. Harry Jaeger, the director of the Servicemen's Department, praised the "heroic devotion of Christian Solomon Islanders" for assisting the Americans in their victories in the southern Pacific Ocean.

> In half a century these treacherous head hunters of the Pacific have become some of the finest Christian people in the world. Today thousands of G. I.'s owe their lives to the aid of these natives who [are] devot[ed] to our English-speaking race. . . .[114]

Jaeger referred to "our forces" in Iwo Jima and applauded the fifty-five thousand Assemblies of God men who were serving in the military by this time. Two months later the Servicemen's Department reported that "65,000 copies [of *Reveille*] will be required for our own Assemblies of God servicemen whose names are on our mailing list."[115]

They hoped that their "loved ones in service"[116] would come home and serve in their churches. However, these who had "patriotically left home to go to war to defend democracy and save the world from dictatorship" might return with some problems.[117] Those who had stayed behind were concerned about aspects of their character.

> Every one of those drunken boys were church members from evangelical churches. Three of them from Full Gospel Churches [Pentecostal]. These boys will be coming home now. THE WAR IS NOT OVER! The victory is not won! It will take the combined energy of every Christian at home, mobilized into one mighty army, to fight the powers of hell seeking to damn our nation.[118]

The fact that the men consumed alcohol caused more consternation for the Assemblies of God than the fact that they killed other human beings. This limiting of ethical focus was apparent in another article in that same *Pentecostal Evangel*.

Wallace Bragg bemoaned the necessity of women working in the defense factories and the way that it had corrupted their morality. However, his concern was not that they were participating in the destruction of human life by manufacturing munitions and armaments.

> During the last few years the mother has left the sacred shrine of American democracy—the home and her family—and has fol-

lowed her husband to the assembly line. Women were needed in the factories; but there were little ones to be cared for. . . . Their mothers, wearing what some call "slacks," but which I call "breeches," had left them while they worked in a defense plant. Slacks are "slack" indeed—slack in everything that is modest and decent. But until we can get more preachers who will land in the great big middle of some of these immodest, obscene conditions we will never retrieve the lost for Christ.[119]

Bragg's only mention of death and destruction related to the bombing of Stalingrad and other European cities. He attributed those catastrophes to the denial of Christ by the Russians and Europeans. "It is all because the love of Jesus Christ has not been known in the homes of th[ose] nations."[120] Participation in war had gained tremendous respectability and discussion regarding its sinfulness had practically ceased.

Combatant Participation in War, 1946-1967

The Cold War, Korean War, and Vietnam War served as the primary well-known conflicts in which America engaged itself from 1946 to 1967. The Assemblies of God supported American military involvement in each one. This era also saw more support for combatant military service in formats other than official Assemblies of God periodicals.

As Assemblies of God persons pursued higher education, they began to write dissertations and books about the history of their fellowship. These histories, along with other books written by Assemblies of God members and chaplains, revealed that they were trying to downplay the noncombatant element of their story. This culminated with the changing of the Assemblies of God Military Service article at the General Council in 1967.

OFFICIAL PERIODICALS

Admiration for Christian military personnel remained the predominant opinion in Assemblies of God periodicals. *The Pentecostal Evangel*, *C. A. Herald*, and *At Ease* (the publication directed at military personnel) each maintained a positive view of military service and highly recommended it to young people.

"Utter submission to his country's service" and "a profound sense of duty" convinced one Assemblies of God author that enlisting in the Army did not conflict with serving God.[121] Instead, the two were parallel. He reiterated a recruiting message from World War I, "If you want to help the enemy, you do not need to join his army nor act as a traitor in any way; all you need to do is to stay at home and do nothing."

An excellent example of the admiration for military service occurred in a narrative written by Frank Gigliotti in 1948.

> The war was on with Germany. America was rushing the cream of her manhood to the nearest points of mobilization, in swift response to the President's call . . . "We are fighting for democracy; and we will not cease until justice and right shall prevail." Young men and old men . . . made these words their own and offered their all for the cause at stake. . . .[122]

One particular Christian soldier was given a Bible and encouraged, "If you want to be a good Christian, always read this Book." He and his Christian buddies then dreamt of "what a licking [they] were going to give the Kaiser."[123] The author of this article described accomplishing their dream by slashing "steel against steel, while hand grenades poured thick upon us, and the sweep of machine-gun fire mowed men down with the wheat. At last we fell upon the road and wrenched it free. Spurred by success, we quelled the fury of resistance."[124] The Bible helped them through it because they read, "Though I walk through the valley of the shadow of death, I will fear no evil, for Thou art with me."[125]

The reinstatement of the draft in 1948 prompted *The Pentecostal Evangel* to offer advice to churches about how to address the situation. The unnamed author mentioned neither conscientious objection nor pacifism but encouraged draftees to enjoy their stint in the military. "The comradery of men in uniform is something never quite duplicated elsewhere. . . . Soft muscles will become hardened by training, and the youthful soldier will acquire a great deal of self-confidence in knowing that he has been able to take the regimented life in stride."[126] He told churches to praise their draftees by having them "come to the front while the pastor and friends have special prayer for them. . . . Tell them you know they are men enough to take it and that you are counting on them."[127] He concluded with a sentiment that has remained prominent since then, "The boys are going again. We must stand behind them!"

In 1948 Ernest S. Williams preached a sermon on the National Radio Hour that was later printed in *The Pentecostal Evangel*. He advocated the idea that a soldier could remain compassionate if he accepted

God into his life. "Without God a military man might easily become void of compassionate feeling, but *whatever pursuit a man may follow*, if he is filled with God's Spirit and will daily seek fellowship with God through prayer, God can keep him tender."[128]

The *C. A. Herald* regularly revealed its esteem for Christian military personnel and several articles that addressed the topic appeared in both the *Herald* and *The Pentecostal Evangel*. One example contained the following evaluation of the relationship between military service and Christianity.

> The accusation that men in the armed forces are notably sinful is indicative of the failure on the part of the churches to reach these young men for God before they donned the uniform. It is this lack of salvation, rather than the military atmosphere that prevails in a camp, from which sinfulness springs. Men who have been soundly converted, born again, set free from the habits of sin, and have dedicated their lives to God, serve their officers with excellence.[129]

Support for the military accompanied by loyalty to the government meant that the Assemblies of God supported American involvement in Korea. During the Korean War, *The Pentecostal Evangel* printed an article that was hostile toward noncombatants. "War may be God's judgment which [conscientious] objectors cannot stop."[130] An editorial at the one-year anniversary of the beginning of the war revealed that they were concerned for America and "our other allies."[131] However, the editors also quoted a Korean interpretation of the war as God's judgment. "I do not know why God raised up the Reds, who are worse than the ROK troops, to punish us. . . . If this war is God's rod to chastise the Koreans and correct them, may it not also be His means of speaking to other nations, including America?"[132]

During the 1950s, *The Pentecostal Evangel* referred to "peace churches" as a group to which they did not belong.[133] They proved this by teaching their Christ's Ambassadors (the youth in the Assemblies of God) how to maintain their Christianity while in the military rather than why they should not serve.[134] The author counseled them to fellowship with other "fine . . . Christian soldiers" and to attend chapel on their base every Sunday.[135] He discouraged attending civilian churches exclusively because it could lead to a misunderstanding.

Such an attitude also lends itself to the mistaken notion that Christianity and soldiering do not mix; that you should keep your Christian profession in town, your soldiering on the post, and never let the twain meet. Nothing could be more destructive of Christian faith and godly living. Rather let your light shine before your comrades-in-arms. It will point them to Christ and illuminate your military path.[136]

Combatant military service was not the only thing that mixed with Christianity. Support for U.S. development of atomic weapons did as well. "It is atomic defense or atomic destruction, one or the other. . . . Therefore the *free world must be armed with atomic weapons* so numerous and so deadly that no nation would dare start World War III."[137] C. M. Ward, one of the most famous Assemblies of God preachers, also encouraged American participation in the "arms race" against the Communists.[138] He defended nuclear tests by quoting an American physicist, "The tests are necessary if the United States is not to be left behind in the development of nuclear weapons."[139]

A memorandum written by Richard G. Champion, a staff member of *The Pentecostal Evangel*, revealed the sentiment regarding noncombatants. He dismissed with disdain a pacifist editorial in the British Assemblies of God publication, *Redemption Tidings*. The editor had exhorted his readers, "Ban all bombs, I say. Assemblies of God are officially a Pacifist movement (though not a movement of pacifists). We feel that our job is to spread the kingdom of God in the earth, and to win souls for Christ."[140] A memo Champion attached to a copy of the material scored it as "an 'ostrich' editorial if I ever read one."[141]

The decade of the 1950s concluded with Ernest S. Williams giving his personal approval to military service.

> Since the war it has been my privilege to be associated as an instructor in Bible college with many young men who fought for their country in the war. I have found these to be most *conscientious* Christians, *exemplary in every way*, yet they do not seem to *feel* they grieved the Lord through accepting military service. *I therefore must leave with human conscience what an individual deems right* for him to do in time of war.[142]

His complete willingness to leave this issue with each person's conscience could be interpreted as tolerant and flexible. He appealed to the "feel[ings]" of the Christian as the justifying factor and made no refer-ence to scriptural support. However, neither he nor any other Assem-blies of God leader during this time applied this method to other ethical questions.[143]

In 1961 an article in *The Pentecostal Evangel* insisted that Christians were not to argue over the morality of war.

> Others will yield to the temptation to debate the issues of war all over again, and tempers are likely to flare. Christians should take a very different course than this. We need to pray earnestly for all who are in authority in municipal, state, and national govern-ments today in order that unnecessary strife may be averted throughout our land.[144]

Indeed, Christian soldiers were missionaries sent around the world on the government's tab.[145] "Many a serviceman has been turned into a missionary by serving Christ while in uniform."[146] Warren McPherson, the Servicemen's Representative for the Assemblies of God from 1954-1964, told young men that their choice regarding military service was between enlisting and getting drafted. "Every physically fit male be-tween 18½ and 26 must serve in some capacity. . . . There are two ways to meet your obligation—you may serve it in the active forces or in the reserves."[147] McPherson did not offer the option of conscientious objec-tion. When someone asked the question, "Can a Man Serve God in the Military?" it produced the resounding response, "it is possible to accom-plish a great work for God while wearing the uniform of our coun-try."[148] McPherson received praise because he "was a living example to contradict the argument many people have that the military is a side-track to sin. He maintained that Christian servicemen *can* live for God in service. . . ."[149]

McPherson's successor, Robert R. Way, continued to emphasize the idea that one could be both a good Assemblies of God Christian and a good soldier. One of his goals for the Servicemen's Department was "to encourage every Christian serviceman to live a victorious life during his tour of active duty."[150] Way assumed leadership responsibilities during the Vietnam conflict and the nature of the material he submitted for publication revealed that he and the Assemblies of God supported American involvement. It also exposed the crusade mentality that the Assemblies of God had adopted regarding war.[151]

Down in the swamp paddy under the sky,
A place full of horror to live or to die . . .
Sniping at enemies as planes roar o'erhead;
We succor the living; we bury the dead. . . .
Down in the Viet swamp, far from our friends,
The flash of a rifle—another life ends. . . .
Yet we're buoyed up in our terrible plight;
For *God is still with us, and our cause is right.*
Down in the swamp hole with one life to give;
Freely it's given *that freedom may live. . . .*
Bearing the brunt of an unending fight,
Doing our utmost for God and the right.
Americans, pray for your sons on the line;
Be true to your country; seek guidance divine.[152]

An Assemblies of God Sunday school superintendent who also served as a Lieutenant Colonel in the United States Air Force became the first living recipient of the Air Force Cross for heroism, "which is the nation's second highest decoration for valor."[153] Robert Way was very proud of this Assemblies of God man who was giving his best "to preserve our freedoms."

> A symbol of the current crisis is one of our own Assemblies of God military men, Lt. Col. James Robinson Risner. This 40-year-old career pilot in the U.S. Air Force, who served as commanding officer of the 67th tactical fighter squadron (the "Fighting Cocks"), has been flying combat aircraft since he was 18. During the Korean War he was an air ace with eight Communist Migs to his credit.[154]

Risner received national attention when his picture appeared on the cover of *Time* magazine in 1965.[155] *The Pentecostal Evangel* published the *Time* cover along with Way's article about Risner. The Assemblies of God had journeyed a long way from their days of pacifism. They now enjoyed the status of a church that unquestionably supported its government in time of war and they had a military hero to prove it.

The Assemblies of God continued to support the Vietnam War and even appealed for more soldiers. "As the Red tide continued to swell, soldiers were sent by the thousands. Today thousands more are needed."[156] However, the Assemblies of God did not think that military might alone could win the war in Southeast Asia. They believed that God could and would help America to win if only Americans would pray.

> What is apt to be the result if a nation at war prays for victory over the enemy? Suppose that Christians everywhere in America would seek divine guidance through prayer and fasting. . . . Unless we hear from heaven in these days of national military involvement, we might just as well go on fighting our wars the way other nations have fought since the beginning of history. . . . What are men and horses, swords and spears (or bombs and missiles), without the hand of God? . . . Has America been praying? The fighting has not diminished! Yes, even mighty nations need to pray for victory—that God will grant wisdom to our President, his cabinet, and all our civilian and military leaders, so that God will be glorified by a meaningful solution with a minimum of additional casualties.[157]

Chaplain Debock exhibited no hesitation in equating bombs and missiles with the hand of God being administered through Christians.

Several articles appeared in the pages of *The Pentecostal Evangel* during 1967 which showed exactly how the Assemblies of God viewed war quite differently than they had fifty years prior. The first was Ernest S. Williams' response to a direct question about Assemblies of God pacifism. "We are told that *many years ago* the Assemblies of God aligned with pacifist groups in opposing the bearing of arms. Is this true; and if it is, has the position been changed?"[158]

Two elements of this question should be noted. First, the view that the pacifist position was antiquated revealed that when the idea was discussed, it was discussed as history. Second, the uncertain inquisitor assumed that, had pacifism actually existed in the Assemblies of God at one time, it very probably had been changed. This idea could easily be gleaned from the content of *The Pentecostal Evangel* articles since World War II. Williams responded by informing the writer that the Assemblies of God had gone on record as "*willing to serve the nation in time of war in every way* that does not require the bearing of arms."[159] The order of the sentence shows that willingness to serve in warfare was the primary emphasis that Williams wanted to make. He knew of no action rescinding that position but concluded with one pointed remark. "However, our young men *almost universally* have refrained from requesting exemption from combat on grounds of conscience."[160]

One month later, one single issue of *The Pentecostal Evangel* devoted five pages and six articles to supporting Christians in the military. The issue combined God with country, evangelization with firepower, and the military police with the baptism in the Holy Spirit to an unprecedented degree. Robert Way tried to show in "Serving God and Country Involves The Other War" that Christian servicemen should "win the war and preserve the peace."[161] Indeed, "firepower and defoliats [sic], helicopters and rivercraft, missiles and heavy artillery" needed to be augmented with "an abundance of love to show the people that we really care."[162] Soldiers testified that "besides fighting for my country, I know the Lord has sent me to Vietnam to witness to others." Assemblies of God church members lauded the contributions of military personnel, "A young MP took charge of the junior department and under his ministry many received the baptism in the Holy Spirit."[163] These exemplary combatant Pentecostals "are not only singing, 'From the halls of Montezuma to the shores of Tripoli,' but they raise their voices with ours in the challenge, 'We've a story to tell to the nations.' They are serving God and country. . . . We are proud of them!"[164]

The broad participation of Assemblies of God youth in the Vietnam War served as a cause for both pride and prayer, "Hardly a church in our fellowship is without vacant seats on Sunday—seats left empty by sons in military service."[165] This issue of *The Pentecostal Evangel* also displayed an advertisement that stood in stark contrast to earlier advertisements. Booth-Clibborn's strongly pacifistic *Blood Against Blood* had been heralded by *The Pentecostal Evangel* during the second decade of the twentieth century, but in 1967 it promoted a book which encouraged the opposite approach to war. Chaplain David Plank's *Called to Serve*, which encouraged combatant military service to Christian young people, received unqualified approval by the reviewer. He believed that Plank should receive a medal for "spiritual guidance and concern for Pentecostal youth . . . [for] his outstanding new manual, *Called to Serve*, a book designed to help Christian youths become good servicemen."[166] He called Plank a "Pentecostal minister-in-uniform" who rightly advised that "with God you can face your future in the military service with confidence." Advice that impressed Caldwell included "you must take what you are given . . . the job you are given, or the combat spot for which you are selected. You must do what you are told."[167] *Called to Serve* was esteemed so highly that Caldwell concluded his review with the following recommendation.

> Here is a book that should be placed in the hands of every Christian young man eligible for the armed forces. . . . You can find no finer, more practical gift for the youth about to leave home and church to enter military service. . . . Make sure your church has copies on hand for presentation to young men on their way to basic training.[168]

The official change in the pacifist position actually took place in August 1967 at the General Council.[169] It was reported to the constituency in October 1967 via *The Pentecostal Evangel.*

> An article on Military Service which remained on the Constitution and Bylaws of the General Council of the Assemblies of God through three [*sic*] world wars has been deleted in favor of a new article which reflects more accurately the current attitude of the fellowship as a whole.[170]

This introductory paragraph admitted that the changing mood of the constituency led to the changing of the article. The reporter made no reference to the attitude of Scripture or its relationship to this issue. He instead related that the former statement had properly pledged "unswerving loyalty" to the government but had improperly committed the entire fellowship to noncombatant or conscientious objector status because it "flatly stated" that Assemblies of God Christians could not participate in the destruction of human life.[171]

The sentiment had changed so the new article preserved "the right of each member to choose for himself" whether or not to kill human life. The reporter then printed the entire resolution and the new article. He expressed no remorse for the loss of the old position.

Books and Pamphlets by Assemblies of God Authors

As the Assemblies of God and the Pentecostal movement grew in size and prestige, several men wrote their versions of its history.[172] A few of these made reference to Pentecostal participation in warfare. One man wrote a book that directly related to military service. None of the writings between 1941 and 1967 complimented the history of nonparticipation.

Stanley Howard Frodsham made no mention of military service in *With Signs Following: The Story of the Pentecostal Revival in the Twentieth Century,* which he wrote in 1946.[173] However, eight years later John

Harrison boasted about the extensive involvement of Pentecostal servicemen in World War II. "The blood of the noble youth from the ranks of the Assemblies of God flowed with that of all others . . . and they wrote a like glorious page in the history of our land with those of the other great churches of America."[174] Harrison unabashedly included the Assemblies of God among the respected and established American churches who supported and defended their nation.[175]

Klaude Kendrick wrote his Ph.D. dissertation in 1959 about the history of the Assemblies of God.[176] The Gospel Publishing House printed it in 1961.[177] Kendrick dealt with many aspects of Assemblies of God history but neither evaluated the statement on military service nor commented on participation in war. However, the gospel Publishing House published another book in 1961 that did mention the pacifistic heritage of the Assemblies of God. Carl Brumback penned *Suddenly . . . from Heaven* and provided his opinion regarding the transition: "World War II witnessed a modification in the attitude of the Assemblies of God toward military service. . . . Between the two global conflicts the view developed that the shedding of blood in war is not the same as the shedding of blood in peace (1 Kings 2:5)."[178]

Brumback provided scriptural support from the Old Testament for the change but then went on to state that most Assemblies of God men did not serve in combatant positions during the war.

> Even so, the *great majority* found that their conscience would not permit them to kill and requested noncombatant service (in preference to the "conscientious objector" status which had proved so disillusioning and distasteful in the First War). Many Assemblies of God men served their country with bravery and distinction in this capacity, ministering to the wounded and suffering in all battle zones.[179]

Whereas J. R. Flower had stated that the majority had served as combatants,[180] Brumback insisted that most had been noncombatants. However, while Brumback certainly had little respect for the distasteful conscientious objector, he did not seem to be ashamed of the noncombatants. It was important for him to point out that they served in areas where they could have been killed. Nevertheless, Brumback identified the foremost contribution of the Assemblies of God during World War II to be their ministry to the servicemen.

The highly acclaimed David Plank penned the book that most powerfully supported military service. In 1967 the Gospel Publishing House printed it and *The Pentecostal Evangel* praised it.[181] Chaplain Plank directed his book toward Assemblies of God Christians who were entering or already in the military, for he considered such service to be "normal and expected."[182] He highlighted the opportunity, adventure, maturity, and training that military service provided.[183] Plank insisted that Christians must use military power for the defense of America's freedoms. "We must render to God an account of our defense of freedom. . . . To assure that this *holy light* [of freedom] shines brightly into the far reaches of the years ahead, America maintains her *military might*."[184] Since God demanded the defense of America, the Christian should accept his or her "call to military duty eagerly and with high hopes."[185] Plank even believed that military service would enhance one's morality and spirituality, because the Armed Forces had "pledged themselves to protect and develop high moral values in the lives of their service men and women."[186] Therefore, military service was both a duty and a privilege even though one "may have to serve in combat." But "personal considerations should never stand in the way of performing a rightful duty" for "God and country."[187]

Only after praising America and freedom did Plank provide a Christian rationale for participation in war. He based his reasoning on the Old Testament and Romans 13. He never mentioned the life or teaching of Jesus.[188] In fact, the example of Jesus was dismissed in a sweeping generalization that characterized Plank's understanding of why someone would object to war. His sarcasm and disdain for this position was clear.

> Perhaps you are one of those who believes that though you have a duty to serve your country, it is not your duty—"as you understand it"—to serve as a combatant bearing arms. You'll stand guard, but without a rifle. "Thou shalt not kill" and other considerations make it impossible for you, as a Christian, in good conscience, to take human life.[189]

The entire life and teachings of Jesus garnered no more than a reference as "other considerations," and Plank never addressed them directly. Instead, he took the easier approach and presented "the following Christian rationale for war which is set forth most clearly and comprehensively in Romans 13."[190] His interpretation of Romans 13 led him to the following conclusions.

> Government . . . has been commissioned by God to suppress evil
> conduct, and to execute His wrath upon wrongdoers with the
> sword, i.e., to kill. There is a "time for war" in which God pun-
> ishes wickedness and prevents it from spreading. . . . Every per-
> son, without exception, is commanded to render obedience to his
> government and rulers. . . . Obedience to the government may
> necessarily require that you serve in its Armed Forces. As a mem-
> ber of its military force you act as its agent, aiding in the discharge
> of its divine commission to suppress evil and punish wrongdoing.
> When on duty you act on behalf of the United States govern-
> ment, not on your own behalf for personal reasons. *Even though
> such duty includes the taking of life, it does not contradict God's law
> of love but somehow fulfills and affirms it.*[191]

Plank's lack of theological precision in the last sentence is to be expected,
since "God's law of love" was not his book's focus. He was more concerned with justifying killing in war than investigating the love of God.

Plank provided another biblical example as support for combatant
participation. He stated that most biblical scholars agreed "thou shalt
not kill" meant "thou shalt not murder." This allowed a soldier to pull
the trigger with a clear conscience, because he did not have "premedi-
tated malice or hatred in his heart."[192] Plank was probably unaware that
most Pentecostal pacifists rarely used the command in Exodus as a rationale for nonparticipation.[193] Their justification was generally based
on the life and teaching of Jesus and the example of the early church.
Nevertheless, these two biblical references provided for Plank the proof
that "the military man does not personally kill in this manner any more
than the citizen who farms the soil and grows the food that feeds the soldier."[194] But Plank did not stop there. He continued to argue that "a
frank consideration of *Christian ethics favors military service.*"[195]

> How can a person accept local police protection for himself, his
> family, his property, and his community, it is reasoned, unless he
> complies with the Christian ethic and extends that same princi-
> ple of protection to others and their families? . . . To deny mercy
> is as reprehensible as acting unmercifully.[196]

Plank did not provide any scriptural support for the "Christian
ethic" of protecting some people by doing violence to other people. In-

stead, he reasoned that allowing oneself to be defended meant that one should defend others. Since this was based on *Christian* ethics, Plank's conclusion about the holy nature of war should not be a surprise. "Here, then, is a Christian defense of combatant military service, the reason a Christian can, in good conscience, participate in a *righteous war.*"[197] Plank had reasoned his way to a crusade approach to war, i.e. aggressive war to establish order or justice on behalf of God.[198]

Nevertheless, Plank informed conscientious objectors that if they still believed they could not participate, they had the blessing of the church.[199] Whereas in the early days of the Assemblies of God the combatant was still accepted despite the official position, now the conscientious objector had to be reassured that he would not be ostracized. This reassurance was necessary because he was ignoring and evading the fact that he was "divinely called to wear a uniform."[200] Plank equated the rejection of war with the rejection of God's call.

Called to Serve was published just months before the 1967 General Council that deleted the pacifist statement on military service. It accurately portrayed the attitude of the fellowship at the time. It also helped explain why the committee appointed to study the statement came under such fire on the floor of the convention when they proposed that the statement did not need to be changed. The next section explores that eruption.

GENERAL COUNCIL ACTION

The General Council of the Assemblies of God has convened a business session during the late summer of each odd-numbered year since 1915. These councils consist of preaching, reports, and resolutions. Ordained ministers and church delegates have voting privileges. The events of each day are recorded, and then they are collectively published as the *Minutes, Constitution and Bylaws.*[201] The biannual councils revealed that concern for military matters surfaced occasionally and various issues relating to military service were considered from 1947-1967.

In view of the significant participation of Assemblies of God men in World War II, the 1947 General Council appointed a committee to evaluate the appropriateness of the article on military service. They realized that perhaps their actions as a fellowship contradicted their stated position. However, the committee reported that they did not find it necessary to change the position.

After considerable thought and prayer on this very vital subject, your committee feels that it will be unable to formulate an article on Military Service that will better represent the attitude of the Assemblies of God than that which is now a part of our General Council By-laws.[202]

This report was adopted without debate. It is possible that at this point the fellowship was not ready to overturn the strongly worded scriptural support for nonviolence. Although at least 65,000 Assemblies of God men had served in both combatant and noncombatant positions during World War II, the Council could not yet delete the "clear teaching of the inspired Word of God" which "prohibit[ed] Christians from shedding blood or taking human life."[203] But the question had been raised.

In 1947 the reference to Exodus was elided without comment from the article on military service.[204] The statement still began and ended with the declaration of "unswerving loyalty to the Government." This loyalty found complementary official support when the 1957 General Council passed a resolution promoting participation in civil defense.

WHEREAS, Our Government has set up the Federal Civil Defense Administration as an agency for the protection of human life and property through the established forms of government, and . . .

WHEREAS, Our religious faith commits us to concern not only for our own lives but also for the life and security of our families, our neighbors, and our nation, and

WHEREAS, We believe that the church cannot be indifferent to the political and historical destiny of the world in which we live, nor withdraw to a pious island and to leave the world unmercifully to its own fate . . .

THEREFORE BE IT RESOLVED, That the General Council of the Assemblies of God . . . urge all pastors to give consideration to their responsibilities to the program of public security in their communities [and] recommend to all its members to assume their moral responsibilities of citizenship and offer their services to local authorities. . . .[205]

This statement declared that the Pentecostal faith promoted a concern for one's own life and those of others. It also committed Pentecostals to involvement in helping shape the political and historical destiny of the world. These sentiments in favor of social concern came from a denomination that had developed, in some sense, from being a "pious island" into a major and accepted mainstream church.

The next action regarding participation in war came in 1965, when the following resolution was presented and approved:

> In view of the fact that there are *widespread questions* regarding the adequacy of our statement on military service as found in Article XXII of the General Council constitution and bylaws; therefore, be it RESOLVED, That a committee be appointed to make a study of this important article and bring its report to the next General Council session.[206]

The resolution did not delineate from whom the questions were coming, but the tone of concern revealed that the general beliefs and actions of the General Council no longer aligned with this historic statement. Admirably, the General Council did not act impulsively. They allowed two years for the committee, to be appointed by the executive presbytery, to research the issue before reporting. This ample amount of time should have provided the opportunity for a thorough review and a trustworthy investigation. However, the presbytery did not appoint the committee until 1966.[207] Furthermore, the committee did not meet together until the actual General Council of 1967 in Long Beach, California.[208] Once they all arrived they discussed the situation and presented their report, which could not have been much more than a week old, to the General Council on Friday afternoon, August 25 1967.

> WHEREAS, The 31st General Council in session requested the appointing of a committee to study the adequacy of our statement on Military Service as found in Article XXII of the Bylaws; and
>
> WHEREAS, Subsequently a duly appointed committee has carefully examined said Article XXII, together with the expressed opinions of chaplains, pastors, evangelists, and correspondence from young men currently involved in the draft; therefore, be it
>
> RESOLVED, That we retain Article XXII as it now appears in the Bylaws; and be it further
>
> RESOLVED, That the following paragraph be added thereto: "We hereby express our desire to continue to extend fel-

lowship and sacramental ministries to those who do not choose non-combatant service."[209]

Before analyzing the statement, we should briefly list some of the major events of 1967 that occurred in the few months before the General Council convened. Martin Luther King Jr. had denounced the Vietnam War in a sermon in New York City on April 4 (he was killed exactly one year later). Muhammad Ali refused military service, and tens of thousands in San Francisco and New York City protested the war. The Six Day War (also known as the 1967 Arab Israeli War) occurred in early June and Israel held the Gaza Strip, the Sinai Peninsula, the West Bank of the Jordan River (including East Jerusalem), and the Golan Heights. The U.S. Supreme Court declared all state laws banning interracial marriages to be unconstitutional. Deadly race riots occurred in Detroit, Newark, Washington, D.C. and other American cities, and an explosion and fire aboard the U.S. Navy aircraft carrier USS Forrestal in the Gulf of Tonkin left 134 dead. About 440 U.S. military personnel died each month in Vietnam in the first eight months of 1967.[210]

In the context of these events, this committee recommended that the Assemblies of God remain a peace church—a church of conscientious objectors. They claimed that they had contacted numerous Assemblies of God ministers and draftees to arrive at this recommendation. Based on the "widespread questions" about the inadequacy of the statement, the preponderance of literature supporting military action, and the thousands of Assemblies of God people in the military, the statement that the committee found support for the pacifistic article certainly seems misinformed. But the committee specifically stated that the "expressed opinions" of many indicated exactly that sentiment.

These opinions must have been gleaned in an unofficial manner, since the committee did not spend much time researching and preparing before the General Council itself.[211] Perhaps lack of preparation led to the inability to frame a new article, so the committee decided to attempt to keep the old one. They thought they could keep the peaceful themes of the old article if they also emphasized their acceptance of those who could conscientiously participate. They thought this could be accomplished by adding a sentence that expressed approval of combatants. The committee had not actually gauged fellowship attitudes, so they did not realize that there would be support for the deletion of the old article. They were not prepared for the reaction their report evoked.

With little awareness of the prevailing sentiment, the goals of the committee were to present a report that appeared well researched, would keep the strongly worded emphasis on nonparticipation, and would also allow fellowship with soldiers.

However, after Chairman Howard Bush read the report, the session erupted into "heated"[212] discussion because the report "didn't go over well."[213] The decision to keep the existing statement had not been expected and was certainly not accepted by those present at the General Council. Even the addition of the sentence that approved combatant military service did not suffice. Some in the audience insisted that "there was fighting and killing in the Old Testament" and others reminded the fellowship that many Assemblies of God men and women served in the military.[214] Howard Cummings, one of the three who eventually joined the committee, supported changing the article.

> I do recall that I spoke out in favor of revising the By-law, as I felt that the General Council, in its ministry to the military, its publications, and its public posture was not a group of conscientious objectors nor non-combatant, either practically or philosophically. I also had my lay delegate sitting beside me who felt even stronger than I, having been injured in combat in WWII.[215]

Dick Mormon from the Stone Church in Chicago added that he was "not in favor of conscientious objection" and that his "church feels very strongly in opposition to CO." Paul Miller of Glendale, Arizona, agreed because he "believe[d] in obligation to bear arms." Cordas C. Burnett, a longtime educator in the Assemblies of God, revealed his fear of being labeled with the "peaceniks." He argued that the old statement should be abandoned because it provided "protection of a few at the cost of the *condemnation of the whole*."[216]

After this "considerable discussion," it was decided that "the resolution be referred back to committee for *further study and clarification* and that the report be brought back to *this* session of the General Council."[217] However, constituents no longer trusted the five-member committee that had presented the unsatisfactory report. A second motion carried that allowed General Superintendent Thomas Zimmerman to appoint three additional members.[218] These new appointments were to be "representative of a cross section of the Fellowship." They were also to ensure that an appropriate resolution would be forthcoming.

The Assemblies of God did not hide this discussion. They did the opposite by broadcasting it to the public, so that all would know they would probably change their stance to support the government and war. The *Independent Star-Telegram* in Long Beach, California, carried an article the next day entitled, "Church Convention Vote Due on Duty in Armed Services."[219] They reported that "the Assemblies of God will vote early next week on a proposed change in the constitution and by-laws to allow young members to serve in combat capacities in the armed forces without going against doctrine."

It did not take long for the new eight-member committee to draft a new proposal.[220] By 11:00 a.m. the following Monday, August 28, 1967, a new resolution had been prepared that presented a new article on military service. The heated discussion of Friday afternoon accompanied by the influence of three new committee members brought forth the following resolution.

> WHEREAS the ideal world condition is that of peace, we as Christian citizens should use our influence in promoting peaceful solutions to world problems; and,
>
> WHEREAS we live in a world in which there may arise international emergencies which will lead our nation to resort to armed conflict in the defense of its ideals, freedom, and national existence;[221] and,
>
> WHERAS, our first loyalty is to God, we recognize nevertheless that human government is ordained by God, and that there are obligations of citizenship which are binding upon us as Christians; and,
>
> WHEREAS, we acknowledge the principle of individual freedom of conscience as it relates to military service; therefore, be it
>
> RESOLVED, That Article XXII of The General Council By-laws be deleted and replaced with the following article: Article XXII. Military Service
>
> As a movement we affirm our loyalty to the government of the United States in war or peace. We shall continue to insist, as we have historically, on the right of each member to choose for himself whether to declare his position as a combatant, a noncombatant, or a conscientious objector.[222]

Once they approved the change, the Assemblies of God advertised their new policy. It appeared in Monday's *Independent Star-Telegram*, "Church Votes OK of Combat Service," and garnered an additional headline on Tuesday as well, "Combat Doctrine Altered."[223]

Several observations are necessary to understand this development. First, the statement admired peace and acquiesced to the idea that Christians should help promote world peace. They did this by mentioning their citizenship as equal to their Christianity. Second, each of the first three warrants referenced citizenship and "our country." Loyalty to the government was prominent and brought "obligations" that bound Christians. This emphasis was evident in the first sentence of the new article. Third, the framers of this resolution and article made no appeal to Scripture or to Jesus. Not a single verse or reference is employed. The only reference to God is qualified by the fact that God required loyalty to the government because God ordained it.

This leads to the fourth observation: The "nevertheless" is implemented in exactly the opposite manner as it had been previously. Previously the Assemblies of God had stated that although they were loyal citizens of their country, they "nevertheless" could not participate in the destruction of human life. That now changed. The new statement proclaimed that although they were loyal to God, they "nevertheless" were obligated to defend their country's ideals, freedoms, and existence. It was a complete reversal, and the famous pacifist word, *nevertheless*, was used to explain it.[224]

Furthermore, the resolution appealed to "individual freedom of conscience" as the philosophical foundation upon which the new statement was built. This concept had not justified the consumption of alcohol, smoking, gambling, dancing, or women wearing slacks. But the authority of one's own conscience served as the trustworthy principle that allowed killing in war.

The theology reflected in the resolution centered on national loyalties and the authority of individual conscience. Theological reflection in the article itself is completely absent. Whereas the original article referred to the "Lord Jesus Christ," the "Prince of Peace," the "Divine commands and precepts," and the "inspired Word of God," the one accepted in 1967 mentioned none of these. It merely reflected the two emphases of the resolution. The wording in the article was significant, since "the right of each member to choose" has since been denied in reference to abortion.[225] There was no theological rationale for the application of the principle of "freedom of choice" to military service other than that God had ordained government.

The procombatant elements that had existed in the Assemblies of God since the earliest days found official expression in this 1967 article change. The standard was each individual conscience. This was a far cry from the official claim of the Assemblies of God that has remained intact since 1914, "The Bible is our all-sufficient rule for faith and practice."[226] *Christianity Today* evaluated the change in the following manner:

> Although its leadership has long denied the church's commitment to pacifism, the biennial General Council of the Assemblies of God put ground under the denial by repudiating its constitution's Article 22 on military service. . . . True pacifism among Pentecostals has never been strong. The Assemblies are aggressive in grooming chaplains and help prepare military chaplain lessons.[227]

The author noted the incongruous nature of pacifism and military chaplaincy, and that focus in the Assemblies of God helped remove pacifist theology and practice.

MINISTRY TO THE MILITARY, 1941-1967

The Assemblies of God dedicated themselves to evangelizing the military during and after World War II. Their distribution of Christian literature during World War II was not surpassed by any other Christian organization.[228] They supplied chaplains and evangelists to every branch of the Armed Forces, built and managed service centers for military personnel, and held revival rallies at military bases around the globe. Their emphasis on evangelizing the military was boldly proclaimed in *The Pentecostal Evangel* throughout the war. At least sixty-five articles appeared between 1941 and 1945 that promoted this type of ministry.[229] Reports were regularly provided about the numbers of soldiers being saved because of Assemblies of God ministries.[230]

By May 1945 the Servicemen's Department boasted thirty-five full time employees, forty-one part-time assistants, eight field representatives, and twenty-two workers in service centers. This staff stayed in contact with 147 prisoners of war, fifty-five thousand Assemblies of God servicemen, and ministered to two hundred thousand soldiers each month at the Victory Service Centers. The department also reported that three thousand military chaplains had requested copies of *Reveille*, which were being sent out free of charge by the millions.[231]

The intensity with which they approached this ministry effectively replaced any concern for the morality of participation in war. Soldiers who converted were not expected to leave the military. They were expected to become better soldiers and effective witnesses for Christ in the military. In effect, they approved of killing in war and treated Jesus as being for soul salvation rather than a moral example of nonviolence. The Assemblies of God knew that soldiers gave the best testimonies and had the best chance at leading other soldiers to God.

> Brother Myer Pearlman, who went through the last war as a private in the United States Army, and who knows how to interpret the truths of Scripture in language the soldier boys will appreciate, has been responsible for both editions of *Reveille*.[232]

The military ceased to be a place where a Christian could not go. To the contrary, it was considered a place to which a Christian must go, both as a loyal citizen of the United States and as a missionary for Jesus. The military had become "the world's greatest mission field."[233]

SUMMARY

By 1967 the last vestiges of any emphasis on pacifism or conscientious objection had completely disappeared from the Assemblies of God. Lay people questioned whether or not the Assemblies of God had ever been opposed to war, because they had never been taught that it was a part of Pentecostal Christianity. Leaders ridiculed conscientious objection and praised combatant service. The attempt to retain the statement in 1967 elicited opposition; the vote to delete it went uncontested.

Most authors downplayed the historical presence of anticombatant sentiments in the Assemblies of God. Instead, they lauded their military chaplaincy and their strong Americanism. Their concern for evangelism effectively replaced their concerns about combatant participation in war. This transformation accompanied the General Council's growing identification with the evangelical church world and secular culture. Between 1941 and 1967, the Assemblies of God made great strides toward entrenching itself into the religious and political establishments. They also moved away from appealing to Christ's example alone for their model. Instead, they appealed more to the Old Testament, the Pauline corpus, and the philosophy of the authority of individual conscience for their ethic of war.

The widespread attitudes of Americanism, militarism, and evangelism continued to dominate the next three decades of Assemblies of God history. They continued to view global military events from an American perspective. However, a faint glimmer of interest in Pentecostal pacifism began to flicker in the 1980s and 1990s among some Assemblies of God ministers.

NOTES

1. Between 1941 and 1945, thirty-six articles either recommended or approved combatant participation in military service. A total of eighty-two articles supporting participation were printed from 1941 to 1967. During that time only two articles clearly promoted conscientious objection or pacifism. These articles are elaborated upon in the following sections of this chapter.

2. *General Council Minutes*, 1947, 13. *General Council Minutes*, 1957, 55-56.

3. At least sixty-seven articles appeared on ministry to soldiers in the 1940s.

4. "The perception that the United States differs qualitatively from other developed nations, because of its unique origins, national credo, historical evolution, and distinctive political and religious institutions." "Foreword: On American Exceptionalism; Symposium on Treaties, Enforcement, and U.S. Sovereignty," *Stanford Law Review* (May 1 2003): 1479.

5. Menzies, *Anointed to Serve*, 328. Thirty-two are listed in the *Directory of Civilian Public Service: May, 1941 to March, 1947* (New York: Fellowship of Reconciliation, 1988, reprint), xviii. See Appendix B for a full list. The number of World War II conscientious objectors listed by denominational affiliation is also available online in Glenn D. Paige, *Nonkilling Global Political Science* (Xlibris, 2002), Appendix D. Http://www.global nonviolence.org/docs/nonkilling/nonkilling_text.pdf (accessed August 11, 2007).

6. By July 1945 sixty-five thousand servicemen were on the *Reveille* mailing list. "Shall 'Reveille' Be Continued," *The Pentecostal Evangel*, 28 July 1945, 7. It is not clear whether they were members or not since in 1945 the Assemblies of God listed their membership at 241,782. That would mean that 27% of the members were in the military in 1945. It is more likely that the *Reveille* mailing list included many more servicemen than Assemblies of God members.

7. On March 9, 2007, Dr. Horton told Shelly McMullin of the Pentecostal Charismatic Peace Fellowship that he had been a conscientious objector during

World War II. The next day I interviewed him briefly, and he is planning to share this important part of his testimony in an article written by Martin Mittelstadt of Evangel University.

8. Gary B. McGee, "Horton, Stanley Monroe," in *Dictionary of Pentecostal and Charismatic Movements*, ed. Stanley M. Burgess and Gary B. McGee (Grand Rapids: Zondervan, 1988).

9. Howard Kenyon, "An Analysis of Ethical Issues in the History of the Assemblies of God" (Ph.D. diss., Baylor University, 1988), 356.

10. Carl Brumback, *Suddenly . . . from Heaven* (Springfield, Mo.: Gospel Publishing House, 1961), 312.

11. Charnal Adrian Bird went through "boot camp" in 1945 but did not carry a weapon and subsequently served as a cook in the Navy. He could not have been included in J. R. Flower's estimate, which came two years before Bird was drafted. Reverend Charnal Adrian Bird, interview by author, 20 December 1999, Hawkins, Texas. Donald Rosengartner served two years as a medic because he would not kill. Helen Rosengartner, interview by author, 30 May 2000, Garland, Texas. Manson David Stokley was an Assemblies of God man who did not serve in the military even as a noncombatant and was instead placed in a CPS camp. Evelyn Smith, interview by author, 30 May 2000, Garland, Texas.

12. Melvin Gingerich, *Service for Peace, A History of Mennonite Civilian Public Service* (Mennonite Central Committee, 1949), 452.

13. *Military Classification For Draftees,* compiled by Anne Yoder, Archivist, Swarthmore College Peace Collection, March 2007, http://www.swarthmore.edu/library/peace/conscientiousobjection/MilitaryClassifications.htm. For a complete listing of classifications see *Selective Service Regulations. Volume Three. Classification & Selection*, 1940 (Subject File: Conscientious Objection/Objectors—Government Documents); also "Memorandum Of the Rights Of Conscientious Objectors Under the Draft Laws As Of December 1, 1942" (Subject File: Conscientious Objection/Objectors—U.S. Sources, 1942).

14. "Universal Warfare," *The Pentecostal Evangel*, 19 April 1941, 4.

15. Ibid.

16. Letter from Stanley H. Frodsham to Leslie C. Wattenburger, 26 November 1941, Frodsham file, J. R. Flower Pentecostal Heritage Center, Springfield, Missouri.

17. Letter from Stanley H. Frodsham to T. L. Ward, Memphis Tennessee, 30 December 1941, Frodsham file, J. R. Flower Pentecostal Heritage Center, Springfield, Missouri.

18. Bernice Proctor, "Our Missionaries in War Areas," *The Pentecostal Evangel*, 24 January 1942, 10. Note the eschatological rationale for their nonviolence.

19. Watson Argue, "The Present War and the World Situation," *The Pentecostal Evangel*, 24 October 1942, 10.

20. Ibid. The Hebrew Scriptures actually report that God himself warred against his own people. See Millard Lind, *Yahweh is a Warrior: The Theology of Warfare in Ancient Israel*. Scottdale, Pa.: Herald, 1980.

21. Watson Argue, "The Present War and the World Situation," *The Pentecostal*

Evangel, 24 October 1942, 10.

22. W. I. Evans, "How the Issues of War Will Be Settled," *The Pentecostal Evangel*, 2 January 1943, 2.

23. Ibid.

24. J. Roswell Flower, "The Plight of the Christian in the Present World War," *The Pentecostal Evangel*, 12 June 1943, 6.

25. Ibid. Emphasis added. Flower also revealed that the Assemblies of God and probably he himself struggled to balance their pacifism with their strong feelings that fighting was necessary.

26. Ibid.

27. Ibid.

28. The rationale he employed is evaluated in the following section of this chapter.

29. Flower, "The Plight of the Christian," 6.

30. Ibid., 7.

31. J. Roswell Flower, "The Plight of the Conscientious Objector in the Present World Conflict," *The Pentecostal Evangel*, 3 July 1943, 7.

32. Ibid.

33. *General Council Minutes*, 1943, 26.

34. J. Roswell Flower, "Concerning the Conscientious Objector," *The Pentecostal Evangel*, 4 March 1944, 7. *General Council Minutes*, 1945, 45.

35. *General Council Minutes*, 1945, 81. *Reveille* was a highly praised serviceman's publication that the Gospel Publishing House distributed to millions of servicemen during World War II. It was evangelistic and nondenominational in nature. *The Pentecostal Evangel* carried dozens of requests for its financial support while only asking for support for the conscientious objectors twice. On Mennonite expenditures, see Paul Toews, *Mennonites in American Society, 1930-1970: Modernity and the Persistence of Religious Community, The Mennonite Experience in America*, vol. 4 (Scottdale, Pa.: Herald Press, 1996)), 138.

36. See Appendix B.

37. Interview with Walter B. Smith, August 15 2007. Personal files of author. Smith, then an Assemblies of God machinist from Winnsboro, Texas, served in two CPS camps and vividly remembers fighting fires in Virginia as the Army shelled the mountains.

38. Ernest S. Williams, "The Hour Demands It!" *The Pentecostal Evangel*, 31 August 1946, 8.

39. *General Council Minutes*, 1947, 13.

40. "Shall 'Reveille' Be Continued?" *The Pentecostal Evangel*, 28 July 1945, 7.

41. Blumhofer, *The Assemblies of God: A Chapter in the Story of American Pentecostalism*, 435.

42. *General Council Minutes*, 1953, 60.

43. See Wilma Ann Bailey, *"You Shall Not Kill" Or "You Shall Not Murder"? The Assault on a Biblical Text* (Collegeville, Minn.: Liturgical Press, 2005) for an exegetical treatment of this passage.

44. "Wartime Wages of the C.O.'s," *The Pentecostal Evangel*, 14 January 1950, 8.

45. "Conscientious Objectors," *The Pentecostal Evangel*, 14 January 1950, 8. This figure represents all the conscientious objectors in the United States. They did not provide the number of Assemblies of God men.

46. This same issue contained his recommendation regarding sharing America's surplus of grain with starving nations, "The suggestion is good. Let us hope it is acted upon." "Should America Hoard Food While Millions Starve?" *The Pentecostal Evangel*, 14 January 1950, 8.

47. "War is the Great Tragedy," *The Pentecostal Evangel*, 8 April 1951, 7.

48. Ibid.

49. "Provision for Conscientious Objectors," *The Pentecostal Evangel*, 1 July 1951, 2.

50. Bob Evans, "Pardoned Twice: How a Nazi War Criminal Found Christ," *The Pentecostal Evangel*, 28 October 1951, 11.

51. Ibid.

52. "The Editorial Viewpoint: War or Peace?" *The Pentecostal Evangel*, 6 January 1957, 2.

53. Ibid.

54. Ibid.

55. William H. Douglas, "Glorifying War?" *The Pentecostal Evangel*, 28 July 1957, 23.

56. Ernest S. Williams, "Your Questions Answered by Ernest S. Williams," *The Pentecostal Evangel*, 5 July 1959, 7.

57. Ibid.

58. Ernest S. Williams, "Your Questions Answered by Ernest S. Williams," *The Pentecostal Evangel*, 7 February 1960, 11.

59. Ibid.

60. Ernest S. Williams, "Your Questions Answered by Ernest S. Williams," *The Pentecostal Evangel*, 20 August 1961, 21.

61. Memorandum from Bert Webb to Bob Cunningham, 31 May 1961; and memorandum from Bert Webb to Bob Cunniningham, 17 July 1961, from the files of *The Pentecostal Evangel* office, Flower Pentecostal Heritage Center, Springfield, Missouri; quoted in Kenyon, 390.

62. Paul E. Lowenberg, "His Hand Stuck to the Sword," *The Pentecostal Evangel*, 19 July 1964, 16.

63. Lowenberg spoke of warfare throughout history in admirable terms and used war stories as illustrations of how Christians were to attack and defeat the devil. Ibid., 17, 18.

64. "New Bylaws on Military Service Adopted by General Council," *The Pentecostal Evangel*, 8 October 1967, 7.

65. A. G. Ward, "A Postwar Revival," *The Pentecostal Evangel*, 10 May 1941, 3.

66. Zelma Argue, ". . . Until I Have Showed Thy Strength Unto This Generation," *The Pentecostal Evangel*, 28 June 1941, 1. Wesley R. Steelberg, "The Stars and Stripes of Calvary," *The Pentecostal Evangel*, 4 July 1942, 1. "The Hope of a Nation," *The Pentecostal Evangel*, 12 June 1943, 8.

67. E. Elsworth Krogstad, "Loyalty to Government and to God in the Present

World Crisis," *The Pentecostal Evangel*, 4 July 1942, 1; quoted in Kenyon, "An Analysis of Ethical Issues," 343.

68. "Fifty Soldiers Saved!" *The Pentecostal Evangel*, 13 September 1941, 16.

69. Noel Perkins, "War and Missions," *The Pentecostal Evangel*, 27 December 1941, 6.

70. "Dedicating Gospels," *The Pentecostal Evangel*, 7 February 1942, 1. George T. B. Davis, "Nation-wide Prayer for Revival and Victory," *The Pentecostal Evangel*, 9 May 1942, 1.

71. Steelberg, 1. This occurred the same year the Assemblies of God helped found the National Association of Evangelicals. The possessive pronoun *our* began to be applied to all American and Allied military activity. The Assemblies of God was beginning to accept ownership. This shift toward establishmentarianism accompanied the involvement with the National Association of Evangelicals and directly corresponded to the growth of patriotism. The Assemblies of God viewed itself as a good American church, just like all the other good American churches. The main difference was that the Pentecostals spoke in tongues. "From 1942 onward there followed a thoroughgoing identification with the spirit [patriotic] and practice [combatant participation in warfare] of this wing of the Christian church [American fundamentalism]." Menzies, *Anointed to Serve*, 189. "Announcing a *Reveille* Servicemen's Department," *The Pentecostal Evangel*, 29 January 1944, 5. "Our Sons in Service," *The Pentecostal Evangel*, 12 August 1944, 16.

72. J. Roswell Flower, "The Plight of the Christian in the Present World War," 6-7. Flower proudly referred to his militant ancestors as he identified wholeheartedly with America.

73. "The Hope of a Nation," *The Pentecostal Evangel*, 12 June 1943, 8.

74. Clarence P. Smales, "Problems of the Serviceman," *The Pentecostal Evangel*, 24 June 1944.

75. Ibid.

76. J. Roswell Flower, "The Plight of the Christian in the Present World War," 6.

77. "Prepare or Perish," *The Pentecostal Evangel*, 16 February 1946, 11.

78. "Honored for American Spirit," *The Pentecostal Evangel*, 27 November 1955, 6.

79. Williams, "Your Questions Answered by Ernest S. Williams," 7. Emphasis added.

80. Ibid.

81. Ibid.

82. Vivian Skipper, "One Nation Under God," *The Pentecostal Evangel*, 5 July 1964, 6. Forty years earlier Bartleman referred to this heresy that is present in every nation that has a god or gods, "the national Gods have been invoked."

83. "Loyal to Both," *The Pentecostal Evangel*, 13 March 1960, 22.

84. J. Bashford Bishop, "Christ and His Enemies," *The Pentecostal Evangel*, 13 March 1960, 22.

85. David W. Plank, *Called to Serve* (Springfield, Mo.: Gospel Publishing House, 1967).

86. Ibid., 19.

87. Ibid., 20.

88. Ibid., 15, 33.

89. Ibid., 17.

90. Delbert Grant, "Khaki Christmas," *The Pentecostal Evangel*, 5 December 1942, 18. W. I. Evans, "How the Issues of War Will Be Settled," *The Pentecostal Evangel*, 2 January 1943, 2. Harry A. Jaeger, "Modern Miracles," *The Pentecostal Evangel*, 22 January 1944, 8.

91. "Work Among the Soldiers," *The Pentecostal Evangel*, 1 November 1941, 16.

92. Ernest S. Williams, "Questions and Answers," *The Pentecostal Evangel*, 22 November 1941, 16.

93. "Dedicated to the Defenders of America," *The Pentecostal Evangel*, 27 December 1941, 14.

94. Raymond T. Richey, "Evangelizing At Our Army Camps," *The Pentecostal Evangel*, 10 January 1942, 12. "Announcing a *Reveille* Servicemen's Department," *The Pentecostal Evangel*, 29 January 1944, 5. "Our Sons in Service," *The Pentecostal Evangel*, 12 August 1944, 16.

95. "Helping the Service Men," *The Pentecostal Evangel*, 21 February 1942, 1. Myer Pearlman, a World War I veteran, was praised as being able to minister "in the language the soldier boys" appreciate.

96. "Revival and Victory Prayer Card," *The Pentecostal Evangel*, 13 June 1942, 12. Delbert S. Grant, "Leading Service Men to Christ," *The Pentecostal Evangel*, 11 July 1942, 10.

97. Letter from Robert A. Brown to J. Roswell Flower, 12 August 1942, Robert Brown file, Flower Pentecostal Heritage Center, Springfield, Missouri. He also wrote, "He has not a scruple to be in non combat service, but his idea is to get clear of all service and go preacheing [sic]. . . . I think he would take your advise , [sic] if you felt led to write him."

98. Argue, "The Present War and the World Situation," 10.

99. Ibid., 11.

100. Ibid. For a detailed consideration of the "Hitler question," see Robert W. Brimlow, *What About Hitler? Wrestling With Jesus' Call to Nonviolence in an Evil World* (Grand Rapids: Brazos, 2006).

101. Flower, "The Plight of the Christian in the Present World War," 6. This cessation of personal responsibility extended only to killing, not to sexuality, cursing, gambling, drinking alcohol, or smoking.

102. Ibid. He relegated peace to the private sphere and accepted violence as both public and necessary.

103. He did not delineate who conceded this.

104. Ibid.

105. Ibid. Flower did not consider the possibility that Christ purchased the liberty of salvation with his own blood rather than with the blood of his enemies.

106. Ibid., 7.

107. "50,000 Men," *The Pentecostal Evangel*, 18 March 1944, 12.

108. "When a Coconut Log Became an Altar," *The Pentecostal Evangel*, 14 October 1944, 9.

109. "Bombardier Barney Comes Back," *The Pentecostal Evangel*, 25 November 1944, 12. Kenneth D. Barney, a bombardier on a B-24 airplane, was a member of the Topeka Assembly of God Church in Topeka, Kansas.

110. Mark Kagan, "Hitlerism Must Lose," *The Pentecostal Evangel*, 25 March 1944, 1.

111. "There's A Job To Be Done: Serving the Men in the Service," *The Pentecostal Evangel*, 19 February 1944, 12.

112. "Twelve Million Men at Stake," *The Pentecostal Evangel*, 13 May 1944, 12. "Winning Men in the Desert Training Area," *The Pentecostal Evangel*, 29 April 1944, 7. "Victory," *The Pentecostal Evangel*, 24 June 1944, 1. Delbert Grant, "*Reveille* and a Revolution," *The Pentecostal Evangel*, 22 July 1944, 9. "Bombardier Barney Comes Back," *The Pentecostal Evangel*, 25 November 1944, 12.

113. Mervin E. Rosell, "War Points the Way," *The Pentecostal Evangel*, 17 February 1945, 1-2.

114. Harry A. Jaeger, "Spiritual Conquest Among the American Doughboys," *The Pentecostal Evangel*, 12 May 1945, 5. Emphasis added.

115. "Shall '*Reveille*' Be Continued," *The Pentecostal Evangel*, 28 July 1945, 7.

116. "Harvest Time," *The Pentecostal Evangel*, 1 September 1945, 5.

117. Lester Sumrall, "The War is Not Over . . . Tho' the Boys are Coming Home," *The Pentecostal Evangel*, 27 October 1945, 1.

118. Ibid., 5.

119. Wallace S. Bragg, "Our Task in a Post-War World," *The Pentecostal Evangel*, 27 October 1945, 2.

120. Ibid.

121. F. M. Bellsmith, "Two Enlistments," *The Pentecostal Evangel*, 23 February 1946, 5.

122. Frank B. Gigliotti, "Blood Stains," *The Pentecostal Evangel*, 18 October 1947, 14.

123. Ibid. The story is about World War I but would probably not have been printed in *The Pentecostal Evangel* during that war. However, by 1947 it voiced the sentiments of the constituency well enough to be published.

124. Ibid.

125. Ibid., 15.

126. "The Boys Are Going Again," *The Pentecostal Evangel*, 14 August 1948, 12.

127. Ibid.

128. Ernest S. Williams, "Christ Invades the Military," *The Pentecostal Evangel*, 11 September 1948, 6. Emphasis added.

129. "Ambassadors Advance! Serving the Servicemen," *The Pentecostal Evangel*, 8 January 1949, 12. "Serving the Servicemen," *C. A. Herald*, January 1949, 2.

130. "Passing and Permanent: War Is the Great Tragedy," *The Pentecostal Evangel*, 8 April 1951, 7.

131. "Editorially: One Year of War," *The Pentecostal Evangel*, 24 June 1951, 2.

132. Ibid.

133. "Passing and Permanent: New Plan for Conscientious Objectors," *The Pentecostal Evangel*, 23 March 1952, 2.

134. F. R. Griepp, "To C. A.'s Entering Military Service," *The Pentecostal Evangel*, 13 December 1953, 6, 11-12.

135. Ibid., 6, 11.

136. Ibid., 12.

137. "The Editorial Viewpoint: The Missile Age," *The Pentecostal Evangel*, 5 May 1957, 2. Emphasis added.

138. C. M. Ward, "The Cold War," *The Pentecostal Evangel*, 14 June 1959, 3, 28-31.

139. Ibid., 3.

140. "Editorial," *Redemption Tidings*, 15 November 1957, 3. No such pacifist sentiment was evidenced anywhere in the United States any longer. The British Assemblies of God allowed the noncombatant ethic to continue longer than the American Assemblies of God at least in part because of the powerful influence of Donald Gee, their pacifist leader who served as assistant chairman (1934-44) and chairman (1945-1948).

141. Memo from Richard G. Champion, attached to copy of the editorial, Richard G. Champion file, Flower Pentecostal Heritage Center, Springfield, Missouri.

142. Ernest S. Williams, "Your Questions Answered by Ernest S. Williams," *The Pentecostal Evangel*, 5 July 1959, 7. Emphasis added.

143. Examples include: it is always right to salute the American flag (Ernest S. Williams, "Your Questions Answered by Ernest S. Williams," *The Pentecostal Evangel*, 5 July 1959, 7), it is never right to drink alcohol ("Intemperance and Insanity," *The Pentecostal Evangel*, 19 December 1954, 7; "Alcohol and Sex Crimes," *The Pentecostal Evangel*, 14 January 1950, 8), it is never right to gamble ("Bingo Boom in New York" and "U.S. Is 'Gamblingest' Nation," *The Pentecostal Evangel*, 7 February 1960, 11), and it is never right to smoke ("Daily Newspaper Bans All Tobacco Advertising," *The Pentecostal Evangel*, 7 February 1960, 11).

144. "Cannons Boom and Christians Pray as Civil War Centennial Begins," *The Pentecostal Evangel*, 8 January 1961, 25.

145. J. Philip Hogan, "Military Missionaries," *The Pentecostal Evangel*, 27 January 1963, 9. Warren McPherson, "Keys to Closed Doors," *The Pentecostal Evangel*, 5 July 1964, 5. Bert Webb, "Ministering to Servicemen in Europe," *The Pentecostal Evangel*, 5 July 1964, 6.

146. Warren McPherson, "Missions and the Military," *The Pentecostal Evangel*, 7 July 1963, 8. McPherson also wrote, "We must build proper attitudes about military service among our boys. . . . Our boys must realize that soldiering is not all destruction. . . . Military service can be a time of missionary service for God. . . . They can serve God in the military."

147. Warren McPherson, "To Join or Not to Join?" *The Pentecostal Evangel*, 1 July 1962, 6.

148. Chaplain Orville McCormack, "Can A Man Serve God in the Military?" *The Pentecostal Evangel*, 1 July 1962, 24-25. The morality of war did not elicit the question, it was brought about by the concern for other moral issues: sexual promiscuity, alcoholism, and smoking.

149. Helen Braxton, "God bless you, Warren," *At Ease*, January 1965, 9. This article had previously appeared in the *C. A. Herald* in 1964. Emphasis in the original.

150. Robert R. Way, "Our Mission to the Military," *The Pentecostal Evangel*, 26 September 1965, 7.

151. Describing the crusade mentality, John Howard Yoder wrote: "The 'survival of the free world' . . . can constitute transcendent-cause claims that are not subject to political measurement, so that the 'holy' mentality is still at work." John Howard Yoder, *When War is Unjust* (Maryknoll, N.Y.: Orbis, 1996), 14.

152. "In South Vietnam: 1965," *The Pentecostal Evangel*, 26 September 1965, 7. Emphasis added.

153. Robert R. Way, "Christmas in Vietnam," *The Pentecostal Evangel*, 19 December 1965, 5-6. The previous Air Force Crosses had been awarded posthumously.

154. Ibid., 5. Risner retired in 1976 as a Brigadier General, having also received the "Distinguished Service Medal, Silver Star with oak leaf cluster, Distinguished Flying Cross with two oak leaf clusters, Bronze Star Medal with 'V' device and oak leaf cluster, Air Medal with seven oak leaf clusters, Joint Service Commendation Medal, Purple Heart with three oak leaf clusters, Presidential Unit Citation Emblem, Air Force outstanding Unit Award Ribbon with two combat 'V' devices, the Republic of Korea Presidential Unit Citation Ribbon, and the Republic of Vietnam Gallantry Cross with 'V' device." http://www.af.mil/bios/bio.asp?bioID=6916 (accessed July 16, 2007).

155. *Time* devoted a five-page article to Risner and his crew that included a picture of him standing next to his F-105. "Who's Fighting in Viet Nam: A Gallery of American Combatants," *Time*, 23 April 1965, 22-26.

156. E. S. Caldwell, "The Battle is the Lord's," *The Pentecostal Evangel*, 13 November 1966, 11.

157. Ronald G. Debock, "The Battle is Not Yours," *The Pentecostal Evangel*, 13 November 1966, 10.

158. Ernest S. Williams, "Your Questions Answered by Ernest S. Williams," *The Pentecostal Evangel*, 28 May 1967, 15. Emphasis added.

159. Ibid. Emphasis added.

160. Ibid. Emphasis added.

161. *The Pentecostal Evangel*, 25 June 1967, 8.

162. Ibid.

163. Ibid.

164. Ibid., 9.

165. "Away—But Not Forgotten," *The Pentecostal Evangel*, 25 June 1967, 9. There were 8,506 Assemblies of God churches in the United States in 1967. Menzies, *Anointed to Serve*, 400.

166. E. S. Caldwell, "Called to Serve," *The Pentecostal Evangel*, 25 June 1967, 10.

167. Ibid., 11.

168. Ibid.

169. The actual resolution and new article regarding Military Service is evaluated in a subsequent section.

170. "New Bylaws on Military Service Adopted By General Council," *The Pente-*

costal Evangel, 8 October 1967, 7.

171. Ibid.

172. The Assemblies of God increased from nonexistence in 1913 to 11,168 ordained ministers (average 70% per year increase since 1914), 8,506 churches (average 22% per year increase since 1925), and 1,027,688 Sunday school enrollees in the United States (average 10% per year increase since 1951) by 1967. The global constituency numbered 3,256,641 (U.S. Sunday school plus non-American membership, average 22% per increase since 1951; the majority of this growth was overseas). Giving to foreign missions increased from $4,879 in 1916 to $6,380,505 in 1967, an average annual increase of 256%. Menzies, *Anointed to Serve*, 399-400, 402, 404-405.

173. Stanley Howard Frodsham, *With Signs Following: The Story of the Pentecostal Revival in the Twentieth Century* (Springfield, Mo.: Gospel Publishing House, 1946). This book was an expansion of B. F. Lawrence's version that originally appeared as *The Apostolic Faith Restored* (Springfield, Mo.: Gospel Publishing House, 1916).

174. John Irvine Harrison, "A History of the Assemblies of God" (Th.D. diss., Berkley Baptist Divinity School, 1954), 156.

175. Other evidence that the Assemblies of God sought respectability was their affiliation with the National Association of Evangelicals in 1942. By 1954, when Harrison wrote his dissertation, this association served as a source of pride. J. Roswell Flower, "Basic Unity of Evangelic Christianity," *The Pentecostal Evangel*, 19 June 1943, 8. J. Roswell Flower, "United Evangelical Action," *The Pentecostal Evangel*, 13 May 1944, 5. J. Roswell Flower, "Why We Joined the NAE," *The Pentecostal Evangel*, 29 March 1947, 12. Stanley H. Frodsham, "Fifth Annual Convention of the NAE," *The Pentecostal Evangel*, 10 May 1947, 6. J. Philip Hogan, "World Evangelical Fellowship," *The Pentecostal Evangel*, 18 October 1953, 6.

176. Kendrick did his Ph.D. in history at the University of Texas and graduated in 1959. He served as president of both Evangel College (Springfield, Mo.) and Southwestern Assemblies of God University (Waxahachie, Tex.).

177. Klaude Kendrick, *The Promise Fulfilled* (Springfield, Mo.: Gospel Publishing House, 1961).

178. Carl Brumback, *Suddenly . . . from Heaven* (Springfield, Mo.: Gospel Publishing House, 1961), 312.

179. Ibid. Emphasis added.

180. Flower, "The Plight of the Christian in the Present World War," 6.

181. David Plank, *Called to Serve* (Springfield, Mo.: Gospel Publishing House, 1967).

182. Ibid., 11. He wrote that eighty percent of American youth would serve in the military.

183. Ibid., 12.

184. Ibid., 15. Emphasis added.

185. Ibid., 17.

186. Ibid., 18. Plank did list the dangers of military life but none of them related to killing, lessening the value of human life, violence, or destruction. The main

problems that Plank saw in the military were, according to his order of presentation: sex (he devoted six pages to this topic; 35-41), homosexuality (two paragraphs; 41), alcohol (which "compromis[es] your Christian testimony;" 41-42), smoking (42-43), profanity (43-44), narcotics/drugs (44-45), gambling (45), and pornography (45-46).

187. Ibid., 19.

188. Significantly, the first reference to Jesus occurred on page 42, when Plank cited his example as the primary reason why Christians should not consume alcohol. "Jesus Christ refused a potion of wine in the hour of His death . . . how much more ought you in the finest hour of your life follow our Lord's example!" It is ironic that Jesus was not worth mentioning when Plank discussed participation in killing but his example served as the ideal when promoting abstinence from alcohol.

189. Ibid., 19.

190. Ibid. "In fact, every Christian serviceman should be familiar with the *scriptural teachings which justify and defend* his membership in the military service and his *participation in war.*" Emphasis added.

191. Ibid., 20. Emphasis added.

192. Ibid., 21.

193. The Assemblies of God even deleted it in 1947.

194. Ibid.

195. Ibid. Emphasis added.

196. Ibid.

197. Ibid. Emphasis added.

198. Ceadel, *Thinking About War and Peace*, 4-5.

199. Ibid.

200. Ibid., 34.

201. The name of this publication has changed occasionally. It is consistently referred to as *General Council Minutes* in this book.

202. *General Council Minutes*, 1947, 13.

203. Ibid., 42.

204. Ibid., 13.

205. *General Council Minutes*, 1957, 55-56.

206. *General Council Minutes*, 1965, 61. Emphasis added.

207. William H. Robertson of Mission Viejo, California, interview by author, 12 February 2000, by telephone.

208. Ibid. The committee members were Howard S. Bush, chairman; Bartlett Peterson, J. L. Gerhart, William H. Robertson, and Chaplain Leonard L. Ahrnsbrak. *General Council Minutes*, 1967, 15. The presbytery did not choose the committee based upon their individual concern for this topic. They simply chose existing officials within the Assemblies of God. However, Robertson also believed he may have been chosen because he visited the Assemblies of God chaplains in Vietnam in 1966. He also believed that they chose Chaplain Ahrnsbrak because he was a chaplain. William H. Robertson of Mission Viejo, California, interview by author, 1 April 2000, by telephone.

209. *General Council Minutes*, 1967, 14.

210. *Casualty Statistics on Southeast Asia, By Month*, Comptroller, Secretary of Defense, United States of America.

211. William H. Robertson, interview by author, 12 February 2000.

212. Howard Cummings of Aurora, Colorado, interview by author, 12 April 2000, by mail, personal files of the author. "Feelings across the U.S. were intense at that time, due to the nation's involvement in Viet Nam and the subsequent opposition to the war, the 'peacenik revolution,' and the anti-authority attitudes which developed."

213. William H. Robertson, interview by author, 12 February 2000.

214. Ibid.

215. Howard Cummings, interview by author, 12 April 2000.

216. Ibid. Emphasis added.

217. *General Council Minutes*, 1967, 15. Emphasis added.

218. *General Council Minutes*, 1967, 15. The three new members were O. B. Harrup, Daniel P. Kolenda, and Howard Cummings.

219. "Church Convention Vote Due on Duty in Armed Services," *Independent Star-Telegram*, 26 August 1967.

220. Robertson stated that the committee did not meet "too long" over the weekend, "I don't remember it so it must not have been much." William H. Roberston, interview by author, 12 February 2000. Cummings believed that the committee met "3 or 4 times." Howard Cummings, interview by author, 12 April 2000.

221. It was significant that this was written as an American statement, despite the fact that the majority of the Assemblies of God constituency (seventy percent) were not citizens of the United States in 1967 (the non-U.S. constituency had eclipsed the U.S. constituency in 1958). Menzies, *Anointed to Serve*, 402, 404. By December 2005 barely five percent of Assemblies of God members were in the United States (U.S. adherents, 2,830,861; foreign adherents, 51,886,816; worldwide constituency, 54,717,677), but the rationale for the military service article had not been amended. Sherri Doty of Springfield, Missouri, Assemblies of God Statistician, interview by author, 29 March 2000, by e-mail. http://world missions.ag.org/ downloads/PDF/CFH/agwm_current_facts_1_06.pdf (accessed February 1, 2007).

222. *General Council Minutes*, 1967, 35.

223. "Church Votes OK of Combat Service," *Independent Star-Telegram*, 28 August 1967. "Combat Doctrine Altered," *Independent Star-Telegram*, 29 August 1967.

224. John Howard Yoder, *Nevertheless: The Varieties and Shortcomings of Religious Pacifism* (Scottdale, Pa.: Herald Press, 1992).

225. "The Assemblies of God is unashamedly pro-life. . . . This stand is founded on the biblical truth that all human life is created in the image of God (Genesis 1:27)." "Pro-life" and the value of human life applied only to abortion, not to capital punishment or war for the Assemblies of God. *The Assemblies of God Perspectives: Contempoary Issues, Social, Medical, Political* (Springfield, Mo.: Gospel Publishing House, 1995), 3, 21-23, 28-29.

226. *General Council Minutes*, 1914, 1. *General Council Minutes*, 1999, 89.

227. James Daane, "Making Non-Pacifism Official," *Christianity Today*, 15 September 1967, 46. He also noted the respectability and size of the Assemblies of God, "The Assemblies belong to the National Association of Evangelicals, the Pentecostal Fellowship of North America, and the Pentecostal World Conference. . . . [They are a] fast-growing denomination whose U.S. membership is well over half a million, whose foreign membership is well over a million and a half, whose publishing house prints more than eleven tons of literature daily and whose denominational budget for the past two years was $29 million." Numerically and financially the Assemblies of God was quite impressive.

228. The Assemblies of God spent $450,000 on the production of *Reveille* and distributed up to six million copies per year. *General Council Minutes*, 1945, 81. Harry A. Jaeger, "Spiritual Conquest Among American Dougboys," *The Pentecostal Evangel*, 12 May 1945, 7. *Reveille* was "the only non-governmental religious publication given free postage to any theatre in the world." Kenyon, 350. The Servicemen's Department also sent 1.26 million personal letters to servicemen by October 1945. "Letters," *The Pentecostal Evangel*, 6 October 1945, 12.

229. See the bibliography for a complete listing.

230. Delbert S. Grant, "Leading Service Men to Christ," *The Pentecostal Evangel*, 11 July 1942, 10. "God Working in the Camps," *The Pentecostal Evangel*, 29 August 1942, 11. "Evangelizing Our Servicemen," *The Pentecostal Evangel*, 5 December 1942, 9. J. Paul Bruton, "Giving the Gospel to the Soldier," *The Pentecostal Evangel*, 20 March 1943, 5. Arthur Knowles, "Our Servicemen's Rally," *The Pentecostal Evangel*, 4 March 1944, 11. "Winning Men in the Desert Training Area," *The Pentecostal Evangel*, 29 April 1944, 7.

231. Harry A. Jaeger, "Spiritual Conquest Among American Doughboys," *The Pentecostal Evangel*, 12 May 1945, 5, 7.

232. "Helping the Service Men," *The Pentecostal Evangel*, 21 February 1942, 6.

233. Warren McPherson, "Missions and the Military," *The Pentecostal Evangel*, 7 July 1963, 8.

CHAPTER SEVEN

ACCOUNTABILITY, SENSIBILITY, AND RESPONSIBILITY: ASSEMBLIES OF GOD ATTITUDES TOWARD WAR AND NATION FROM 1968-2007

INTRODUCTION

Vietnam. The Soviet Union. Gulf War I. September 11, 2001. Afghanistan. Gulf War II. And more. From 1968-2007 and beyond, the American Assemblies of God continued to conform to the nationalistic values of dominant American society and consistently supported all the wars the U.S. fought. Combatant participation in warfare experienced its greatest support and praise during this time. During the 1970s, 1980s, and 1990s, an Assemblies of God veteran of Vietnam, Dave Roever, gained national and international recognition as a loyal American citizen who fought and was injured for liberty, democracy, and the American way. Ministry and support continued to be the primary ways that the General Council related to the military.

The years following 9-11 do not need their own chapter in this book, because even the intense patriotism and war fervor that swept the nation during this time was directly in line with what the Assemblies of God had already been saying and practicing. There had always existed at least a strand of conscientious objection, noncombatant service, or pacifism in *The Pentecostal Evangel*, but any such positive references disappeared altogether during the era covered in this chapter. Not a single question was raised that might hinder Christian service in the military.[1]

The objective of this chapter is threefold. First, to document and evaluate the growth and eventual supremacy of Americanism in the Assemblies of God. Second, the chapter reveals the widespread contemporary support for military action and combatant defense of American ideals by conscientious Pentecostals. Dave Roever, one of the more significant perpetuators of Pentecostal participation in warfare during the 1980s and 1990s, serves as an ideal example of the product of the post-World War II American Assemblies of God. Third, since the military chaplaincy contributed to the demise of pacifism, this chapter will chronicle and appraise briefly the emphasis placed on this ministry.

THE VICTORY OF NATIONALISM, 1968-2007

Marion Dearman published a study in 1974 showing that Pentecostals had become socialized to the dominant values of American society.[2] He noted the intense patriotism among the Pentecostals he interviewed.

> What is Caesar's and what is God's get fused together in the crucible of fundamentalist religion. At least this seems to be true for Pentecostals. People should be forced to salute and pledge allegiance to the flag, an informant told me, "because the Bible says that we should give unto Caesar what is Caesar's. . . ." Respect and allegiance toward the nation and obedience toward its laws are considered necessary for the Christian.[3]

This passionate national loyalty characterized the Assemblies of God during this period and is clearly seen in *The Pentecostal Evangel* and other denominational literature. Pictures of the American flag became commonplace and numerous articles promoted American pride as well as duty and fidelity to the nation. The Assemblies of God practiced civil religion like many other American denominations and had long since abandoned Stanley Frodsham's declaration, "National pride, like every other form of pride, is abomination in the sight of God."[4]

The close association of God and country is evident in a 1968 article with the all-capitalized and boldfaced title, "**I'M GLAD I'M AN**

AMERICAN." This article appeared two months after Dr. Martin
Luther King Jr. was assassinated (April 4, 1968) and three weeks after
Robert Kennedy was killed. The Viet Cong had carried out the Tet Offensive, students had taken over Columbia University in New York and
shut the school down for a week, and the Civil Rights Act of 1968 had
just passed. In this context a retired high school teacher conveyed his
hopes for a return to the old days when patriotism and Christian faith
went hand-in-hand. He lamented the separation of Christianity and
government and opposed the nonviolent direct actions of the civil rights
and antiwar movements.

> But then we had no demonstrators, no protestors, no sit-down
> strikes, no opposition to real education, *no objections to real patri-
> otism.* . . . Then came a few "professors" in each school . . . [who]
> were spreading socialism, communism, modernism, and infi-
> delity to many, many young minds. They taught us to be tolerant
> and broadminded toward everything—especially toward com-
> munism. . . . Leftwingers, socialists, liberalists, and agnostics have
> no kinship with the fine people who taught me patriotism and
> faith in God.[5]

This view of government during the Vietnam War manifested itself
in letters to the editors of *The Pentecostal Evangel* as well. The editors introduced just such a correspondence with the following words: "In these
days of draft-card burning, rebellion, and confusion, young men hardly
know where to turn."[6] Thankfully, they could provide an answer from
one of their readers.

> When the big cannon fires at headquarters and the national an-
> them is played and Old Glory comes down at the end of the day,
> one feels proud that he's training to help this country. Today I al-
> most cried as I watched the flag come down. You can't imagine
> the pride that swelled within me, just to think I'm a soldier. What
> we're training for isn't easy, but it's well worth it.[7]

The embarrassment surrounding the presidency of Richard Nixon
and the disapproval of Jimmy Carter probably contributed to the slight
decline of patriotic language during the 1970s.[8] Nevertheless, Thomas
Zimmerman, General Superintendent of the Assemblies of God from
1959-1985, provided his opinion when he praised the prayers and faith
of Americans and approved patriotism. He was concerned about im-

proving this great nation that belonged to "us."

> In 1787 prayer helped determine the future of our country in a significant way. . . . Both houses of Congress to this day begin their morning sessions with prayer. . . . We should all take inventory of our lives to discover whether we are obeying God's Word and making our country stronger. . . . We [are] told to pray for our country and to obey its laws.[9]

There was a resurgence of patriotic articles and nationalism in the 1980s, and this continued through the 1990s. Republican presidents probably helped generate this attitude among Assemblies of God constituents, who generally sided with the conservatives and voted Republican.[10] Patriotic articles tapered off after 1992, when Bill Clinton was elected.[11]

Nevertheless, the patriotism that came forth did so in an uncompromising manner. A chaplain praised two "Top Navy Men/Top Christians" for "proudly serving their Lord and their country in the U.S. Navy."[12] In 1982 the American and Christian flags were represented at equal heights along with an article entitled, "Banners of Faith."[13] Neither the editors nor the author considered the possible problem of serving under a plurality of banners. They proudly displayed the cross and the eagle at the top of the flagpoles.

Fidelity to America was rooted in the defense of freedom. Freedom, since it is "not free," demanded killing and anyone who served America in such a way deserved great honor. *The Pentecostal Evangel* praised the Americans who fought in the Revolutionary War and encouraged its readership to be grateful for them.

> Gallant citizens of Charleston on June 28, 1776, had fought the British at Fort Moultrie on Sullivan's Island. The pride of the British fleet was destroyed, and about 2,000 British troops were killed. . . . [Michael Christzberg] would fight for freedom [in the Revolutionary War] . . . and five generations and over 200 years later, one of his descendants is an Assemblies of God minister telling *Evangel* readers that almost forgotten story. . . . As we honor our military men this Sunday, let us remember them in our prayers and be thankful for their willingness to give their time and talents—and if necessary, their lives—for our defense and freedom.[14]

The movement of the Assemblies of God into mainstream American culture was continually evidenced in the way authors talked about America. "U.S. soldiers, sailors, airmen, and marines—totaling more than 2 million—serve as protection to our great nation and to world peace."[15] However, nationalism rarely stood alone; it was generally accompanied with a reference to the divine. An Assemblies of God chaplain praised soldiers with similar words a year later, "[you serve] around the world as *ambassadors of God and protectors of our great nation* through military services."[16] Good Christians should reenlist so "that they might serve both Uncle Sam and the unevangelized."[17]

They had difficulty separating God from country. A large picture of an American flag accompanied an article by Kenneth Barney that related some of the most zealous nationalism ever presented in *The Pentecostal Evangel* up to that time. He began with the following declaration. "I am an unashamed flag-waver. I have no time for those who bad-mouth our nation. My spine tingles and my eyes get damp when I sing 'The Star-Spangled Banner.'"[18] However, he claimed that his "intense patriotism" and "love for [his] country" did not blind him to the deterioration of America's "moral fabric."

He located this deterioration in drug addiction, abortion, divorce, and homosexuality, "Homosexuals were hiding in closets [when all was proper] instead of brazenly demanding rights."[19] He declared that the best time in American history was during World War II, when thousands of American youth were fighting. That was the ideal to which he wanted to return, because that was unity without "economic, social, and political dilemmas so complex no one can offer any real solutions."[20] He concluded his article about the "nation founded on Christian principles" by swearing one hundred percent allegiance. "America is too great a nation with too glorious a history to passively surrender its future to Satan. *I love my country with every fiber of my being*, and I long to see its terrible spiritual sickness healed by the great Physician."[21] One measured one's depth of loyalty to God by measuring one's loyalty to America. This was necessarily the case, because otherwise he had not a single thread of himself left with which to love God.

Appreciation for and satisfaction in American military strength did not need to be restrained. One Assemblies of God employee wrote, "Words cannot adequately express the pride I felt as I watched hundreds of highly trained troops parachuting from a military transport plane, the skill of engineers and technicians at work, the dedication during training, and many other activities."[22] Armed paratroopers elicited no thought of a conflict with Christianity. Instead Assemblies of God members could boast that "we who live in the United States are protected by the most powerful military force in the world."[23]

The Assemblies of God made a point to honor veterans as "people of valor. They have served in peace and in war and have sacrificed to *preserve the freedom of our beloved homeland.*"[24] This adored mother country provided the "cherished treasures of liberty and justice" so the Declaration of Independence and the Pledge of Allegiance received praise.[25]

One of the best portraits of the intensity of Assemblies of God patriotism came from a church in Louisiana. Each year since 1974 they have held an "I Love America Extravaganza." This celebration received national recognition and praise from *The Pentecostal Evangel* in 1990 and 1991. The first headline reiterated the duality of allegiance theme by quoting the pastor of Westbank Cathedral (Assembly of God), "'God-and-country days' vital to nation."[26] This featured article had a 3 x 5½ inch picture of the pastor speaking from a pulpit with an eagle clutching a flag shield on the front of it. There were also seven flags visible, bunting, and liberty bells. Pastor Radke explained the gala.

> After serving my country in World War II and after visiting 45 nations of the world, I can see how God has kept His hand upon our nation and how fortunate I am to be an American. . . . Our children deserve the same opportunity to grow up in a community and society that is patriotic and God-fearing like we had the privilege of doing. We feel a "God-and-country" day such as our extravaganza is very appropriate to pull the community together in appreciation for America and what our country means to each of us.[27]

The rally featured a fly over by "a squadron of F-15 fighter jets," "a team of parachutists," fireworks, the Fourth Marine Aircraft Wing Band playing "patriotic music," speeches by U.S. congressmen and other public officials, and two naturalized citizens telling "why they were glad to be American citizens."[28] This was one Assembly of God's contribution toward promoting Americanism and protecting the status quo. Their efforts were well received by the community and the Assemblies of God as a whole.

The entrance of America into Operation Desert Shield/Storm in 1990-91 provided yet another opportunity for the Assemblies of God to express their enthusiastic patriotism. The "us versus them" mentality prevailed in instructions about praying. "Pray that God will set a hedge of protection for all the *allied* military forces abroad. . . . Pray for the President, governmental officials, and the United Nations delegates. . . . Pray for wisdom in the Pentagon and in all armed forces officials [as they plan how to win the war]."[29] One page later another writer expressed her support for America by agreeing with President George H. W. Bush: "I felt his pride in our American troops and their successful military actions so far. I shared his concern that they know we stand behind them and fully support them as a country."[30]

One week later, March 24, 1991, a half-page-size picture of President Bush topped an article entitled, "It Is a Just War."[31] The content of this speech will be evaluated later, but the fact that it and an excerpt from his 1991 State of the Union address appeared in the pages of *The Pentecostal Evangel* shows the depth of allegiance the Assemblies of God gave to their president and to America. The State of the Union excerpt affirmed both liberty and obligation: "Let future generations understand the burden and blessings of freedom. Let them say, we stood where duty required us to stand. Let them know that together, we affirmed America, and the world, as a community of conscience."[32] Such affirmation of America continued in a variety of ways. Letters from soldiers were published. "I am willing to die for our country because it was founded by good Christian men and women. So don't ever feel I am the victim of the *government I love and serve.*"[33] Assemblies of God fighter pilots radioed their towers, "'God bless America.' That's how I feel about it."[34]

Following the Gulf War, the Assemblies of God constituents continued to express their patriotism in ways that revealed it was ingrained as an unquestionable tenet of their Christianity. Patriotism had become a part of the faith. The National Guard presented "the colors" at an Assembly of God church service.[35] A photographer who took a picture of veterans in an Assembly of God church unwittingly revealed the centrality and prominent place of honor enjoyed by the American flag (centered and elevated above the platform) and the subordinate position of the Christian flag (on the floor to the left of the platform).[36]

At the end of the twentieth century, an Assembly of God congregation in Iowa gloried in the fact that several Republican presidential candidates addressed their "Faith, Family, and Freedom Rally" as they cheered in support.[37] Although the Assemblies of God claims to be "apolitical," the constituency as a whole is very involved in sustaining Americanism.[38] This is demonstrated by the "Americanism Pledge" that faculty at Southwestern Assemblies of God University are supposed to sign.

> I herewith affirm my loyalty to, my devotion for, and my prayers in behalf of, the United States of America. Without political implication, but with the realization of the strategic position which is afforded me for the proper and professional *promotion of true Americanism*, I will unalterably oppose subversion in any form by both discussion and example. I will also attempt to instill within my students a sense of matured responsibility toward American citizenship by the interpretation of the Christian ethic as related to governmental power.[39]

The university did not define "Americanism" for the faculty, but simple definitions include "the belief that American values are the most ideal of cultural values or an attitude that gives special importance for the United States of America" and "allegiance to the United States and its customs and institutions."[40]

In Praise of the Military:
Combatant Participation in War, 1968 to 2007

Although the Assemblies of God manifested its willingness to fight during World War II, there still existed some reservations, be they ever so small. Any such reservations among the leadership and official publications disappeared completely following the 1967 change in the military service article. In fact, unreserved praise was given to almost anything that had to do with military service, especially combatant service, which defended America or her ideals. The Korean and Vietnam Wars had received widespread support, but the intense military language and symbolism of the 1970s, 1980s, 1990s, and early twenty-first century surpassed anything up to that point.[41] Combatant military service moved from being allowed and supported to being highly promoted as ideal, honorable, and what any "conscientious" Christian would do.[42] After the events of September 11, 2001, this high regard for military service only continued. The only four references to pacifism or conscientious objection during this period claimed that the former drove people to alcohol, resentment, and bitterness against the church,[43] while the latter was an "extreme"[44] "personal conviction."[45]

Support for Combat, 1968-1979

Assemblies of God Chaplain Stanford Linzey's nineteen-page pamphlet claimed that "'To serve or not to serve' is *not* the question. Our country has a draft which recruits men like you from communities and cities across the nation."[46] Linzey demanded that Pentecostals fight for their country.[47]

> Our democratic society has decided we need military defense for our own protection and common good. Freedom is not inherited. It is fought for and won by blood. . . . This is not only a duty or responsibility but a privilege and an honor for one to protect his loved ones and country. . . . [The communists] are militant. And likewise, we must be strong.[48]

Linzey argued that Christians in America must match the militancy of the communists in the USSR. He used his enemies' actions as a measure for himself and arrived quite naturally at defencism—if you want peace, prepare for war. He applied the sixth commandment to personal murder and mentioned Jesus only in the following context: "In the event of war (and Jesus said we would always have them), or in the event we are called into military service, we can maintain a clear conscience before God and do our duty to the nation as Christians."[49] Jesus only became the guide when something he said could be used to show that wars were regular occurrences. Since Jesus said there would be wars, we might as well arm ourselves and be ready to do our duty.

Linzey considered that the conscientious objector probably "hid under the cloak of religion because [he was] afraid."[50] He viewed conscientious objection as a personal issue that could not be recommended to anyone else. "[If you think] that participation is *wrong for you*" then you still have to "do your part somewhere in the effort" because "our religion ought to make us strong for the tasks we are expected to perform."[51] Linzey, with the blessing of the Assemblies of God, combined combatant military service and Pentecostalism into a cohesive patriotic whole.

The enthusiastic militarism of the Assemblies of God manifested it-self in an editorial in *The Pentecostal Evangel* just one month into the Viet Cong Tet Offensive during the Vietnam War in 1968. Richard Champion bemoaned "limited war against a ruthless enemy" and in-sisted that "this country should either go all-out to defeat the Commu-nists in Vietnam by whatever means are necessary, or else withdraw its forces."[52] He probably did not intend to quote Malcolm X's famous statement, "by any means necessary,"[53] but he did intend to demand "all-out" violence as the swiftest way to end the war, as long as Christians also prayed. "When will the Christians of America muster the same courage, the same determination, the same spirit of self-sacrifice that its sons are showing in the fight for a free Southeast Asia?"[54] He described the soldiers in glorious terms, positioned them as examples to be emu-lated, and linked spiritual and physical war as mutually dependent. In fact, he believed that Christians could control the length of the war by prayer: "God can change the situation in Vietnam and bring our boys home—but his hands are tied by the sins of his people, especially the sin of prayerlessness. . . . The more they would pray, the sooner the bloody conflict in Vietnam would end."[55] Prayer and escalated violence to-gether, both of which were the responsibility and duty of Christians, formed the best way to bring the conflict to a successful conclusion.

The Assemblies of God portrayed military service quite positively. Stories of Assemblies of God military personnel abounded, and the warnings were against skipping church and not witnessing. "The tragedy is that many Assemblies of God people come into the military and never get involved [in church activities]."[56] These Assemblies of God soldiers numbered 35,000 as of January 1970, and their denomi-nation was heavily involved in proudly "fueling the fires of homefront support."[57] "Assemblies of God airmen"[58] and other soldiers were viewed as missionaries who had to deal with the different moral codes of Vietnam. "Southeast Asia has posed a more difficult problem for our servicemen than even military combat. The outlook and moral values of these Buddhist people are much different from ours."[59] The author re-ferred to the stereotype of sexual laxity among the Vietnamese, "the Asian view of life," as posing a greater threat than fighting. His concern was not for the morality of combat but for the difficulty of abstaining from promiscuity. He thought it was much easier to kill someone and stay alive during a war than it was to avoid sexual immorality.

The Assemblies of God praised anyone who honored the Vietnam soldiers and proclaimed their dislike for anyone who did not support the war. An *Evangel* editorial quoted *The Reader's Digest* and agreed with its opinion.

> "Amid an unpopular and bloody war, our soldiers have often become Samaritans, engaged in those small, selfless acts of mercy that never seem to make the headlines." So reads the foreword of an article in *The Reader's Digest* for June. It is a welcome relief from the TV news and press reports that seem to discredit the young men serving in Vietnam more often that giving them the honor and support they well deserve.[60]

The Assemblies of God worked hard to give that honor and support that they felt the soldiers deserved by regularly mentioning their own. "Among the highest ranking officers known to be in captivity is an Assemblies of God layman, Air Force Colonel Robinson Risner, who was captured in September 1965."[61]

Almost every article about the military during the Vietnam War highlighted "Christian servicemen," "military Jesus people,"[62] "victorious Christians in the Armed Forces,"[63] and "Spirit-filled GIs."[64] These were the "best missionaries" and since "war and the whole military machine that supports it will be with us until the end" the Assemblies of God might as well use it to spread the gospel. The numerous references to the inevitability of war revealed that the Assemblies of God had accepted the violent nature of the world and no longer believed that they were supposed to provide an alternative. The executive director of Assemblies of God Foreign Missions considered that this was the way that God made "the wrath of man to praise Him. Out of the sufferings and sorrows of war He can bring blessing and honor to his name." Pentecostals participated in that which brought about the suffering and sorrow but they also helped bring about the blessing because they served "under two banners.[65]

The testimony of an Assemblies of God Army Captain gave insight into why a Christian should kill even though he was aware of the results.

> The piercing screams of young men whose bodies lay punctured and shattered behind my seat almost drowned out our jet-engine. . . . The putrid and sour stench of erupting abdominal

wounds, the overpowering aroma of gas gangrene, and the vile smell of cavities ripped open in wounded and dying. . . .[66]

These results could be attributed to the divine plan, because "there is no such thing as a bullet inscribed, 'To whom it may concern.' God alone determines the length of a man's days."[67] Shooting an enemy and then dressing his wounds made perfect sense, because the former act was for the divinely ordained government and the latter was done as a loving Christian. Soldiers just did their duty for their country and let God end people's lives when he wanted. However, the war also made the captain realize "just how wonderful a human life really is—even if it's an enemy's."[68]

Even after the conflict in Vietnam ended, the emphasis on "our Christians . . . wearing our country's uniforms" continued.[69] The duality of allegiance surfaced repeatedly in relation to military service. "A believer can and should be a good soldier when it comes to soldiering, and a good Christian when it comes to every other aspect of life. His marching will reflect the sergeant's cadence, but his walk will be directed by the voice of Another."[70] Not only did the Assemblies of God proudly serve under two banners, they also marched to two cadences, depending on which aspect of life they were living.

Colonel Risner, the famous Assemblies of God former prisoner of war, spoke at the Thirty-Fifth General Council in 1973 and elicited standing ovations for his intense patriotism and exemplary combat service. *The Pentecostal Evangel* printed his speech and the gospel Publishing House distributed his book.[71] Risner endured seven years and four months as a prisoner of war after being shot down over Vietnam. He told the General Council that he "was the proud commander of a proud fighting unit" and "a member of the United States Air Force, [and] of the strongest, most powerful, richest country in the world."[72] He praised the military men who did not betray their country even though tortured extensively and any "who gave his life fighting for what you and I believe in."[73] He concluded by affirming his faith and his vocation.

> I told you that I stand here knowing that God is real. I didn't come here because I *believe* He's real. I came here because I *know* He's real and because I have no choice. I go where God wants me to go. I'm still in the Air Force. I'm a career military officer.[74]

The General Council had no reservations about featuring a proud fighter pilot as their honored speaker, and an Assembly of God church in Bellevue, Nebraska, received praise for consisting of ninety percent Air Force personnel.[75]

Articles in *The Pentecostal Evangel* contained increasingly violent content and details about combat. Pictures of automatic weapons, hand grenades, military helicopters, F-16 jets, aircraft carriers, and armed soldiers also continued to increase and served as attention grabbing accompaniments to military articles.[76] One example portrayed three Viet Cong soldiers with AK-47s and hand grenades sneaking up on two American GIs carrying M-16s.[77] The article related the story of an Assemblies of God soldier in Vietnam who fought the enemy and prayed to God with a special Christian friend in his combat unit.

> My unit, the Fourth Special Forces Company (Para-Rescue), had been awakened late one night. . . . We were putting on our combat gear by instinct. . . . (Kenny began praying with me and guiding me. With his help I grew stronger spiritually and came closer to the Lord than I had ever been. . . .) The intensity of firepower was too great. It had to be North Vietnamese Regulars. We were 14 against 200. I didn't like the odds. . . . Out of the 14 in our group, two were dead and three were seriously wounded. That left nine of us able to fight. . . . We [Kenny and the author] knew each other well, not only as brothers in Christ, but as combat buddies. We were a team. . . . Then I saw him. It was a Vietnamese, and he was as scared as I was. Instinctively I jumped—everything became slow motion. I saw the grenade he tossed at me. Kenny was shooting, "dropping" the Vietnamese soldier. I was still in the air trying to get distance between me and the grenade.[78]

The intertwining of violent killing and Christianity was done so naturally that there was no concern about the morality of it. In fact, the author employed John 5:13 to show that Jesus himself complimented what they did, "Greater love hath no man that this, that a man lay down his life for his fiends."

Support for Combat, 1980-1989

The Armed Forces served as a place to show the world how Christians could excel because of their morality and dedication. In 1980 two Assemblies of God Navy officers received praise for "living the Christian life in the testing ground called the military."[79] They claimed that their Christianity did not hamper their ability to serve in the Navy but enhanced it and that the greatest "tension" as a Christian in the military related to moral failures such as swearing and adultery.

The Assemblies of God published plenty of evidence that they were comfortable with serving two masters. An ordained minister also worked in a Tactical Air Warfare Center for Electronic Warfare and Reconnaissance. He preached the gospel and calculated methods to employ to destroy America's enemies. The casual manner with which they presented this is best heard in their own words.

> Things have seemed to work out well for Chief Teas as far as combining his Air Force career and his ministry are concerned. . . . *Living his life under two masters, the Air Force and the Lord, hasn't been a problem.* In fact, the two have somehow found a way to blend together very well, often as a result of his hard work and devotion to both. . . . The man in blue is now, and will continue to be, a man of God's cloth.[80]

The years leading up to the Persian Gulf War of 1991 witnessed praise for Christian soldiers in the Revolutionary War,[81] special salutes to Vietnam veterans,[82] gratefulness for America's strong national defense,[83] boasting about Assemblies of God high school students heading to West Point,[84] and numerous testimonies about how violence and Christianity could work together. Occasionally an especially strongly worded article would appear. One such reflection related how an Assemblies of God man taught soldiers how to participate in "chemical, biological, and nuclear warfare."[85] Furthermore, "good soldiering in no way hinders his testimony for Jesus Christ; rather, it enhances his witness." The author thanked all the Assemblies of God men and women "diligently serving their country in uniform and fervently serving God as living witnesses . . . around the world as ambassadors of God and protectors of our great nation through the military services."[86]

In 1987 the special Military Personnel edition of *The Pentecostal Evangel* reiterated the unrestrained adoration the Assemblies of God had for the Armed Forces. It was dedicated to "military men and women who faithfully serve their country and Christ . . . [as] a strong missionary force."[87] The next page declared that "Our country's military personnel faithfully protect the freedom we enjoy."[88] A two-page article related the story of a Vietnam veteran who rejected Christianity for thirteen years because of an encounter with some non-Assemblies of God preaching.

> "I served my country and thought they would support my patriotism. Instead that morning the priest denounced soldiers who served in Vietnam as killers and murderers of women and children." Bill, the only soldier present, sat stunned. Unable to tolerate the tirade, he walked out, complaining under his breath, "If this is what Christianity is, then I don't need Christians."[89]

He eventually found an Assembly of God that accepted him and began serving the Lord while serving in the military. "God began burdening Bill about the prevalence of profanity, especially in staff meetings he attended. . . . This distressed his spirit." So Bill showed that he was a conscientious Christian by confronting the colonel: "I'm a Christian, and there are a number of Christians here who are upset because of the cursing and taking the Lord's name in vain."[90] The kind of Christianity that Bill learned from the Assemblies of God allowed him to approve killing but led him to disapprove vulgarity.

In 1988 Jesse Moon, an Assemblies of God professor and author, wrote a thirty-five page pamphlet entitled *War and the Christian*.[91] Although Moon recognized that pacifism reigned in Christianity for the first three centuries,[92] he nevertheless concluded that "the Christian Ethic of War is one of just war."[93] Moon listed ten reasons why Christians might choose to be nonviolent, but he refuted each one.[94] Instead, he provided seven reasons why the Christian should support the just war, none of which were distinctively Pentecostal. In fact, Moon never mentioned the pacifist heritage of the Assemblies of God.

Moon supported combatant participation because (1) the Old Testament showed that God approved warfare; (2) Romans 13 gave permission to governments (and therefore Christians) to engage in warfare; (3) Jesus cleansed the temple with violence; (4) there were Christian soldiers in the New Testament; (5) Jesus told his disciples to buy swords; (6) Reinhold Niebhur said war was the lesser of two evils; and (7) the fact of multiple relationships forced Christians to choose which ones were more important—and that meant defending your own kind.[95]

Moon dismissed the Sermon on the Mount because it needed to be interpreted by the Old Testament and did "not exhaustively treat social and personal responsibilities of the Christian today . . . one of which is the war question."[96] He decided that "love may resist and even use force for punitive reasons" and this allowed Christians to participate in warfare.[97] He even claimed that a Christian acted as a "minister of God" when "acting as an officer of the State" by killing the enemy and "quelling injustices."[98] This Assemblies of God minister and respected professor told his readers that they served God by fighting for their government and participating in the violence of a just war.

Recognition of the violence of war certainly did not negate Christian participation for Pentecostals. One Assemblies of God officer related his experience on the border between Czechoslovakia and West Germany.

> The soldiers I commanded were tasked with the defense and surveillance of a strip of land . . . [that was] a treacherous region, accented with barbed wire, cement bunkers, fields fertilized with mines, and at times, human blood. Beyond the next rise lay a division of Soviet tanks, soldiers, and aircraft.[99]

Another Assemblies of God officer led an "Attack Squadron" while serving aboard the *U.S.S. Enterprise*. The twenty thousand Assemblies of God members in the military in 1989 believed that "war and sacrifice were necessary to win [and preserve] the independence so boldly declared" by America's founders.[100]

Support for Combat, 1990-2007

The deployment of U.S. troops to the Middle East for Operation Desert Shield in 1990 provided another opportunity for the Assemblies of God to reveal their nearly unconditional support for American military action. During and immediately after the first Persian Gulf War, *The Pentecostal Evangel* expressed loyalty to all the military personnel and printed some very militaristic articles. By October 1990 about two percent of the U.S. troops in the Persian Gulf were Assemblies of God.[101] Another article showed an almost full-page picture of American combat jets flying over the desert.[102]

Since so many Assemblies of God ministers and laypeople were participating in combat, the churches in America devoted themselves to boosting morale by decorating their churches in red, white, and blue. They revealed their casual attitude toward killing and its necessary relationship to Christianity. "And while our deployed men are waging war with military machines, we are helping fight the battle by praying for those deployed and helping their families while they are away."[103]

The extent to which the Assemblies of God involved itself in military action was particularly evident in First Assembly in Goldsboro, North Carolina. The statements of the pastor and the author of the article revealed that killing for America and going to an Assembly of God church complemented each other well.

> [It] is a "military" church, and the Persian Gulf conflict has had a strong impact on it. Some 50 members are in Saudi Arabia. Many of them are frontline fighter pilots. . . . Because of concerns for the combat troops' safety, Painter chose not to name any of them. . . . Most of the 50 missing members are key workers in the church. . . . About 50 percent of the 800 people who attend First Assembly are military personnel. . . . First Assembly has become a rallying point in the community for support for the war in the gulf. Just recently there was a rally here which drew about 8,000 people in support of the war effort. Our church was a very active part of that. . . . The men and women in Saudi Arabia are the men and women who have built our country and our churches. The American servicemen are the finest in the world. . . . They are just as talented at . . . working in a Royal Rangers group [Assemblies of God boys club like Boy Scouts] as they are at flying an F-15. They are men full of God. You'd be delighted to know these men who are flying for your country. They are absolutely first-class Christians. . . . We have reason to be pleased that our Fellowship has produced such men.[104]

Fighter pilots served as role models for many Assemblies of God young men and women, and their combatant service received high praise. The church zealously encouraged the city to support the war. Any persuasion the church exhibited served in favor of defeating the Iraqis and building morale.

In a related article, the pastor of this church recommended military personnel as the ones *most* like the New Testament Christians.

> Painter said he has found service personnel a valuable asset to the congregation. . . . He emphasized that God's method in the Early Church was "transitional" people who would move around and carry the gospel to new regions. "The military person is ideal for

this," he said. "He is a transitional person, frequently on the move."[105]

Ironically, he now employed the New Testament in a restorationist manner to prove the opposite of what many early Pentecostals had believed. Whereas the early Pentecostals had imitated the early church's nonviolence, the Assemblies of God of the 1990s felt more comfortable imitating their geographically transient nature.

Although the Assemblies of God had not devoted much effort to evaluating the just war tradition, *The Pentecostal Evangel* printed two of President George H. W. Bush's speeches that named the Gulf War a just war. Although no Assemblies of God person wrote the speeches, they did devote three pages to Bush's defense of the war, and they provided no alternative position. The statements that Bush made contradicted neither that which already appeared in *The Pentecostal Evangel* nor the general attitude of the Assemblies of God.

> It's the regime of Saddam Hussein against the rest of the world. Saddam tried to cast this conflict as a religious war. But it has nothing to do with religion per se. It has, on the other hand, everything to do with what religion embodies—good versus evil, right versus wrong, human dignity and freedom versus tyranny and oppression. The war in the Gulf is not a Christian war, a Jewish war, or a Moslem war—it is a just war.[106]

The editors also decided to print a small portion of Bush's State of the Union Address, part of which read, "If we fight in anger, it is only because we have to fight at all."[107]

Assemblies of God soldiers knew that they would have to kill, but they resolutely accepted that fact as a necessary element of their Christianity. "I don't regret joining the military. It has been a good career, though some may say that I earn my living by the death of others. And yet I am reminded, and now remind you, history has shown that, as long as Christ tarries, evil men will invest their lives in reigning over the weak."[108] An Assemblies of God pilot expressed the exhilaration of combat and the way God helped him fight.

> "I carried a small Bible in a pocket of my G-suit," the F15-E fighter pilot said. . . . "Your faith in God rises up during combat missions more than you'll ever know . . . it was exciting over there." Once the air war began [he] was led into battle over Iraq

the first night of the war. . . . "We hit a lot of munitions targets . . . once they decided to go after Scud missiles, we were given the task of 'Scud-busting.' We also did a lot of tank attacks later in the war. The night capability of the plane is just fantastic."[109]

Since this Pentecostal pilot thought that military combat was "exciting" and "fantastic," his answer to a question about serving God and going to battle was not surprising. "I think of it as a job that had to be done and I feel I would rather have godly men leading us to war than those who don't believe in Him."[110] This was amazing evidence of the Constantinian shift within the Assemblies of God—from no Christians in the military to preferably only Christians in the military. The Assemblies of God constituency summed up the Gulf War as follows.

> January 1991—war! And though news reports indicated things were going better than expected, we were still concerned. Those were our husbands, wives, fathers, mothers, sons, daughters, brothers, sisters, and friends fighting for the freedom of a country invaded by another. . . . Finally victory came. . . . We proudly and thankfully say, "Welcome home!"[111]

Nevertheless, facing the reality of killing prompted one woman to encourage church members to help the six thousand[112] returning Assemblies of God military personnel. "Be open to listen if they want to share feelings of guilt at causing another's suffering or their grief at losing a dear friend. Avoid voicing your apprehension about how the war may have changed them."[113]

This same issue contained the results of a Gallup Poll that indicated, "Three-fourths of the American public believes the Persian Gulf War was 'just,' but less than half believes the war met all six criteria for formally defining a 'just war.'"[114] Based on the manner in which the Assemblies of God treated the war, there was probably a higher percentage of Assemblies of God constituents who considered it a just war than the general public. One hundred percent of the articles dealing with the war were in favor of it; no voice against the war ever appeared. The Assemblies of God at this time was evidently more militant than America.

During the decade of the 1990s, the Assemblies of God continued to be militaristic, and the popular literature reflected their support of violence with both pictures and articles. However, they also began to deal with the topic of homosexuality in the military. As members of the National Association of Evangelicals, they reprinted and supported its statement in favor of banning homosexuals from the military. For this position they referred to Scripture (three references from the Old Testament and five from the New Testament). They expressed their convictions to President Bill Clinton with the following declaration:

> Because of our strong commitment to biblical truth, we state our unequivocal opposition to lifting the current ban. We believe that such presidential action would defy the moral law of God and the standard of natural law, subvert military law, and also undermine the integrity of the armed forces of the United States of America.[115]

One month later, they praised the Officers' Christian Fellowship for supporting the ban against homosexuals. Their letter to General Colin Powell, chairman of the Joint Chiefs of Staff, expressed their principles.

> Our rejection of homosexuality is based on an understanding of God's revealed truth in the Bible. . . . The current policy is both logical and sound and should be continued. . . . We pledge our support to you as you seek to maintain the highest moral standards within our Armed Forces.[116]

By this time killing was not an issue, but many struggled with "whether they should resign from the military if the ban on homosexuals is lifted." Morality, God, and the Bible were chief concerns, "We should pray that God will give elected officials wisdom and courage to lead our nation in ways that conform to His moral law. But we should stand fast as His servants of love and truth."[117] After having abandoned their own Bible-based peace witness, the Assemblies of God believed they had the prophetic voice to speak out and be heard on this issue. But how they quoted the Bible changed dramatically in eighty years—from "Scripture tells us not to kill" to "Scripture says gay people will hurt our ability to kill as effectively as we need to."

The rest of the 1990s contained stories of "our military might," "fighter cover,"[118] "military honor guards" and "21-gun salutes" in Assembly of God churches,[119] and testimonies of American soldiers being saved by God while killing some of their Somali "enemies."[120] When others critiqued the military verbally or in print the Assemblies of God quickly defended it.

The military is receiving some bad press. The focus has been on Tailhook, downsizing, and the possibility of homosexuals being permitted in the military. Despite these problems, the military has many high-ranking men and women of honor and dignity. Many are committed Christians.[121]

Thirty years after the article change in 1967, the Assemblies of God finally provided a rationale for their position regarding combatant military service. It appeared in a pamphlet and in *The Pentecostal Evangel*. By 1997 the majority of the laity, clergy, and leadership had forgotten that they even had a heritage of pacifism.[122] In fact, the director of the Assemblies of God Chaplains Department, Charles Marvin, shared with me, "I'm on the adjunct faculty at AGTS [Assemblies of God Theological Seminary] and teach the class offered to those planning to become chaplains. Your work is therefore of interest to me; I wasn't aware, for instance, that in 1917 the AG took an absolute pacifist position." Since some Assemblies of God scholars had begun to write about pacifism in the early Assemblies of God, perhaps their writings provoked the need for an explanation in 1997. Nevertheless, this explanation only supported what had already become obvious.

> As a Movement we affirm our loyalty to the government of the United States in war or peace. We shall continue to insist, as we have historically, on the right of each member to choose for himself whether to declare his position as a combatant (one who willingly serves in positions of violence), a noncombatant (one who serves only in nonviolent ways), or a conscientious objector (one who refuses to participate in any form of military service because of personal convictions regarding war).[123]

Their elaboration on each of the three positions reveals that the first option allowed "violence" and the last option was "personal." They then explained why they preferred the first choice for the Assemblies of God.

> The implications of the above statement are clear. The Assemblies of God is committed to a position of loyalty to the government. Second, *that loyalty is not imperiled by the presence of war*. And, third, all members are encouraged to exercise their *personal convictions* in how they will respond during times of war.[124]

Violence and killing for one's nation did not prohibit fidelity to one's nation, because violence was a disputable matter about which each individual could decide for himself or herself. This is by default a pro-combatant position. Affirming the option of violence in war automatically grants approval. In response to possible questions, the authors continued,

> What are the biblical principles which support this position? 1. The Scriptures call for civic loyalty: "Everyone must submit himself to the governing authorities, for there is no authority except that which God has established" (Rom. 13:1, NIV). 2. On occasion, those *authorities must bear arms*: "He does not bear the sword for nothing. He is God's servant, an agent of wrath to bring punishment on the wrongdoer" (Rom. 13:4). 3. The *Scriptures call for the employment of personal conscience in all matters*: "Each of us will give an account of himself to God" (Rom. 14:12).[125]

The first and second rationales revealed that the Assemblies of God was part of the establishment and had to defend it. The third scriptural rationale is remarkable, because it would apply to few other ethical issues that the Assemblies of God addressed. This is so even though they used the far-reaching adjective "all." The Assemblies of God published statements against any consumption of alcohol (under the title "Abstinence"),[126] against abortion, against lotteries and gambling, against pornography, against suicide, and against euthanasia. Each of these allowed no room for "conscience" but was presented as clearly wrong according to the Scriptures. Capital punishment was the only other ethical issue where disagreement was allowed. "There is room in the church for honest differences of opinion concerning the use of capital punishment."[127]

The authors then addressed Exodus 20:13, the Scripture they considered might be used against combatant participation in warfare. Again, the representatives of the Assemblies of God neglected to address the example and teachings of Jesus as presented in the Gospels. Instead, they interpreted the sixth commandment as referring to murder and explained other situations that required killing.

> The Hebrew word used here (*raisach*) in the ancient manuscripts is descriptive of willful and personal vengeance. While the outcome may be similar to the killings of war, the motive and driving force are quite different. The language of Exodus 20:13 does not suggest that we are to disallow participation in war, even if that

participation involves killing. The preservation of peace and tranquility sometimes makes this response imperative.[128]

When the Assemblies of God in the 1990s needed to know what to do about war, they looked to the Hebrew Scriptures and the first few verses of Romans 13. They also decided that peace and tranquility, which were rather vague and undefined terms, necessitated violence. However, they did not provide a scriptural rationale for that position. While claiming to hate war, the Assemblies of God officially supported it and promoted it whenever they felt it was necessary, because only the return of Jesus would bring peace.

> The Assemblies of God as a Movement deplores war. Therefore, we are committed to its avoidance as much as accountability, sensibility, and responsibility allow. This will be the necessary posture, until the Prince of Peace—Jesus Christ—establishes His reign over a world that is now characterized by violence, wickedness, and war.[129]

This is a significant statement. First, it meant that Jesus Christ had not established his reign of peace over their lives or their church. They would submit only when the entire world submitted; as long as the world kills, so should the church. Second, it meant that not only the world but also the Assemblies of God was characterized by violence, wickedness, and war, since they approved all of it when it made good sense. That which they say they despised they condoned and performed. The U.S. government could argue for wars using responsible and sensible language, and since Jesus is not back yet, Pentecostals would join right in the fighting.

Their failure to live according to the terms of their eschatology (there will be peace in the end) showed their rejection of the idea that the rule of the Prince of Peace had broken into the present, a common peace church perspective. In other words, one could fully follow the Messiah only in his bodily presence. Although it is a common Christian profession that the church is the body—flesh and blood—of Jesus on earth in the present, the Assemblies of God ceased to see this as a reason not to kill people. This entire article received the endorsement, "the above statement is based upon our common understanding of scriptural teaching."[130]

A survey of American Assemblies of God ministers conducted in April 2001 revealed that ninety-three percent agreed with the statement,

"It is appropriate for a Christian to support war." Sixty-five percent of these pastors agreed that "The principles of Jesus support war." Even more, a significant seventy-one percent, said that they themselves "would kill in a war." These were not Pentecostal lay people who supported war and would kill; these were the pastors of the Assemblies of God churches in America five months before September 11, 2001.[131]

After the tragic and morally unjustifiable attacks on September 11, sympathy for Americans swept the world and patriotism swept the country. The Assemblies of God, like most other American Christians, supported the war in Afghanistan that followed. Since then they have continued to back President Bush's military policies, including the 2003 invasion of Iraq by the United States and the subsequent years of war. Martin Ceadel defines crusading as a first-strike preemptive war against another country to establish peace and justice, and Gulf War II certainly qualifies as such, for President George W. Bush himself called it a first-strike preemptive war.

Iraq was already experiencing the longest bombing campaign in U.S. and U.K. history—1991-2003. The U.S. military conducted daily flyovers of the no-fly zones in the north and south of Iraq and frequently targeted sites. The Pentagon admitted that 280,000 sorties were flown in the decade after 1991; 24,000 combat missions were flown over the southern no-fly zone alone between 1998 and 2000. Over a million pounds of high-tech bombs were dropped on 400 targets in 1999.[132] And the U.S. and U.K. heavily bombed Baghdad in September 2002; this was a month before Congress gave authority to use force, two months before the U.N. brought the matter to a vote, and six months before the war officially began. Assemblies of God support for the post 9-11 wars at least matched their support for the Vietnam War, the Cold War, and Gulf War I.

Although much denominational literature could be cited to show this, it will be sufficient to quote part of a resolution passed by Southwestern Assemblies of God University's board of regents in response to faculty members signing a Pentecostal letter to President Bush asking him not to invade Iraq in March 2003. They unanimously agreed to "express concern regarding any faculty member taking a public stand in opposition to the war situation currently facing America."[133]

DAVE ROEVER

The support for combat by the Assemblies of God is exemplified by the writing and speaking of Dave Roever. When I was a young man, I loved hearing Dave Roever speak and thoroughly enjoyed playing war. We owned all of Dave's videos and books and watched him regularly because he is so funny and inspiring; I remember many of his jokes, and they still make me smile. "I get up every morning and run around the block. Then I slide it back under the bed and crawl back in." Dave went to Southwestern Assemblies of God University with my parents in the 1960s; I went there too. When I was teaching at Southwestern in 1995, I had Dave Roever as a student in a couple of classes, since he was finishing the degree he had put on hold because of the Vietnam War. We chatted a few times, and I was as impressed with him in person as I always had been from afar. He is the embodiment of an American Pentecostal war hero.

Dave Roever was injured terribly, almost fatally, while fighting in Vietnam. Since his recovery he has addressed over six million high school students, thousands of churches, and the General Council of the Assemblies of God in full session. He has written three books that tell his story, collaborated in twenty videos, and made a movie about his life with World Wide Pictures.[134] As of this writing, he still holds over one hundred meetings per year in which he primarily tells his story and preaches. He has told his life story thousands of times to millions of people and always does so in a hopeful, encouraging, and humorous way as an ordained Assemblies of God minister who proudly served his country in Vietnam. Probably the majority of the 2.5 million Assemblies of God people in the United States know Dave Roever's story and greatly admire him.

Roever grew up in an Assemblies of God pastor's home in Texas. When he was only a child, he believed that God had called him to the ministry. He attended Southwestern to pursue that calling. The armed forces drafted him because of poor grades.[135] As a product of the 1960s Assemblies of God, his response to the draft was typical, but the language he used to relate it was ironic.

> My immediate reaction was to apply for a ministerial exemption. All I had to do was pick up the phone, call the district Superintendent of the Assemblies of God, and say, "Rev. Anderson, I need an exemption letter for my draft board...." But—and that's the biggest "but" of my life—*my conscience got hold of me.*[136]

Roever continued to experience the prodding of his conscience. He had a dream that he wandered among the wounded and dying in Vietnam while a voice kept saying, "Why not me?" and "Why isn't that me?" He evaluated it as follows.

> I'm sure it was my conscience saying to me, *Why weren't you among those killed in the DMZ? What gives you the right to be sleeping in this bed with your wife in your arms, living in a comfortable house, while those guys are out suffering and dying for your liberty?* I felt responsible for those guys.[137]

This call to fight for America outweighed his call to pursue the ministry at Southwestern, so after a sleepless night he decided, "I couldn't ignore the voice of my conscience. I'm not sure how long I lay there in bed, but I finally looked at Brenda, woke her up, and said, 'I'm going into the military. . . . Am I a minister? I'm hoping to be one, but I'm not one yet.'"[138]

As a thoroughly Assemblies of God man of the 1960s, Roever's conscience led him toward the military rather than away from it. He joined the Navy because he thought that would help him avoid Vietnam, "I had no desire to hurt anybody . . . I wanted to perform my duty to my country, but I did not want to go to Vietnam."[139] He could have been a medic or a noncombatant if that had been presented to him as a viable option. Instead, he underwent basic training plus sixteen weeks of missile training and twelve weeks of river patrol training.[140]

Roever devoted much of his book to discussing his combat training, providing details about all the weapons he used, and describing his attitude.

> *I've got to fight back or I'm going to die.* . . . By the time I got to Vietnam the sound of gunfire was so common to me, those flashes in the dark so familiar, that when I finally heard the real thing, I never once felt like ducking and running. My only thought was that I had two seconds. If I didn't return fire in two seconds they would be on target and I was dead. But the instant I started returning fire, they had the same problem as I did.[141]

His prisoner of war training taught him to hate the North Vietnamese and practically idolize America. He related the events following their liberation from their practice POW camp.

The North Vietnamese flag flying over that place came down fast. When the GIs pulled the flag down, we attacked it. We shredded that flag until there was nothing left but threads. Then they raised the American flag and a bugler started playing, "Battle Hymn of the Republic." I bawled, I was so happy. We all cried and hollered and hugged each other. It was over. We had succeeded. Oh man, what a feeling. It made me love America as I had never loved America before.[142]

Roever reflected the perspective that the moral problems related to war were primarily sexual. "The *real* war was fought in the bars and brothels of Saigon because it was there that many men sold their souls. Saigon was in a war zone alright: the war zone of the soul."[143] He worked on river patrol, so he engaged in many fire fights and combat situations. He slept with his weapon and made himself an extra one by shortening an M-1 so that he could maneuver it in cramped spaces. He knew that he killed people but accepted that it was necessary.

We pounded those banks like you wouldn't believe. . . . In a fire-fight like that, you don't see people, you just see the tracer bullets from the automatic weapons, and you fire back at the source of that tracer. You go for it, man, and you just pump your own tracers in there. You just keep pumping; and all the while you're begging, *Please, God, don't let them take my head off.* You pump for everything you're worth, because the more you fire, the more they duck into their trenches. . . . You just keep circling until it's over or you're out of ammunition. Most everybody screams and hollers, exploding with tremendous rage.[144]

Roever tried to stay sensitive, "One question always haunted me: Did I kill that guy in the bunker? The one who must have been running away because he got it in the back? Did I kill any of the dead?"[145]

Although Roever participated in combat, his morality did not allow him to take drugs, drink alcohol, or be promiscuous. But he recognized the relationship between killing and substance abuse.

My values didn't allow me the luxury of anesthetizing the pain. I went straight to my bunk, put my face in my pillow and cried and cried and cried. I kept saying, "For God and country, for God and country, for God and country. . . ." But that was the last time I cried. I became callous, too.[146]

This hardening may have contributed to the way he told the story of one of his close encounters with a hand grenade. "The sucker that had thrown that thing had missed from only a few feet away. Incredible. I unloaded at the bank of that river. I probably dumped a thousand rounds on that sucker. I knew he was in there and that made me mad. Here I was just minding my own business, and he almost killed me."[147]

Roever's Christianity allowed him to recognize that "hatred for the enemy could really bring out the evil in a man's soul" and that "too many of our fellows let the war silence their consciences" but that did not negate the fact that war was necessary.[148] While Roever served in Vietnam, he consistently preached to his crewmates. He believed that he pricked their consciences by expounding on biblical passages about sin, repentance, forgiveness, and "a changed life."[149]

He did not get any responses, and he probably never thought that it might be because his participation in warfare negated his claims of morality. Killing but not drinking may not have come across as an entirely consistent message. Roever himself finally felt like he disappointed God only when he eventually consumed some alcohol, "With my drunkenness, however, came the feeling of betraying my Lord—just like Judas."[150] His conscience told him war was acceptable but drinking was not. In fact, while in Vietnam, Roever received his credentials with the Assemblies of God. He believed God told him, "I don't like what you did [drinking], but I forgive you; now get on with your life [war and preaching]."[151]

The life that he continued, as a credentialed minister, involved callously destroying an old tomb,[152] calling in air strikes to decimate the enemy,[153] and wanting to "drop the bomb" and "exterminate all the brutes" in Vietnam.[154] But then he suffered the injury that changed his life forever. A phosphorous grenade he was holding exploded six inches from his head and melted the flesh off his face. He lost his right eye, right ear, and the use of most of his right hand. He spent fourteen months in hospitalization and was expected to die.[155] His recovery, humor, storytelling abilities, and zeal to preach opened the many doors to ministry that he enjoyed during the last thirty-five years. As he told his story of pain, despair, and hope in God he always related his love for his country and the necessity of warfare. The millions to whom he spoke always heard him share his famous analysis.

I hate war. I hate the pain. I don't like disfigurement. I hate war. It rapes. It plunders. It disfigures. It dismembers. It destroys. But, I also want you to know—I love freedom. My love of liberty is the most compelling force in my life both physically and spiritually. So what I'm going to say comes from my heart, and nobody needs to agree with me. It's America, and you have the right to disagree. . . . One of the reasons I went to Vietnam is to preserve your right to disagree with everything I stand for. . . . I believe in one nation under God . . . and as a Vietnam veteran I'm proud of my scars and stripes. I'm proud I served my country, and I am proud to be an American. And contrary to some people's pathetic opinion of what our job as military men in Vietnam was, I wasn't sent over there to kill anybody. I was sent there to stop the killing of the innocent people of South Vietnam and I'm glad to tell you, this man and many others like me served with an awful lot of pride to do our job to protect and prevent the further devastation of a free people.[156]

Dave Roever was one of the most sought-after speakers in the Assemblies of God in the 1980s and 1990s. He commanded the respect of the entire movement and addressed the General Council in 1985. At no time did he reveal that he ever contemplated the possibility that he should not have fought for his country because of his Christianity or Pentecostalism. He communicated this to the millions in his audiences by promoting an intense patriotism that demanded the despair of war. The Assemblies of God had journeyed from strongly discouraging combatant participation to hailing a combatant as one of their finest ministers.[157] In fact, he said that he knew of no Assemblies of God conscientious objectors, that nobody in the Assemblies of God had ever expressed concern about his patriotism or support for the military, and that "most, if not all" people in the Assemblies of God supported "war efforts abroad."

MINISTRY TO THE MILITARY AFTER 1968

Since 1968 the Assemblies of God has continued to channel resources into evangelizing the unbelievers and encouraging the Christians in the military. By the end of 1969 there were forty-five fulltime Assemblies of God military chaplains. The number has increased to more than three hundred.[158] *The Pentecostal Evangel* regularly printed a story whenever a new chaplain received his or her commission.[159] The

Assemblies of God devoted the first Sunday of each July to an annual Servicemen's Day, and *The Pentecostal Evangel* published a variety of articles about ministering to these "most effective missionaries [who] wear military uniforms."[160]

The missions-oriented nature of the Assemblies of God allowed them to constantly view the military as "a whitened harvest field with far too few workers."[161] This denomination, which usually did not emphasize officially joining the church, issued a call for membership because of the chaplaincy situation.

> If you attend an Assemblies of God church and have not become a member, you may be denying your sons and others in the military the blessing of a full-gospel ministry. . . . Quotas for military chaplains are based on denominational membership. . . . "Major denominations' membership is sometimes twice or three times the number of those who actually attend the churches . . . and therefore their quota for chaplains is high." On the other hand, in many of the Assemblies of God churches "only one-third to one-half of the total 'attenders' actually are members. Therefore, our quota is low."[162]

The Assemblies of God increased their number of chaplains because of four factors. First, they approved of combatant military service. Second, they considered the military to be "one of the largest mission fields"[163] and "a vast mission field."[164] Third, they founded the Assemblies of God Theological Seminary in 1973 primarily to grant the Master of Divinity degree (a prerequisite to becoming a military chaplain).[165] Fourth, the Assemblies of God led "all evangelical churches in membership gained during the [1970s], with an increase of 62 percent."[166]

This "vast" military mission field consisted of about 2.1 million persons in 1990.[167] Only half of that number had any religious affiliation.[168] This relatively small number of people, less than the population of Houston, Texas, commanded the attention of dozens of articles, millions of dollars, hundreds of personnel, and possibly the forfeiture of an important theological and ethical doctrine and practice of early Pentecostalism.[169]

The increase in military chaplaincy is inversely proportional to the decrease in a concern for a Pentecostal peace witness. It is proportional to the increase in militaristic civil religion and Americanism. Military ministry is important, but its value should be weighed against what had to be sacrificed to make it successful. Evaluated from the perspective of an early Pentecostal pacifist, the unquestionable support of the military and the blessing it receives from the Assemblies of God would be considered unfortunate, to say the least.

SUMMARY

After 1968 the Assemblies of God toughened into a pro-military and pro-American denomination that allowed little room for the conscientious objector. They protected their status as an established and respected church by encouraging ministry to and support for the military. They also argued consistently and with good intentions against those who might recommend conscientious objection.

NOTES

1. I was born in 1972 and reared in the Assemblies of God and could not even fathom the thought of a Christian being opposed to killing for America.

2. Marion Dearman, "Christ and Conformity: A Study of Pentecostal Values," *Journal for the Scientific Study of Religion*, 1974: 437-453. Although Dearman studied members of the United Pentecostal Church in particular he believed that his conclusions could be applied to the American Pentecostal movement in general. The evidence within this chapter regarding the Assemblies of God supports Dearman's claim.

3. Ibid., 446.

4. Stanley H. Frodsham, "Our Heavenly Citizenship," *The Weekly Evangel*, 11 September 1915, 3. Also, "God's people must all get to this place, where national prejudices must die and where the glory of the Lord only will be sought." J. Roswell Flower, "What Will the Harvest Be? Article in Last Week's *Evangel* Receiving Just Criticism," *The Weekly Evangel*, 14 August 1915, 2.

5. Floyd J. Highfill, "I'm Glad I'm An American," *The Pentecostal Evangel*, 30 June 1968, 23.

6. "Proud of His Country," *The Pentecostal Evangel*, 10 November 1968, 28.

7. Ibid. The son of an Assemblies of God pastor wrote this.

8. I remember singing the following childish tune in elementary school during the Carter administration, "Our president has a first name, it's J-I-M-M-Y. Our president has a second name, it's C-A-R-T-E-R. I hate to say it everyday and if you ask me why I'll say, 'Cause Jimmy Carter has a way of messing up the USA.'"

9. Thomas F. Zimmerman, "The Christian and His Country," *The Pentecostal Evangel*, 29 June 1975, 6.

10. Edith L. Blumhofer, *The Assemblies of God*, vol. 2 (Springfield, Mo.: Gospel Publishing House, 1989), 179.

11. I found only one article from the 1970s that specifically promoted loyalty to government. There were ten articles in the 1980s and six from 1990-1992. Only three occurred between 1993 and 1999.

12. Charles W. Marvin, "Top Navy Men/Top Christians," *The Pentecostal Evangel*, 22 June 1980, 13.

13. Ernie Lawrence, "Banners of Faith," *The Pentecostal Evangel*, 7 March 1982, 7. The editors described Lawrence as "a retired Air Force master sergeant and former Air Force Public Affairs superintendent."

14. Calvin M. Durham, "He Fought For Freedom," *The Pentecostal Evangel*, 4 July 1982, 5.

15. "Military Ministries," *The Pentecostal Evangel*, 23 October 1983, S-14. Darwin Evans, "A Tribute to Lay-Soldiers," *The Pentecostal Evangel*, 4 August 1985, 25. Emphasis added.

16. Darwin Evans, "A Tribute to Lay-Soldiers," *The Pentecostal Evangel*, 4 August 1985, 25. Emphasis added.

17. Ruby Enyart, "Continued Victory in Retreat," 26 June 1988, 17. Soldiers encouraged other soldiers, "I urge Christians assigned to military service to work for the Lord, while you serve your country." Martin A. Hoffman, "To Christians in Military Service," *The Pentecostal Evangel*, 9 November 1997, 22.

18. Kenneth D. Barney, "God, Save America," *The Pentecostal Evangel*, 29 June 1986, 4. Barney served as the adult editor of the Church School Literature Department for the Assemblies of God.

19. Ibid., 5.

20. Ibid.

21. Ibid. Emphasis added.

22. James P. Allen, "The Greater Power," *The Pentecostal Evangel*, 29 June 1986, 8.

23. Ibid.

24. Roger D. Wolff, "Serving Our Nation's Veterans," *The Pentecostal Evangel*, 8 November 1987, 17. Emphasis added.

25. Lemuel D. McElyea, "Who Upholds America's Treasures?" *The Pentecostal Evangel*, 25 June 1989, 10.

26. "Church's 'I Love America Extravaganza' Draws 5,000 to Stadium," *The Pentecostal Evangel*, 1 July 1990, 12.

27. Ibid.

28. Ibid.

29. Larry Bryan, "How to Pray About the Gulf War," *The Pentecostal Evangel*, 17 March 1991, 6. Emphasis added. Bryan's last item for prayer was "the Iraqi people" but he provided no elaboration about the nature of that prayer other than citing Matthew 5.44, "But I say to you, love your enemies. . . ." So he viewed the Iraqi people as enemies.

30. Jodi Detrick, "What Does It Mean?" *The Pentecostal Evangel*, 17 March 1991, 7. Detrick was more concerned about Bush's comments regarding a "new

world order" and a possible one-world government than about the ethics of war, and she made no connection between the new world order and the war in Iraq.

31. George H.W. Bush, "It is a Just War," *The Pentecostal Evangel*, 24 March 1991, 10.

32. George H.W. Bush, "We Stood Where Duty Required," *The Pentecostal Evangel*, 24 March 1991, 11.

33. "Love Letters From a Soldier," *The Pentecostal Evangel*, 7 April 1991, 6. Emphasis added.

34. "Faith in God, Word of God Were Strength In Battle, Fighter Pilot Says," *The Pentecostal Evangel*, 30 June 1991, 14.

35. Janice Moore, "The Price of Freedom," *The Pentecostal Evangel*, 13 November 1994, 20.

36. Ibid. There were actually seven American flags in these pictures and only one Christian flag.

37. Alan Keyes, Gary Bauer, and Steve Forbes attended. David Yepsen and Jeff Zeleny, "Republicans Court Abortion Foes," *The Des Moines Register*, 23 January 2000, 1.

38. *Assemblies of God Perspectives—Contemporary Issues: Social, Medical, and Political*, 26. The 1997 statement on military service is evaluated later in this chapter.

39. *Southwestern Assemblies of God University Institutional Policy Manual* (Waxahachie, Tex.: Southwestern Assemblies of God University, 1999), 127. Emphasis added. It should be noted that the university did not enforce the signing of this pledge until late fall of 2001. Since I was faculty at the time, I wrote "as appropriate" at the end and signed it.

40. Americanism, www.wikipedia.org, accessed December 1, 2006. *The American Heritage Dictionary of the English Language*, 4th. ed. (Boston, Mass.: Houghton Mifflin, 2003). Also see David Gelernter, *Americanism: The Fourth Great Western Religion* (New York: Doubleday, 2007).

41. Although over seventy articles were published during this period that strongly supported combatant participation in warfare, only the most salient will be examined.

42. See the section on Dave Roever in this chapter.

43. Robert R. Way, "A Soldier's Concern Prompted . . . The Colonel's New Order," *The Pentecostal Evangel*, 28 June 1987, 12.

44. John Maempa, "War and Peace," *The Pentecostal Evangel*, 3 December 1995, 5.

45. Stanford Linzey, *Filling Your Boots* (Springfield, Mo.: Gospel Publishing House, 1968), 8. Although there is no date on the book itself I confirmed the date with Linzey. Standford Linzey of Escondido, California, interview by author, 13 February 2000, by telephone. "Contemporary Issues," *The Pentecostal Evangel*, 12 January 1997, 22.

46. Linzey, *Filling Your Boots*, 2. Emphasis in the original.

47. *Called to Serve* (Springfield, Mo.: Gospel Publishing House, 1967).

48. Linzey, *Filling Your Boots*, 2.

49. Ibid., 7-8.

50. Ibid., 8.

51. Ibid. Emphasis added.

52. Richard G. Champion, "How Wars are Won," *The Pentecostal Evangel*, 4 March 1968, 4.

53. Although Malcolm X stated this many times, a prime example is Malcolm X, *Malcolm X Speaks*, compiled by Betty Shabazz (New York: Merit Publishers, 1965), 165.

54. Ibid.

55. Ibid.

56. Richard Fulmer, "Revival Cells in the Military," *The Pentecostal Evangel*, 20 July 1969, 7.

57. "Ministry to Servicemen Helps Meet Vital Need," *The Pentecostal Evangel*, 18 January 1970, 29.

58. "Building a Church 'Like the One Back Home' For Servicemen at Ramey Air Force Base," *The Pentecostal Evangel*, 29 March 1970, 9.

59. "Servicemen are Missionaries Too," *The Pentecostal Evangel*, 29 March 1970, 16.

60. "Clothing the Orphans," *The Pentecostal Evangel*, 28 June 1970, 2. The article praised the humanitarian efforts of American servicemen led by an Assemblies of God chaplain and condemned the "atrocities of the heartless forces who are trying to conquer South Vietnam and turn it into an atheistic communist state."

61. "Frank Borman Addresses Congress on War Prisoners," *The Pentecostal Evangel*, 13 September 1970, 26. "Thousands of our sons, brothers, and husbands are away from home in the Armed Forces. Many are in active combat zones while others are stationed at isolated, lonely outposts." Warren McPherson, "Have You Been to See the Battle?" *The Pentecostal Evangel*, 27 June 1971, 10. "Even after Vietnam is forgotten, thousands of our young men will still be serving all over the world. Help us reach this unique mission field—our own sons—by giving to the Servicemen's Division." "No Other Way," *The Pentecostal Evangel*, 25 June 1972, 9.

62. Don Hall, "Here We Are Lord; Send Us!" *The Pentecostal Evangel*, 26 March 1972, 7.

63. Donald Schorsch, "Not Somehow, But Triumphantly, Lord!" *The Pentecostal Evangel*, 25 June 1972, 8.

64. J. Philip Hogan, "Serving Under Two Banners," *The Pentecostal Evangel*, 25 June 1972, 13. References to "Spirit-filled military men" continued after the war. Richard C. Fulmer, "Fellowship in the Spirit," *The Pentecostal Evangel*, 26 June 1977, 14.

65. Hogan, "Serving Under Two Banners," 13.

66. Robert B. Robeson, "Right On, Sir! Right On!" *The Pentecostal Evangel*, 22 October 1972, 20.

67. Ibid.

68. Ibid.

69. Norman Correll, "Help Them Keep Step With Jesus," *The Pentecostal Evangel*, 24 June 1973, 10.

70. Ibid.

71. Robinson Risner, "Communications—Our Lifeblood," *The Pentecostal Evangel*, 7 October 1973, 6-9. Robinson Risner, *The Passing of Night* (New York: Random House, 1973).

72. Risner, "Communications—Our Lifeblood," 6.

73. Ibid., 8.

74. Ibid., 9. Emphasis added.

75. Larry Altman, "Air Force Personnel Build A Church," *The Pentecostal Evangel*, 23 April 1978, 10. The congregation consisted of approximately 800 members.

76. Over one hundred such pictures occurred in positive contexts between 1968 and 1999.

77. Mark (Dusty) Ellis, "That Others May Live," *The Pentecostal Evangel*, 25 June 1978, 8-9.

78. Ibid.

79. Charles W. Marvin, "Top Navy Men/Top Christians," 13.

80. Dave Sutherlin, "Air Force Sergeant Excels in Dual Role," *The Pentecostal Evangel*, 29 June 1980, 10. Emphasis added.

81. Calvin M. Durham, "He Fought for Freedom," 5.

82. "Churches Urged to Salute Vietnam Veterans," *The Pentecostal Evangel*, 10 October 1982, 26.

83. Ruby M. Enyart, "Meeting the Spiritual Needs of the Military," *The Pentecostal Evangel*, 26 June 1983, 12.

84. "Two From Florida Assembly Head for Military Academy," *The Pentecostal Evangel*, 25 October 1987, 27.

85. Darwin E. Evans, "A Tribute to Lay-Soldiers," 4 August 1985, 25. This article featured a picture of a line of soldiers laying on sandbags and firing their M-16s.

86. Ibid.

87. "Faithful," *The Pentecostal Evangel*, 28 June 1987, 8. A 6 ½ inch x 6 ½ inch picture of a soldier holding an M-16 with a cross necklace laying across it covered most of the page. The caption read, "Many men and women in the U.S. Armed Forces are faithful Christians who share Christ with others."

88. *The Pentecostal Evangel*, 28 June 1987, 9.

89. Robert R. Way, "A Soldier's Concern," 12.

90. Ibid., 13. "He quoted Scriptures, affirmed his commitment to the Lord, and cited previous military orders."

91. Jesse K. Moon, *War and the Christian* (Springfield, Mo.: by the author, 1988). Moon served on the faculty and administration at Southwestern Assemblies of God University, Waxahachie, Texas, and Central Bible College (Assemblies of God), Springfield, Missouri.

92. Ibid., 9.

93. Ibid., 35.

94. Ibid., 19-23. He listed the reasons that people opposed war: 1) the Sermon on the Mount, 2) the Decalogue, 3) the Great Commission, 4) Christians should not kill Christians, 5) war was diametrically opposed to the life of Jesus, 6) war was opposite the Golden Rule, 7) Christ on the cross was love overcoming evil and the cross is the power of nonresistance, 8) Jesus' kingdom was not of the world so it did

not have to be defended, 9) war was wasteful, and 10) there are no solutions and war is the worst attempt.

95. Ibid., 24-26.

96. Ibid., 28.

97. Ibid., 29.

98. Ibid., 31.

99. Joseph G. Jarret, "Of Evil Walls," *The Pentecostal Evangel*, 25 June 1989, 7.

100. Lemuel D. McElyea, "Who Upholds America's Cherished Treasures?" 11.

101. Lemuel D. McElyea, "Serving in the Middle East," *The Pentecostal Evangel*, 28 October 1990, 21. Two thousand out of one hundred thousand troops were Assemblies of God. Only one percent of the U.S. population was Assemblies of God at that time (2½ million of 250 million).

102. Larry Bryan, "War Over Iraq," *The Pentecostal Evangel*, 17 March 1991, 6.

103. Phil Simun, "What Can We Do?" *The Pentecostal Evangel*, 17 March 1991, 9.

104. "50 From North Carolina Assembly Deployed in Persian Gulf, Many as Pilots," *The Pentecostal Evangel*, 17 March 1991, 24-25, 30.

105. "'Military Church' Provides Opportunity," *The Pentecostal Evangel*, 17 March 1991, 26, 30.

106. George H. W. Bush, "It is a Just War," 11. He also said, "We all know that war never comes cheap. War is never without the loss of innocent life. And that is war's greatest tragedy."

107. George H. W. Bush, "We Stood Where Duty Required," 11.

108. "Love Letters From a Soldier," 6.

109. "Faith in God, Word of God Were Strength in Battle, Fighter Pilot Says," *The Pentecostal Evangel*, 14.

110. Ibid.

111. Jodi Ohlin, "Welcome HOME!" *The Pentecostal Evangel*, 8.

112. Ibid.

113. Carol L. Bruning, "Reunited!" *The Pentecostal Evangel*, 30 June 1991, 4. Emphasis added.

114. "At a Glance," *The Pentecostal Evangel*, 30 June 1991, 14.

115. "NAE Issues Statement on Homosexuals in the Military," *The Pentecostal Evangel*, 25 April 1993, 25.

116. "Officers' Christian Fellowship Urges Military to Uphold Homosexual Ban," *The Pentecostal Evangel*, 9 May 1993, 25, 30.

117. Ibid., 30.

118. Bob Hudson, "In Enemy Hands," *The Pentecostal Evangel*, 27 June 1993, 5.

119. Janice Moore, "The Price of Freedom," *The Pentecostal Evangel*, 13 November 1994, 20. "Ohio Assembly Celebrates Military Personnel Day With Community," *The Pentecostal Evangel*, 8 October 1995, 29.

120. David C. Causey, "Divine Protection in Somalia," *The Pentecostal Evangel*, 26 June 1994, 21.

121. William L. Patrick, "God is at Work in the Military," *The Pentecostal Evangel*, 27 June 1993, 11.

122. The director of the Chaplains Department in 1988 told Howard Kenyon that he was unaware that the Assemblies of God had ever been officially pacifist. Kenyon, "An Analysis," 380. Most of the ministers and laity that I encounter are still unaware that the Assemblies of God had at one time disapproved of Christian combatant participation in warfare. Charles Marvin of Springfield, Missouri, interview by author, 30 March 2000, e-mail, personal files of author.

123. "Contemporary Issues," *The Pentecostal Evangel*, 12 January 1997, 22. Parentheses in the original.

124. Ibid. Emphasis added.

125. Ibid. Emphasis added.

126. *Position Papers: Abstinence* (Springfield, Mo.: Gospel Publishing House, 1985).

127. *Perspectives: Contemporary Issues: Social, Medical, Political*, 23.

128. Ibid., 29. "Contemporary Issues," *The Pentecostal Evangel*, 12 January 1997, 22.

129. Ibid.

130. Ibid. However, some in the Assemblies of God disagreed with this position, and their writings are evaluated in a later section of this chapter.

131. Paul Alexander, "Spirit Empowered Peacemaking: Toward a Pentecostal Charismatic Peace Fellowship." *Journal of the European Pentecostal Theological Association*. Vol. 22, (2002): 78-102.

132. James W. Crawley, "Little-noted air war over Iraq grinds on, with criticism rising," *The San Diego Union-Tribune* (December 27, 1999).

133. "Summary of Interaction with Dr. Paul Alexander Concerning His Involvement in a Petition Against the United States Initiation of a War with Iraq." Personal files of the author. Marlon Millner authored the letter, "Send Judah First: A Pentecostal Perspective on Peace," and several dozen Pentecostal pastors, students, laity, and teachers signed it. http://www.pcpf.org/index.php?option=com_content&task=view&id=261&Itemid=45.

134. Louise Willard Derrick, Personal Assistant of Dave Roever, interview by author, 3 March 2000, by telephone. He told his story in each of his three books. Dave Roever and Harold Fickett, *Welcome Home, Davey* (Waco, Tex.: Word Books, 1986). Dave Roever with Karen Crews Crump, *Nobody's Ever Cried For Me* (Forth Worth, Tex.: Roever Communications, 1992). Dave Roever with Kathy Koch, *Scarred* (Fort Worth, Tex.: Roever Communications, 1995).

135. Dave Roever and Harold Fickett, *Welcome Home, Davey*, 30. Roever was working at the General Dynamics plant in Fort Worth, Texas, that manufactured F-111s for use in Vietnam.

136. Ibid., 31. Emphasis added.

137. Ibid. Emphasis in the original.

138. Ibid., 32.

139. Ibid.

140. Ibid., 34.

141. Ibid., 43. Emphasis in the original.

142. Ibid., 52.

143. Ibid., 60. Emphasis in the original.

144. Ibid., 65. Emphasis in the original.

145. Ibid., 66.

146. Ibid., 70.

147. Ibid., 73. It is remarkable that Roever thought sitting in a fully armed gunboat during a war was "minding his own business."

148. Ibid., 76, 77.

149. Ibid., 78.

150. Ibid., 82.

151. Ibid., 84.

152. Ibid., 93.

153. Ibid., 103.

154. Ibid., 104. He took these quotes from others but wrote that he agreed with how they felt.

155. Ibid., 137.

156. *Dave Roever: From Tragedy to Triumph*, 65 minutes, Roever Communications, 1988, videocassette. This videocassette set video footage from the Vietnam War (shooting, bombs, mortars, napalm, hand grenades, dead, wounded, jets, etc.) to patriotic music ("America the Beautiful") while Roever proclaimed his message. He followed this with a tribute to veterans that consistently elicited prolonged standing ovations from the Assemblies of God crowds across the nation. Before Roever told his personal story, two musicians performed a song written for Vietnam veterans. "Men who served their countries in wars of distant past, were welcomed home with victory songs that they were home at last. . . . But shame befalls a nation as the story now unfolds, the ones who fought the Vietnam War were never welcomed home. You fought a war you could not win, yet the price was still the same. With pain, and death, and dignity, you bore America's name. We stand to give our heroes praise, you are America's pride. We honor you for you gave in paying freedom's price. . . . But when you crossed the miles of sea to land on godless shores, the Stars and Stripes you bore with pride were now in flames unfurled. . . . You gave a chance to those who dreamed of life and liberty, and some would say that war was wrong, and some will call it right, but who are we to scorn the ones who paid with loss of life. And heroes do not come to be because they win or lose, they're honored for their sacrifice and the pathway that they choose. There is a price to pay and *sometimes war must be, God bless the ones who paid the price, for peace and liberty.*" Emphasis added.

157. Roever did not know that the Assemblies of God had any pacifist or conscientious objector heritage until the interview I conducted with him on April 20, 2000. Furthermore, in response to the question "What is your opinion of those Christians who don't participate in killing in warfare and base their nonviolence on the lives and teachings of Jesus and his followers?" he stated, "The people who base their lack of support for war efforts that free those in bondage and deliver the abused are as guilty of murder by omission as those who kill innocent people by commission. Ask any policeman who has just intervened to stop the murder of a family member of an objector . . . I personally accept the objector's point of view if he will

serve in a nonviolent, supportive way for those who are willing to die for his freedom to make such a choice." Roever did not address Jesus, his teachings, or his followers when he answered the question. Dave Roever of Fort Worth, Texas, interview by author, 20 April 2000, e-mail, personal files of author.

158. Menzies, *Anointed to Serve*, 276. Charles Marvin of Springfield, Missouri, interview by author, 29 March 2000, e-mail. There were an additional fifty-two Assemblies of God chaplains in the Armed Forces Reserves and sixty-three retired chaplains in 1999.

159. "38th. A/G Military Chaplain Appointed," *The Pentecostal Evangel*, 18 November 1973, 25. "David Anderson is 39th. A/G Military Chaplain," *The Pentecostal Evangel*, 24 March 1974, 26. Theodore E. Gannon, "Assemblies of God Chaplains Now on Active Military Duty," *The Pentecostal Evangel*, 26 June 1977, 11. Theodore E. Gannon, "Assemblies of God Chaplains Now on Active Duty," *The Pentecostal Evangel*, 24 June 1979, 11. "AGGS Student Commissioned for Military Seminarian Program," *The Pentecostal Evangel*, 29 June 1980, 26. "Graduate School Student Commissioned for Military Seminarian Program," *The Pentecostal Evangel*, 24 May 1981, 26. Lemuel D. McElyea, "Chaplain Candidate Program Promotes Quality: God's Men in the Military," *The Pentecostal Evangel*, 19 August 1984, S-4. "Assemblies of God Military Ministry Statistics," *The Pentecostal Evangel*, 28 June 1987, 9.

160. Warren F. McPherson, "Harvest Field With Few Workers," *The Pentecostal Evangel*, 18 May 1975, 20.

161. Ibid.

162. "'Help Us Minister to the Military,' Chaplain Urges," *The Pentecostal Evangel*, 31 January 1971, 28.

163. Cynthia D. Felix, "Army Religious Education Director—A Challenging Ministry," *The Pentecostal Evangel*, 14 May 1989, 18.

164. Charles C. McCullough, "U.S. Military Personnel in Europe: A Vast Mission Field," *The Pentecostal Evangel*, 26 June 1983, 21.

165. Blumhofer, *The Assemblies of God*, vol. 2, 126.

166. Ruby M. Enyart, "Meeting the Spiritual Needs of the Military," *The Pentecostal Evangel*, 26 June 1983, 12.

167. Lemuel D. McElyea, "Reaching Those in Uniform," *The Pentecostal Evangel*, 24 June 1990, 10. The same number was recognized in 1983. Enyart, "Meeting the Spiritual Needs of the Military," 12.

168. McElyea, "Reaching," 10.

169. There were 390 personnel (chaplains, reservists, pastors, seminarians) ministering to the military in 1987. "Assemblies of God Military Ministry Statistics," *The Pentecostal Evangel*, 28 June 1987, 9.

EIGHT

DISCOVERING A LARGELY FORGOTTEN PENTECOSTAL HERITAGE: ANALYSES OF THE LOSS OF ASSEMBLIES OF GOD PACIFISM

INTRODUCTION

The 1970s, 1980s, 1990s, and early twenty-first century witnessed a relative surge in academic analysis of Pentecostals by both Pentecostal and non-Pentecostal scholars. Several of these authors either mentioned or briefly evaluated early Assemblies of God pacifism and the changes that the fellowship underwent. Most provided their analyses without considering whether a return to Pentecostal pacifism was possible, but a few contemplated the prospects. This chapter first provides an examination of those who addressed pacifism. It then focuses on those particular Assemblies of God scholars who have raised questions about the theological validity of the transformation from peace witness to war-making. All of these Assemblies of God folk went to graduate school, which drew them not further away but nearer to the crucifism of their less formally educated Pentecostal forebears.[1] The chapter concludes with a survey of the contributions of five scholars who examined the history of the Assemblies of God attitude toward war and patriotism and appraises attempts to reintroduce Pentecostal pacifism to the Assemblies of God.

293

ANALYSES OF PENTECOSTAL PACIFISM

William Menzies (1971)

In 1971 the Gospel Publishing House released William Menzies' *Anointed to Serve*. Menzies devoted three pages to explaining the Assemblies of God position regarding "Military Service."[2] He related that in 1917 the leadership "established the official position of the Assemblies of God as pacifist" but that "a radical change occurred in the attitude of Assemblies of God people respecting military service sometime in the interval between World War I and World War II, despite official pronouncements."[3] He cited Flower's estimate that less than twenty Assemblies of God members had been conscientious objectors in World War II while "more than 50,000" had served.[4] By the Korean War there was "little need" for the conscientious objector provision, and during the Vietnam War the alteration came declaring that "the denomination no longer officially affirmed a pacifist position."[5] Menzies referenced the change positively when he explained fellowship with the National Association of Evangelicals.

> For what reasons had the Evangelicals extended the invitation to the Pentecostals to share in the development of the NAE? There are several contributing factors. One was the role of the Assemblies of God in World War II. Assemblies of God men were thrown together with others in the military services, creating a mutual feeling of respect between Evangelicals and Pentecostals. Without question, the contact of Pentecostals with the larger church world occasioned by the grim circumstances of the war broke down many barriers on both sides. Another avenue of openness occasioned by the conflict was service of Assemblies of God ministers for the first time in the army chaplaincy corps, *a venture the pacifist-oriented denomination had not engaged in heretofore.*[6]

Menzies considered that the Assemblies of God association with the "larger church world" was a good development since they helped found the National Association of Evangelicals. He also recognized that gaining respect from older Christian denominations was not of great concern for the early Pentecostal pacifists and that losing pacifism was a good move for the growing denomination. Indeed, the Assemblies of

God had happily moved away from some of their earlier distinctives.

> Still another reason was simply that it had become apparent that Pentecostals were here to stay. The image of permanence, missing in the early days, was emerging. Perhaps this was strengthened by the recognition by leading Pentecostals of past evidences of isolationism, exclusivism, and even fanaticism within the ranks, failures they deplored. For these reasons, and possibly others, the Assemblies of God was received into the fellowship of moderate Evangelicalism. *From 1942 onward there followed a thoroughgoing identification with the spirit and practice of this wing of the Christian church.*[7]

Menzies explained that the Assemblies of God was just like other mainstream churches; they were becoming a more respected part of conventional American Christianity.

Walter Hollenweger (1972, 1997)

Walter Hollenweger provided a non-Assemblies of God perspective in 1972 with the publication of *The Pentecostals: The Charismatic Movement in the Churches.*[8] As a member (and eventually Secretary of Evangelism) in the World Council of Churches, a Pentecostal clergyman in the Swiss Reformed Church, and a professor at the University of Birmingham (UK), Hollenweger provided a unique and powerful interpretation of the significance of Pentecostalism for the church. He used the Assemblies of God as a prime example for his critique of the way American Pentecostals dealt with militarism and other ethical issues.

> The older leaders, such as Williams and Riggs, maintain for the moment the rejection of worldliness. It is true that Williams leaves open the question whether military service can be reconciled with the Christian conscience. Everyone must decide according to his own conscience. But that one should not play volleyball on a Sunday afternoon is quite clear to him; it is a compromise with the world: "How then are we an example of reverence for God, for his worship, and of his day as set apart for worship?"[9]

Hollenweger did not hesitate to compare their approach to Sunday sports to their approach to war, and he continued his critique of Assemblies of God ethics and social conscience.

At a period when many American Christians—and many Swedish Pentecostals—have seen the questionable nature of the Vietnam War and published declarations to this effect, there is no sign of such ideas in *The Pentecostal Evangel*. On the contrary, the title page frequently carries pictures of Pentecostal army chaplains in Vietnam. The accompanying articles tell of their fruitful evangelization and services amongst the soldiers and civilians. While German Pentecostals are increasingly rejecting military service in favour of a substitute civilian form of service, a different tendency can be observed in the Assemblies of God. Biblical arguments are used in favour of the retention of capital punishment, and America is regarded as the best country on earth.[10]

He noted the relationship between militarism and patriotism and claimed that the Assemblies of God was less concerned about the issues even than other American Christians. He continued his point that Germans, of all people(!), were more conscientious about war than the American Assemblies of God.

Whereas during the first world war, and to some extent also during the second world war, German Pentecostals joined with other German Christians in manifesting an astonishing enthusiasm for war, they are resolutely putting this attitude behind them at the present day. On the other hand, American Pentecostals are trying to prove their loyalty and conformity to the American government by forgetting their critical past.[11]

Hollenweger praised the fact that early Pentecostals had a critical piece in their theological approach that allowed them to evaluate governments from an independent perspective. He called this Pentecostalism's "critical root." Without actually calling for a return, he spoke approvingly of Pentecostal nonviolence and critiqued patriotic militarism.

Hollenweger weighed in again in 1997 with a 400-page critical evaluation of Pentecostalism.[12] He stated that most early Pentecostals were pacifists but that possibly only a minority of the early Assemblies of God were pacifists.[13] He claimed that those who opposed war did so because of its inherent structural injustice, its political idolatry, and its economic exploitation of the poor for the benefit of the rich.[14] Hollenweger did not mention their use of Scripture regarding participation in war but later devoted an entire section to Pentecostal hermeneutics that could be applied to this issue (though he did not do so explicitly).[15] He lamented aloud the fact that Pentecostals had lost such an important aspect of their heritage.

> So far the Pentecostals have moved away from their own roots. How is it possible that modern American revivalism, with its deep roots in the nineteenth-century holiness movement, can be either so ignorant of or so antagonistic to many of its own tenets, as for example its stand for equal rights for women and slaves, and its fight for peace and justice? How is it possible that a powerful religious movement which directed its religious energies to the solution of the structural ills of its time could become so individualistic and almost blind to its own past?[16]

Hollenweger clearly disagreed with Robert Mapes Anderson (see below) about the nature of early Pentecostal concern for social evils. But the voice of concern was indeed silenced, and Hollenweger gave credence to William Faupel's theory that it related to a change in eschatology.

> Originally the holiness preachers had believed that the rapture would take place after the millennium (postmillennialism). They had also believed that their endeavor for holiness would contribute something to the establishment of the kingdom of God on earth. . . . When this proved to be unsuccessful, and instead of the millennium the Great War and the economic crisis arrived, postmillennialism was replaced by premillennialism, i.e., by the expectation of the rapture *before* the millennium. It was now necessary to prepare the believers for the rapture which would save them *out* of the world before everything broke down.[17]

Hollenweger viewed premillennialism as the "most potent obstacle to an involvement in the struggle against structural evils." Pentecostals ceased resisting the evils of violence and war, but some in the Assemblies of God once again began viewing it as a problem that needed to be corrected.[18]

Augustus Cerillo (1978)

Augustus Cerillo, an Assemblies of God professor, commented on the loss of pacifism in "Moving Up: Some Consequences of the New A/G Social Status" in 1978.[19] He agreed with Menzies that changing the attitude toward war helped entice the National Association of Evangelicals.

Indeed, we might see parallels between this personal cultural conformity and the denomination's quest for national acceptance. Two examples hopefully suffice. Has not our earlier and socially unpopular pacifism been replaced by a rather uncritical support of the nation's military and foreign policies? And a not unreasonable intuitive leap allows me to believe that we mute our Pentecostal zeal just sufficiently to guarantee increasing acceptance by the National Association of Evangelicals.[20]

He echoed the concern of Hollenweger about the loss of critical thought and expressed his own idea that "Pentecostal zeal," or the prophetic voice, is quenched in the trade-off for recognition and growth.

Robert Mapes Anderson (1979)

The next commentator on Pentecostal pacifism came from a widely respected atheistic historian. Robert Mapes Anderson's work greatly assisted the study of Pentecostalism, and his approach provided a valuable critique. When he wrote that "the Pentecostal drive for acceptance and respectability that began after World War II seemed to be succeeding" and "the movement initially constituted a radical critique of the status quo, but . . . it was soon transformed, in effect, into a conservative bulwark of the social system," his opinions were heard.[21]

After pointing out that he believed early Pentecostals had little or no social conscience, he evaluated their attitudes toward war.[22] However, his interpretation revealed that he had only superficially encountered all that early Pentecostals had written about war. "The *Christian Evangel* expressed typical Pentecostal sentiments when it greeted the outbreak of the first world war with scarcely disguised jubilation."[23] Although Pentecostals thought the war signified the imminent return of Jesus Christ to the earth the typical Pentecostal did not celebrate the destruction, blasphemy, murder, and hell of war. Nevertheless, Anderson recognized the conscientious objection of the early Pentecostals and placed it in the context of "the rejection of the world," i.e. sectarian pacifism. He noted that "Pentecostal leaders strenuously protested their loyalty, obedience, and subservience to the government and its laws in all other respects."[24] Whereas Menzies and Cerillo had linked the loss of pacifism with the desire to be accepted by the church world, Anderson linked it more to their loyalty to the government (which also comes from a desire to be accepted by the larger world).

Submission to state authority was no mere wartime expedient, but rather a consistent orientation of the Pentecostal movement. . . . In time these sentiments undermined and reversed the Pentecostals' initial position on military service. . . . The Pentecostal acceptance of combatant military duty signaled the death of all resistance and the near total subservience of the movement to the authority of the state. The kind of patriotism and glorification of war that Bartleman had excoriated in 1915 were embraced by [the] Assemblies of God.[25]

Anderson claimed that the gradual rise in social status and acceptability led to the gradual loss of "sect" and "outsider" traits. "Those Pentecostal groups, like the Assemblies of God, that first achieved a modicum of stability and realized some improvements in their social circumstances, were the first in which ecstasy began to subside."[26] The peace witness, which was one of these radical elements, also collapsed.

Anderson's analysis, though not intended to do so, served as a challenge to Pentecostal theologians and ethicists.

Their initial opposition to bearing arms in World War I should not obscure their overall respect and subservience to "the powers that be." Aside from these early, modest challenges to secular authority, the Pentecostals have been ideal workers and citizens in every respect except the cultivation of ecstasy. . . . Even the presumed "radical" or "extremist" practices of tongues, exorcism, and healing are conservative in effect, because they have kept the Pentecostals busily engaged in activities which have no impact whatever on the fundamental political economy or social relations of American society, and because they serve to reconcile the Pentecostals to things as they are. Because these practices are so "different" they have appeared to challenge the status quo, but they have been mere rituals of rebellion, cathartic mechanisms which in fact stabilize the social order.[27]

He made the accusation that speaking in tongues, the Assemblies of God distinctive, was all words and no action. Anderson forcefully brought his investigation to an end with the restatement of his thesis and its sad implications.

The root source of the Pentecostal movement was social discontent. Its initial millenarian vision contained within it a rejection of the social order and a hope for a new, more just society, but the belief that the Millennium would come without human effort was inimical to the real life interests of the Pentecostals. The radical social impulse inherent in the vision of the disinherited was transformed into social passivity, ecstatic escape, and, finally, a most conservative conformity.[28]

These accusations left Pentecostals wondering if they truly were radical at all and prompted them to begin examining their own heritage more critically.

Jay Beaman (1982, 1983, 1989)

Only three years later, Jay Beaman penned his M.Div. thesis at the North American Baptist Seminary, "Pentecostal Pacifism: The Origin, Development, and Rejection of Pacific Belief Among the Pentecostals."[29] He then presented a paper at The Society for Pentecostal Studies annual meeting in 1983 entitled, "Pacifism and the World View of Early Pentecostalism."[30] This paper brought more details of the issue before scholars within the Pentecostal movement. A few years later the Center for Mennonite Brethren Studies published his thesis as a book with the same name.[31]

Beaman's work was relatively broad in scope (he attempted to classify and evaluate over thirty Pentecostal denominations) and was significant because it was the first serious attempt to deal with the issue of Pentecostal pacifism. He noted in his introduction that, "No one has yet made a study of the origins of pacifism in the Pentecostal movement. It is not a major concern with most Pentecostals today."[32] His work also inspired others to continue the investigation by providing a good bibliography and important observations.

Beaman argued that pacifism was widespread and dominant in Pentecostalism in the early years, since at least thirty groups adopted noncombatant positions.[33] He noted relationships between pacifism and women in ministry, missionary zeal, poverty, and eschatology.[34] He located the origins of Pentecostal pacifism primarily with the holiness movement and to a slight degree from the influence of Dwight L. Moody.[35] He attributed the loss of pacifism to upward mobility and cultural accommodation which were best seen in combatant duty in World War II, the development of the chaplaincy, and the identification with the National Association of Evangelicals.[36]

Beaman did not concern himself with tracing the development in any one denomination, but he did briefly examine the Assemblies of God. He devoted six pages to recounting significant events relative to military service between World War II and 1981.[37] By bringing together various themes of early Pentecostalism and telling the broad story of the disappearance, Beaman did an invaluable service. He also encouraged Pentecostals with his conclusion.

> Pentecostals need to ponder whether they can long maintain their distinctive views about the church and the Holy Spirit, while conforming to mainstream Evangelical socio-religious views. By asking in what ways their earlier pacifism formed a part of their whole belief system, Pentecostals may come to see that this loss signaled other losses too. It may be time to ask in what way this movement, founded upon a desire to be open to the re-newing ministry of the Holy Spirit, can continue to have a prophetic role in the life of the church.[38]

His call for a return to their prophetic role provoked reviews and dialogue and even motivated some Assemblies of God ministers to examine their own heritage more thoroughly, so that they could suggest avenues toward restoration.[39]

John Howard Yoder (1983, 1989)

John Howard Yoder, the well-known and widely influential Mennonite theologian and ethicist, mentioned Pentecostal pacifism in one of his own works in 1983.[40] While discussing the nineteenth century, he evaluated Pentecostalism because "it is a continuation of what was already going on in the Wesleyan revival experience. Pentecostalism began as a revival within the culture produced by revival."[41] As a revival for revivalists, it was willing to change, needed to be different, and had "the notion of literal obedience to a word of Scripture without rationalizing, without having to study through why it should be taken this way."[42] Yoder agreed with Anderson that the socially lower-class Pentecostals had little interest in social responsibility and that they downplayed creeds, organization, and history. Yoder affirmed previously asserted reasons why Pentecostals became pacifists.

> [Pentecostalism] becomes rather directly and simply pacifist in the first generation. The simplest reason is that they take the

whole Bible straight. It starts out saying "thou shalt not kill. . . ." It is probably related to this [that] Pentecostalism was not only pacifist but also racially integrated for a generation. . . . Yet their success led them to stop just experiencing unity in revival and to start to strategize about how to grow better.[43]

Then Yoder explained why he thought that these radical elements disappeared from Pentecostalism.

But this originality (both the pacifism and the racial integration) was not deeply rooted. They don't believe in being deeply rooted. If you think history doesn't matter, and theology doesn't matter, church structures don't matter, there need be no sense of history in society which could make sense of a radically ethical position in the world. There was no critique of Americanism as such. . . . The Pentecostals, being a new revival movement in the western half of the Bible belt, didn't have any peace church neighbors to lean on and to learn from. They had no alternative view of the meaning of power, the meaning of nationalism.[44]

Without history and without community, Yoder viewed the Pentecostals as on their own with only tongues to help them. Their pacifism "softened" immediately when they sent ministers to evangelize the soldiers during World War I. This desire to grow, a questionable motive if the message is diluted, led to the development of seminaries.

By the second World War there was such a special push to get people into the chaplaincy that seminaries were created for the first time, because the chaplaincy required a seminary degree. They didn't believe in seminary for their churches, but to get people into the army they would give them a seminary degree.[45]

Yoder's analysis did not receive much response until 1996, but others continued to mention the subject as they wrote more historically aware studies. However, he also kindly provided the foreword for Jay Beaman's *Pentecostal Pacifism* in 1989. He made it clear that he believed the Pentecostals did nothing but "sell out" to the world when they forfeited their pacifism. However, he admired their early emphasis and found it more interesting than traditional "Peace Church" pacifism. "Charismatic pacifism is a component of the first-generation transformation wrought by the synergy of enthusiasm and prima facie biblicism."[46] In contrast to "established" pacifism, the Pentecostal pacifists did not have to worry about whether their nonviolence could be urged on the world.

> The pacifist who has come to that stance by first-generation convincement can be freed from such doubts. "You are freed from violence" is a part of the miracle of renewal. Pragmatism about social values to be defended politically is no more decisive than is determinism about whether hearts can be changed or sins forgiven.[47]

Perhaps this is part of the genius of Pentecostal pacifism—first-generation converts to Christian nonviolence (even if they are fourth- or fifth-generation Pentecostals) see that love of enemy is just part of what it means to be "saved," to follow Jesus in the power of the Holy Spirit. Pentecostals specialize in evangelism and if peacemaking is part of the gospel then new converts passionately adopt and proclaim their newfound freedom from violence. However, Yoder argued that Pentecostals did not integrate nonviolence into their message of the good news:

> Pentecostalism's changes have become a classical specimen of the "sect cycle," making within barely two generation some fundamental accommodations to establishment like those which took early Christianity centuries. The prima facie biblicism did not mature into a solid ethical hermeneutic. The prophetic discernment of the evils of social stratification yielded with astonishing ease to personal prosperity and institutional respectability. The millennial hope no longer functioned as existential grounds for nonconformity to the world. . . . The ministry of women and "laity" subsided behind the credentialing of ministers (partly for military purposes). This parallels the loss of Pentecostalism's initial interracial character.[48]

Yoder questioned whether the "subjectivism" inherent within Pentecostalism allowed the movement to relegate military service to conscience and to accept "uncritical patriotism."[49] Even though he chastised Pentecostals for their change, he concluded by putting it all in perspective. "These modes of patriotic accommodation are in no way peculiar to Pentecostals. That is just the point; they are mainstream Christendom responses, unworthy of the nonconformist originality and spiritual independence with which the movement began."[50] Yoder undoubtedly intended this last sentence to stir the hearts and minds of Pentecostals who would read Beaman's book.

Gary B. McGee (1986, 1991)

Gary McGee noted early Assemblies of God pacifism in the first volume of his two-volume opus about the history and theology of Assemblies of God foreign missions.[51] It appeared in the context of "The Effect of War on Missionaries" and referenced the works of both Jay Beaman and Roger Robins. McGee first cited early Assemblies of God loyalty to government, then referred to their opposition to "participation in the war effort" because of the nearness of the Second Coming.[52] In an endnote McGee suggested Beaman's thesis as a "more comprehensive study of the changing attitudes of the General Council of the Assemblies of God toward war."[53] McGee did not analyze the situation himself and devoted only one sentence of his text to the topic.

In 1991 McGee answered a question about war for the *Assemblies of God Heritage* magazine.[54] He told the readers that "many Pentecostals were pacifists in the early years of the movement" and that the General Council "declared its opposition to participation in the war because it involved the destruction of human life." He also noted that the military service article did not condemn those who chose to fight. He explained that they changed the statement in 1967 because most people thought World War II was a just war, there was "growing political conservatism," and the Assemblies of God increasingly identified with the NAE (who supported the use of arms).

Edith Blumhofer (1989)

Edith Blumhofer, who served for a time as the official Assemblies of God historian, devoted ten pages to Assemblies of God views of war in her two-volume work, *The Assemblies of God: A Chapter in the Story of American Pentecostalism.*[55] In addition to describing their pacifism, she noted that early Pentecostals were comfortable with militaristic religious symbols, that they interpreted war in eschatological terms, and that they struggled with their "dual allegiance."

> As citizens of another kingdom, Pentecostals were uninterested in their culture; yet, they soon learned to move handily from operating under the pilgrim model to expressing their concerns as Christian soldiers. These two themes mingle to make the story of

Assemblies of God attitudes toward war and country complex. Pacifists declared their identity as pilgrims; others, while concurring, claimed an obligation in that pilgrimage to counter evil.[56]

She argued that the 1917 resolution did not attempt to deal theologically with the issue but intended to insure exemptions.[57] At the time of her writing she noted that the Assemblies of God had still not developed a "just war theory or theology."[58] Blumhofer argued that diversity ruled the early Assemblies of God regarding war but that only a few expressed concerns over the "loss" of pacifism.[59] Her final analysis was that "the war experience exposed inconsistent views of Christian identity. If that of pilgrims and strangers suited some, others found the battling soldier, at times, more congenial . . . [and] most would opt—with considerable pride—to serve their country."[60]

RECOVERING THE THEOLOGY
AND PRACTICE OF PENTECOSTAL PACIFISM

Since 1980, five Assemblies of God ministers have written significant pieces that reveal the rekindling of an interest in Pentecostal pacifism both for their denomination and for Pentecostalism as a whole. One resolution that encouraged the same sentiment has been presented and rejected at a General Council. All but the latter of these contributions issued from men who had acquired graduate education that exposed them to their Pentecostal heritage. Each had read the works of the scholars in the section above. They varied in their approaches, yet they each expressed a desire to recapture or develop a significant Pentecostal social ethic in which a critique of war would be an integral part.

Murray W. Dempster (1980)

Murray Dempster has devoted himself to encouraging and constructing a Pentecostal social ethic.[61] He has written four articles, three addresses, and one book chapter dealing directly with Pentecostal pacifism and has provided numerous other works on ethical concerns. Immediately following Robert Anderson's *Vision of the Disinherited* in 1979, Dempster addressed Pentecostals and the draft.[62] He recalled

the long and torturous journey of Pentecostal moral conscience toward military service that codified itself during the turbulent

time of the late 60s and the early 70s. . . . That journey of conscience ended . . . when the General Council issued a death sentence to its historic pacifist stance on war.[63]

By pointedly calling the action a "death sentence," he foreshadowed
the frustration of others who would study this topic. Dempster objected
to the claim in the resolution of 1967 that it represented the historical
position of the Assemblies of God.

Such a claim arbitrarily revises history apparently to avoid making a change in the eternal word of revelation, or perhaps to avert
the embarrassment of admitting that an earlier interpretation of
the truth was faulty. But a change in the A/G position it was, and
an unacknowledged banishment of Pentecostal heritage it remains.[64]

He based his strongly worded evaluation on the fact that the rationale employed to defend this position had changed drastically. Since neither the authority of Scripture nor any specific biblical texts were mentioned,

The Pentecostal believer's conscience on war no longer needed to
be formed specifically by biblical teaching but was now to be informed by knowledge of certain political, theological and ethical
propositions. . . . The poverty of explicit biblical thinking in this
rationale is an utter embarrassment to people who give first priority in a "Statement of Faith" to affirming the authority of Scripture.[65]

Dempster wanted the Assemblies of God to provide a biblical foundation for their support of the authority of individual conscience regarding combatant participation in warfare. He did not write that it was
impossible but insisted that "it is significant and tragic that no attempt
has been made to do so."[66] As an ordained Assemblies of God minister,
he challenged his denomination to evaluate and defend its position on
military service from a biblical perspective. Several other Assemblies of
God scholars produced work about Assemblies of God pacifism before
Dempster contributed again, but the next significant event occurred at
the General Council in 1981.

Michael Chase and Joel Kruggel (1981)

Michael Chase and Joel Kruggel were ordained ministers from Illinois who presented a resolution to the General Council in 1981 that did not even make it to a vote. Their resolution was significant because it revealed that pacifism, though wounded and bleeding, was not completely dead in the Assemblies of God. They hoped to get the Assemblies of God to support the World Peace Tax Fund, a fund that would allow U.S. taxpayers to direct their taxes toward nonmilitary expenditures. Chase and Kruggel did not try to persuade the Assemblies of God to abstain from war, to change their position about war, or to support tax evasion. They simply thought that since the Assemblies of God allowed its members to be conscientious objectors they might support this kind of legislation. Chase and Kruggel even implemented some of the language from the original pacifist resolution of 1917 to help persuade their audience. It is probable that few, if any, of the delegates in 1981 realized that when they rejected this resolution they rejected statements the Assemblies of God had previously supported. Most of the resolution follows so that it can be fully appreciated.

> WHEREAS, The Scriptures exhort: "Let us therefore make every effort to do what leads to peace" (Rom. 14:19, NIV) and to "make every effort to live in peace with all men" (Heb. 12:14, NIV); and our Lord Jesus taught "blessed are the peacemakers" (Matt. 5:9); and
>
> WHEREAS, There are those in our Assemblies of God fellowship, and among our fellow Christian believers, who while purposing to fulfill all the obligations of loyal citizenship, nevertheless feel constrained by the Holy Spirit and the teaching of Scriptures that they cannot conscientiously participate in war and armed resistance which involves the actual destruction of human life, nor conscientiously pay taxes for military expenditures and the production of weapons (especially nuclear weaponry) which will result in the destruction of human life; and
>
> WHEREAS, The present tax system in the United States is working a grievous injustice against people who, while not required to bear arms, must still pay for others to do so and for the continuing and widening arms race; and
>
> WHEREAS, We as Christians are called to be salt and light in this world and to speak prophetically to our society with the

gospel message of salvation and peace, and therefore should look for alternatives to war to settle international conflicts; and

WHEREAS, A bill to establish a World Peace Tax Fund, i.e., H.R. 4897 and S. 880, has been introduced in Congress which would amend the Internal Revenue Code to provide that taxpayers conscientiously opposed to participation in war may elect to have their income, estate, or gift tax payments spent for nonmilitary and peace-related purposes; therefore, be it

RESOLVED, That the 39th. General Council of the Assemblies of God go on record in support of the swift passage of legislation establishing a World Peace Tax Fund, and to urge individual members of the Assemblies of God to write their appropriate legislators.[67]

The response to the reading of this resolution revealed that the constituency would employ any excuse to avoid having to support conscientious objectors. Although the Council could have amended any or all of the resolution that was deemed unacceptable, instead they decided that "this is a political matter, and as a General Council we ought not to take a stand for or against any political issue, no matter how popular or unpopular it might be."[68] The Assemblies of God refrained from taking responsibility when the issue was killing in war because they no longer considered it to be a theological or ethical issue—but merely a political one.

However, the opposite position has since appeared. In a widely distributed pamphlet entitled "Political Involvement and the Church: Does the Assemblies of God Involve Itself in Political Issues?" political involvement was encouraged and supported.

The Assemblies of God encourages its members and adherents to influence society and the political process by voting, maintaining strong moral convictions and holy lifestyles (Matt. 5:13), praying for government officials (1 Tim. 2:2), *encouraging and promoting legislation that strengthens the nation morally,* and *speaking out both corporately and individually* against any political issue that would have an adverse affect upon the kingdom of God or His moral absolutes.[69]

The specific issues that they wanted constituents to address were abortion and homosexuality, but their instructions covered much more than just those two topics. However, the idea of supporting legislation that promoted "world peace" did not fit the category of "strengthens the nation morally." Nevertheless, Chase and Kruggel did at least attempt to bring back to the Assemblies of God an earlier Pentecostal understanding of "Scripture," the "Holy Spirit," and the "prophetic."

Roger Robins (1984, 1986)

Shortly after Jay Beaman finished his M.Div. thesis, Roger Robins, who was working on his own M.Div. at Harvard Divinity School, wrote an article specifically about Assemblies of God attitudes toward war during World War I.[70] Robins wanted more Pentecostals to be able to "genuincly feel the pulse of early Assemblies of God thoughts on war and peace."[71] Therefore, he provided a significant amount of primary materials so that the passion of the early Pentecostals would be clear. He evaluated his sources as evidence that, although there was "a sharp thematic disconsonance, . . . pacifistic sentiment seems to have been predominant within the Assemblies of God ranks."[72] Nevertheless, he recognized that there was "a strand of patriotic sentiment which may have been but which was not necessarily pacifistic."[73] Robins also noted the strong evangelistic vision of the early Assemblies of God.

He decried E. N. Bell's "blatantly non-pacifistic" views and acknowledged that pacifism held a "somewhat tenuous" position in the early years, even though the bulk of the literature revealed that the Assemblies of God "certainly leaned toward pacifism in spirit."[74] Robins then shifted from a historical evaluation to addressing contemporary Pentecostalism (and specifically the Assemblies of God).

> As Pentecostals we are now no less than then called to discern what it means to be faithful to God's Word on this issue. As we carry on the dialogue, with ourselves as well as with others, we could do well to notice a remarkable pattern in these documents.[75]

The pattern to which Robins referred revealed the direction that he believed the Assemblies of God should travel.

> Where there is argumentation in favor of pacifism, that argumentation is biblically rooted, eschatologically informed, and it frequently appeals to the work of the Spirit in sanctification, conversion, and in the creation of a new people or of a new age. That

is to say that the argument is characterized by qualities which are central to our self-understanding as Pentecostals. On the other hand, argumentation against pacifism is characterized by political considerations, rationalism and humanism. That is to say the argumentation is characterized by elements drawn from intellectual traditions which we have generally not regarded as adequate sources for determining doctrinal or ethical truth.[76]

Robins concluded by encouraging Pentecostals to examine the way they argued as well as what they argued for or against, and to examine their origins so that they could once again follow the leading of the Spirit when dealing with the issue of war. Thus, Robins issued a call to consider whether something valuable had been lost.

Whereas Robins' previous article appeared in a non-Assemblies of God publication, Wayne Warner, the editor of the *Assemblies of God Heritage* magazine, allowed him to present this history to their limited readership in 1986.[77] This event in 1986 was one of only two of its kind in an Assemblies of God periodical in the 1970s, 1980s, or 1990s. Since Robins penned this article for the nonacademic, he introduced the topic in a unique way. He quoted the Assemblies of God reference to Quaker principles in support of their pacifism in 1917 and then began his article.

> Do you recognize the movement described above? Could it be Mennonite? Brethren? Guess again! With this paragraph, taken from the August 4, 1917, issue of *Weekly Evangel*, the editors of that paper described their own Pentecostal movement as they themselves understood it.[78]

He claimed that "we do have a forgotten heritage . . . in the ardent pacifism that marked much of Pentecostalism in its emergent years." Robins claimed that pacifism was "clearly the predominant view," and he actually challenged the politics and ethics of his Assemblies of God readers.

> The pacifism of first-generation Pentecostals was part of a broader worldview that allowed, and even demanded, a stronger critique of society's power structures than is common among Pentecostals today. . . . This "Pentecostal populism" of the first-generation souls is hardly compatible with the conservative politics espoused by many of their grandchildren![79]

Nothing like this challenge appeared in the pages of *The Pentecostal Evangel* during this time. Robins continued by asking some tough questions that only a few have been willing to address.

> The pacifist conviction of early Pentecostalism is indeed a largely forgotten heritage. *It is a heritage, however, that we must redeem from forgetfulness.* Change is inevitable for any historical body. But if we are to change wisely, we must do so knowingly, aware of where we are headed and where we have been. . . . If Pentecostals have moved from pacifism to militarism, we must ask, has this been accomplished by careful, discerning attention to Scripture and the Holy Spirit—that is, by attention to the same authorities early Pentecostals claimed for their position of peace? Or has the transition simply been a part of our general assimilation into mainstream American culture?[80]

Robins issued the first call directly to the Assemblies of God, in one of their own publications, to review their heritage and perhaps recover their critique of war. But he was not the only Assemblies of God person who investigated the issue.

Howard Kenyon (1988)

Howard Kenyon devoted his Ph.D. dissertation research to demonstrating that "the Assemblies of God has developed a set of moral principles lacking the distinctiveness of a thoroughgoing Pentecostal social ethic."[81] He analyzed race issues, gender issues, and participation in warfare and concluded that "a Pentecostal ethic should be eschatological and prophetic—rooted in the theological notion of the 'Age of the Spirit.'"[82]

Kenyon wrote two chapters (116 pages) on Assemblies of God pacifism and the nature of its demise.[83] He did not investigate its origins because that was outside the scope of his study, and he dealt only briefly (one page) with developments since 1967. However, he claimed that "a minority element within the General Council continues to cling to the pacifist perspective, even though the position is generally suspect as being unscriptural and disloyal to government."[84] He was probably at least partly referring to himself, since he has remarked that, "I've always said I was a pacifist."[85] But this minority did not negate the fact that he believed the Assemblies of God was characterized by a "total repudiation of the 1917 resolution."[86] Kenyon argued that "pacifism, loyalty, and evangelism [were] rejected in favor of . . . loyalty and freedom of conscience. Since 1967 the Assemblies of God has shown no sign of movement on the position."[87]

Kenyon found that the Assemblies of God used evangelism to the military as their guide when discussing war. To minister to the soldiers, they approved of their occupation. To be accepted by the church world, they approved of patriotism. Acceptability, not biblical principles, determined their stance on war.[88] Kenyon concluded that the Assemblies of God had forfeited their prophetic role to become pastoral.[89] "It is unfortunate that the fellowship's pacifist heritage has been lost so quickly. It is not only the belief in pacifism which has been discarded, but also a healthy commitment to the Word and to the prophetic—regardless of the feasibility of the results."[90]

He did not let the Assemblies of God off easily. He remarked that their "pioneer spirit [was] replaced by a defensive self-image and acceptance of status quo," the "denomination today often seems to have forgotten heaven in search of an earthly kingdom," and "Scripture and Pentecostal heritage were sacrificed on the altar of social expediency."[91] Kenyon called for a return to the three themes necessary in a Pentecostal ethic: liberation, reconciliation, and justice.[92] He agreed with Dempster that Pentecostals could not mimic Evangelicals and thus trivialize their ethics by personalizing them at the expense of social concern.[93] Finally, Kenyon made the connection between Pentecostalism and Stanley Hauerwas' narrative approach to theological ethics. "Being" and "doing" were inextricably linked so the Assemblies of God should follow the Spirit and live their story to be truly Pentecostal.[94] Unfortunately, Howard Kenyon's dissertation did not receive wide circulation, and few referenced his work. Nonetheless he did serve as another Assemblies of God voice calling for a reinvestigation of Pentecostal pacifism.

Dwight Wilson (1988)

The *Dictionary of Pentecostal and Charismatic Movements* that appeared in 1988 devoted two full pages to "Pacifism."[95] Dwight Wilson, professor of history at Bethany Bible College and an ordained Assemblies of God minister, penned the article. He freely critiqued the loss. Wilson stated that the decline of pacifism "basically corresponded to the trends in public opinion in the population at large."[96] He wrote that Pentecostal pacifists, who were predominant before World War I, did not actively seek peace but only refrained from war because the end of time quickly approached. Even this disappeared because Pentecostals eventually decided that "established government power was divinely ordained" and could therefore make a Christian go to war.[97]

Wilson did not just tacitly describe the history. He reserved his most cutting analysis for the Assemblies of God. He blamed the "chaplain's lobby within the AG [as] the major force after the war [that] change[d] the denomination's official position so as to conform to practice."[98] He also provided his own evaluations and revealed his opinions.

> As the popular romanticism of the general population leaned in the direction of antinuclear views and opposition to the Vietnam War, *the conservatism of the AG toughened*. . . . This development may be contrasted, however, with a growing anti-militarism in the postwar German and British Pentecostal churches, the British leadership strongly supporting the banning of atomic weapons. . . . Thus while some Pentecostals retained residues of the general pacifism of an earlier era, *others [the Assemblies of God] had even gone beyond nonpacifism and had hardened into an antipacifist position, continuing to merely reflect, rather than to instruct, public opinion.*[99]

Wilson referred to the failure of the 1981 World Peace Tax Fund resolution as proof that the Assemblies of God had severed themselves from their heritage. With such a strongly worded article in such a prominent place (The *Dictionary* sold over forty thousand copies),[100] one would think that responses would emerge. Dempster again came to the forefront for the next few years and hammered away at the Assemblies of God solidification of pro-war sentiment.

Murray Dempster (1989, 1990, 1991, 1992)

In 1989 Dempster reviewed Jay Beaman's *Pentecostal Pacifism*. He praised it, augmented it, and called for more research on the topic. Dempster recognized the four elements that Beaman claimed transformed Pentecostal pacifism: upward social and economic mobility, the impact of World War II, the participation of the Assemblies of God in the National Association of Evangelicals, and the institutionalization of the chaplaincy.[101] He agreed that these contributed but that the transformation needed more exploration, "The greatest contribution of Beaman's study may turn out to be the future research into this subject which his work hopefully will stimulate."[102]

He thought that the origins of pacifism stood as the first area in need of research. Dempster especially suggested that Quakerism, "while the most enigmatic to track, may shed some light on the content and the language-use found in the 1917 pacifism statement."[103] Dempster recommended the extent of Pentecostal pacifism as the second aspect needing further development. He claimed that the early writings had "an advocacy character" that revealed they were trying to persuade their readers rather than simply affirming a majority position.[104] Third, Dempster questioned whether there was ever such a "social reality" as "Pentecostal pacifism." Rather, different Pentecostal pacifists held their positions for a variety of reasons, and these never coalesced into one distinct teaching.[105] He then augmented Beaman's assertion and echoed Yoder's evaluation that

> pacifism disappeared among Pentecostals because these pacifists never established a theologically informed ethical heritage to perpetuate their pacifistic beliefs to subsequent generations. Their eschatologically driven world view . . . may have been chiefly responsible for this inattention to theological reflection.[106]

This observation pointed to the possibility that current Assemblies of God theologians could in fact develop a "theologically informed ethical heritage" that would reveal the connection between nonviolence and Pentecost, the cross and the upper room. Eschatology would still be necessary but from a different perspective; rather than discouraging theological reflection, it would inform it.

The publication of Beaman's book inspired Dempster to write more than just a review. The following spring he published an article aimed at "Reassessing the Moral Rhetoric of Early American Pentecostal Pacifism" in which he developed the themes he had mentioned in the above review.[107] He expressed sorrow at the "growing militaristic attitudes about war and peacemaking in American Pentecostal circles today" and noted that most Pentecostals "express astonishment when they first discover that the Pentecostal movement in the United States was almost entirely officially pacifist."[108] He blamed this on the silence of Assemblies of God historians but revealed hope because "word about early Pentecostal pacifism is starting to spread."[109] Although he did not intend to argue for the relevance of pacifism for Pentecostals today, he knew "that question will always be lurking around the corner."[110]

Dempster examined the way early Pentecostal pacifists viewed their moral responsibility to the larger society, and he located three principal arguments they used to support their pacifism. First, they viewed pacifism as an integral aspect of restoring the New Testament church—"[a] tangible moral sign that the Pentecostal church had recovered the eschatological character of New Testament Christianity."[111] Second, pacifism served as a moral critique of the existing social and political order —"[it] critique[d] the power structure of the world order in concrete action."[112] Third, pacifism served as a moral affirmation of the universal scope of the value of human life—"[a] concrete moral authenticity to the gospel."[113] He quoted five "absolute" Pentecostal pacifists to support his analysis: Arthur and Samuel Booth-Clibborn, Frank Bartleman, Stanley Frodsham, and Charles Parham. Dempster drew all three themes together in his summary of their position.

> The church is an eschatological community of pilgrims already living as citizens of the future age. Given its eschatological character, the church resists being assimilated into the values and behaviors of the world and its power structure. Instead the church embodies the values and behaviors of the new humanity "in Christ," which values include the worth of all human life created by God and for whom Christ died.[114]

But Dempster then claimed that early Pentecostals never tied pacifism in with their pneumatology; therefore, it vanished. "Nowhere was the argument made that to be a Pentecostal was to be a pacifist . . . a Spirit-empowered witness and a sense of moral responsibility for society were never brought together into an integrated whole."[115] Dempster lamented this fact because this terrible "bifurcation" had a "lethal impact on the task of constructing a Pentecostal social ethic."[116]

Dempster claimed that Pentecostals limited the Spirit's empowerment to *kerygma* (preaching) and *koinonia* (fellowship) while forgetting their "*diakonic* [servanthood] mission." His final analysis perfectly described his own Assemblies of God and also revealed his hopes for the future.

A church that only views its mission in terms of preaching the good news and nurturing its own spiritual life has a proclivity to degenerate into a self-absorbed verbal community . . . a religion of ritual and piety but no ethical content. . . .

But the pacifists, for all intents and purposes, are gone—people of eschatological mentality, with moral conviction about the individual and institutional nature of human sin, and deeply aware of the value of human life. A study of their demise may shed some light on the character of *today's Pentecostal church, a church committed to the evangelism of the world and to the fellowship of believers but with an underdeveloped social conscience.* But more importantly, "Discovering a Pentecostal Heritage . . ." in the *pacifism* advocated by early Pentecostal leaders *may lead to the recovery of a prophetic social ethic* capable of directing the church's moral engagement with society. Such a recovery might also restore the opportunity for Pentecostals to shape the contours of a social ethic from a pneumatological understanding of the church's mission and ministry in the world on behalf of Jesus Christ.[117]

Dempster expressed his desire for a recovery of the broad social concern he found present in early Pentecostalism, and he thought pacifism could serve as the route to recovery. Although he thought the concern was mostly gone, his own works revealed that it was still present.

In 1991 Dempster published another article that contained much of the same content as the previous one and again revealed that he hoped pacifism could be reclaimed.[118] He celebrated Beaman's work but argued that Pentecostal pacifism was not just sectarian and did not disappear simply because of sociological reasons. He again presented the three theological emphases mentioned above and then provided his revision of Beaman's "cultural assimilation thesis." Dempster claimed that pacifism lost out because it was never the majority position, it was instead a position held by "a prophetic minority."[119] "Before they [the prophetic minority] had an opportunity to cultivate a pacifist tradition based on shared theology and ethics, history had overtaken them and the patriotic war spirit invaded the house never to leave."[120] He continued to promote this perspective by participating in conferences such as "Pacifist Traditions in American Churches (other than historic Peace Churches)" at Goshen College and "The Fragmentation of the Church and its Unity in Peacemaking" at Notre Dame University.[121] His perspective eventually made it into *Proclaim Peace: Christian Pacifism From Unexpected Quarters*.[122]

It is possible that Dempster saw himself as being part of a new prophetic minority within Pentecostalism, specifically the Assemblies of God, which would call for a Spirit-empowered moral vision. For his work helped inspire another Assemblies of God scholar to issue the most direct appeal for Pentecostal pacifism since the early twentieth century.

Joel Shuman (1996)

While working on his Ph.D. dissertation under the direction of Stanley Hauerwas at Duke University, Shuman authored an article with the shameless title, "Pentecost and the End of Patriotism: A Call for the Restoration of Pacifism Among Pentecostal Christians."[123] He acknowledged the influence of Murray Dempster, John Howard Yoder, and Stanley Hauerwas and attempted to restore the prophetic element he and others thought had been lost.[124] For the purposes of this book, it is significant that Shuman directed his remarks specifically to the American Assemblies of God.

> This essay is intended to be prophetic in nature . . . it is meant to "reinforce a vision of the place of the believing community in history, which vision locates moral reasoning. . . ." *The 1967 decision of the Assemblies of God officially to abandon its historical position as a pacifist church was a grievous error* . . . the Assemblies of God ceased to exist in a way consistent with the radical eschatological vision which energized it from its beginning. . . . My arguments here are concerned with the Assemblies of God, simply because this is the community of which I am a member and with which I am most familiar.[125]

Having made it clear that he addressed the Assemblies of God, he further elucidated his purpose with a direct appeal.

> Where Dempster denies, however, that his primary goal is to "provide a basis from which to assess the normative *relevance of pacifism for today*," I shall make the provision of such a basis *my principal objective*. I want to offer, in other words, a theological rationale for my assertion that the gradual and eventually complete loss of its pacifism is among the most compelling signs that

the Assemblies of God has, at least in practice, abandoned its self-understanding as a community of radical Christian witness. For in this regard *I agree* with Stanley Hauerwas, who has said *that nonviolence is "the hallmark of the Christian moral life . . .* not just an option for a few, but incumbent on all Christians who seek to live faithfully in the kingdom made possible by the life, death, and resurrection of Jesus."[126]

Shuman linked pacifism with the radical Christian witness that Pentecostalism hoped to exemplify. He blamed the demise of pacifism on (1) the loss of identity as an eschatologically driven church; and (2) the acceptance of American nationalism and democratic liberalism. These events occurred because (a) the Assemblies of God accepted the lie that America was founded on Christian principles and was therefore favored by God and (b) the Assemblies of God gained acceptance "into the highly nationalistic American evangelical mainstream" (by joining the NAE).[127]

Shuman not only pointed out the errors, he also provided solutions to these problems. Although he did not enumerate them as follows, the following arrangement delineates his concerns. First, Pentecostals once again needed to restore the disestablishmentarianism of early Christianity/Pentecostalism. "A general attitude of social and political disestablishment was . . . seen as an integral part of the Pentecostal renewal."[128] This attitude should include non-nationalism and non-patriotism because "pride in nation and race was an abomination."[129] It should also reject the quest for power that so limited the prophetic voice of respected churches, i.e. the "establishmentarian Christianity that Pentecostalism's restorationist heritage led it to repudiate."[130] That kind of Christianity believed, erroneously, that "the state is at the very least the necessary establisher and protector of a cluster of personal and institutional freedoms which are necessary for the good of the church."[131] Shuman followed Yoder's analysis of Constantinian accommodation and applied it specifically to the Assemblies of God: they believed that God's reign was evident because of a "Christian America" which acted on behalf of God to protect the church; as America prospers so prospers the church.[132] Worship of America had to cease.

Second, Pentecostals needed to base their position on war in Scripture for "the initial statement of the General Council is explicitly theological in its language and logic" and referred to numerous New Testament Scriptures that "were to be modeled by a faithful community."[133] However, the military service resolution of 1967 "is void of any such references" and appealed instead to abstract principles that were "patently fallacious on historical and philosophical, as well as theological, grounds."[134] Furthermore, Shuman alleged that the closer Pentecostals got to the state, the further they got from Scripture.[135] A return to Scripture would be a return to the proper non-patriotic pacifism inherent in the early radical witness of the church.

Third, the Assemblies of God needed to evaluate whether their "evangelistic passion" allowed them to forsake important aspects of their heritage. Especially since the new members had been raised as nationalistic Americans and had only changed their views on tongues, "the growth and subsequent institutionalization of the Pentecostal movement was rapid enough . . . that the community was unable to continue defining itself in ways consistent with its restorationist heritage."[136]

Fourth, the Assemblies of God's desire for acceptability that manifested itself when they helped found the National Association of Evangelicals needed to be reversed. He noted Blumhofer's observation that "it is hardly a coincidence that Assemblies of God views on war and country changed significantly at about the same time the denomination affiliated with the NAE."[137] Shuman pointed out that the first president of the National Association of Evangelicals (formed April 1942) was highly patriotic, strongly anti-Catholic, and assumed that "there is a sort of philosophical principle undergirding both Christianity and the United States Constitution and that this principle is in a sense more significant than the gospel, which is but a historical manifestation of the principal."[138] This view necessitates warfare to defend itself while the gospel does not.

The last two suggestions that Shuman made formed the basis for his contention that the story of Pentecost should be central to Christian nonviolence and that Pentecostals should be the ones to bring this back to the church. He believed that "a return to pacifism still exists" for the Assemblies of God because of both "the eschatological nature of its origins and the priority it gives the book of Acts among the New Testament Scriptures."[139]

Shuman argued that the arrival of the Holy Spirit had been understood as an eschatological event that empowered the believers to be "a radical community of witness to the life, death, and resurrection of

Jesus."[140] This provided the basis for a strong commitment to pacifism, and although he believed the link was not made by early Pentecostals, it could still be done.[141] He appealed to Stanley Hauerwas' approach that recognized the importance of the narrative character of Christian life and belief.

> "There is no more fundamental way to talk of God," he claims, "than in a story. . . ." Christians are "justified" and "sanctified" through our participation in this story. . . . Participation in the stories of Israel and Jesus rightly calls into question the supposition that Christians must calculate ways to protect themselves and to control their own existences; it names as a lie the notion that human existence in a world filled with violence necessarily relativizes the way of life presented in Jesus' life, death, and resurrection.[142]

Shuman then argued that Pentecostals, because they privileged the story of Acts, were "uniquely well positioned" to testify to the power of the Spirit which enabled one to live peaceably in "a new world [as] a new people."[143]

> Our participation in the Christian story offers an altogether different possibility for our existence, a possibility grounded in the claim that as we make the story of Jesus . . . our own, we are brought into the immediacy of God's kingdom . . . in which we are called to learn how to live. We are thus able to see the world from a distinctively eschatological perspective.[144]

According to Shuman, Pentecostal unity reversed Babel's divisions and showed that people no longer had to kill someone who differed from them or disagreed with them. This opened "a new possibility of human, social, and therefore political relationships" which were symbolized by God's one language that was heard by all in their own tongue (*glossolalia*).[145] At Pentecost the human story culminated with God's triumphant victory over violence that had been caused by the divisions of Babel: "God had begun the final work of gathering together the world's scattered peoples into one new people."[146]

The power of this interpretation is that Shuman joined the proud Assemblies of God distinctive, speaking in tongues, with Hauerwas' argument that it was more than just words.

The glossolalia of Pentecost represents the Spirit's creation of a new language that is not restricted to the utterance of words. "It is instead a community whose memory of its Savior creates the miracle of being a people whose very differences contribute to their unity. . . ." The community which looks forward [eschatologically] to the time when God will complete the work of gathering together. . . ."[147]

Shuman cited Hauerwas' observation that Christians had an "alternative to Babel, to fear of one another, and finally then to war. . . . We do not just have an alternative, we are the alternative. We do not just have a story to tell but in the telling we *are* the story being told."[148] Shuman drew his composition to a close with a conclusion intended to stir the hearts and minds of his Pentecostal readers.

Pentecostals, of all such people, ought to be faithful embodiments of this story. For it is our "distinctive testimony" that at Pentecost God made possible the existence of a community whose willingness to live "filled with the Spirit" makes present to the world the reality of God's kingdom. A reality so centered around so peaceable a vision certainly precludes any level of participation in killing. May we be transformed by the recovery of this vision.[149]

Thus, almost thirty years after the Assemblies of God officially abandoned their pacifist heritage, one Assemblies of God person directly challenged them to recover it.

SUMMARY

Several scholars, both inside and outside of the Assemblies of God, mentioned the pacifist transition in various contexts but did not suggest that the path to militarism could ever change. Nevertheless, a small trickle of Assemblies of God scholars began to investigate the issue and finally recommended that the loss of pacifism had been a dreadful mistake. Each of these Assemblies of God people who suggested that pacifism was an important element of Pentecostalism did so while and after studying Pentecostal history and theology. Perhaps the struggle inherent in education pushed them to consider that their denomination had changed in a theologically and ethically unfortunate manner. Even though their analyses have been largely overlooked by most within the Assemblies of God, their faithful work has inspired a reemergence of a concern for a Pentecostal peace and justice witness that is now developing into a growing movement.[150]

NOTES

1. Murray Dempster holds the Ph.D. in social ethics from the University of Southern California, Roger Robins holds the M.Div. from Harvard Divinity School, Howard Kenyon holds the Ph.D. in religion (theological ethics) from Baylor University, Dwight Wilson holds the Ph.D. from the University of California, Santa Cruz, and Joel Shuman holds the Ph.D. in theological ethics from Duke University. Jay Beaman, a non-Assemblies of God Pentecostal who researched Assemblies of God pacifism, holds the M.Div. from North American Baptist Seminary and the Ph.D. These are the ones who write, but it does not mean that those with less formal education do not and cannot interpret scripture in ways that lead them away from combatant participation in war. This was certainly the case in the early Pentecostal movement.

2. William W. Menzies, *Anointed to Serve* (Springfield, Mo.: Gospel Publishing House, 1971), 326-328.

3. Ibid., 326-327.

4. Ibid., 327.

5. Ibid., 328.

6. Ibid., 188. Emphasis added. The Assemblies of God actually did minister to the military in World War I, see chapter two of this book.

7. Ibid., 189. Emphasis added.

8. Walter J. Hollenweger, *The Pentecostals: The Charismatic Movement in the Churches* (Minneapolis, Minn.: Augsburg Publishing House, 1972). He had written his ten-volume Th.D. dissertation, "Handbuch der Pfingstbewegung," at the University of Zurich in 1965 and portions of it were revised and republished in German, English, and Spanish.

9. Ibid., 36. His analysis is set in the context of ethical legalism. "The Assemblies of God began by making rigorist demands upon its members. Make-up, the theatre, the cinema, and even secondary schools (high schools) and universities lay outside the social horizons of its founders and religious taboo was therefore placed on them. This changed in time. The men earned more money, and consequently the women wanted to be better dressed and the children wanted to take their education further. In this respect the leaders of the Assemblies of God are constantly on the retreat because they will not risk losing their influence on future generations."

10. Ibid., 37.

11. Ibid., 401.

12. Walter J. Hollenweger, *Pentecostalism: Origins and Developments Worldwide* (Peabody, Mass.: Hendrickson Publishers, Inc., 1997). He referred to the works of Jay Beaman, Murray Dempster, Roger Robins, and Joel Shuman. Apparently

Howard Kenyon's dissertation did not receive enough circulation to reach his notice.

13. Ibid., 187-188. Hollenweger referred to Murray Dempster's thesis that pacifism was lost because it was only held by a "prophetic minority."

14. Ibid. He tied it to social concern, contra Robert Anderson and John Howard Yoder, non-Pentecostals considered below.

15. Ibid., 307-325.

16. Ibid., 189.

17. Ibid. Emphasis in the original.

18. In 1997 Jay Beaman had an opportunity to defend his interpretation that the majority of early Pentecostals were pacifists. Murray Dempster had disagreed with him by arguing that only a prophetic minority held pacifistic ideals. Beaman responded by posing six "serious questions" that needed to be answered in order for the minority theory to be true. Each of his questions and the responses of this author are in chapter one of this book. Jay Beaman, "Pacifism Among the Early Pentecostals, Conflicts Within and Without: A Response to Murray W. Dempster and Theodore Kornweibel Jr.," in *Proclaim Peace: Christian Pacifism From Unexpected Quarters*, ed. Theron F. Schlabach and Richard T. Hughes (Champaign, Ill.: University of Illinois Press, 1997), 82-93.

19. August Cerillo Jr., "Moving Up: Some Consequences of the New A/G Social Status," *Agora* 1 (Winter 1978): 8-11.

20. Ibid., 11.

21. Robert Mapes Anderson, *Vision of the Disinherited: The Making of American Pentecostalism* (Oxford: Oxford University Press, 1979), xi, xii.

22. This has been contested by Kenyon, Dempster, Hollenweger, and myself.

23. Anderson, *Vision of the Disinherited*, 202.

24. Ibid.

25. Ibid., 203-204.

26. Ibid., 231.

27. Ibid., 239-240.

28. Ibid., 240.

29. Jay Beaman, "Pentecostal Pacifism: The Origin, Development, and Rejection of Pacific Belief Among the Pentecostals" (M.Div. thesis, North American Baptist Seminary, 1982).

30. Jay Beaman, "Pacifism and the World View of Early Pentecostalism," paper presented to The Society for Pentecostal Studies, Cleveland, Tenn., November 1983.

31. Jay Beaman, *Pentecostal Pacifism: The Origin, Development, and Rejection of Pacific Belief Among the Pentecostals*, with a forward by John Howard Yoder (Hillsboro, Kan.: Center for Mennonite Brethren Studies, 1989).

32. Ibid., viii.

33. Beaman, "Pacifism and the World View of Early Pentecostalism," 1, 4.

34. Ibid., 5, 18, 23, 28.

35. Beaman, *Pentecostal Pacifism*, 4-14.

36. Ibid., 107, 109.

37. Ibid., 112-118.

38. Ibid., 123.

39. These are evaluated in the next section of this chapter.

40. John Howard Yoder, *Christian Attitudes to War, Peace, and Revolution: A Companion to Bainton* (Elkhart, Ind.: Goshen Biblical Seminary, 1983).

41. Ibid., 307.

42. Ibid.

43. Ibid., 308.

44. Ibid., 308-309.

45. Ibid., 309.

46. John Howard Yoder, foreword to *Pentecostal Pacifism*, by Jay Beaman (Hillsbore, Kan.: Center for Mennonite Brethren Studies, 1989), iii.

47. Ibid.

48. Ibid., iii-iv.

49. Ibid., iv.

50. Ibid., v.

51. Gary B. McGee, *This Gospel Shall Be Preached: A History and Theology of Assemblies of God Foreign Missions*, vol. 1, *A History and Theology of Assemblies of God Foreign Missions to 1959* (Springfield, Mo.: Gospel Publishing House, 1986). Gary B. McGee, *This Gospel Shall Be Preached: A History and Theology of Assemblies of God Foreign Missions*, vol. 2, *A History and Theology of Assemblies of God Foreign Missions since 1959* (Springfield, Mo.: Gospel Publishing House, 1989).

52. McGee, *This Gospel Shall Be Preached: A History and Theology of Assemblies of God Foreign Missions*, vol. 1, *A History and Theology of Assemblies of God Foreign Missions to 1959* (Springfield, Mo.: Gospel Publishing House, 1986), 93. This was a quote from Roger Robins, "Attitudes Toward War and Peace in the Assemblies of God: 1914-1918," 1982, 6 (Typewritten).

53. Ibid., 226.

54. Gary B. McGee, "Questions & Answers," *Assemblies of God Heritage* 11, no 2 (Summer 1991), 6.

55. Edith L. Blumhofer, *The Assemblies of God: A Chapter in the Story of American Pentecostalism*, vol. 1, *To 1941* (Springfield, Mo.: Gospel Publishing House, 1989), 344-355. Edith L. Blumhofer, *The Assemblies of God: A Chapter in the Story of American Pentecostalism*, vol. 2, *Since 1941* (Springfield, Mo.: Gospel Publishing House, 1989), 11.

56. Blumhofer, *The Assemblies of God*, vol. 1, 347.

57. Ibid., 352. Shuman disagreed and said the statement was very theological, see the next section of this chapter.

58. Either she was not aware of Moon's analysis or she recognized that it was not officially sanctioned by the General Council. They began an attempt to address this by discussing war and military service in *Assemblies of God Perspectives: Contemporary Issues: Social, Medical, Political* in 1995. Michael Beals, an Assemblies of God minister, has also addressed just war tradition in "Toward a Constructive Pentecostal Perspective of the Just War Tradition: New Direction for the Moral Migration of the Assemblies of God," Ph.D. dissertation, Fuller Theological Seminary, 2002.

59. Blumhofer reported that E. S. Williams, former General Superintendent, expressed his sadness at the loss of the peace witness to her in a personal interview in

1976. Blumhofer, *The Assemblies of God*, 435.

60. Blumhofer, *The Assemblies of God: A Chapter in the Story of American Pentecostalism*, vol. 1, *To 1941*, 355.

61. Dempster has served at Vanguard University (Assemblies of God) as professor of social ethics, Vice President for Academic Affairs and Dean, Provost, and now President. He also served as the editor of *Pneuma: The Journal of the Society for Pentecostal Studies*.

62. Murray W. Dempster, "Peacetime Draft Registration and Pentecostal Moral Conscience," 1 *Agora* (Spring 1980): 2-3. Dempster served as one of the editors of *Agora* at this time and this article was a slightly revised reprint of his unpublished "From Conscientious Objection to the Just War: The Ironic Journey of Pentecostal Social Conscience," Special Vietnam Moratorium Day Assembly, Southern California College, 1970.

63. Ibid., 2.

64. Ibid.

65. Ibid., 3.

66. Ibid.

67. "Resolution 22. World Peace Tax Fund," *General Council Minutes*, 1981, 70-71.

68. Ibid., 71.

69. *Assemblies of God Perspectives—Contemporary Issues: Social, Medical, and Political* (Springfield, Mo.: Gospel Publishing House, 1995), 50. Emphasis added.

70. Roger Robins, "A Chronology of Peace: Attitudes Toward War and Peace in the Assemblies of God: 1914-1918," *Pneuma: The Journal of the Society for Pentecostal Studies* (Spring 1984): 3-25. He graduated in June 1984.

71. Ibid., 3.

72. Ibid., 14.

73. Ibid.

74. Ibid., 23.

75. Ibid.

76. Ibid., 24.

77. Wayne Warner of Springfield, Missouri, interview by author, 20 March 2000, e-mail. Robins conducted research at the Assemblies of God Archives in Springfield, Missouri and became acquainted with Warner. Warner subsequently invited him to submit an article on this topic since *Pneuma* printed Robins previous article.

78. Roger Robins, "Our Forgotten Heritage: A Look at Early Pentecostal Pacifism," *Assemblies of God Heritage*, Winter 1986-87, 3.

79. Ibid., 4.

80. Ibid. Emphasis added.

81. Howard N. Kenyon, "An Analysis of Ethical Issues in the History of the Assemblies of God" (Ph.D. diss., Baylor University, 1988), iii.

82. Ibid.

83. Ibid., 284-400. His dissertation consisted of a preface and eight chapters (424 pages).

84. Ibid., 395. He referred specifically to Chase and Kruggel's resolution of 1981.

85. Howard Kenyon, interview by author, 26 February 2000, by telephone. Kenyon's grandfather was a Pentecostal with pacifistic tendencies during World War I. He refused to play "The Star Spangled Banner" in high school in 1916 because it "was war tainted," and he was not allowed to graduate.

86. Kenyon, "An Analysis," 396.

87. Ibid., 396-397.

88. Ibid., 400.

89. Ibid., 399.

90. Ibid., 400.

91. Ibid., 401, 403.

92. Ibid., 421.

93. Ibid., 422.

94. Ibid., 423-424.

95. Dwight J. Wilson, "Pacifism," in *Dictionary of Pentecostal and Charismatic Movements*, ed. Stanley M. Burgess, Gary B. McGee, and Patrick H. Alexander (Grand Rapids, Mich.: Zondervan, 1988), 658-660. Wilson cited Anderson, Beaman, Hollenweger, Menzies, and Robins as his sources for this article.

96. Ibid., 658.

97. Ibid.

98. Ibid., 659.

99. Ibid. Emphasis added.

100. Gary B. McGee of Springfield, Missouri, interview by author, 24 April 2000, e-mail, personal files of author.

101. Murray Dempster, "Jay Beaman, *Pentecostal Pacifism: The Origins, Development and Rejection of Pacific Belief among the Pentecostals* (Hillsboro, Kan.: Center for Mennonite Brethren Studies, 1989), 142 pp. $10.00 paper. Reviewed by Murray W. Dempster," *Pneuma* 11, no. 1 (Fall 1989): 60.

102. Ibid., 60-61.

103. Ibid., 61.

104. Ibid., 62-63.

105. Ibid., 63.

106. Ibid., 63-64.

107. Murray W. Dempster, "Reassessing the Moral Rhetoric of Early American Pentecostal Pacifism," *Crux* 26, no. 1 (March 1990): 23-36. This article issued from work he had done for the 7th. Annual Pentecostal Lectureship at Regent College, Vancouver, Canada, October 12-13, 1988. Nevertheless, he did not publish it until after he reviewed Beaman's book.

108. Ibid., 23.

109. Ibid.

110. Ibid.

111. Ibid., 26-28.

112. Ibid., 28-30.

113. Ibid., 30-32.

114. Ibid., 32.

115. Dempster, "Reassessing," 32.

116. Ibid.

117. Ibid., 33. Emphasis added.

118. Murray W. Dempster, "'Crossing Borders:' Arguments Used By Early American Pentecostals in Support of the Global Character of Pacifism," *The Journal of the European Pentecostal Theological Association* 10, no. 2 (1991): 63-80.

119. Ibid., 75.

120. Ibid. 76. Emphasis in the original.

121. "Pacifism in Pentecostalism: The Case of the Assemblies of God" at Conference on "Pacifist Traditions in American Churches (other than historic Peace churches)," jointly sponsored by Goshen College and Pepperdine University at Goshen College, Goshen, Indiana, September 24-26, 1992; "Pacifism as a Divisive Issue in the Pentecostal Tradition," at A Consultation on "The Fragmentation of the Church and its Unity in Peacemaking," sponsored by the Faith and Order Working Group of the National Council of Churches/USA and by the Joan B. Kroc Institute for International Peace Studies at Notre Dame, held at the University of Notre Dame, Notre Dame, Ind., June 13-17, 1995.

122. "Pacifism in Pentecostalism: The Case of the Assemblies of God," in *Proclaim Peace: Voices of Christian Pacifism from Unexpected Sources,* ed. Theron F. Schlabach and Richard T. Hughes (Champaign, Ill.: University of Illinois Press, 1997), 31-57.

123. Joel Shuman, "Pentecost and the End of Patriotism: A Call for the Restoration of Pacifism Among Pentecostal Christians," *Journal of Pentecostal Theology* 9 (1996): 70-96.

124. Kenyon had made the same observation in 1988 but neither Dempster nor Shuman referenced his work.

125. Shuman, 70-71. Emphasis added.

126. Ibid., 71-72. Emphasis added.

127. Ibid., 73, 85-86.

128. Ibid., 75.

129. Ibid.

130. Ibid., 78.

131. Ibid., 79.

132. Ibid., 80-82.

133. Ibid., 76. He disagreed with Blumhofer's assessment that the statement originated purely out of pragmatic necessity.

134. Ibid., 89. Shuman countered the idea that the church needed the state by insisting that "the church has existed and can continue to exist as a minority community at odds, rather than in partnership, with the state."

135. Ibid., 90. "As the church has deepened and complicated its alliances with government, that deepening has demanded an ever-increasing reliance on principles and ideals and a corresponding abandonment of the scriptural accounts of Jesus and the church."

136. Ibid., 83, 85. He referred to Yoder's analysis that Pentecostals lost pacifism because they did not have peace church associations to help them retain it.

137. Ibid., 87.

138. Ibid.

139. Ibid., 90.

140. Ibid., 91.

141. My analysis shows that the connection had been made to a limited extent by some early Pentecostal pacifists (the Booth-Clibborns), see chapter four.

142. Shuman, "Pentecost and the End of Patriotism," 92. He quotes Stanley Hauerwas, *The Peaceable Kingdom* (Notre Dame, Ind.: University of Notre Dame Press, 1983), 25.

143. Shuman, "Pentecost and the End of Patriotism," 93.

144. Ibid. Shuman also employed the work of George Lindbeck, *The Nature of Doctrine* (Philadelphia: Westminster Press, 1984), 116-118.

145. Shuman, "Pentecost and the End of Patriotism," 94-95.

146. Ibid., 95.

147. Ibid.

148. Ibid. Stanley Hauerwas, "The Church as God's New Language," in *Christian Existence Today* (Durham, NC: Labyrinth, 1988), 48. Emphasis in the original.

149. Ibid., 96.

150. Pentecostal and Charismatics for Peace and Justice—www.pcpf.org.

NINE

BUT WHAT ABOUT JESUS? THE ETHICAL TRANSFORMATION OF THE ASSEMBLIES OF GOD

The transformation from peace to war in this story led to implications that still define the American Assemblies of God. This book considers these implications. But I must confess that I have little interest in whether pacifism was a majority or minority position in the early years of the Assemblies of God. That numbers game is less significant than the actual theology and practice of Jesus-shaped love of enemy that motivated so many early Pentecostals. Even if only one person takes up the cross and follows Jesus, it is still a witness to the Way, Truth, and Life.

Historical arguments come and go. I make my case for crucifism theologically—as did the early Pentecostals—not based on a statistically verifiable number of my ancestors who believed a certain way. For the majority is often wrong about all manner of important beliefs and practices (slavery, segregation). The majority, might by numbers, does *not* make right. My historical arguments are simply historical—my theological arguments are much more important because they call us to a faithful way of living regardless of what our ancestors did.

Factors in the Loss of Pacifism

This last chapter summarizes elements of this story of the Assemblies of God and pacifism by focusing on the desire for acceptability and effectiveness, Jesus and biblical interpretation, and the meaning of Pentecost. The loss of pacifism happened slowly as the Assemblies of God made choices which had consequences they could not see at the time, such as appealing to the authority of individual conscience as the ultimate authority rather than Jesus or reliance upon and interpretation of Scripture. Not wanting to alienate the non-pacifists, they chose conscience as authoritative with the best of intentions. Because of their commitment to Jesus' Great Commission they ministered to soldiers, not realizing at the time that this would develop into unqualified support of the military as a Christian vocation. They respected conscience, sought effective ministry, and desired acceptance without sinister motives.

Many scholars have noted that the Assemblies of God desired acceptability from the American culture and government as well as from the fundamentalist religious establishment. They wanted to be radical while worshipping in the privacy of the church building, but it was harder to be radical in public regarding controversial issues about which their religious and patriotic friends had contradictory views. Subordinating public and potentially embarrassing ethical stands under doctrinal distinctives eased the tension with surrounding culture. So they held to radical orthodoxy (right worship—speaking in tongues) but not radical orthopraxy (right living—nonviolence).

The Assemblies of God increasingly began to interpret Scripture and Jesus in ways that supported the secular and religious status quo. References to the teachings of Jesus regarding violence disappeared from conversations about war. They focused on one Pauline reference and Hebrew Scripture passages for assistance regarding war and used narrative for doctrine—for narrative is the one and only possible way to argue that speaking in tongues is the one and only initial physical evidence of being baptized in the Holy Spirit.[1] But the Assemblies of God stopped using the narrative of Jesus' life or the early church for their ethics of war and peacemaking.

The significance of this latter move is that the Assemblies of God lost elements of Pentecost. Sadly, by disregarding the nonviolence of Jesus, they exchanged the Spirit-empowered message of suffering love for a more popular and less critical Americanized religion. They abandoned their prophetic voice by which they critiqued the domination and oppression of the social order. They significantly lost their ability to view patriotism and violence from the perspective of kingdom out-siders, for they had transformed themselves into political insiders. Re-grettably, Spirit-empowered peace witness degenerated into mere verbal proclamation, and eschatology helped them accept Christian participa-tion in "war, wickedness, and violence" as inevitable and necessary.

ACCEPTABILITY AND EFFECTIVENESS

With good objectives and amid the extreme nationalism of World War I, the more patriotic Pentecostals reminded the majority of the ne-cessity of loyalty to the government. The tremendous pressure from the Espionage and Sedition Acts helps clarify why E. N. Bell, the Texas Dis-trict Council, and the authors of the 1917 Military Service article would express their respect for the secular establishment. They were not neces-sarily catering to a nationalistic minority; they were surviving as a fledg-ling pacifist organization amid an all-encompassing war. In the same resolution, the executive presbytery passed that argued for exemptions from military service, they also employed respectful patriotic language by "affirming . . . unswerving loyalty to the Government of the United States."[2] Thus, they presented both a love for their country and the re-fusal to fight for it in the same resolution. Out of these tensions the de-sire for governmental approval eventually emerged victorious, but it did not start that way.

They pledged loyal support for the president, "your Excellency," and passed resolutions that expressly related their desire to be accepted and approved by the state. In 1918 they again declared their "unswerv-ing loyalty" and hoped for a "successful conclusion" to the war.[3] By 1927 they had bracketed their conscientious objection between two declara-tions of unswerving loyalty. Seeking approval from the government led eventually to the abandonment of a Christian ethic that directly, though nonviolently, confronted that government. The majority of the early As-semblies of God did not specifically abandon pacifism to support Amer-ica; they simply went along with the ongoing transition of the Assem-blies of God into an American church, and with the Americanization of the world.

During the debate about the military service article at the General Council in 1967, the statement of one Assemblies of God minister seems clearly to reveal that a quest for acceptance motivated their opposition to conscientious objection. Supporting conscientious objectors meant "protection of a few at the cost of *condemnation of the whole*."[4] The specific issue of opposition to killing in warfare embarrassed them, because it brought condemnation from the American churches with which the Assemblies of God had associated. In fact, the chaplains who in 1965 recommended the removal of the pacifist article cited the reality that it diminished the effectiveness of evangelistic efforts among military personnel.[5]

The Assemblies of God began in an attempt to restore New Testament Christianity to the church and to the world. Many believed that this restoration included a critique of violence and injustice. Dempster wisely noted that their pacifism served as their concrete moral sign that they had the character of the New Testament Christians. However, others limited the restoration to speaking in tongues, healings, and other gifts of the Holy Spirit.

Both approaches conflicted with the religious establishment in America. However, those who accepted the former did so in a public manner that criticized the way the American churches supported their "Christian" government. Those who limited restoration to the latter manifestations of the Spirit could enjoy their experiential Christianity in the privacy of their own churches. As the Assemblies of God grew, those who critiqued war had diminishing significance. When the Assemblies of God desired to affiliate with other American evangelical churches in the 1940s, their peace witness, though still present, weakened even more. Yet even this limited conscientious objection did not match the ethics of the churches with which they desired to associate. The leaders who led the Assemblies of God toward the religious establishment did not highlight their pacifist heritage, and they let the controversial peace witness expire in the 1950s and 1960s.

Thankfully, twenty-first century ecumenism is moving toward testimony sharing and friendship that encourages Christians to speak authentically out of their experience and their traditions.[6] This should mean that Historic Peace Churches need not fear losing their nonviolent pacifism as they engage in interchurch fellowship, as long as they do not try to seek acceptability by abandoning it. Seeking approval is quite different from Christian unity and ecumenical dialogue.

The Assemblies of God impressed American evangelicals with their support of World War II by sending sixty-five thousand soldiers (not mentioning that many were noncombatants) and over sixteen million pieces of free Christian literature to the Allied forces while employing over one hundred personnel in their Servicemen's Department.[7] They participated in the formation of the National Association of Evangelicals in 1942 and increasingly conformed to the American church that many had hoped to reform. They became a conservative and established American denomination on the outside (regarding their politics), and reserved their radical practices (tongues speech and ecstatic worship, etc.) for the inside.

The well-intentioned ministry to the military that began in World War I eventually developed into a chaplaincy department that brought ever increasing prestige to the Assemblies of God. Pentecostals knew without a doubt that God empowered them to witness to everybody and the military was a ripe mission field. But they did not nuance their ministry to protect against the loss of their witness for cross-bearing rather than weapons-bearing as the faithfulness that Jesus called them to. One of the unintended consequences of their effective ministry to the soldiers was that the United States military converted the Assemblies of God into one of its greater supporters. If first-generation pacifists had foreseen the changes that eventually befell the Assemblies of God, they likely would have developed strategies to make disciples of all nations that did not require the compromises they ultimately made.

JESUS AND SCRIPTURE

The Assemblies of God eventually began to interpret Scripture the way established Christendom churches do, which means that they are certainly not alone in rendering Jesus irrelevant for social ethics. As John Howard Yoder noted, no particular condemnation needs to fall on the American Assemblies of God, since they simply began to act like other mainline traditions.

At their origins, however, they were differently oriented. They consistently read the whole counsel of Scripture in light of the fact that Jesus, the clear revelation of God, had arrived. They began their articles with such questions and declarations as "What saith Scripture on this all important matter?"[8] "The arguments [are] based solely on the authority of God's Holy Word"[9] and "I took the stand that I did as a C. O. [because] I could not see any other stand to take as a Christian who is measuring his walk by the Word of God."[10] The 1917 resolution appealed to Jesus and contained references to Scripture in every paragraph.[11]

The Pentecostals who professed pacifist theology and practice had a christocentric hermeneutic. They interpreted the instructions and life of Jesus seriously and applied them to themselves, regardless of the consequences.

> I don't believe in the face of all these Scriptures Christians should believe it to be right to engage in fights or kill one another. It is not what we think about it, but we are pledged already as Christians *to obey Christ* and the *teachings of the New Testament*. If we are fully on the Lord's side on this question, we will have to say what the Lord says about it.[12]

Their respect for the New Testament and for Jesus meant that they would take the reproach of Christ upon themselves even to the point of death and caused them to interpret Hebrew Scriptures in light of the more complete revelation in Jesus. The Pentecostal pacifists publicly proclaimed the nonviolent resistance inherent in the good news of Jesus.

Whenever any Assemblies of God people argued against the pacifists or the conscientious objectors, they would consistently employ a rationale that appealed to defending the innocent, obeying the government, or honoring the authority of one's own conscience. When they referred to Scripture, they quoted the Hebrew Scriptures, the first few verses of Romans 13, and other verses that seemed to support doing what the government said. They even said that the Hebrew Scriptures controlled what Jesus' and the Sermon on the Mount could mean. So they employed a different, non-christocentric hermeneutic. They consistently avoided both the Gospels and references to Jesus. Beginning with the support of the European War in 1914, "[otherwise] not a life in Christendom would be safe. The State is of God,"[13] and continuing to the present, "We are committed to [war's] avoidance as much as accountability, sensibility, and responsibility allow,"[14] the American Assemblies of God has a different way of referencing Jesus than it did at its origins.

John Howard Yoder listed a number of historic ways that Christians have rendered Jesus irrelevant for social ethics.[15] First, some Christians argue that Jesus' rejection of violence, of self-defense, and of accumulating wealth were only for a brief interim period that did not take into account the survival of society. The duration of society itself invalidates Jesus' teachings, since they cannot be used to run a successful government in a fallen world. The survival of society is therefore more important than Jesus' teachings.

Second, other Christians say that Jesus was a simple rural figure who radically personalized all ethical problems. His vision is not possible in an urban or global context, since Jesus did not address complex organizations, institutions and offices, and power struggles. Therefore, Jesus is irrelevant because the world is more complicated now.

Third, Jesus and his followers lived in a world they could not control. Their lack of being able to exercise social responsibility left them only to be witnesses as a faithful minority. But Christianity has made great progress since Constantine's conversion in the fourth century, and "Judeo-Christian" values permeate Western culture. Thus Christians now have to make choices that Jesus did not face, and we must accept responsibilities that were inconceivable in Jesus' time. Therefore, our ability to control the present and the future require that we disregard Jesus.

Fourth, other Christians argue that Jesus' teachings were ahistorical, symbolic, and spiritual. He talked about spirituality, not social matters; atonement not obedience; not social change but a new private self understanding. Faith is viewed as inward and not to be expressed outwardly in society.

Fifth, Jesus came only to give his life for the sins of humanity; this justification of sins by Christ's self-giving death on the cross is correlated with one's being forgiven but should never be correlated with our own ethics. Justification is a miracle; it does not show us what proper behavior looks like. Therefore, the kind of life Jesus led or the death he died is ethically irrelevant.

The Assemblies of God does not offer a sophisticated explanation of why Jesus' life, teachings, death, or resurrection do not provide guidance for Christians' treatment of their enemies or for a rejection of violence, but their stance employs a combination of the reasons identified by Yoder. This contemporary outlook poses a stark contrast to the way first-generation Pentecostals appealed to Jesus for direction regarding participation in war. American Pentecostals, like the majority of other American Christians, have outgrown the narratives of Jesus and Acts and have adopted what they consider to be a more responsible managing of the affairs of the world. They now live in a different story.

It is not that the Assemblies of God is unethical or have no ethics. It is rather that the ethical norm has shifted from appeals to Jesus to a norm in line with politically conservative or fundamentalist teachings that support a nationalistic American agenda. Whereas in the early period they discussed killing and war with reference to Jesus, they now deal with war by quoting the first part of Romans 13 and by appealing to conscience based on Romans 14.

In my view, the appeal to conscience as the ultimate authority in approving combatant participation over the recognized teaching of Jesus exposes a tension within the ethical stance of the Assemblies of God. Only for the issues of war and capital punishment is individual conscience the norm. On other issues dear to the American Evangelical politically conservative agenda—abortion, drinking alcohol, lotteries, gambling, and tobacco—the stand of the church is clear, and the authority of conscience is never mentioned.[16]

In 1997 the Assemblies of God explained that they supported combat because "The Scriptures call for civic loyalty: 'Everyone must submit himself to the governing authorities, for there is no authority except that which God has established' (Rom. 13:1 NIV)."[17] As we consider whether the Assemblies of God has departed from its earliest vision of basing ethics on Jesus, there are some appropriate questions that should be asked about this particular passage. Does it mean all nations all of the time, all kings and presidents and dictators in particular, all governmental systems? Does this reference mean that Saddam Hussein was a governmental authority God established? That Adolph Hitler was established by God? That Bill Clinton and George W. Bush were governmental authorities God set up? Their use of this text justified German Christian participation in the Third Reich in the 1930s and 1940s, since those Christians were simply submitting to the divinely sanctioned governmental authority. They did not address when or if it was ever appropriate to disobey the governing authorities, for instance, if the government said Christians should do something that contradicted God's will. Even that simple caveat was gone in 1997.

Or does everything every government asks of its citizens become God's will based on Romans 13? Does "submission" then mean obedience? Paul did not tell the Roman Christians to *obey* the government. Can one disobey the governing authorities like Shadrach, Meschach, and Abednego yet still submit to the fiery furnace?[18] Can we disobey like

Peter did when he kept preaching, "Who am I to obey? God or man? Let God be true and every man a liar," and yet then he still submitted to being imprisoned? Could an American Pentecostal both *disobey* the government and *submit* to the government at the same time? Could she say no and submit to the consequences?

"Civic loyalty" should probably not mean disobeying the way of Jesus. Could Romans 13 have been Paul's way of telling Christians not to revolt against Roman rule even though it was oppressive and tyrannical? Perhaps participating in ongoing regime change attempts would get them killed, not for their faithfulness but for their unfaithfulness? Romans 13 also says that "love does no harm to its neighbor; therefore, love is the fulfillment of the law." But that part of Romans 13 and these questions were not even considered in a context in which American government is so intimately and closely aligned with God. Romans 13 simply serves as a proof text to justify Christian military service.

"Personal conscience in all matters" and "honest differences of opinion" seem only to apply to killing in war and killing criminals. The Assemblies of God clearly chooses their Scriptures selectively to bolster the status quo and its interests. According to my understanding of the importance of Jesus, this contemporary view seems to be a departure from the call to peacemaking Jesus issued. Once the Assemblies of God made it into the establishment and thoroughly adopted American civil religion, they either had to deal with the arguments of the pacifists or ignore them.

IMPLICATIONS: THE LOSS OF PENTECOST?

Pentecost encompassed three elements early Pentecostal pacifists recognized.[19] First, it meant being empowered to take the life and example of Jesus very seriously, even to the point of picking up the cross and following him in death. Jesus said, "If any one would come after me, he must deny himself and pick up his cross."

Second, it meant a prophetic and Spirit-empowered critique of social, racial, economic, institutional, religious, and state-sanctioned sin.

Third, Pentecost provided a transforming eschatology that allowed followers of Jesus to live in accordance with the ultimate end of all things. They could embrace the peaceful kingdom of God amid a violent and chaotic world because Jesus had come and shown them how to live (and die). The ways of the world do not determine the Way of the followers of Jesus—we can live Jesus' way *now* because we are in the world but not of (defined by) the world.

These elements are weakened in the American Assemblies of God today. However, the Assemblies of God did not willfully set out to abandon the pacifist heritage. The shift was gradual and occurred with the best of intentions, without a clear realization of what was happening—the Assemblies of God sincerely thought they were right when they changed the pacifist article in 1967. Jesus' example of self-giving love continued to be emphasized for missions and other works of compassion, but unfortunately qualified so that Pentecostals were taught to kill their enemies. Gradual choices along the way meant that critiques of consumerist greed, nationalistic idolatry, and the insanity of war were replaced by divinely sanctioned participation in all three. Most Assemblies of God Christians, like most Americans, support the seeking of riches, the love of country, and the killing that seems to make it possible. The reality shaping eschatology of the early pacifists has been overwhelmed by an eschatology that professes, "Jesus is coming back soon, but just in case he doesn't we need to kill our enemies."

The Assemblies of God has always claimed to be a Pentecostal church that lives in accordance to the way of Jesus: "The Assemblies of God shall represent, as nearly as possible, the body of Christ as described in the New Testament."[20] But today the impact of Pentecost has been limited to speaking in tongues and other experiences that do not confront the violent status quo. The Assemblies of God prefers to "fight the devil" by attacking state lotteries while fully participating in that which its members themselves describe as "violence, wickedness, and war."[21b] They accept the parts of New Testament Christianity that allow them to be good Americans but have rejected the nonviolence of New Testament Christianity and early Pentecostalism. First-generation Assemblies of God conscientious objectors believed Pentecost was an empowerment to live and die like Jesus, but it has perhaps become simply an entryway into ecstatic experiences. Even though ecstatic experiences are wonderful (I am in the fifty percent of Assemblies of God folk who pray in tongues) the gift of the Spirit on Pentecost also enabled a border-crossing, self-giving, reconciling, cross-bearing witness.

The loss of the peace witness brings into question whether the Assemblies of God can honestly consider itself a restoration of the New

Testament church. Alliance with America and the quest for acceptability, coupled with selective reliance on Jesus and Scripture, reveals that they are not as radical as they claim to be. To claim to be like first-century Christians while proudly participating in violence and warfare is less than commendable. It seems the Assemblies of God has three options if seeking to be honest about a self-understanding as a Holy Spirit-led renewal movement.

First, we can be more humble about presenting ourselves as a representation of the body of Christ as described in the New Testament. We have neither accepted nor adequately explained away the broad early Christian/Pentecostal witness to nonviolence. Since we have not officially attempted to deal with our own historical peace witness, which was an earnest attempt to restore primitive Christianity, we could simply admit that we are just doing the best we can and do not have it all figured out. In other words, avoid the controversial conversations about war and nationalism and just temper our hopes to live out New Testament Christianity.

Second, if we do insist on describing ourselves as a New Testament church, then we must resurrect the peace witness and reincorporate nonviolence into our understanding of Christianity and Pentecost, since it was integral to the early church. According to the founders of the denomination, and the majority of New Testament biblical scholars, the early Christians did indeed believe Jesus had taught them to be crucifists.[22] To say that we are Christians like the early Christians would mean that we should teach, preach, and practice nonviolence. A contemporary Pentecostal peace witness could be drafted by Assemblies of God ministers and constituents, published, and distributed. It should be the official position of the church once again, while also welcoming all into fellowship—even those who disagree.

A third option would be for the Assemblies of God to explore how we can be "restored," "Pentecostal," and "New Testament" without embodying the nonviolence inherent in the early witness of the church. Since the current position on military service allows for "combatants, noncombatants, and conscientious objectors" each of these should present their understanding of Jesus, Scripture, faith, and practice so that it can be critiqued by the others. This could include a careful and respectful discussion of just war tradition, Christian pacifism, and just peacemaking.[23] These issues could be revisited by Assemblies of God missionaries, pastors, lay persons, theologians, biblical scholars, and ethicists. Such a process would almost certainly nuance and strengthen the witness of the Assemblies of God regarding our participation in warfare. Furthermore, explanations of all three perspectives should be presented in official Assemblies of God literature.

SUGGESTIONS FOR FURTHER RESEARCH

For every question that this book may help answer, it elicits more that indicate areas than need further research. First, the relationship between ethics and doctrine needs to be examined in the Assemblies of God. If "authority of conscience" can be applied to war, could it also be applied to unique doctrines within the Assemblies of God? For instance, peacemaking and nonviolence were major teachings in the New Testament that numerous writers expressed, yet the Assemblies of God relegated them to personal conscience. However, speaking in tongues as the one and only evidence of being filled with the Holy Spirit (the famous doctrine of the Assemblies of God) is supported only by Luke (in Acts), then with only three direct references. Nothing in the Hebrew Scriptures, Paul, Matthew, Mark, John, Peter, or James helps the Assemblies of God make its case. All they have is a story, but that is enough. Tongues as "initial physical evidence" has significantly less biblical support than nonviolence, but more than enough for the Assemblies of God to make it mandatory.

In other words, if I employ a classical Pentecostal approach to narrative to support this doctrine (Luke teaches it by the way he tells the story) then the way has been paved to argue quite easily for nonviolence. Yet nonviolence is a matter of conscience, not a matter of biblical interpretation. Could tongues as initial physical evidence also be a matter of conscience rather than of biblical interpretation?

Second, an entire book could be devoted to the effects the Assemblies of God military chaplaincy program has had upon the ethics and nationalism of the denomination. The degree to which it has been a factor in helping transform the Assemblies of God into an Americanized church rather than a globally oriented and non-nationalistic movement should be examined.

Third, the recovery of a peace testimony within Pentecostalism in general and the Assemblies of God in particular needs to encouraged and supported. The positive elements within Pentecostalism that are conducive to a peace testimony should be highlighted and linked to crucifism. Appeals to the example of Jesus, scriptural authority, the power of the Holy Spirit, and prophetic radical witness all remain within the language of the Assemblies of God. We value narrative and use it to establish doctrine. But these positive aspects have been limited and muted so as to fit within the belief systems of violence affirming Christians. Could a large and established denomination bring back a long-forgotten emphasis and admit that we made a mistake when we removed it? We tried to do so with racial reconciliation by repenting of racism.[24] The prospects for such a repentance regarding militarism and nationalism should be considered as well.

CONCLUSION

The number of people who were or are Jesus-following crucifists is much less significant than the actual theology and practice of Jesus-shaped love of enemy that motivated so many of the early Pentecostals. For in their early years the Assemblies of God believed Pentecostal Christianity included loving enemies and not killing them. These conscientious objectors wrote a biblically and theologically informed peace witness during World War I that lasted for fifty years. However, the number of Pentecostals who supported Americanism and war continued to increase as the movement aged. The Assemblies of God associated with churches that promoted nationalistic ideals, and the crucifists slowly and quietly disappeared. Acceptance into mainstream politically conservative American evangelicalism necessitated that the Assemblies of God agree with their ethical issues, such as who to kill.

Meanwhile they were allowed to differ on doctrinal issues related to the way they acted when in their own church buildings, such as speaking in tongues. These latter elements eventually became the defining marks of Pentecostalism. The majority of the members of the Assemblies of God accepted the necessity of war by World War II and became an increasingly militant church throughout the rest of the century. They eventually even condemned conscientious objectors, not realizing they condemned their own founders. They came to express sincere militarism and Americanism as forcefully as early Pentecostal pacifists had rejected them.

Reading this story could cause some frustration because of the way the Assemblies of God has changed. Some could even think that they have to choose between Jesus and Pentecostalism, and some might be willing to abandon the latter for the former. But Pentecostals do not have to make that choice. They can believe in and follow Jesus as cross-bearing, Holy Spirit-filled, tongue-talking, enemy-loving, nonviolent witnesses to the Way, Truth, and Life.

The Assemblies of God constituents have not completely lost a love for Jesus, emphasis on Spirit empowerment, and the belief that we can be disciples right now in this sinful world. These elements still exist, but the amount of emphasis placed on them has decreased, and the way they are expressed has shifted. This book has described the choices the Assemblies of God made that led to the shift. But since it resulted from choices we as a denomination made, perhaps the shift can be reversed by different choices in the future.

This book also speaks to the Historic Peace Churches. It is my hope that they can see in this story how easily the Christian pacifist nonviolent witness can be lost. Warning signs abound. The story in this book can enable them to diagnose their own situations so they can prayerfully and courageously strengthen their witness. The Historic Peace Churches' visible and bold proclamation in both word and deed to the nonviolence inherent in the gospel of Jesus Christ is a gift to the world.

Pentecostals are reinvestigating the importance of a peace testimony and Pentecostal peacemakers exist today.[25] Pentecostal peacemakers are also becoming more vocal, but the degree of their persuasiveness has yet to be seen. Individual Christians, the Assemblies of God, and other denominations *can* make different choices that better embody the way of Jesus. I hope and pray that there will be growing awareness that Jesus' teachings regarding peacemaking and violence deserve careful consideration.

NOTES

1. *General Council Minutes*, 1999, 92.

2. J. W. Welch, "An Explanation," *The Weekly Evangel*, 19 May 1917, 8.

3. "Expression of Loyalty to the Government," *General Council Minutes*, 1918, 9.

4. Cordas C. Burnett, as quoted by Howard Cummings of Aurora, Colorado, interview by author, 12 April 2000, by letter, personal files of the author. Emphasis added. Burnett served as National Secretary for the Assemblies of God Education

Department and as president of Bethany Bible College (Assemblies of God).

5. Dwight J. Wilson, "Pacifism," in *Dictionary of Pentecostal and Charismatic Movements*, ed. Stanley M. Burgess, Gary B. McGee, and Patrick H. Alexander (Grand Rapids, Mich.: Zondervan, 1988).

6. John Dart, "Ecumenism's New Basis: Testimony," *The Christian Century* 124, no. 17 (21 August 2007): 12-13.

7. Harry A. Jaegar, "Spiritual Conquest Among the American Doughboys," *The Pentecostal Evangel*, 12 May 1945, 5, 7. "Helping the Servicemen," *The Pentecostal Evangel*, 21 February 1942, 6.

8. "The Crisis," *The Weekly Evangel*, 21 April 1917, 7. The author then quoted from Matthew 5-7, Luke 6, and Philippians 3.

9. Samuel H. Booth-Clibborn, "The Christian and War. It is too Late?" *The Weekly Evangel*, 28 April 1917, 5. Booth-Clibborn referenced Hebrews 13, John 1, Matthew 5 and 18, Philippians 3, Romans 12, and Revelation 7.

10. "Compulsory Military Service: An English Conscientious Objector's Testimony," *The Weekly Evangel*, 28 April 1917, 7.

11. "The Pentecostal Movement and the Conscription Law," *The Pentecostal Evangel*, 4 August 1917, 6. The presbytery employed Luke 2.14, Hebrews 12.14, Exodus 20.13, Matthew 5.39, and Matthew 5.44.

12. Lydia Hatfield, "The Law of Christ for Believers," *The Christian Evangel*, 12 July 1919, 3. Emphasis added. See Bracy V. Hill II, "A Search for a Scriptural Hermeneutic in Early Pentecostal Pacifism," unpublished Ph.D. seminar paper, Baylor University, 2005.

13. "Is European War Justifiable?" *The Christian Evangel*, 12 December 1914, 1.

14. *The Assemblies of God Perspectives: Contemporary Issues: Social, Medical, Political* (Springfield, Mo.: Gospel Publishing House, 1995), 29.

15. John Howard Yoder, *The Politics of Jesus: Vicit Agnus Noster* (Grand Rapids:, Mich.: Eerdmans, 1995), 4-8.

16. *The Assemblies of God Perspectives: Contemporary Issues: Social, Medical, Political*, 3-43.

17. "Contemporary Issues: Does the Assemblies of God Have a Position on War and Conscientious Objectors?" *The Pentecostal Evangel*, 12 January 1997, 22.

18. Daniel 3:1-30.

19. Evidence for these themes is found in chapter one in the presentation of similarities between Quakers and early Pentecostals as well as in the theological origins of Pentecostal pacifism.

20. *General Council Minutes*, 1999, 88.

21. *Perspectives*, 29.

22. See Richard Hays, *The Moral Vision of the New Testament: Community, Cross, New Creation* (San Francisco, Calif.: HarperSanFrancisco, 1996); N.T. Wright, *The New Testament and the People of God* (Minneapolis, Minn.: Augsburg Fortress Press, 1996), and N.T. Wright, *Jesus and the Victory of God* (Minneapolis, Minn.: Augsburg Fortress Press, 1997).

23. For a helpful overview of these see Glen Stassen and David Gushee, "Just War, Nonviolence, and Just Peacemaking" in *Kingdom Ethics: Following Jesus in Con-*

temporary Context (Grand Rapids, Mich.: InterVarsity, 2003), and Glen Stassen *Just Peacemaking: Transforming Initiatives for Justice and Peace* (Louisville, Ky.: Westminster John Knox Press, 1992).

24. The Assemblies of God led the way in founding the all-white Pentecostal Fellowship of North America in 1948. However, they disbanded it in 1994 and replaced it with the multiethnic Pentecostal and Charismatic Churches of North America. The Assemblies of God officially apologized for its racism and is attempting to reverse it. *Reconciliation: The Official Journal of the Pentecostal / Charismatic Churches of North America* (Summer 1998).

25. In 2007 Dr. Don Argue, president of Northwest University (Assemblies of God) in Kirkland, Washington signed a letter that supported reinvigoration of Israeli-Palestinian peace talks (working toward "the viability of a Palestinian State") and affirmed that both Israel and Palestine have historic rights to the land. "Letter to President Bush From Evangelical Leaders," *New York Times*, 29 July 2007.

AFTERWORD

When people hear about my research on Assemblies of God pacifism and my interest in peacemaking and justice seeking as a Pentecostal Christian, they often ask, with concerned looks on their faces, something like, "So how is that being received in the Assemblies of God?" I smile and say, "It got me fired."

Not really. I don't say that, and it didn't get me fired. However, in March 2006 Southwestern Assemblies of God University (Waxahachie, Tex.) told me that I would not be getting another full-time faculty contract. I asked nicely for one several times, but my sixteen-year journey with my alma mater had come to a close. My parents, grandfather-in-law, aunts, uncles, cousins, wife, and brother had attended. I had been Student Congress president and Missions Association president as an undergraduate student (1990-1993) and served on the faculty for nine years (1995-1996, 1998-2006).

But they finally had enough of my quiet, yet consistent, questioning of nationalism and war. Believe me when I say that it does not matter how softly you speak, how much you smile, or how much you talk about Jesus. If you question Christian support of Americanism and warfare, you are going to have trouble. But I understand the challenges and tensions they faced; leading a denominational university is hard. Constituencies have to be considered, and my views on Jesus, the war in Iraq, and American exceptionalism differed from many of the churches who sent students (and money). Even though I tried, I no longer fit.[1]

But that's not the entire story. Another Assemblies of God university offered me a job immediately, and there are many missionaries, pastors, and especially young people who think the time has come to be authentically Jesus-shaped internationally aware peacemakers and justice-seekers regardless of the consequences.[2] I am one of them. But following Jesus is messy, and I often do not know what I am doing; I have made a lot of mistakes while trying to encourage peace with justice. I am a first-generation convert to crucifism, and I am learning, stumbling, and getting back up as I go.

The hundred-year-long story about Pentecostals and war got very personal for me on September 11, 2001. I was teaching at Southwestern and had just the year before finished my dissertation on pacifism (which has become this book). On July 17, 2001, I had presented my first conference paper, "Spirit Empowered Peacemaking: Toward a Pentecostal Charismatic Peace Fellowship."[3] Like early Pentecostals, I did not like the word *pacifist*. Nevertheless, I had been convinced by their early witness, John Howard Yoder, Stanley Hauerwas, and my own study of Scripture. I had become a Pentecostal crucifist—a follower of Jesus' way of nonviolent, cross-carrying, enemy love.

On the morning of 9-11 I was teaching a systematic theology class and did not dismiss because we did not know what had happened. After class we found out. I went to Greek class. We prayed, interceded actually (that means we prayed out loud and wept). I felt strongly that I should go talk to the president; I could see the tide of nationalism and violence rising, and I wanted to try to calm it before chapel began at 11:00 a.m.

I told the president as we briskly walked across campus toward the auditorium, "We have to remember who *we* are, we're followers of Jesus; we have to remember who we are. A lot of people will be saying a lot of things that are hateful; we have to remember who we are."

The first hour and a half of chapel was prayer and a lot of apocalyptic, prophecy fulfillment talk. It involved the Middle East, the rapture, Israel, the battle of Armageddon, tribulation, the antichrist, the United States, patriotism, war, and Muslims. I was squirming and feeling a definite "leading of the Holy Spirit" to address the students and faculty, a gathering of about one thousand people. I avoided this feeling and tried to talk myself out of it. I shifted in my seat and prayed. I put my head in my hands and prayed. I finally went up and asked the president if I could speak; he handed me the microphone.

I sat down in the middle of the stage, crossed my legs, and spoke very quietly, doing the best I could in that context,

> I love you guys. I have a dream, and a vision, and a purpose. And it's to tell the truth, amen? Just to tell the truth. We just want to follow Jesus faithfully, that's what we want to do. And I just want to point out, in all humbleness; in fact, I'm going to have to sit down to say this, because you have to take me for who I am, in all humility—we have participated in some sins. We have talked about confession, and that's a good thing, but we need to know what to confess.
>
> We are a very rich church, and that can actually be a problem rather than a good thing. That can lead us to greed, and some oppression, and exploitation and liking it. Do you hear what I'm saying? Am I being honest with you? That we've gotten involved in that? We're very very greedy, we like money a lot. I think that's a problem. And as we are this kind of people and call ourselves Christian, then we can be critiqued appropriately.
>
> And when someone sees our . . . *hypocrisy* is an easy word . . . when they see our living like this. . . . Around the world, there are 38 million Assemblies of God people, only two million are in the United States. Thirty-six million are in the rest of the world, South America, Asia, Africa, Europe, these are our brothers and sisters in Christ, when they see this, they wonder.
>
> What we can do in this time is examine ourselves. There's going to be a lot of picking the speck out of other people's eyes, but maybe we could use this as a time to pick the beam out of our eyes, amen? To critique ourselves, to let God speak to us regarding who are we to be as faithful followers of Jesus. That we can be who we are supposed to be in all situations, in a time of mourning, human mourning. This is a human tragedy, beyond an American tragedy, this is a human tragedy.
>
> So I just pray and I want you to pray that you will examine your understanding of the church, your understanding of your allegiances and your loyalties, what are the purposes and visions and dreams that we have, that they are good, that they are in line with what God wants us to be. And that we can confess some sin that the church has participated in . . . arrogance, liking power, liking control, it's fun to be in control, it's fun to dominate, it's

nice, you get what you want. And I'm not sure that's how Jesus led the church. So if we can critique ourselves even in those things. . . .

Now let me quote the president [of the university] quoting Brother Rosdahl, "revival begins with confession." It's true. You have your personal sins, but there are also social sins like racism that we participate in. There's no room for this in our body, amen? Because we are a chosen people, a holy nation, a royal priesthood. That's who we are first and foremost.

I fought against saying this, and I've said it very softly, but I know that God had this for us this morning, and that things said here are appropriate. And we won't say that God caused 9-11 to happen, by no means, no, but retaliation for retaliation for retaliation for retaliation—that happens in the world, right? If someone hits you, you hit them back. Eye for eye, tooth for tooth. What people have thought they're doing is they're taking the eye of America because they think America has taken their eye, America has taken their tooth. And now they're taking our tooth, and that is the system of when you get it, you give it back.

What did Jesus call us to do? When someone takes your eye, what do you do? You forgive them, right? We won't take this into what will happen now, but I'll tell you what will happen. Now America will respond, and that will be responded to, and that system of escalating violence will continue.

This is what happens, the "why" the World Trade Center and the Pentagon were bombed is because they're seen as the symbols of what makes America what it is—we expand ourselves economically and militarily, so they attack the economic and military centers. It's an attack on that, okay? As Christians, we say, "Yes, that's what happens. You reap what you sow. You hit, you get hit back." Look, it's written to the largest scale it's ever been written.

And now what do *we* do? We be faithful followers of Jesus, let's confess our participation in it and let God move us forward to being faithful followers of Jesus.[4]

I spent most of my "capital" that day; I was broke. That was my coming out of the closet as a peacemaker at my alma mater in front of all the people who had educated, loved, and hired me. There were faculty who did not talk to me for years, and some who tried to get me fired.

I have no idea if what I did or said was good or right, I just know that I had been reading a lot of Frank Bartleman, Arthur Booth-Clibborn, the early Assemblies of God peace witness, John Howard Yoder, and Jesus. I thought all of us Pentecostals just wanted to be radical Spirit-filled followers of the Messiah, regardless of the consequences, and I felt compelled to speak. To Southwestern's credit, they let me teach there another five years. I am still an Assemblies of God minister, and one way I intend to serve the kingdom of God is by staying with the institution of my heritage.

I am hopeful that the Assemblies of God and other Pentecostal denominations will reexamine their statements and position papers on war and nation. Doing so can dramatically enhance our witness to the gospel of Jesus Christ if we listen to our ancestors in the faith and to the testimony of Scripture—especially if we articulate a clear just war theory and an explanation of conscientious objection and noncombatant service.

I also hope that thousands and thousands of Christians join Pentecostals and Charismatics for Peace and Justice to work and pray together for peace with justice.[5] Researching this book created such a monumental change in my life that I was compelled (I think led by the Holy Spirit) to suggest the formation of an organization that would be a catalyst to help fulfill what God wants to do in the world. The motto is "Jesus Shaped Spirit Empowered Peace and Justice," and the mission is "to encourage, enable, and sustain peacemaking as authentic and integral to Pentecostal/Charismatic Christianity, witnessing to the conviction that Jesus Christ is relevant to all tensions, crises, and brokenness in the world. PCPJ seeks to show that addressing injustice and making peace as Jesus did is theologically sound, biblically commanded, and realistically possible." PCPJ consists of pastors, missionaries, laity, students, teachers, and many others from more than twenty denominations who work to—

- educate the hundreds of millions of Pentecostals and Charismatics in the world regarding their nonviolent and reconciliation focused biblical and Pentecostal heritage;
- educate us in the methodologies and practices of nonviolence;
- inform us of local, national, and international issues regarding injustice, oppression, and exploitation;
- facilitate action that brings about peace with justice through writing, speaking, preaching, dialoguing, demonstrating, civil disobedi-

ence, and other nonviolent methods of effecting positive change;

• serve as a social network of Spirit-filled and Spirit-empowered followers of Jesus that encourages and promotes discussions and Christian action related to war, capital punishment, human rights, gender, ethnicity, immigration, nationalism, discrimination, economics, and violence of any kind;

• cooperate with other peace fellowships and organizations to build peace and work for justice.

The PCPJ has members who are just war theorists, some who are crucifists, and we all seek to be just peacemakers.[6] The second century of Pentecostalism is just beginning, and perhaps it can bear witness to the reemergence and resurgence of a powerful Pentecostal peace-with-justice witness that blesses the world far beyond what we could ever imagine.

NOTES

1. I want to add that I had no moral failures, students evaluated my teaching above ninety percent every year I was there, and I was specifically told that I would not get another contract because of my political and theological views. It also was not a budget issue—they hired another person to replace me.

2. Being a little gun shy, I did not take the job at the Assemblies of God university but went to Azusa (Calif.) Pacific University instead.

3. Presented to the European Pentecostal Charismatic Research Association/ Theology Faculty of the Catholic University of Leuven, July 17-21, 2001, in Leuven, Belgium. Published as "Spirit Empowered Peacemaking: Toward a Pentecostal Charismatic Peace Fellowship," *Journal of the European Pentecostal Theological Association* 22 (2002): 78-102.

4. Audio CD of chapel service at Southwestern Assemblies of God University, Waxahachie, Texas, September 11, 2001.

5. Http://www.pcpj.org. The following quotations and many other resources can be found at this website.

6. Glen Stassen, *Just Peacemaking: Transforming Initiatives for Justice and Peace* (Louisville: Westminster/John Knox Press, 1992). Glen Stassen, ed., *Just Peacemaking: The New Paradigm for the Ethics of Peace and War* (Cleveland: Pilgrim Press, 1998, 2004, 2008).

Appendix A

Data obtained from Jacob D. Mininger, *Religious C.O.'s Imprisoned at the U.S. Disciplinary Barracks, Ft. Leavenworth, Kansas* (1919). Available from Mennonite Church USA Archives, Goshen, Indiana.

Name	Address	Denomination	Camp Sent From	No. of Years Sent.	Date of Imprison-ment	Date of Re-lease
Clemens, Eddie (colored)	60 E. 132nd St., N.Y. City	Pentecostal Assemblies of God	Upton, Ft. Jay			
Emlery, Melvin	Lone Wolf, Okla.	Pentecostal	Travis	10 years	June 13, 1918	
Leonhardt, Henry		Apostolic Faith				
Lucius, Henry	Okla.	Church of God, Apostolic Holiness	Pike			
Montgomery, Clinton	Plantersville, Miss.	Church of God in Christ		3 years	Oct. 7, 1918	
Meister, David W.	Manchester, Okla.	Christian Apostolic	Travis	25 years	June 15, 1918	
Nygaard, Sauder M.	Grygla, Minn.	Pentecostal	Ft. Ontario	10 years		
Olson, Elmer N.	Goodridge, Minn.	Pentecostal	Dodge	15 years		
Parrett, Charley	Bond, Ky	Pentecostal Church of God	Wads-worth			
Roberts, Charles S.	Rabbit, Okla.	Apostolic Faith	Travis	25 years		
Rothberg, Knud Carlo		Pentecostal	Upton			
Sass, Reingold	Milwaukee, Wis.	Pentecostal Assemblies of God	Green-leaf			
Strohm, Noah	Sabetha (Kans.?)	Apostolic Faith				
Smith, Wm. O.	Roodhouse, Illinois	Pentecostal Assembly of the World	Taylor	10 years	July 17, 1918	Jan. 27, 1919
Snyder, Sherman	Jennings, Md.	Pentecostal	Meade	15 years	Nov. 25, 1918	
Schulz, Wm.	603 Pine St., St. Joeph, Mich.	Pentecostal Assembly	Custer			
Stauffer, J. Virgil	Wakarusa, Ind.	Pentecostal Assemblies of God				Jan. 27, 1919
Weiershau-sen, Geo. C.		Pentecostal				
Wheeler, Oscar O.	Sandstone, W. Va.	Pentecostal				

Appendix B

Pentecostal conscientious objectors in World War II. Data obtained from the *Civilian Public Service Directory*.

Last Name	First Name	Pent. Affil.	Occupation	CPS Camps	Birth	City	State	Age	Dates of Service
Adlesic	Ralph	AG	Mason	23, 83	1919	Cuyahoga Falls	OH	23	1/21/42-1/21/46
Albritton	Edgar	PCGA	Laborer and fruit packer	31	1910	Lindsay	CA	33	8/10/43-9/14/43
Ambrose	Henry	PAW	Paint finisher	8	1917	Norwood	OH	24	6/23/41-12/23/41
Andrews	Clifford	Pent.	Minister and gardener	33	1909	Oklahoma City	OK	33	6/26/42-11/8/45
August	Herman	Pent.	Garment worker	89, 94	1917	New York City	NY	25	3/31/42-7/24/43
Barron	Marvin	Pent. Hol.	Timber worker	108, 37	1925	Section	AL	19	8/25/44-7/6/45
Bates	James	Pent.	Farmer	128, 108	1926	Whitesboro	TX	20	3/1/46-; not listed
Baughman	Earl	Pent.	Salesman	128, 108	1913	Gracemont	OK	31	6/8/44-; not listed
Baughman	Jacob	Pent. Evang.	Mechanic	57, 138	1923	Marshalltown	IA	20	5/11/43-6/21/46
Becker	Reuben	Pent. Hol.	Laborer	5	1918	Helena	OK	24	11/17/42-12/3/43
Belau	Harry	AG	Logger	2, 76	1918	Westwood	CA	23	9/2/41-1/6/43
Berg	Cecil	Pent.	Farmer	60, 76	1918	Modesto	CA	25	1/19/43-6/14/44
Berg	Orville	Pent.	Farmer	21, 56, 97, 42, 36, 134	1919	Manteca	CA	22	12/5/41-12/22/45
Bernhardt	Franz	Pent.	Carpenter	36, 27	1905	Albuquerque	NM	37	6/2/42-11/1/45
Boehs	Wilmer	CGIC	Farming	33, 5	1922	Fairview	OK	21	3/10/43-3/18/46
Brandon	Jesse	Pent. Hol.	Textile worker	45	1900	Danville	VA	42	11/17/42-6/30/43
Buller	Raymond	CGIC	Farmer	5, 64	1919	McPherson	KS	22	6/5/41-11/19/45
Butler	George	Pent.	Carpenter helper	7	1920	Livingston	TX	21	7/21/41-10/31/41
Busse	Martin	Pent.	Paper salesman	11	1913	Long Island	NY	29	3/31/42-10/2/42
Bynes	William	CGIC	Not listed	23	1920	New Brunswick	NJ	22	2/21/42-9/30/42
Caldwell	James	Pent.	Laborer	2, 76	1914	Aberdeen	ID	27	8/14/41-10/24/42
Calvert	William	Apost. Christ. Church	Grocery clerk	19, 34	1918	Collingsdale	PA	23	10/8/41-2/3/43
Campbell	Victor	Pent.	Hospital maint.	21	1906	Great Falls	MT	37	3/10/43-2/16/44
Cardone	John	Pent.	Auto mechanic	16, 56, 80	1923	Phil.	PA	20	5/28/43-6/14/46

Cardone	Nicholas	Pent.	Mechanic	3, 52, 50, 46	1919	Phil.	PA	22	9/18/41-12/11/45
Carrico	Frederick	Pent.	Mechanic	52	1926	The Plains	VA	19	5/4/45-; not listed
Chapman	Loyd	Rog. Quak.	Wood working machinist	37	1920	Huntington Park	CA	24	7/11/44-7/3/45
Clark	Russell	AG	Lumber-jack	2	1916	Westwood	CA	25	9/12/41-12/8/41
Cline	Melvin	AG	Laborer	35	1918	West Salem	OR	24	7/16/42-9/3/43
Cortez	Robert	Apost. Christian Church	Farm laborer	31	1925	Tulare	CA	18	7/28/43-10/28/43
Craig	Murray	Pent.	Farmer	46, 108	1924	Farmland	IN	21	7/19/45-; not listed
Crouch	Everett	Rog. Quak.	Laborer	2, 76, 43	1915	Westminster	CA	26	6/23/41-11/27/44
Crouch	Leonard	Rog. Quak.	Stone cutter	10	1915	Rockville	CT	26	10/8/41-1/3/42
Crowe	Hesley	Pent.	Laborer	32, 50	1915	Portland	ME	27	5/19/42-10/22/43
Curtis	Louis	CFGI	Machinist	134	1918	Hayward	CA	26	10/3/44-3/4/46
Davidson	Bertrum	Open Bible Standard	Farmer	21	1916	Terrebonne	OR	26	10/14/42-4/20/46
Davis	William	Free Pent. Hol.	Textile mill worker	108	1920	Chavies	AL	25	3/7/45-12/26/45
Davolt	Clyde	Fire Baptized Hol.	Not Listed	5	1913	McCune	KS	28	8/15/41-9/23/41
Delaney	Marcus	Pent.	Laborer	29	1901	Benning Station	DC	41	9/15/42-6/25/43
DeVol	William	Foursq. Gospel	Waiter	11, 46	1919	Glens Falls	NY	23	1/21/42-10/17/45
Dirksen	Jacob	Pent.	Painter/Minister	2	1911	Los Angeles	CA	30	6/9/41-10/11/41
Eicher	Eugene	CGIC	Farmer	5, 55	1927	Foley	AL	18	5/4/45-; not listed
Ekelard	Robert	Pent.	Delica-tessen clerk	11, 53, 115	1919	Staten Island	NY	22	12/9/41-12/15/45
Ellis	William	Pent.	Sawmill laborer	7, 88, 128	1907	Lufkin	TX	35	9/3/42-11/15/45
Feggans	William	Pent.	Chauffeur	46, 57, 76	1919	Phil.	PA	25	8/30/44-5/22/46
Ferragino	Ralph	Pent.	Plumber	121, 134, 27	1926	Phil.	PA	19	2/20/45-; not listed
Ford	Harold	Pent.	Minister	25, 97, 28, 57, 18	1922	Marshalltown	IA	21	1/19/43-5/27/46
Furlan	Joseph, Jr.	Pent.	Clothes presser	57	1909	Milwaukee	WI	34	3/10/43-5/17/43
Garrison	William	AG	Not Listed	7	1919	Berryman	MO	22	6/23/41-9/27/41
Gaubatz	Edward	Pent.	Shoe repairman	2, 21	1918	Oakland	CA	23	9/2/41-12/27/43
Godwin	Donald	Faith Tab.	Hosiery worker	16, 56, 88, 111,	1920	Phil.	PA	22	12/22/42-; not listed

Green	Paul	CGIC	Farm laborer	17, 42, 62	1918	Muskegon	MI	23	7/12/41-12/8/45
Green	Robert	Church of the Gospel	Mechanical engineer	46, 98	1918	Pittsburg	MA	25	9/1/43-6/20/46
Green	Thomas	CGIC	Janitor	28, 69	1925	Detroit	MI	19	2/11/44-7/15/46
Greer	Loy	Pent.	Gas station worker	108	1923	Paragould	AR	21	6/15/44-5/22/46
Grundy	Elwin	Pent.	Cabinet maker	46, 108	1921	Mystic	CT	23	4/18/44-10/5/44
Hartz	David	Full Gospel	Laundry worker	31	1917	San Jacinta	CA	26	4/20/43-6/15/43
Henry	Andrew	CG of Apost. Faith	Minister	16	1908	Phil.	PA	36	2/1/44-2/22/44
Henry	Wilmer	Church of the Living God	Nursery gardener	8, 35, 109, 100	1908	Indiana	PA	34	3/19/42-11/20/45
Hicks	James	Pent. Fire Baptized Holiness	Textile worker	29, 121, 134	1918	Anderson	SC	24	5/28/42-3/5/46
Hines	Henry	CGIC	Block factory worker	32	1911	Newton-ville	NJ	31	4/22/42-5/17/43
Holt	John	Pent.	First helper furnace	48, 16	1917	Pittsburg	PA	26	10/19/43-5/12/44
Holybee	Donovan	Full Gospel	Labor contractor	107, 31	1917	Hayward	CA	27	8/19/44-6/21/46
Horst	Adam	AG	Auto mechanic	21	1907	Glendive	MT	35	6/3/42-5/1/43
Howard	Glen	Pent.	Const. worker	107	1923	Exeter	CA	21	2/18/44-3/27/46
Howe	Joseph	AG	Farmer	7, 56, 42	1917	Holland	TX	25	8/27/42-3/11/46
Irizarry	Elas	Assemb. of Christian Churches	Student	46, 94	1922	New York City	NY	21	5/4/43-6/16/46
Isaac	Charles	Pent.	Laborer	46, 20, 31, 45	1918	New York City	NY	25	5/4/43-6/14/46
Iten	George	AG	Clerk	21, 103, 115, 140	1917	Burbank	CA	24	12/5/41-12/20/45
Johnson	Alfred	Pent.	Truck driver	128, 148	1914	Green Bay	WI	30	12/5/44-; not listed
Johnson	John H.	Faith Tab.	Janitor	48	1922	Phil.	PA	21	1/14/43-3-6-43
Johnson	John N.	Faith Tab.	Separator in dress factory	16, 56, 21, 42	1925	Phil.	PA	19	6/15/44-; not listed
Judd	Edwin	Pent.	Crane operator	128	1923	Oregon City	OR	21	5/9/44-11/15/44
Kadow	Daniel	Church of the Living God	Not Listed	2, 76	1914	Algona	WA	27	8/20/41-12/6/43
Kapp	Otto	Foursq. Gospel	Golf course maint.	6	1906	Matteson	IL	35	6/26/41-10/10/41

Koehn	Harvey	CGIC	Farmer	57, 5	1918	Galva	KS	24	10/23/42-4/15/46
Kolenda	Louie	AG	Tool grinder	17, 42, 56	1919	Clio	MI	23	1/23/42-1/28/46
Laroya	Severino	Filipino Full Gospel	Laborer	55	1907	Pasadena	CA	36	9/10/43-12/5/44
Larson	Phillip	Apost. Faith	Lumber man	128	1911	El Monte	CA	33	7/8/44-; not listed
Leath	John	Apost. Faith	Student	37, 76, 108	1926	San Bernardino	CA	19	5/18/45-; not listed
Lozans	John	CGIC	Farmer	2, 76	1915	Greeley	CO	27	6/2/42-2/18/46
Mac Dougall	Archie	Faith Tab.	Railroad employee	46, 59	1914	Phil.	PA	28	10/15/42-11/12/43
Madero	Angel	Pent.	Laborer	37, 128, 148	1927	Los Angeles	CA	18	6/5/45-; not listed
Marks	Arthur	Pent.	Gardener	37	1900	Corvallis	OR	42	12/2/42-6/19/45
Maynard	Robert	Pent.	Window washer	56	1898	Spokane	WA	44	11/13/42-5/5/43
Mc Clintock	Harold	Pent.	Farmer	37, 107, 31	1926	Westmorland	CA	18	11/21/44-; not listed
McKinney	George	AG	Student welder	21, 36, 2, 134	1920	Los Angeles	CA	21	12/5/41-12/19/45
Milks	Leonard	AG	Arc Welder/Mechanic	24, 16, 42	1913	Little Valley	NY	29	5/15/42-2/27/46
Milnes	Arthur	Faith Tab.	Factory foreman	16, 116	1917	Phil.	PA	24	9/18/41-11/29/45
Milnes	Robert	Faith Tab.	Textile worker	16, 116	1925	Phil.	PA	19	5/12/44-7/9/46
Morper	Oather	AG	Labor specialist	111, 128, 33, 128	1910	Oklahoma City	OK	34	5/9/44-5/27/46
Morrison	Junior	AG	Farmer	36, 134	1925	Eloy	AZ	19	1/28/44-5/20/44
Muff	Howard	Pent.	Stockroom clerk	128, 148	1927	Oregon City	OR	19	4/11/46-; not listed
Murray	Wilfred	CG of Apost. Faith	Railroad section hand	7, 33	1913	Mulberry	KS	30	10/19/43-5/27/46
Nelson	Selmer	Pent.	Farmer	55, 111, 128	1907	Canby	OR	35	8/18/42-11/10/45
Nett	Sam	Pent. CG	Painter	36	1916	Del Paso Heights	CA	27	3/19/43-1/11/44
Newton	Howard	Pent.	Plumber	45, 100, 45	1910	Phil.	PA	34	11/11/44-1/15/46
Nixon	James	Faith Tab.	Usher	45, 107, 63, 24	1926	Memphis	TN	18	9/5/44-; not listed
Olsen	Roy	AG	Logger	21	1905	Molalla	OR	37	6/2/42-5/20/43
Olson	Sidney	Pent. AG	Farmer	18	1927	Superior	WI	19	1/25/46-; not listed
Pagno	John	Pent.	Barber	94, 49	1915	Solvay	NY	26	6/26/41-7/23/42
Paiva	Leon	AG	Machinist	36	1905	San Mateo	CA	37	7/10/42-12/13/43

Patterson	Floyd	Pent.	Roofing contractor	107	1914	South Gate	CA	31	5/18/45-5/30/46
Patton	Gerald	Pent.	Farmer	7, 97	1914	Petersburg	TX	28	12/20/42-; not listed
Perry	Daniel	AG	Farmer	5, 66	1919	Weldona	CO	22	10/8/41-11/28/45
Prince	Marvin	CG of Apost. Faith	Arc welder	7, 33	1922	Mulberry	KS	22	3/17/44-; not listed
Ragonese	Joseph	Pent.	Farmer/Carpenter	108, 52	1917	Syracuse	NY	28	7/20/45-; not listed
Raney	Leonard	Pent.	Farmer	7, 103, 5, 111	1919	Seminole	OK	24	1/28/43-5/26/46
Ray	Jesse	Apost. Faith	Ranchman	5, 55, 90	1917	Greeley	CO	24	6/16/41-12/3/45
Reimer	Edward	Full Gospel	Mechanic	31	1909	Reedley	CA	34	6/28/43-6/30/45
Reinert	Charles	Faith Tab.	Cabinet maker	52	1917	Phil.	PA	28	6/21/45-2/246
Reinert	John	Faith Tab.	Hosiery knitter	18, 19, 89, 94	1917	Phil.	PA	24	8/28/41-12/5/45
Reinert	Paul	Faith Tab.	Mill worker	89, 46, 94, 46	1923	Phil.	PA	20	4/28/43-5/10/46
Reinert	William	Faith Tab.	Milk business	8	1919	Phil.	PA	23	2/20/42-10/29/42
Reynolds	Gaylon	Pent.	Farmer	111	1924	Casey	IL	21	2/6/45-; not listed
Roberts	Maurice	CG of Apost. Faith	Farmer	33	1923	Liberal	MO	22	10/19/45-8/11/46
Rogers	Fred	Pent.	Metal worker	121, 34, 108	1927	Knoxville	TN	18	9/20/45-; not listed
Rutledge	Wilbur	CG of Apost. Faith	Grocery clerk	7, 33	1923	Liberal	MO	21	4/11/44-5/27/46
Schultz	Jonas	CGIC	Farmer	33, 97, 5	1919	Neodesha	KS	23	7/31/42-3/30/46
Seals	John	Pent.	Machinist	121	1916	Morristown	TN	28	8/10/44-4/13/46
Shattuck	Claude	AG	Student	111, 128, 135	1924	Seattle	WA	19	8/10/43-7/11/46
Shaw	Elmer	AG	Typist clerk	7, 105	1917	Geary	OK	24	8/27/41-11/27/45
Shaw	Warren	AG	Farmer	7, 103, 98	1921	Geary	OK	21	8/11/42-3/28/46
Simensky	John	Pent.	Laborer	53, 37, 76, 46	1914	Brooklyn	NY	29	3/12/43-5/17/46
Smith	Floyd	AG	Laborer	16	1908	Geneva	OH	35	2/9/43-4/6/43
Smith	Herman	CGIC	Farmer	33, 5	1918	Ringwood	OK	24	7/9/42-8/19/43
Smith	Paul	Pent.	Student	28, 100, 18	1921	Roodhouse	IL	22	1/15/43-; not listed
Smith	Walter	AG	Machinist	29, 121	1914	Winnsboro	TX	31	5/3/45-5/16/42
Stanfill	Coy	Pent.	Farmer	7	1923	Scott's Hill	TN	20	6/11/43-2/8/44
Sullivan	Covy	Pent.	Farmer/Laborer	7, 109	1917	Beacon	TN	24	6/23/41-12/10/45
Thomas	Mamon	CGIC	Farm worker	37, 76	1927	Blythe	CA	18	7/20/45-; not listed

Thomas	Mamon	CGIC	Farm worker	37, 76	1927	Blythe	CA	18	7/20/45-; not listed
Thrush	Clifford	Apost. Faith	Factory worker	17	1915	Alma	MI	26	6/27/41-8/7/41
Toews	Harvey	CGIC	Farm laborer	5, 64	1920	Chickasha	OK	22	2/5/42-1/28/46
Towes	Lloyd	CGIC	Farm laborer	5, 64	1918	Chickasha	OK	24	2/5/42-1/28/46
Troutman	Ralph	Faith Tab.	Chauffeur, Carrier	121, 134, 34	1926	Phil.	PA	19	3/20/45-; not listed
Tucker	Emanuel	CGIC	Laborer	6	1921	Chicago	IL	22	5/4/43-7/21/43
Villa	Arthur	Pent.	Gardener	21, 95	1915	El Monte	CA	26	12/3/41-3/6/44
Walker	Alfred	Pent.	Pent. minister	57	1916	Aurora	IL	27	10/27/43-3/6/46
Watkins	George	Pent.	Railroad employee	56	1914	Whitefish	MT	28	2/4/42-10/12/44
Wedel	DeWayne	CGIC	Farmer	64, 55	1927	Bonners Ferry	ID	19	3/7/46-; not listed
Wedel	Harry	CGIC	Dairy farmer	64, 138	1925	Tampa	KS	20	5/14/45-; not listed
Welsch	Ronald	CG of Apost. Faith	Stock clerk	57, 18	Not listed	Akron	OH	Unknown	4/4/45-7/25/46
Williams	Shirley	Pent.	Church worker	20, 31, 45	1912	New York	NY	32	2/1/44-7/12/46
Williams	Amos	CGIC	Not Listed	46, 37, 76, 46	1925	Ulline	IL	19	9/5/44-; not listed
Wilson	William	Church of Christ of Apost. Faith	Presser in factory	20	1913	Phil.	PA	31	2/11/44-4/12/44
Young	Russell	Faith Tab.	Typewriter mechanic	121, 34	1923	Phil.	PA	22	6/20/45-; not listed

Pentecostal Affiliations
AG: Assemblies of God
CFGI: Church of the Full Gospel, Inc.
CG: Church of God
CGIC: Church of God in Christ
PAW: Pentecostal Assemblies of the World
PCGA: Pentecostal Church of God in America
Pent. Hol.: Pentecostal Holiness
Rog. Quak.: Rogerine Quaker

BIBLIOGRAPHY

Primary Sources

Books

Abrams, Ray. *Preachers Present Arms*. Scottdale, Pa.: Herald Press, 1969.

Barclay, Robert. *An Apology for the True Christian Divinity as the Same is Held Forth and Preached by the People, in Scorn, Called Quakers*. 1678. Reprint, Glasgow: R. Barclay Murdoch, Dunn and Wright Printers, 1886.

Bartleman, Frank. *Christian Citizenship*. Los Angeles: by the author, circa 1922.

———. *From Plow to Pulpit, From Maine to California*. Los Angeles: by the author, 1924.

———. *How Pentecost Came to Los Angeles: As It Was In the Beginning*. Los Angeles: by the author, 1925.

———. *Another Wave Rolls In (formerly "What Really Happened at Azusa Street?")*. 1925. Reprint, Monroeville, Pa.: Whitaker Books, 1962

———. *Two Years Mission Work in Europe Just Before the War 1912-1914*. Los Angeles: By the author, n.d.

Booth-Clibborn, Arthur Sidney. *Blood Against Blood*. 3rd. ed. New York: Charles C. Cook, 1914.

Booth-Clibborn, Catherine. *They Endured.* London: Marshall, Morgan Scott, Lts., n.d.

Booth-Clibborn, Samuel. *Should a Christian Fight? An Appeal to Christian Young Men of All Nations.* Swengel, Pa.: Bible Truth Depot, n.d., circa 1917.

Booth-Clibborn, William. *The Baptism in the Holy Spirit: A Personal Testimony.* Portland, Ore.: Booth-Clibborn Book Concern, 1936.

———. The Baptism in the Holy Spirit: A Personal Testimony, *4ᵗʰ ed. Dallas, Tex.: Voice of Healing Publishing, 1962.*

———. *Saved by Sight: The Vision Without Which We Perish.* Northridge, Calif.: Voice Christian Publications, 1968.

Brumback, Carl. *What Meaneth This? A Pentecostal Answer to a Pentecostal Question.* Springfield, Mo.: Gospel Publishing House, 1947.

Dresser, Amos. *The Bible Against War.* Oberlin: By the Author, 1849.

French, Paul C. *We Won't Murder.* New York: Hastings House, 1940.

Gee, Donald. *Wind and Flame.* Croydon: Health Press, Ltd., 1967.

General Council Minutes. Springfield, Mo.: Gospel Publishing House, 1914-1999.

Gurney, Joseph John. *A Peculiar People: The Rediscovery of Primitive Christianity.* 1824. Reprint, Introduction by Donald Green. Richmond, Ind.: Friends United Press, 1979.

Hughs, George. *Fragrant Memories of the Tuesday Meeting and the Guide to Holiness.* New York: Palmer and Hughes, 1886.

Lawrence, Bennet F. *The Apostolic Faith Restored.* With a foreword by John W. Welch. St. Louis, Mo.: Gospel Publishing House, 1916.

Meyer, Ernest L. *"Hey! Yellowbacks!": The War Diary of A Conscientious Objector,* reprint ed. The Peace Movement in America Series, Foreword by Willima Ellery Leonard. New York: Jerome S. Ozer, 1972.

Parham, Charles F. *The Everlasting Gospel.* Baxter Springs, Kan.: Apostolic Faith Bible College, 1911.

Paulk, Earl. P. *Your Pentecostal Neighbor.* Cleveland, Tenn.: Pathway Press, 1958.

Plank, David W. *Called to Serve.* Springfield, Mo.: Gospel Publishing House, 1967.

Risner, James Robinson. *The Passing of Night.* New York: Random House, 1973.

Roever, Dave. *The High School Experience.* Roever Communications, 1987. Videocassette.

———. *Dave Roever: From Tragedy to Triumph*. Roever Communications, 1988. Videocassette.

———. *Scars That Heal: The True Life Story of Dave Roever*. World Wide Pictures, 1993. Videocassette.

Roever, Dave and Harold Fickett. *Welcome Home, Davey*. Waco, Tex.: Word Books, 1986.

Roever, Dave and Karen Crews Crump. *Nobody's Ever Cried For Me*. Fort Worth, Tex.: Roever Communications, 1992.

Roever, Dave and Kathy Koch. *Scarred*. Fort Worth, Tex.: Roever Communications, 1995.

Smith, Hannah Whithall. *The Christian's Secret of a Happy Life*. 1870; reprint Westwood, N.J.: The Scarecrow Press, 1980, 1985.

———. *The God of All Comfort*. 1875; reprint Chicago: Moody Press, 1956.

Southwestern Assemblies of God University Institutional Policy Manual. Waxahachie, Tex.: Southwestern Assemblies of God University, 1999.

Taylor, George F. *The Spirit and the Bride*. Dunn, N.C.: by the author, 1907.

Thrift, Minton. *Memoir of the Rev. Jesse Lee*. New York: Bangs and Mason, 1823; reprint, Arno Press, 1969.

Upham, Thomas. *Manual of Peace*. New York: Leavitt, Lord, and Company, 1836.

Wesley, John. *The Works of the Rev. John Wesley, A.M.* vol . 1 *Sermons*. New York: Eaton and Mains, 1910.

Witness to Pentecost: The Life of Frank Bartleman, with a preface by Cecil M. Roebeck, Jr. The Higher Christian Life: Sources for the Study of the Holiness, Pentecostal, and Keswick Movements, ed. Donald W. Dayton, no. 5. New York: Garland Publishing, 1985.

Articles and Unpublished Materials

"21 Chaplains Attend Conference at Springfield." *The Pentecostal Evangel*, 19 May 1963, 12.

"23rd and 24th Assemblies of God Chaplains Commissioned." *The Pentecostal Evangel*, 1 July 1962, 26.

"30th Assemblies of God Military Chaplain Named." *The Pentecostal Evangel*, 15 January 1967, 31.

"38th A/G Military Chaplain Appointed." *The Pentecostal Evangel*, 18 November 1973, 25.

"50 from North Carolina Assembly Deployed in Persian Gulf Many as Pilots." *The Pentecostal Evangel*, 17 March 1991, 24.

"1,000 Testaments for the Soldiers." *The Pentecostal Evangel*, 21 June 1941, 13.

"50,000 Men." *The Pentecostal Evangel*, 18 March 1944, 12.

"A-Bomb Shelters." *The Pentecostal Evangel*, 8 April 1951, 7.

"A Challenge." *The Pentecostal Evangel*, 17 October 1942, 1.

"A Conversion in the Philippines." *The Pentecostal Evangel*, 23 June 1945, 5.

"'A Double for our Son.'" *The Pentecostal Evangel*, 12 August 1944, 7.

"A Few Lines from Our Soldier Boys." *The Christian Evangel*, 19 October 1918, 14.

"'A Home Away from Home.'" *The Pentecostal Evangel*, 19 May 1945, 7.

"A Hundred Years' War?" *The Pentecostal Evangel*, 28 January 1950, 10.

"A King with Many Titles." *The Weekly Evangel*, 11 September 1915, 2.

"A Warning from MacArthur." *The Pentecostal Evangel*, 13 January 1952, 2.

"Addresses Congress on War Prisoners." *The Pentecostal Evangel*, 8 November 1970, 26.

"A/G Chaplain Discusses Drug Abuse in Army." *The Pentecostal Evangel*, 4 July 1971, 15.

"A/G Chaplain Ministers in Vietman." *The Pentecostal Evangel*, 31 June 1971, 28.

"A/G Chaplain Wins Major Award." *The Pentecostal Evangel*, 13 December 1998, 27.

"A/G Chaplains Named to Commission." *The Pentecostal Evangel*, 18 May 1969, 29.

"A/G Military Chaplain Retires." *The Pentecostal Evangel*, 28 August 1994, 26.

"Aggressive Spiritual Warfare." *The Pentecostal Evangel*, 3 March 1945, 4.

"AGGS Student Commissioned for Military Seminarian Program." *The Pentecostal Evangel*, 29 June 1980, 26.

"Alcohol and Sex Crimes." *The Pentecostal Evangel*, 14 January 1950, 8.

Allen, James P. "Former Barracks Enlisted for a Different Kind of War." *The Pentecostal Evangel*, 22 January 1984, 8.

———. "The Greater Power." *The Pentecostal Evangel*, 29 June 1986, 8.

Allen, William G. "War Behind the Smoke Screen." *The Pentecostal Evangel*, 6 December 1930, 3.

Alsup, Debra. "Christmas in a War Zone." *The Pentecostal Evangel*, 15 December 1990, 11.

Altman, Larry. "Air Force Personnel Build a Church." *The Pentecostal Evangel*, 23 April 1978, 10.

"Ambassadors Advance!" *The Pentecostal Evangel*, 2 April 1949, 9.

"Ambassadors Advance!" *The Pentecostal Evangel*, 16 July 1949, 12.

"Ambassadors Advance! Serving the Servicemen." *The Pentecostal Evangel*, 8 January 1949, 12.

"American Servicemen in Europe Find Pentecostal Fellowship." *The Pentecostal Evangel*, 4 March 1979, 12.

"Amid the Horror of War." *The Pentecostal Evangel*, 29 June 1969, 14.

"Among the Wounded." *The Pentecostal Evangel*, 15 April 1944, 12.

"Amongst the Soldier Boys." *The Weekly Evangel*, 18 August 1917, 2-3.

"Amongst the Soldier Boys." *The Christian Evangel*, 29 June 1918, 14.

"And Some People Wonder Why." *The Pentecostal Evangel*, 19 August 1944, 9.

Anderson, Edwin R. "Greatest War of History." *The Pentecostal Evangel*, 13 September 1970, 12.

Anderson, Mardria. "Serving Okinawa's Military Personnel." *The Pentecostal Evangel*, 24 April 1983, 16.

Andraeas, Alan L. "Desert Storm Church Call." *The Pentecostal Evangel*, 7 July 1991, 10.

Andrews, James H. and Anna. "Messengers of Peace to Those Who are at War." *The Pentecostal Evangel*, 24 January 1931, 10.

"Announcing a *Reveille* Servicemen's Department." *The Pentecostal Evangel*, 29 January 1944, 5.

"Another A/G Chaplain Receives Regular Military Commission." *The Pentecostal Evangel*, 5 March 1961, 10.

"Another War in 1927?" *The Pentecostal Evangel*, 1 April 1922, 7.

"Another War Prophet." *The Weekly Evangel*, 27 May 1916, 7.

"Are You Doing Your Bit?" *The Pentecostal Evangel*, 13 June 1942, 3.

"Are You Off to the Front?" *Weekly Evangel*, September 11, 1915, 1.

Argue, Watson. "The Present War and the World Situation." *The Pentecostal Evangel*, 24 October 1942, 10-11, 14.

Argue, Zelma. ". . . Until I have Showed They Strength Unto This Generation." *The Pentecostal Evangel*, 28 June 1941, 1.

———. "'Nevertheless David Took the Castle.'" *The Pentecostal Evangel*, 12 June 1943, 1, 8-9.

"Arming them with the Gospel Too!" *The Pentecostal Evangel*, 10 October 1942, 21.

Armstrong, Edward. "Sane and Insane Practices." *Word and Witness*, July 1915, 5.

"Arrow of the Lord's Deliverance." *The Pentecostal Evangel*, 19 April 1924, 4.

"Article No. 6 Changed." *Minutes of the General Council of the Assemblies of God*. Springfield, Mo.: Gospel Publishing House, 1918, 10.

"As Costly As War." *The Pentecostal Evangel*, 4 February 1950, 9.

"Assemblies Chaplain Adds Second Oak Leaf Cluster to Army Commendation Medal." *The Pentecostal Evangel*, 24 November 1968, 30.

"Assemblies Chaplain Received Regular Navy Commission." *The Pentecostal Evangel*, 29 June 1958, 12.

"Assemblies Chaplains Confer." *The Pentecostal Evangel*, 26 June 1966, 8.

"Assemblies Chaplains Convene." *The Pentecostal Evangel*, 25 June 1967, 30.

"Assemblies Chaplains in Europe Attend Religious Retreat." *The Pentecostal Evangel*, 1 July 1956, 11.

"Assemblies Chaplains Minister Worldwide." *The Pentecostal Evangel*, 10 March 1968, 27.

"Assemblies Chaplains Serve in Vietnam." *The Pentecostal Evangel*, 25 June 1976, 30.

"Assemblies of God Chaplain Conducts Religious Retreat in Japan." *The Pentecostal Evangel*, 29 April 1956, 11.

"Assemblies of God Chaplain Earns Commendation." *The Pentecostal Evangel*, 6 March 1960, 9.

"Assemblies of God Chaplain Wins Commendation." *The Pentecostal Evangel*, 20 December 1959, 12.

"Assemblies of God Chaplains Meet." *The Pentecostal Evangel*, 19 April 1959, 12.

"Assemblies of God Chaplains Now on Active Military Duty." *The Pentecostal Evangel*, 26 June 1977, 11.

"Assemblies of God Chaplains Now on Active Military Duty." *The Pentecostal Evangel*, 24 June 1979, 11.

"Assemblies of God Military Ministry Statistics." *The Pentecostal Evangel*, 28 June 1987, 9.

Assemblies of God Perspectives—Contemporary Issues: Social, Medical, and Political. Springfield, Mo.: Gospel Publishing House, 1995.

"Assemblies Pilot Receives Award." *The Pentecostal Evangel*, 1 October 1967, 7.

"At a Glance." *The Pentecostal Evangel*, 30 June 1991, 14.

"Attitude Check!" *The Pentecostal Evangel*, 27 June 1971, 5.

"The Attitude of the General Council Toward Military Service." *The Pentecostal Evangel*, 12 October 1941, 13.

"Away—But Not Forgotten." *The Pentecostal Evangel*, 25 June 1967, 9.

B., A. G. "The Impending Conflict." *The Pentecostal Evangel*, 2 October 1926, 4-5.

Bard, B. T. "Respite from Civil War." *The Pentecostal Evangel*, 13 March 1926, 10.

Barl, Oscar. "Reports From the Field: Fort Riley, Kansas." *The Weekly Evangel*, 19 October 1918, 14.

Bartleman, Frank. "Present Day Conditions." *Weekly Evangel,* 5 June 1915, 3.

———. "The European War." *Weekly Evangel*, 10 July 1915, 3.

———. "What Will the Harvest Be?" *Weekly Evangel*, 7, August 1915, 1-2.

———. "War and the Christian." *Word and Work* (circa. 1915): 83.

———. "In the Last Days." *Work and Work*, September 1916, 393.

———. "Christian Preparedness." *Word and Work*, circa. 1916, 114.

Barney, Kenneth D. "Bombardier Barney Came Back." *The Pentecostal Evangel*, 25 November 1944, 12.

———. "War Declared!" *The Pentecostal Evangel*, 25 June 1978, 4.

———. "Standing Firm 'In the Evil Day.'" *The Pentecostal Evangel*, 8 July 1984, 4.

———. "God Save America." *The Pentecostal Evangel*, 29 June 1986, 4.

———. "Raging Nations, Reigning Christ." *The Pentecostal Evangel*, 9 October 1994, 4.

Beacham, Paul F. "Light on the Subject." *Pentecostal Holiness Advocate,* 21 November 1952, n.p.

"'Behold, These Three Years.'" *The Weekly Evangel*, 10 November 1917, 6-7.

Bell, E. N. "Wars and the Missionaries." *The Christian Evangel*, 12 September 1914, 1.

———. "There is Safety in Counsel." *Word and Witness*, October 1915, 1.

———. "Preachers Warned." *The Weekly Evangel*, 5 January 1918, 4.

———. "Questions and Answers." *The Weekly Evangel,* 26 January 1918, 9.

———. "A Tremendous Day is To-Day." *The Weekly Evangel,* 23 February 1918, 6-7.

———. "Destroy This Tract." *The Christian Evangel,* 24 August 1918, 4.

———. "Questions and Answers." *The Christian Evangel,* 7 September 1918, 2.

———. "Questions and Answers." *The Christian Evangel,* 19 October 1918, 5.

———. "The League of Nations." *The Christian Evangel,* 8 March 1919, 2.

Bell, L. Nelson. "Unused Weapons." *The Pentecostal Evangel,* 16 August 1970, 11.

Bellsmith, F. M. "Two Enlistments." *The Pentecostal Evangel,* 23 February 1946, 5.

"Bennett Minutes of the First Conference (1744)." Quoted in Richard Cameron, *Methodism and Society in Historical Perspective,* Volume I of "Methodism and Society." New York: Abingdon, 1961.

Berg, R. Stanley. "Our Chaplain in England." *The Pentecostal Evangel,* 27 May 1944, 9.

———. "Returning Dividends." *The Pentecostal Evangel,* 16 February 1946, 11.

———. "'Go . . . Tell.'" *The Pentecostal Evangel,* 20 April 1946, 10.

Bernard, Williams. "'The Weapons of Our Warfare.'" *The Pentecostal Evangel,* 16 February 1929, 2, 6.

Berry, William I. "A Note of Appreciation By a U.S. Marine." *The Pentecostal Evangel,* 22 October 1927, 11.

Bickle, Joy A. "Commander in Chief." *The Pentecostal Evangel,* 19 December 1993, 22.

"Bingo Boom in New York." *The Pentecostal Evangel,* 7 February 1960, 11.

Bird, Stephen A. "Ministering on Board 'Super Sara.'" *The Pentecostal Evangel,* 10 November 1985, 16.

Bishop, J. Bashford. "Christ and His Enemies." *The Pentecostal Evangel,* 13 March 1960, 22.

"Bishop Mason With the Lord." *The Pentecostal Evangel,* 13 May 1962, 27.

Black, Gregory L. "Urgent Fury." *The Pentecostal Evangel,* 19 August 1984, 7.

"Blood Against Blood. Should Christians Go to War?" *Weekly Evangel,* 3 July 1915, 3.

"Blood Against Blood. Should Christians Go to War?" *Weekly Evangel,* 10 July 1915, 3.

Bloom, Eva Louise. "News From China's War Zone." *The Pentecostal Evangel,* 26 February 1938, 9.

———. "News From China's War Area." *The Pentecostal Evangel,* 4 June 1938, 7.

Boddy, J. T. "The Prince of Peace." *The Pentecostal Evangel,* 25 December 1920, 1.

Bonar, Andrew A. "How Reliable is Conscience?" *Weekly Evangel,* 22 October 1950, 18.

"Books For You to Read." *Pentecostal Evangel,* 2 August 1924, 16.

"Books to Avoid." *The Pentecostal Evangel,* 18 June 1927, 3.

Booth-Clibborn, Arthur Sidney. "Obstructing the View of the Lord Jesus." *The Christian Evangel,* June 29 1918, 2.

———. "A Pentecostal Hymn." *The Christian Evangel,* 27 July 1918, 5.

———. "'Nigh, Even at the Doors!'" *The Christian Evangel,* 7 September 1918, 1-2

———. "'Nigh, Even at the Doors!'" *The Christian Evangel,* 5 October 1918, 6-7.

———. "European Pentecostal Notes." *The Pentecostal Evangel,* 6 March 1920, 11.

———. "Gentileism." *The Pentecostal Evangel,* 13 November 1920, 4.

———. "The Call to Separation." *The Pentecostal Evangel,* 27 November 1920, 4.

Booth-Clibborn, Mrs. Eric. "Obedient Unto Death." *The Weekly Evangel,* 2 January 1926, 12.

Booth-Clibborn, Samuel. "The Christian and War. Is it Too Late?" *The Weekly Evangel,* 28 April 1917, 5.

———. "The Christian and War." *The Weekly Evangel,* 19 May 1917, 4-5.

Borst, Lawrence and Bertha. "Ministering to the War Wounded in Fiji." *The Pentecostal Evangel,* 6 November 1943, 11.

Bowles, Ralph G. "No More Wasted Years for Me." *The Pentecostal Evangel,* 25 June 1967, 11.

Boyd, Chaplain Dudley. "Faith a Necessity." *At Ease,* January 1965, Vol. 5 # 1, 10.

"The Boys are Going Again." *The Pentecostal Evangel,* 14 August 1948, 12.

Bragg, Wallace S. "Our Task in a Post-War World." *The Pentecostal Evangel,* 27 October 1945, 2-3, 7.

Braxton, Helen. "God Bless You, Warren." *At Ease*, January 1965, Vol. 5 #1, 8-10.

Bridges, James K. "Winning the Values War in a Changing Culture." *The Pentecostal Evangel*, 19 January 1997, 22.

"Brief Notes from the War Areas." *The Pentecostal Evangel*, 17 May 1941, 9-10.

Brooks, Hiram Jr. "Witnessing to Servicemen." *The Pentecostal Evangel*, 23 May 1942, 10.

Brown, Robert A., Mrs. ". . .Soldiers. . ." *The Pentecostal Evangel*, 7 December 1929, 5.

Brown, Robert A., letter to J. Roswell Flower, 12 August 1942. J. R. Flower Pentecostal Heritage Center, Springfield, Missouri.

Bruning, Carol L. "Reunited!" *The Pentecostal Evangel*, 30 June 1991, 4.

Bruton, J. Paul. "Giving the Gospel to the Soldier." *The Pentecostal Evangel*, 20 March 1943, 5.

Bryan, Larry. "How to Pray About the Gulf War." *The Pentecostal Evangel*, 17 March 1991, 6.

———. "War Over Iraq." *The Pentecostal Evangel*, 17 March 1991, 6.

Bryant, Kristine. "Twenty Years of Military Service." *The Pentecostal Evangel*, 4 March 1984, 10.

"Building a Church 'Like the One Back Home' for Servicemen at Ramey Air Force Base." *The Pentecostal Evangel*, 29 March 1970, 9.

"Building the Church in a War Zone." *The Pentecostal Evangel*, 3 December 1995, 9.

Burgess, Gene. "Sergeant Versolenko's Search is Ended." *The Pentecostal Evangel*, 24 June 1979, 22.

Bush, Florence I. "Trouble in Palestine." *The Christian Evangel*, 7 nob 1914, 1.

Bush, George H.W. "It is a Just War." *The Pentecostal Evangel*, 24 March 1991, 10.

———. "We Stood Where Duty Required." *The Pentecostal Evangel*, 24 March 1991, 11.

"By Faith the Walls of Jericho Fell." *The Pentecostal Evangel*, 6 February 1926, 1.

"CBC Students Provide Coffeehouse Ministry for Military Base." *The Pentecostal Evangel*, 29 June 1980, 12.

Cadwalder, Hugh. "War and Missions." *The Pentecostal Evangel*, 28 September 1940, 9.

Caldwell, Edward S. "The Battle is the Lord's." *The Pentecostal Evangel*, 13 November 1966, 11.

——. "Called to Serve." *The Pentecostal Evangel*, 25 June 1967, 10.

"Candidate for President of U.S.A., 1964: Bishop Tomlinson's Program Gains Ground." *The Church of God,* 15 October 1963, 1, 3-4.

"Cannons Boom and Christians Pray as Civil War Centennial Begins." *The Pentecostal Evangel*, 8 January 1961, 24-25.

Carlyle, George. "The Great Trubulation." *The Christian Evangel*, 5 September 1914, 1.

Carmichael, Amy. "Prayer for War Days." *The Pentecostal Evangel*, 2 January 1943, 2.

Carmichael, George H. "If War Does Not Hinder." *The Pentecostal Evangel*, 9 September 1950, 8.

Causey, David. "Divine Protection in Somalia." *The Pentecostal Evangel*, 26 June 1994, 20.

"CDR Stanford E. Linzey, Jr. Celebrating 20th Year in U.S. Navy." *The Pentecostal Evangel*, 23 July 1967, 30.

Chafee, Edmund B. "The Early Church and the Sword." *The Pentecostal Evangel*, 27 January 1940, 3.

Champion, Richard G. "How Wars are Won." *The Pentecostal Evangel*, 4 March 1968, 4.

Chandler, Marlee. "On the Front Lines for God." *The Pentecostal Evangel*, 23 February 1992, 12.

"Chaplain Adams Named 37th Assemblies Chaplain." *The Pentecostal Evangel*, 20 October 1968, 29.

"Chaplain Administers Oath to Son." *The Pentecostal Evangel*, 22 June 1975, 28.

"Chaplain Baptizes Marines in Philippine Sea." *The Pentecostal Evangel*, 18 August 1957, 7.

"Chaplain Contributes to Middle East Peace." *The Pentecostal Evangel*, 24 June 1994, 25.

"Chaplain Corps Began with Revolution." *The Pentecostal Evangel*, 5 October 1975, 15.

"Chaplain Honored for Outstanding Service." *The Pentecostal Evangel*, 12 February 1967, 30.

"Chaplain Linzey Baptizes Courtney." *The Pentecostal Evangel*, 24 December 1967, 28.

"Chaplain (Lt. Col.) Orville L. McCormack gets Handshake from Maj. Robert A. Hahn." *The Pentecostal Evangel*, 11 February 1968, 29.

"Chaplain on 'Voice of America.'" *The Pentecostal Evangel*, 1 July 1956, 11.

"Chaplain Plank Appointed to Naval Academy." *The Pentecostal Evangel*, 30 June 1968, 18.

"Chaplain S. E. Linzey Conducts Joint Protestant Worship." *The Pentecostal Evangel*, 3 July 1960, 1.

"Chaplain Urges Contact with Personnel in Military During Holiday Season." *The Pentecostal Evangel*, 10 October 1982, 26.

"Chaplain With a Guitar." *The Pentecostal Evangel*, 27 February 1966, 24.

"Chaplain Writes from the Southwest Pacific." *The Pentecostal Evangel*, 5 December 1942, 21.

"Chaplaincy Department Reports on Materials Shipped to Persian Gulf." *The Pentecostal Evangel*, 12 May 1991, 29.

"Chaplains Conference Provides Spiritual Enrichment." *The Pentecostal Evangel*, 27 June 1965, 7.

"Chaplains Corps to be Doubled." *The Pentecostal Evangel*, 20 October 1950, 6.

"Chaplains in Operation Desert Storm." *The Pentecostal Evangel*, 7 June 1991, 12.

"Chaplains Killed in Korea." *The Pentecostal Evangel*, 13 April 1952, 2.

"Chaplains Minister to American Troops in Alaska." *The Pentecostal Evangel*, 17 August 1958, 8.

"Chaplains Serve in Vietman." *The Pentecostal Evangel*, 27 February 1966, 23.

"Chief of Air Force Chaplains Visits CBI." *The Pentecostal Evangel*, 11 May 1952, 23.

Chittim, Ross. "I Saw the A-bomb." *The Pentecostal Evangel*, 13 January 1952, 6.

"The Christian and War." *The Pentecostal Evangel*, 29 July 1939, 2.

Christmann, Harold L. "Adventuring With God." *The Pentecostal Evangel*, 19 November 1967, 2.

———. "I Have Seen God's Power." *The Pentecostal Evangel*, 25 December 1966, 29.

"Church Call." *The Pentecostal Evangel*, 16 December 1944, 9.

"Church Convention Vote Due on Duty in Armed Services." *Independent Press-Telegram* (Long Beach, CA), 26 August 1967, sec. B, p. 4.

"Church of Tomorrow." *The Pentecostal Evangel*, 17 November 1945, 12.

"Churches Urged to Salute Vietnam Veterans." *The Pentecostal Evangel*, 10 October 1982, 26.

"Church's 'I Love America Extravaganza' Draws 5,000 to Stadium." *The Pentecostal Evangel*, 1 July 1990, 12.

Clark, William. "G.I. Joe Meets Solomon Island Saints." *The Pentecostal Evangel*, 6 January 1945, 4.

Clary, Claude. "A Few Lines From Our Soldier Boys." *The Christian Evangel*, 19 October 1918, 14.

"Clothing the Orphans." *The Pentecostal Evangel*, 28 June 1970, 2.

"Clyde Brown named 31st Assemblies Chaplain." *The Pentecostal Evangel*, 30 April 1967, 30.

Collins, Archer P. "Baptized Baptist Preacher." *The Christian Evangel*, 23 January 1915, 1.

———. "'Competency of the Soul Under God' or Soul Liberty." *The Christian Evangel*, 6 September 1919, 3.

———. "Signs of Our Times." *Word and Witness*, 20 October 1913, 1.

"Commission of Chaplains, Servicemen's Division to be Administered Separately." *The Pentecostal Evangel*, 12 March 1967, 30.

"Communist Leaders in Prison." *The Pentecostal Evangel*, 14 January 1950, 8.

"Compulsory Military Service: An English Conscientious Objector's Testimony." *The Weekly Evangel*, 28 April 1917, 7.

"Conference-Retreat for Chaplains Provides Spiritual Refreshing." *The Pentecostal Evangel*, 11 August 1968, 30.

"Conflict and the Reward." *The Pentecostal Evangel*, 2 June 1917, 8.

"Conflict and the Ultimate Victory." *The Pentecostal Evangel*, 11 December 1926, 1.

"Conflict and Victory." *The Weekly Evangel*, 16 February 1918, 3.

"The Conquering Christ." *The Pentecostal Evangel*, 13 October 1934, 8.

"Conscientious Objectors." *The Pentecostal Evangel*, 14 January 1950, 8.

"Contemporary Issues: Does the Assemblies of God Have a Position on War and Conscientious Objectors?" *The Pentecostal Evangel*, 12 January 1997, 22.

"The Conversion of a Nazi Storm Trooper." *The Pentecostal Evangel*, 16 October 1943, 6-7.

Correll, Norman. "Help Them Keep in Step with Jesus." *The Pentecostal Evangel*, 24 June 1973, 10.

"The Cost of War." *The Pentecostal Evangel*, 16 December 1951, 2.

"The Cost of War." *The Pentecostal Evangel*, 22 February 1953, 2.

Cox, A. B. "In Prison and Out Again." *The Christian Evangel*, 29 June 1918, 14.

"The Crisis." *The Weekly Evangel*, 21 April 1917, 7.

Cunningham, Robert C. "Talk with the Chaplain." *The Pentecostal Evangel*, 13 January 1945, 3.

———. "Should America Hoard Food While Millions Starve." *The Pentecostal Evangel*, 14 January 1950, 8.

———. "A Theological Problem." *The Pentecostal Evangel*, 6 May 1950 4.

———. "Provision for Conscientious Objectors." *The Pentecostal Evangel*, 1 July 1951, 2.

———. "Editorially: One Year of War." *The Pentecostal Evangel*, 24 June 1951, 2.

———. "Passing and Permanent: New Plan for Conscientious Objectors." *The Pentecostal Evangel*, 23 March 1952, 2.

———. "The Editorial Viewpoint: War or Peace?" *The Pentecostal Evangel*, 6 January 1957, 2.

———. "The Editorial Viewpoint: The Missile Age." *The Pentecostal Evangel*, 5 May 1957, 2.

———. "A Time for Action." *The Pentecostal Evangel*, 20 May 1962, 3.

———. "April Deadline." *The Pentecostal Evangel*, 8 April 1962, 3.

———. "Fall-out Shelters." *The Pentecostal Evangel*, 14 January 1962, 3.

Cuyler, Stanley W. "Building Strong Military Families." *The Pentecostal Evangel*, 28 June 1981, 5.

Daane, James. "Making Non-Pacifism Official." *Christianity Today*, 15 September 1967, 46.

"Daily Newspaper Bans All Tobacco Advertising." *The Pentecostal Evangel*, 7 February 1960, 11.

"David Anderson is 39th A/G Military Chaplain," *The Pentecostal Evangel*, 24 March 1974, 26.

Davis, George T. B. "Nation-wide Prayer for Revival and Victory." *The Pentecostal Evangel*, 9 May 1942, 1, 3.

"The Death Penalty." *Pentecostal Evangel*, 24 January 1960, 4.

DeBock, Ronald G. "The Battle is Not Yours." *The Pentecostal Evangel*, 13 November 1966, 10.

"Dedicated to the Defenders of America." *The Pentecostal Evangel*, 27 December 1941, 14.

"Dedicating Gospels." *The Pentecostal Evangel*, 7 February 1942, 1.

"Deliverance to the Captives." *The Pentecostal Evangel*, 9 June 1923, 1.

"Deliverances From Death and Answers to Prayer in the War Zone." *The Weekly Evangel*, 22 April 1916, 7.

"Destination Unknown." *The Pentecostal Evangel*, 21 August 1943, 13.

D'Estournelles de Constant, "The Sinister Education of War," *The Weekly Evangel*, 20 January 1917, 2.

Detrick, Jodi. "What Does It Mean?" *The Pentecostal Evangel*, 17 March 1991, 7.

"Directory of Fellowships: Fellowships and Hospitality Homes for Overseas Military Personnel." *The Pentecostal Evangel*, 17 December 1989, 30.

Discipline of the Wesleyan Methodist Connection, 1844, 93. Quoted in Donald W. and Lucille Sider Dayton, *An Historical Survey of Attitudes Toward War and Peace Within the American Holiness Movement*, 7. Winona Lake, Ind.: 1973.

"Distributing *Reveilles*." *The Pentecostal Evangel*, 22 August 1942, 5.

"Divine Surgery." *The Christian Evangel*, 8 March 1919, 3.

Doney, C. W. "The Gospel of the Kingdom," *Word and Witness*, 20 March 1914, 2.

———. "Three Christian Soldiers." *The Pentecostal Evangel*, 2 December 1916, 3.

———. "Salvation for the Soldier Boys." *The Weekly Evangel*, 23 June 1917, 2.

Douglas, Dolores S. "Take Now Thy Son." *The Pentecostal Evangel*, 26 June 1966, 3.

Douglas, William H. "Glorifying War?" *The Pentecostal Evangel*, 28 July 1957, 23.

Duck, Dewain. "Under Enemy Fire." *The Pentecostal Evangel*, 27 June 1976, 12.

———. "Packets of Love." *The Pentecostal Evangel*, 3 July 1988, 38.

Durham, Calvin M. "He Fought for Freedom." *The Pentecostal Evangel*, 4 July 1982, 5.

"Echoes from the Battlefield." *The Weekly Evangel*, 9 February 1918, 1, 7.

"Editorial." *Redemption Tidings*, 15 November 1957, 3.

Egert, Chester C. "Peace in Somalia." *The Pentecostal Evangel*, 9 May 1993, 16.

"Elected Chaplain." *The Pentecostal Evangel*, 14 October 1944, 9.

Ellis, Mark (Dusty). "'That Others May Live.'" *The Pentecostal Evangel*, 25 June 1978, 8.

"Encourage a Serviceman Through Correspondence." *The Pentecostal Evangel*, 26 June 1967, 11.

Enns, Robert and Al Dueck. "Mennonite Brethren in Three Countries: Comparative Profiles of an Ethno-Religious Tradition." *Direction* 17 (Spring 1988): 30-59.

"Enrolled in Career Course." *The Pentecostal Evangel*, 27 February 1966, 25.

Enyart, Ruby M. "Continued Victory in Retreat." *The Pentecostal Evangel*, 26 June 1988, 16.

———. "Meeting the Spiritual Needs of the Mlitary." *The Pentecostal Evangel*, 26 June 1983, 11.

"Evangelizing Our Servicemen." *The Pentecostal Evangel*, 5 December 1942, 9.

Evans, Bob. "Pardoned Twice: How a Nazi War Criminal Found Christ." *The Pentecostal Evangel*, 28 October 1951, 11.

Evans, Darwin E. "Tribute to Lay-Soldiers." *The Pentecostal Evangel*, 4 August 1985, 5.

Evans, William I. "How the Issues of War Will Be Settled." *The Pentecostal Evangel*, 2 January 1943, 2-3.

"Europe at War—and the Gospel at Work." *The Pentecostal Evangel*, 1 March 1941, 8.

Enyart, Ruby M. "Ministering to the Military." *The Pentecostal Evangel*, 14 June 1987, 22.

"Faithful." *The Pentecostal Evangel*, 28 June 1987, 8.

"Faith in God, Word of God Were Strength in Battle, Fighter Pilot Says." *The Pentecostal Evangel*, 30 June 1991, 14.

Felix, Cynthia D. "Army Religious Education Director – a Challenging Ministry." *The Pentecostal Evangel*, 14 May 1989, 18.

"Fellowship Presents Special Flag to U.S. Army Chaplaincy School." *The Pentecostal Evangel*, 12 March 1989, 29.

Fessler, George. "Ministry to a Captive Audience." *The Pentecostal Evangel*, 28 June 1981, 10.

———. "'Where it all begins.'" *The Pentecostal Evangel*, 20 March 1988, 15.

"Fifty Soldiers Saved!" *The Pentecostal Evangel*, 13 September 1941, 16.

"Fight is Still On." *The Pentecostal Evangel*, 4 September 1926, 1.

Finch, Ella E. "Victory In Spite of the War." *The Pentecostal Evangel*, 21 July 1923, 13.

"First Woman Military Chaplain." *The Pentecostal Evangel*, 26 August 1973, 25.

"Five Newest Assemblies of God Chaplains." *The Pentecostal Evangel*, 27 February 1966, 22.

"Five New Chaplains." *The Pentecostal Evangel*, 8 November 1953, 15.

Flanders, Danny J. "'It Shall Not Come Nigh Thee.'" *The Pentecostal Evangel*, 17 June 1944, 1.

Flower, J. Roswell. "Rumors of Wars." *The Christian Evangel*, 14 August 1914, 2.

———. "Prophetic War Horses Sent Out." *The Christian Evangel*, 29 August 1914, 1.

———. "The Need of the Hour," *Word and Witness*, August 1914, 1.

———. "Editorial Note." *The Christian Evangel*, 31 October 1914, 1.

———. "War-A Fulfillment of Prophecy." *The Christian Evangel*, 31 October 1914, 1.

———. "The Kings of the East." *The Christian Evangel*, 7 November 1914, 1.

———. "Should Christians Go To War?" *The Christian Evangel*, 16 January 1915, 2.

———. "What Will the Harvest Be? Article in Last Week's Evangel Receiving Just Criticism." *The Weekly Evangel*, 14 August 1915, 2.

———. "The Lord's Supper," *Word and Witness*, August 1915, 5.

———. "Little Talks with the Office Editor." *The Weekly Evangel*, 27 May 1916, 2.

———. "The Plight of the Christian in the Present World War." *Pentecostal Evangel*, 12 June 1943, 6-7.

———. "Basic Unity of Evangelical Christianity." *The Pentecostal Evangel*, 19 June 1943, 8.

———. "The Plight of the Conscientious Objector in the Present World Conflict." *Pentecostal Evangel*, 3 July 1943, 2-3.

———. "Concerning the Conscientious Objector." *The Pentecostal Evangel*, 4 March 1944, 7.

———. "United Evangelical Action." *The Pentecostal Evangel*, 13 May 1944, 5.

———. "Why We Joined the NAE." *The Pentecostal Evangel*, 29 March 1947, 12.

Flower, Mrs. A. R. "Daily Portion From the King's Bounty." *The Weekly Evangel*, 21 April, 1917, 7.

———. "Daily Portion From the King's Bounty." *The Weekly Evangel*, 4 August 1917, 7.

Flower, Mrs. J. Roswell. "The Wicked Husbandmen." *The Christian Evangel*, 8 August 1914, 2.

Floyd, Ann. "Military Presence – and God's Presence." *The Pentecostal Evangel*, 7 July 1991, 9.

Fornwalt, Russell J. "Ending the Interpersonal Cold War." *The Pentecostal Evangel*, 26 August 1965, 13.

Fox, George. *Epistles*. No. 188, 1659. Quoted in Peter Brock, *The Quaker Peace Testimony, 1660-1914*. York, England: Sessions Book Trust, 1990.

Frackler, Mark. "Don't Keep the Faith." *The Pentecostal Evangel*, 24 June 1973, 11.

"Frank Borman Addresses Congress on War Prisoners." *The Pentecostal Evangel*, 13 September 1970, 26.

"Fred H. Renfroe—38th Assemblies of God Chaplain is Assigned to Active Duty." *The Pentecostal Evangel*, 29 June 1969, 28.

"Freeman Joins U.S. Army Chaplaincy Corps." *The Pentecostal Evangel*, 10 September 1967, 29.

"Frightening Possibilities." *The Pentecostal Evangel*, 6 May 1950, 4.

Frodsham, Arthur W. "Bound and Loosed." *The Weekly Evangel*, 16 February 1918, 8.

Frodsham, Stanley H. "Our Heavenly Citizenship." *The Weekly Evangel*, 11 September 1915, 3.

———. "Our Heavenly Citizenship." *Word and Witness*, 12 October 1915, 3.

———. "Our Distinctive Testimony." *The Weekly Evangel*, 27 December 1919, 8.

———. "From the Pentecostal Viewpoint." *The Pentecostal Evangel*, 21 June 1924, 4-5.

———. "Editor's Notebook." *The Pentecostal Evangel*, 28 November 1931, 4.

———. "Editor's Notebook." *The Pentecostal Evangel*, 20 February 1932, 4.

———. "The Christian Warfare." *The Pentecostal Evangel*, 31 October 1936, 5.

———. "Fifth Annual Convention of the NAE." *The Pentecostal Evangel*, 10 May 1947, 6.

Funderburk, Frank. "Laws of Warfare." *The Pentecostal Evangel*, 25 June 1967, 12.

Fuchida, Mitsuo. "I Bombed Pearl Harbor." *The Pentecostal Evangel*, 23 September 1950, 4-5.

Fulmer, Richard C. "Revival Cells in the Military." *The Pentecostal Evangel*, 20 July 1969, 6.

———. "Fellowship in the Spirit." *The Pentecostal Evangel*, 26 June 1977, 14.

"Future Wars." *The Pentecostal Evangel*, 7 May 1932, 13.

"G. I. Generosity in Korea." *The Pentecostal Evangel*, 30 May 1954, 2.

Gannon, Theodore E. "Christian Commitment to Military Ministry." *The Pentecostal Evangel*, 27 June 1976, 11.

———. "'Under Orders.'" *The Pentecostal Evangel*, 24 June 1979, 10.

———. "Assemblies of God Chaplains Now on Active Duty." *The Pentecostal Evangel*, 24 June 1979, 11.

———. "Assemblies of God Chaplains Now on Active Duty." *The Pentecostal Evangel*, 24 June 1979, 11.

———. "Everywhere Preaching . . . In the Military." *The Pentecostal Evangel*, 29 June 1980, 13.

Ganz, Lily. "Prisoner of War Returns Home." *The Pentecostal Evangel*, 13 May 1944, 11.

Gay, Bro. and Sis. J. G. "Amongst the Soldier Boys at Ft. Stevens, Ore." *The Christian Evangel*, 7 September 1918, 7.

Gee, Donald. "Conscientious Objection." *The Pentecostal Evangel*, 8 November 1930, 6-7.

———. "War, the Bible, and the Christian." *The Pentecostal Evangel*, 8 November 1930, 6-7.

———. "Conscientious Objection." *The Pentecostal Evangel*, 15 November 1930, 2-3.

————. "War, the Bible, and the Christian." *The Pentecostal Evangel*, 15 November 1930, 2-3.

————. "Conscience." *The Pentecostal Evangel*, 13 August 1938, 1.

————. "Conscientious Objection." *The Pentecostal Evangel*, 4 May 1940, 4.

"General Convention of Pentecostal Saints and Churches of God in Christ. Hot Springs, Arkansas, April 2 to 12, 1914," *Word and Witness*, 20 December 1913, 1.

"Gentle Reminder." *The Pentecostal Evangel*, 26 June 1977, 21.

Gentlemen's Magazine, 1775, 561. Quoted in William Warren Sweet, *Methodism in American History*, 82. New York: Abingdon-Cokesbury Press, 1933.

"Getting the Gospel Going." *The Pentecostal Evangel*, 30 March 1946, 12.

Gierke, William F. A. "Only Ten Years Ago." *The Pentecostal Evangel*, 24 December 1938, 3, 11.

Gigliotti, Frank B. "Blood Stains." *The Pentecostal Evangel*, 18 October 1947, 14-15.

"Gilbert Bender is 32nd Chaplain." *The Pentecostal Evangel*, 13 August 1967, 29.

"Glorifying War?" *The Pentecostal Evangel*, 28 July 1957, 23.

"Go Forward." *The Pentecostal Evangel*, 2 October 1920, 3.

"God Working in the Camps." *The Pentecostal Evangel*, 29 August 1942, 11.

"God's Spirit Moving Among the Military." *The Pentecostal Evangel*, 1 August 1976, 13.

Goldman, W. Darryl. "Gateway to Heaven." *The Pentecostal Evangel*, 11 December 1983, 14.

"Good Soldiers of Jesus Christ." *The Weekly Evangel*, 9 February 1918, 4.

Goodwin, Billy M. "Like a Mighty Army." *The Pentecostal Evangel*, 25 June 1978, 6.

Gordon, A.J. "The Ministry of Women." *The Alliance Weekly*, 1 May 1948, 277. Quoted in Howard Kenyon, "An Analysis of Ethical Issues in the History of the Assemblies of God," 190. Ph.D. diss., Baylor University, 1988.

Gortner, J. Narver. "Why Does Not God Intervene and Stop This War?" *The Pentecostal Evangel*, 6 February 1943, 1, 5-7.

————. "Brother Warwick Appointed Chaplain." *The Pentecostal Evangel*, 10 June 1944, 9.

Goss, H. A. "Shall We Pay Tithes? If So, To Whom?" *Word and Witness*, 20 May 1913, 2.

"Graduate School Student Commissioned for Military Seminarian Program." *The Pentecostal Evangel*, 24 May 1981, 26.

Grant, Delbert S. "Leading Service Men to Christ." *The Pentecostal Evangel*, 11 July 1942, 10-11.

———. "God Working in the Camps." *The Pentecostal Evangel*, 29 August 1942, 11.

———. "Guarded Gates Become Open Doors." *The Pentecostal Evangel*, 12 September 1942, 6.

———. "Khaki Christmas." *The Pentecostal Evangel*, 5 December 1942, 18-19.

———. "When a Prize Ring Became a Pulpit." *The Pentecostal Evangel*, 20 May 1944, 1.

———. "*Reveille* and a Revolution." *The Pentecostal Evangel*, 22 July 1944, 9, 13.

Graves, Carl F., Mr. and Mrs. "War and Missions." *The Pentecostal Evangel*, 13 January 1945, 6.

Gray, James A. "A Voice from England." *The Christian Evangel*, 3 October 1914, 1.

———. "War—A Fulfillemnt of Prophecy." *The Christian Evangel*, 31 October 1914, 1.

"The Great War and the Speedy Return of Our Lord." *The Weekly Evangel*, 10 April 1917, 1.

Griepp, Frank R. "Know Your Chaplain." *The Pentecostal Evangel*, 13 December 1953, 6.

———. "To C.A.'s Entering Military Service." *The Pentecostal Evangel*, 13 December 1953, 6, 11-12.

Hafley, Jennie W. "Reveille." *The Pentecostal Evangel*, 6 June 1942, 11.

Hageman, William. "Diary of a Chaplain's Assistant." *The Pentecostal Evangel*, 29 June 1958, 16.

Hale, F. A. "Amongst the Soldier Boys." *The Pentecostal Evangel*, 29 June 1918, 14.

Hall, Don. "'Here We Are, Lord: Send Us!'" *The Pentecostal Evangel*, 26 March 1972, 6.

Hall, L. C. "The Great Crisis Near at Hand." *Word and Witness*, 20 November 1913, 1.

Hankerson, Elijah H., III. "The Church of God in Christ." *The Pentecostal Evangel*, 31 May 1998, 9.

Hansen, H. E. "War Conditions Affect the Work in North China." *The Pentecostal Evangel*, 7 March 1925, 10.

"Hard But Glorious." *The Pentecostal Evangel*, 11 November 1944, 9.

Hardin, Ben. "The Gospel Among Servicemen." *The Pentecostal Evangel*, 7 October 1944, 2-3.

Harrup, Scott. "Peter Kuzmic Discusses the Church and War in the Former Yugoslavia." *The Pentecostal Evangel*, 3 December 1995, 7.

"Harvest Time." *The Pentecostal Evangel*, 1 September 1945, 5.

"Has the War Ended Missions?" *The Pentecostal Evangel*, 14 February 1942, 8-9.

Hatfield, Larry. "Just Tell Them About Jesus." *The Pentecostal Evangel*, 14 October 1984, 16.

Hatfield, Lydia. "The Law of Christ for Believers." *The Christian Evangel*, 12 July 1919, 3.

"H-Bomb and Evangelism." *The Pentecostal Evangel*, 30 May 1954, 2.

"H-Bomb Could Destroy USA." *The Pentecostal Evangel*, 30 May 1954, 2.

"He is Coming." *The Christian Evangel*, 3 October 1914, 1.

"'He Will Keep the Feet of His Saints.'" *The Pentecostal Evangel*, 21 February 1942, 6.

Heetebry, Adrian M. "Reaching for Servicemen in Fiji." *The Pentecostal Evangel*, 17 October 1942, 8.

"'Help us Minister to the Military,' Chaplain urges." *The Pentecostal Evangel*, 31 January 1971, 28.

"Helping the Service Men." *The Pentecostal Evangel*, 21 February 1942, 1.

Hensley, Gary. "Wilderness Ministry." *The Pentecostal Evangel*, 28 July 1991, 20.

Hernandez, John and Maritza. "Jesus Lives in Miami's War Zone." *The Pentecostal Evangel*, 11 June 1995, 21.

Hicks, W. Percy. "Will There be World Peace?" *The Pentecostal Evangel*, 16 February 1929, 6.

Highfill, Floyd J. "I'm Glad I'm An American." *The Pentecostal Evangel*, 30 June 1968, 23.

Hoffman, Martin A. "To Christians in Military Service." *The Pentecostal Evangel*, 9 November 1997, 22.

Hogan, J. Philip. "World Evangelical Fellowship." *The Pentecostal Evangel*, 18 October 1953, 6.

———. "Military Missionaries." *The Pentecostal Evangel*, 27 January 1963, 9.

———. "Serving Under Two Banners." *The Pentecostal Evangel*, 25 June 1972, 13.

Hoke, Donald E. "War Can Be Averted." *The Pentecostal Evangel*, 14 January 1951, 11.

Holloway, D. P. "The Approaching Day of Doom." *The Pentecostal Evangel*, 15 August 1954, 3, 9.

"Holy Spirit Blesses at Military Retreats Held in Asia Pacific Region." *The Pentecostal Evangel*, 11 February 1990, 27.

"Honored for American Spirit." *The Pentecostal Evangel*, 27 November 1955, 6.

"The Hope of a Nation." *The Pentecostal Evangel*, 12 June 1943, 8.

Horban, Michael P. "Terror of Conscience and the Way of Peace." *The Pentecostal Evangel*, 11 March 1973, 2.

———. "Answer of a Good Conscience." *The Pentecostal Evangel*, 24 April 1983, 12.

"Howard Shaffett is 40th A/G Chaplain." *The Pentecostal Evangel*, 16 November 1969, 28.

Hudson, Bob. "In Enemy Hands." *The Pentecostal Evangel*, 27 June 1993, 4.

Hurst, Randy. "Spiritual Military Intelligance." *The Pentecostal Evangel*, 26 October 1997, 12.

———. "Warfare Tactics." *The Pentecostal Evangel*, 26 October 1997, 14.

"'I Love America' Celebration to Honor Returning Troops." *The Pentecostal Evangel*, 23 June 1991, 24.

"The Impending Conflict." *The Pentecostal Evangel*, 21 July 1917, 8.

"I Sat Where They Sat." *The Pentecostal Evangel*, 15 November 1959, 18.

"Important Notice." *The Christian Evangel*, 31 October 1914, 4.

"In and Round About the Trenches in France." *The Weekly Evangel*, 20 October 1917, 4.

"In South Vietnam: 1965." *The Pentecostal Evangel*, 26 September 1965, 7.

"Intemperance and Insanity." *The Pentecostal Evangel*, 19 December 1954, 7.

"In the Power of His Might." *The Pentecostal Evangel*, 19 January 1924, 3.

Innes, T. Christie. "Defense Against Blitz!" *The Pentecostal Evangel*, 11 September 1948, 5.

"Is European War Justifiable?" *The Christian Evangel,* 12 December 1914, 1.

"Israel's Military Might Ranked Fourth in the World by Analysts." *The Pentecostal Evangel,* 1 May 1983, 12.

"It All Started with One Man." *The Pentecostal Evangel,* 27 December 1981, 5.

"It Takes a Serviceman." *The Pentecostal Evangel,* 31 December 1949, 12.

"It's *Reveille* Time Again!" *The Pentecostal Evangel,* 12 August 1944, 16.

"Jack K. Golie—35th Assemblies Chaplain Appointed." *The Pentecostal Evangel,* 11 February 1968, 29.

Jaeger, Harry A. "Modern Miracles." *The Pentecostal Evangel,* 22 January 1944, 1, 8-9.

———. "Spiritual Conquest Among American Doughboys." *The Pentecostal Evangel,* 12 May 1945, 5, 7.

Jamieson, Samuel A. "Conscience." *Weekly Evangel,* 30 August 1924, 3.

———. "The True Military Armament." *The Pentecostal Evangel,* 29 July 1951, 6-7.

———. "The True Military Armament." *The Pentecostal Evangel,* 26 June 1966, 22-23, 29.

Jarret, Joseph G. "Of Evil Walls." *The Pentecostal Evangel,* 25 June 1989, 7.

"Jerry Webb Appointed 34th A/G Chaplain." *The Pentecostal Evangel,* 22 October 1967, 30.

"Jewish Extermination." *The Pentecostal Evangel,* 23 November 1940, 11.

"Jews to Pray for War's End." *Weekly Evangel,* 11 September 1915, 2.

"John Lindvall Named Chaplain for New Field Command." *The Pentecostal Evangel,* 16 November 1969, 28.

"John Smith Receives Bronze Oak Leaf Cluster." *The Pentecostal Evangel,* 15 January 1967, 31.

Johnson, Bernhard. "Standing Strong in the Battle." *The Pentecostal Evangel,* 7 May 1995, 8.

Johnson, Elva M. "A Song for Marching." *The Pentecostal Evangel,* 30 November 1958, 17.

Johnson, Melvin T. "Who's the Enemy?" *The Pentecostal Evangel,* 23 May 1993, 4.

Johnson, Paul H., III. "'Reverse Jonah.'" *The Pentecostal Evangel,* 19 June 1988, 22.

"Jules Ballas Joins Army Chaplain's Corps." *The Pentecostal Evangel,* 11 August 1957, 11.

Kagan, Mark. "Hitlerism Must Lose." *The Pentecostal Evangel*, 25 March 1944, 1, 7.

"Keep Missions First." *The Pentecostal Evangel*, 27 February 1926, 10.

"Keep Praying." *The Pentecostal Evangel*, 12 August 1944, 16.

Kelley, George M. "Missionaries in Peril." *The Pentecostal Evangel*, 11 December 1920, 12-13.

Kindersley, Guy M. "Can Peace Come From Such Seed?" *The Pentecostal Evangel*, 15 May 1920, 10.

"Kingdom of God Comes, 12:00 Noon July 4th: Righteouness, Peace on Earth as in Heaven." *The Church of God*, 1 July 1964, 1-2.

Kirkpatrick, William F. "Amongst the Soldier Boys." *The Christian Evangel*, 27 July 1918, 7.

———. "Amongst the Soldiers." *The Christian Evangel*, 19 October 1918, 1.

———. "In the Trenches at Houston, Texas." *The Pentecostal Evangel*, 10 August 1918, 3.

Klapach, Frank S. "Ministering in the Military." *The Pentecostal Evangel*, 19 March 1995, 17.

Klippenstein, Lawrence. "Exercising a Free Conscience: The Conscientious Objectors of the Soviet Union and the German Democratic Republic." *Religion in Communist Lands* 13 (Winter 1985): 284-285.

Knowles, Arthur. "Our Servicemen's Rally." *The Pentecostal Evangel*, 4 March 1944, 11.

Krist, Robert. "Peace and Power." *The Pentecostal Evangel*, 31 August 1986, 18.

Krogstad, E. Elsworth. "Loyalty to the Government and to God in the Present World Crisis." *The Pentecostal Evangel*, 4 July 1942, 1.

Kullman, Morris. "Conflict of the Ages." *The Pentecostal Evangel*, 14 November 1925, 6.

Kuzmic, Peter. "God Protects." *The Pentecostal Evangel*, 3 December 1995, 11.

Kvamme, B. Martin. "God's Grace in Time of War." *The Pentecostal Evangel*, 2 January 1932, 8.

"Lack of Morality, Spiritual Poverty, Grease Slide Toward an Atomic War." *The Pentecostal Evangel*, 13 September 1970, 25.

Lane, Albert C. "One Year in Service with Men in Uniform." *The Pentecostal Evangel*, 26 August 1944, 1.

Langston, E. L. "The Present War and Prophecy." *The Pentecostal Evangel*, 25 May 1940, 5.

Larson, Richard E. "First Assemblies of God Church in the Panama Canal Zone Ministers to Civilian and Military Americans." *The Pentecostal Evangel*, 29 June 1969, 16.

"Latin America Faces the Post-War Period." *The Pentecostal Evangel*, 19 October 1946, 10-11.

"The Latter Days." *Word and Work*, 29 September 1907, 23.

Lawrence, Ernest W. "'Banners of Faith.'" *The Pentecostal Evangel*, 7 March 1982, 7.

"Lawsuit in Courts Threatens Tradition of Military Chaplains." *The Pentecostal Evangel*, 3 April 1983, 13.

Lebeck, Albert J. "Will the Present Day Merging Lead to the Mark of the Beast?" *The Pentecostal Evangel*, 6 June 1931, 4-5.

"Lemuel Boyles—30th A/G Military Chaplain Named." *The Pentecostal Evangel*, 15 January 1967, 31.

"Letter From Italy." *The Pentecostal Evangel*, 5 February 1944, 11.

"Letters." *The Pentecostal Evangel*, 6 October 1945, 12.

Lewis, David A. "War in Heaven." *The Pentecostal Evangel*, 30 June 1968, 2.

———. "War on Prophecy." *The Pentecostal Evangel*, 17 December 1989, 6.

"'Light on the Present Crisis.'" *The Weekly Evangel*, 1 July 1916, 6-7, 9.

Lincoln, Abraham. "Letter to the General Conference of 1864." Quoted in William Warren Sweet, *Methodism in American History*, 299. New York: Abingdon-Cokesbury Press, 1933.

Lindvall, John A. "Pentecost in Europe." *The Pentecostal Evangel*, 7 December 1946, 2.

Linzey, Stanford E. *Filling Your Boots*. Springfield, Mo.: Gospel Publishing House, 1968.

———. "'Led to a 'Dark Place,' Chaplain Says." *The Pentecostal Evangel*, 17 May 1998.

———. *God Was At Midway*. San Diego, Calif.: Black Forest Press, 1999.

"Live By The Word," *Word and Witness*, 20 March 1913, 2.

Long, Jim. "Speed-the-Light Reaches a Dying Marine." *The Pentecostal Evangel*, 22 June 1980, 3.

"Love Letters from a Soldier." *The Pentecostal Evangel*, 7 April 1991, 6.

Lowenberg, Paul E. "His Hand Stuck to the Sword." *The Pentecostal Evangel*, 19 July 1964, 16-18.

"Loyal to Both." *The Pentecostal Evangel*, 13 March 1960, 22.

"Loyalty Bonds." *The Christian Evangel*, 1 June 1918, 8.

Mader, Herman J. "War Conditions in China." *The Pentecostal Evangel*, 20 December 1924, 11.

Maempa, John T. "Living the War." *The Pentecostal Evangel*, 17 March 1991, 3.

———. "War and Peace." *The Pentecostal Evangel*, 3 December 1995, 5.

Mahaney, Marjory. "News From the War Zone." *The Pentecostal Evangel*, 28 December 1940, 9.

Manley, Kevin A. "Religious Program Specialist in the U.S. Navy." *The Pentecostal Evangel*, 27 June 1982, 9.

Markstrom, Paul R. "What the Work/Hurting Needs is Jesus." *The Pentecostal Evangel*, 19 August 1984, 7.

Martin, M. "Lessons Taught During the Air Raids." *The Weekly Evangel*, 6 April 1918, 1.

Marvin, Charles W. "Top Navy Men/Top Christians." *The Pentecostal Evangel*, 22 June 1980, 13.

Mayo, Jimmie. "Pentecostal Conscripts." *The Pentecostal Evangel*, 23 November 1941, 11.

McAlister, James. "Startling Signs of the Times." *The Pentecostal Evangel*, 10 July 1920, n.p.

McCafferty, William Burt. "Some One is Coming." *The Christian Evangel*, 12 September 1914, 1.

———. "Should Christians Go to War?" *The Christian Evangel*, 16 January 1915, 1.

———. "'There Shall Be Wars and Rumors of War.'" *The Pentecostal Evangel*, 6 September 1924, 5.

McCarty, Dorothea L. "Effect of War in India." *The Christian Evangel,* 5 December 1914, 4.

McClay, Robert. "Standing True to Scriptural Principles." *The Pentecostal Evangel*, 6 February 1932, 1, 8-9, 13.

McCormack, Orville L. "Can a Man Serve God in the Military?" *The Pentecostal Evangel*, 1 July 1962, 24-25.

McCullough, Charles C. "U.S. Military Personnel in Europe: A Vast Mission Field." *The Pentecostal Evangel*, 26 June 1983, 21.

———. "Missionary to the Military." *The Pentecostal Evangel*, 7 July 1991, 7.

McDowell, David H. "A Call to Arms." *The Pentecostal Evangel*, 8 August 1931, 4-5.

McElyea, Lemuel D. "For God and Country." *The Pentecostal Evangel*, 26 June 1983, 10.

———. "Military Ministries." *The Pentecostal Evangel*, 23 October 1983, 4.

———. "God's Men in the Military." *The Pentecostal Evangel*, 19 August 1984, S-5.

———. "Chaplain Candidate Program Promotes Quality: God's Men in the Military." *The Pentecostal Evangel*, 19 August 1984, S-4.

———. "Mission of the Chaplaincy." *The Pentecostal Evangel*, 4 August 1985, 4.

———. "With Them." *The Pentecostal Evangel*, 9 August 1987, 14.

———. Ministry to Our Armed Forces." *The Pentecostal Evangel*, 20 March 1988, 14.

———. "Who Upholds America's Cherished Treasures?" *The Pentecostal Evangel*, 25 June 1989, 10.

———. "Serving in the Middle East." *The Pentecostal Evangel*, 28 October 1990, 21.

———. "Reaching Those in Uniform." *The Pentecostal Evangel*, 7 July 1991, 12.

———. "Retreats Advance the Gospel." *The Pentecostal Evangel*, 29 December 1991, 22.

McGee, Gary B. "Questions and Answers." *Assemblies of God Heritage*, Summer 1991, 6.

McNabb, Talmadge F. "My Debt to Faithful Friends." *The Pentecostal Evangel*, 9 August 1959, 12.

———. "Heaven Came Down at Berchtesgaden." *The Pentecostal Evangel*, 14 February 1971, 25.

———. "Another Side of the GI Story." *The Pentecostal Evangel*, 24 June 1973, 4.

McPherson, Warren F. "Serving our Servicemen." *The Pentecostal Evangel*, 8 January 1961, 25.

———. "To Join or Not to Join." *The Pentecostal Evangel*, 1 July 1962, 6-7.

———. "Missions and the Military." *The Pentecostal Evangel*, 7 July 1963, 8-9.

———. "Keys to Closed Doors." *The Pentecostal Evangel*, 5 July 1964, 5.

———. "The Case for Military Chaplains." *The Pentecostal Evangel*, 5 July 1964, 12-13.

————. "Have You Been to See the Battle?" *The Pentecostal Evangel*, 27 June 1971, 10.

————. "Harvest Field with Few Workers." *The Pentecostal Evangel*, 18 May 1975, 20.

————. "Command to Occupy!" *The Pentecostal Evangel*, 29 June 1975, 6.

————. "Military Service Policy Restudied by Assemblies." n.p., n.d., n.p.

Meppelink, Charles D. "Military Retreat a Spiritual Oasis." *The Pentecostal Evangel*, 15 January 1995, 18.

"Message Two." *The Christian Evangel*, 12 July 1919, 3.

Michael, Stanley V. "Revivaltime Evangelist Receives War Bonnet." *The Pentecostal Evangel*, 30 March 1958, 12.

"Militant." *The Pentecostal Evangel*, 31 August 1946, 8.

"Military Beats the Church in Americans' Votes of Confidence." *The Pentecostal Evangel*, 22 March 1987, 24.

"Military Chaplain Marches in German Parade." *The Pentecostal Evangel*, 24 July 1994, 28.

"Military Chaplains Needed." *The Pentecostal Evangel*, 19 December 1954, 7.

"'Military Church' Provides Opportunity." *The Pentecostal Evangel*, 17 March 1991, 25.

"Military, Institutional, and Industrial Chaplains Join in First-ever Chaplains Conference." *The Pentecostal Evangel*, 21 August 1983, 28.

"Military Personnel Day." *The Pentecostal Evangel*, 28 June 1998, 20.

"Military Personnel Day, June 6." *The Pentecostal Evangel*, 29 June 1997, 28.

Millard, Stanley. "Ministering to the Military." *The Pentecostal Evangel*, 29 June 1975, 9.

Mininger, J. D. *Religious COs Imprisoned at the U.S. Disciplinary Barracks, Ft. Leavenworth, Kansas.* Jacob D. and Hettie (Kulp) Mininger Collection, Papers, 1879–1941, box 22. Mennonite Church USA Historical Archives, Goshen, Ind.

"Ministry to Servicemen Helps Meet Vital Need." *The Pentecostal Evangel*, 18 January 1970, 29.

Mink, J. E., Mrs. "World-wide War." *The Christian Evangel*, 24 October 1914, 3.

"Missionaries to the Military Honored for 29 Years of Service." *The Pentecostal Evangel*, 24 January 1993, 29.

Moore, Janice. "Price of Freedom." *The Pentecostal Evangel*, 13 November 1994, 20.

Moore, Sarah Foulkes. "Fighting the Good Fight of Faith." *The Pentecostal Evangel*, 9 December 1939, 3, 6.

Morrison, J. C., Mr. and Mrs. "Sorrows of War." *The Pentecostal Evangel*, 7 May 1927, 11.

"Most Americans Rejected Notion Persian Gulf War was Bible's End-times Battle, According to Gallup Survey." *The Pentecostal Evangel*, 2 June 1991, 14.

"Mrs. Talmadge F. McNabb Pins the Silver Oak Leaves. . . ." *The Pentecostal Evangel*, 25 December 1966, 29.

Mulvagh, J. C. "Flag of God." *The Pentecostal Evangel*, 27 February 1972, 10.

"NAE Issues Statement on Homosexuals in the Military." *The Pentecostal Evangel*, 25 April 1993, 25.

Nelson, Ruth. "Winning Souls for Jesus." *The Pentecostal Evangel*, 14 October 1984, 18.

"New Bylaws on Military Service Adopted by General Council." *The Pentecostal Evangel*, 8 October 1967, 7.

"The New Conscription Law." *The Pentecostal Evangel*, 12 October 1940, 13.

"New Navy Chaplain Reports for Duty." *The Pentecostal Evangel*, 23 November 1958, 10.

"New Navy Chaplain Reports for Duty." *The Pentecostal Evangel*, 4 September 1960, 10.

"New Plan for Conscientious Objectors." *The Pentecostal Evangel*, 23 March 1952, 2.

"News Release." *The Church of God* (News Release Issue), 15 October 1963, 1.

"New Requirements for Army Chaplains." *The Pentecostal Evangel*, 16 August 1953, 2.

"News From the War Areas." *The Pentecostal Evangel*, 25 April 1942, 9.

Newby, Leonard. "Light on the present Crisis." *The Weekly Evangel,* 1 July 1916, 6.

"The Next War." *The Pentecostal Evangel*, 25 June 1927, 8-9.

Nicholson, Grace P. "Civil War in North China." *The Pentecostal Evangel*, 27 February 1926, 10.

"No Smoking or Drinking." *The Pentecostal Evangel*, 9 September 1950, 7.

"No 'Universal Military Training.'" *The Pentecostal Evangel*, 13 April 1952, 2.

"Notes From War Areas." *The Pentecostal Evangel*, 31 January 1942, 11.

"Now It Can Be Told." *The Pentecostal Evangel*, 4 March 1944, 11.

"Offensive Warfare." *The Christian Evangel*, 16 November 1918, 3.

"Officers' Christian Fellowship Urges Military to Uphold Homosexual Ban." *The Pentecostal Evangel*, 9 May 1993, 25.

Ohlin, Jodi. "Welcome Home!" *The Pentecostal Evangel*, 30 June 1991, 8.

"Ohio Assembly Celebrates Military Personnel Day with Community." *The Pentecostal Evangel*, 8 October 1995, 29.

"One Christian's Witness." *The Pentecostal Evangel*, 29 June 1975, 8.

"One Year of War." *The Pentecostal Evangel*, 24 June 1951, 2.

"Operation: Opportunity." *The Pentecostal Evangel*, 30 July 1957, 16.

"'Operation Restore Hope' Brings Aid to Somalia." *The Pentecostal Evangel*, 21 August 1994, 29.

Opperman, Daniel C. O. "Who is the Blame?" *Word and Witness*, 20 March 1913, 2.

Orengo, Gloria J. "Serving God and Country." *The Pentecostal Evangel*, 28 June 1981, 4.

Orr, J. Edwin. "A Working Army Chaplain." *The Pentecostal Evangel*, 1 September 1945, 5.

"Our Attitude Toward War and Military Service." *The Pentecostal Evangel*, 2 May 1936, 4-5.

"Our Boys Abroad." *The Pentecostal Evangel*, 31 March 1945, 8.

"Our Colored Brethren." *The Pentecostal Evangel*, 8 July 1950, 12.

"Our God-given Task." *The Pentecostal Evangel*, 26 June 1943, 3.

"Our Ministers in Uniform." *The Pentecostal Evangel*, 8 March 1953, 12.

"Our Mission to the Military." *The Pentecostal Evangel*, 26 September 1965, 7.

"Our Missionaries in War Areas." *The Pentecostal Evangel*, 24 January 1942, 10-11.

"Our Nation's Military." *The Pentecostal Evangel*, 3 June 1990, 26.

"Our Pastors in Uniform." *The Pentecostal Evangel*, 8 July 1944, 9.

"Our Pastors in Uniform." *The Pentecostal Evangel*, 15 September 1945, 1.

"Our Sons in Service." *The Pentecostal Evangel*, 22 July 1944, 12.

"Our Sons in Service." *The Pentecostal Evangel*, 12 August 1944, 16.

"Our Sons in Service." *The Pentecostal Evangel*, 19 August 1944, 9.

"Our Sons in Service." *The Pentecostal Evangel*, 9 December 1944, 12.

"Our Warfare in the Spirit." *The Pentecostal Evangel*, 12 January 1935, 13.

"Overcoming the Roaring Lion." *The Pentecostal Evangel*, 30 September 1922, 7.

Owens, Jerry L. "Morning the War Began." *The Pentecostal Evangel*, 28 June 1992, 8.

"Pacifist Pastor Gets 15 Years." *Boston Globe,* 22 March 1918, 1, 6.

Packer, Marvin. "A/G Chaplain Appointed to Pentagon." *The Pentecostal Evangel*, 29 November 1998, 7.

Panton, D. M. "Coming War." "Democracy and the End." *The Weekly Evangel,* 17 April 1915, 1.

———. "Democracy and the End." *Word and Witness*, May 1915, 5.

———. *The Pentecostal Evangel*, 25 November 1922, 10-11.

———. "Universal War." *The Pentecostal Evangel*, 4 July 1936, 2-3.

Park, Harland A. "Working On in War Zone." *The Pentecostal Evangel*, 1 July 1939, 10.

———. "War Not Stopping Missionary Work." *The Pentecostal Evangel*, 30 September 1939, 8-9.

Parli, Hermann A. "Love . . . and a Communist." *The Pentecostal Evangel*, 6 May 1950, 4.

"Pastor, Congregation Tour Air Force Base in Ohio as Part of Ministry to Reserves." *The Pentecostal Evangel*, 22 December 1991, 24.

Patrick, Saralyn. "So You Want to be a Chaplain." *The Pentecostal Evangel*, 16 June 1991, 22.

Patrick, William L. "From a Chaplain's Diary." *The Pentecostal Evangel*, 27 June 1976, 8.

———. "God is at Work in the Military." *The Pentecostal Evangel*, 27 June 1993, 10.

Patterson, J. H. "Good Soldier of Jesus Christ." *The Pentecostal Evangel*, 11 August 1917, 4.

Paul, Ernest A. "The Great War Thru the Lens of Prophecy." *The Pentecostal Herald,* March 1917, 1-2.

———. "The Great War (Through the Lens of Prophecy)." *The Weekly Evangel,* 6 April 1918, 6-7.

"Peace Comes to the Third Marine Division." *The Pentecostal Evangel*, 17 November 1945, 12.

Pearlman, Myer. "War News Upset Habakkuk Too!" *The Pentecostal Evangel*, 26 July 1941, 1, 4.

Peel, Albert, ed. "A Conscientious Objector of 1576," *Transactions of the Baptist Historical Society* 7: ½ (1920): 123. Quoted in Peter Brock, *The Quaker Peace Testimony, 1660-1914*, 4. York, England: Sessions Book Trust, 1990.

Penn, William. *No Cross, No Crown*. Quoted in Hugh Barbour and J. William Frost, *The Quakers*. Denominations in America, 44. Westport, Conn.: Greenwood Press, 1988.

The Pentecost. 1 (November 1908): 1.

"Pentecostal Bible School Suffers Heavy Damage in Yugoslavian War." *The Pentecostal Evangel*, 19 January 1992, 25.

"Pentecostal Churches destroyed in Yugoslavian Civil War." *The Pentecostal Evangel*, 29 December 1991, 24.

"Pentecostal Conscripts." *The Pentecostal Evangel*, 23 November 1940, 11.

The Pentecostal Evangel, 4 July 1942, 5.

"Pentecostal Groups Oppose UMT and Vatican Ambassador." *The Pentecostal Evangel*, 25 November 1951, 15-16.

"The Pentecostal Movement and the Conscription Law." *The Weekly Evangel*, 4 August 1917, 6-7.

"The Pentecostal Movement and the Conscription Law." *The Weekly Evangel*, 5 January 1918, 5.

"Pentecostal Saints Opposed to War." *Weekly Evangel*, 19 June 1915, 1.

"Peril of Universal Military Training." *The Pentecostal Evangel*, 13 April 1952, 2.

Perkins, Noel. "Call to War." *The Pentecostal Evangel*, 6 June 1931, 8.

———. "The War Situation in China." *The Pentecostal Evangel*, 20 February 1932, 10.

———. "War and Missions." *The Pentecostal Evangel*, 20 July 1940, 8.

———. "War and Missions." *The Pentecostal Evangel*, 31 August 1940, 6.

———. "War and Missions." *The Pentecostal Evangel*, 2 November 1940, 6.

———. "War and Missions." *The Pentecostal Evangel*, 7 December 1940, 6.

———. "War and Missions." *The Pentecostal Evangel*, 27 December 1941, 6.

———. "Our Missionaries in the War Areas." *The Pentecostal Evangel*, 11 April 1942, 7.

———. "Meeting the World's Need." *The Pentecostal Evangel*, 11 October 1947, 2-3, 7.

Pierce, Christine K. "Birth Throes." *Pentecostal Evangel*, 4 February 1922, 1-2.

"Philip Nichols is 39th A/G Chaplain." *The Pentecostal Evangel*, 19 October 1969, 31.

Plank, David W. "Hero in a Prison Camp." *The Pentecostal Evangel*, 16 April 1961, 10.

———. "God's Strategic Naval Assignments." *The Pentecostal Evangel*, 1 September 1968, 10.

Plymire, Victor G. "The Horrors of War and Famine." *The Pentecostal Evangel*, 4 May 1929, 10.

———. "In War-Torn Regions." *The Pentecostal Evangel*, 21 November 1925, 7.

Polman, G. R. "A. A. Boddy Goes to the Front." *Weekly Evangel,* 19 June 1915, 1.

Porter, David. "How Peace Will Come." *The Pentecostal Evangel*, 11 March 1984, 20.

Position Papers: Abstinence. Springfield, Mo.: Gospel Publishing House, 1985.

Position Papers: Homosexuality. Springfield, Mo.: Gospel Publishing House, 1979.

Position Papers: Theology of Ministry. Springfield, Mo.: Gospel Publishing House, 1993.

"Power Over All the Power of the Enemy." *The Christian Evangel*, 8 March 1919, 6.

"Pray!" *The Pentecostal Evangel*, 12 May 1945, 7.

"Pray for Military Chaplains in Action!" *The Pentecostal Evangel*, 21 March 1993, 16.

"Pray for Our Chaplains and Military Personnel." *The Pentecostal Evangel*, 17 March 1991, 16.

"Pray Much – and Pray Now!" *The Pentecostal Evangel*, 12 February 1944, 12.

"Prayer Warfare." *The Pentecostal Evangel*, 21 February 1920, 5.

"Preaching the Gospel at the Front." *The Weekly Evangel*, 9 June 1917, 13.

"Preaching to the Soldier Boys." *The Weekly Evangel*, 16 February 1918, cover.

"Preparations for the Return to Palestine." *Word and Witness*, August 1915, 2.

"'Prepare or Perish.'" *The Pentecostal Evangel*, 16 February 1946, 11.

"Preparing For War." *The Pentecostal Evangel*, 14 January 1950, 8.

"President Wilson's Own Words." *The Weekly Evangel*, 6 April 1918, 1.

Preston, John A. "Work Among the Mexicans in the War Zone." *The Weekly Evangel*, 22 May 1915, 4.

"Pre-war Theology Right." *The Weekly Evangel*, 27 October 1917, 9.

Price, Belle. "Praying for the Soldiers." *The Weekly Evangel*, 7 July 1917, 11.

Proctor, Bernice. "Our Missionaries in War Areas." *The Pentecostal Evangel*, 24 January 1942, 10.

"Protect Your Children." *Word and Witness*, September 1915, 8.

"Proud of His Country." *The Pentecostal Evangel*, 10 November 1968, 28.

"Provision for Conscientious Objectors." *The Pentecostal Evangel*, 1 July 1951, 2.

"Q: Does the Assemblies of God Have a Position on War?" *The Pentecostal Evangel*, 12 January 1997, 22.

Radley, Clarence T. "In a State of War." *The Pentecostal Evangel*, 10 July 1926, 19.

Ramsay, Charles. "Postwar Invasion." *The Pentecostal Evangel*, 30 March 1946, 3.

———. "Postwar Invasion." *The Pentecostal Evangel*, 11 October 1947, 3.

Ramsay, R. G. "Amusements and the Church." *The Pentecostal Evangel*, 4 July 1942, 5.

"Reaches Military People." *The Pentecostal Evangel*, 24 June 1984, 14.

"Recapturing America's Values, Winning the New Civil War." *The Pentecostal Evangel*, 29 March 1992, 29.

Reconciliation: The Magazine of the Pentecostal and Charismatic Churches of North America (Winter 1998).

Reed, H. E. "Methodist Preacher Receives the Baptism." *The Christian Evangel*, 24 October 1914, 4.

"Remember to Pray for Our Assemblies of God Chaplain in Vietnam." *The Pentecostal Evangel*, 18 September 1966, 15.

"Republicans Court Abortion Foes." *The Des Moines Register*, 23 January 2000, 1.

"Reserve Units and National Guard Need Chaplains." *The Pentecostal Evangel*, 27 May 1956, 10.

"*Reveille.*" *The Pentecostal Evangel*, 21 February 1942, 7.

"*Reveille.*" *The Pentecostal Evangel*, 2 May 1942, 16.

"'*Reveille*'for Our Draftees." *The Pentecostal Evangel*, 14 November 1942, 11.

"*Reveille* for Tokyo." *The Pentecostal Evangel*, 27 October 1945, 9.

"*Reveille* No. 9 on the Press." *The Pentecostal Evangel*, 20 November 1943, 9.

"*Reveille* No. 9 Ready for Mailing." *The Pentecostal Evangel*, 2 November 1943, 9.

"Revival Overseas." *The Pentecostal Evangel*, 14 April 1945, 1.

"Revival and Victory Prayer Card." *The Pentecostal Evangel*, 13 June 1942, 12.

"Richard W. Hartman." *The Pentecostal Evangel*, 26 January 1969, 31.

Richardson, David and Marilyn Ross. "World Blew up Around Me." *The Pentecostal Evangel*, 25 June 1989, 8.

Richey, E. N. "Telegram from Houston, Texas." *The Pentecostal Evangel*, 2 February 1918, 3.

Richey, Raymond T. "United Prayer and Workers' League." *The Weekly Evangel*, 8 September 1917, 5.

———. "Amongst the Soldier Boys." *The Weekly Evangel*, 13 October 1917, 15.

———. "Work Amongst the Soldiers." *The Weekly Evangel*, 22 December 1917, 10.

———. "Amongst the Soldier Boys." *The Weekly Evangel*, 16 February 1918, 7.

———. "Among the Soldier Boys." *The Weekly Evangel*, 30 March 1918, 15.

———. "Amongst the Soldier Boys." *The Weekly Evangel*, 16 February 1918, 7.

———. "Amongst the Soldier Boys." *The Weekly Evangel*, 10 August 1918, 10.

———. "Amongst the Soldier Boys." *The Weekly Evangel*, 2 November 1918, 14.

———. "'Peace on Earth, Good Will Toward Men.'" *The Christian Evangel*, 28 December 1918, 9.

———. "Evangelizing at our Army Camps." *The Pentecostal Evangel*, 10 January 1942, 2-3, 12.

Risner, James Robinson. "Communications—Our Lifeblood." *The Pentecostal Evangel*, 7 October 1973, 6-9.

"Robert Carney named 36th Assemblies Chaplain." *The Pentecostal Evangel,* 16 June 1968, 31.

Roberts, L. V. "Prophetic War Horses Sent Out." *The Christian Evangel,* 29 August 1914, 1.

Robeson, Robert B. "Day I Will Remember." *The Pentecostal Evangel,* 26 December 1982, 4.

———. "Right On, Sir! Right On!" *The Pentecostal Evangel,* 22 October 1972, 20.

Rogers, John. "My Turning Point: Delivered From the Horrors of Vietman." *The Pentecostal Evangel,* 22 January 1995, 16.

Rosell, Mervin E. "War Points the Way." *The Pentecostal Evangel,* 17 February 1945, 1, 7.

Rupel, Frederick M. 'Victory in the Desert." *The Pentecostal Evangel,* 7 July 1991, 11.

"Russia and the A-Bomb." *The Pentecostal Evangel,* 28 January 1950, 10.

"Russia Preparing for War." *Pentecostal Evangel,* 26 July 1924, 7.

"Sacramento Pastor Jailed on Charge of Sedition." *Sacramento Bee,* 21 December 1917.

Sandberg, Anne. "Spirit-given Weapons for Spiritual Warfare." *The Pentecostal Evangel,* 9 January 1966, 7-8.

Schell, William G. "The Daily Lives of the Early Christians." *The Weekly Evangel,* 30 October 1915, 1.

———. "The Daily Lives of Early Christians." *The Weekly Evangel,* 6 November 1915, 1.

Schoeneich, B. A. "Sorrows of War." *The Pentecostal Evangel,* 13 August 1927, 11.

———. "War Makes Work in Nicaragua Difficult." *The Pentecostal Evangel,* 20 February 1932.

Schorsch, Donald. "Not Somehow, but Triumphantly, Lord!" *The Pentecostal Evangel,* 25 June 1972, 8.

"Scientists Urge Dispersal of Large Cities." *The Pentecostal Evangel,* 27 November 1955, 6.

Scofield, C. I. "The War in the Light of Prophecy." *The Weekly Evangel,* 28 October 1916, 6-7.

Scott, Douglas G. "The Chaplaincy—a Branch of the Church." *The Pentecostal Evangel,* 2 November 1952, 20.

————. "Our Sons in this Military Era." *The Pentecostal Evangel*, 19 June 1955, 5, 11-12.

Scull, Samuel S. "Christian Courage." *The Pentecostal Evangel*, 30 April 1949, 2, 6-7.

"Selective Service Act Governing Class IV-D." *The Pentecostal Evangel*, 8 April 1951, 11.

"Service Center at Tacoma, Washington." *The Pentecostal Evangel*, 4 December 1943, 9.

"Service Evangelism in Britain." *The Pentecostal Evangel*, 1 January 1944, 13.

"Servicemen are Missionaries Too." *The Pentecostal Evangel*, 29 March 1970, 16.

"Servicemen's Work to be Continued." *The Pentecostal Evangel*, 6 July 1946, 9.

"Servicing the Service Men." *The Pentecostal Evangel*, 12 December 1942, 6-7.

"Serving Our Servicemen." *The Pentecostal Evangel*, 13 January 1945, 5.

"Serving the Servicemen." *The Pentecostal Evangel*, 18 December 1948, 13.

"Serving the Servicemen." *The Pentecostal Evangel*, 8 January 1949, 12.

"Serving the Servicemen." *The Pentecostal Evangel*, 10 September 1949, 16.

Sexton, E. A. "College vs. Gifts of the Spirit." *The Bridegroom's Messenger*, 1 October 1907, 1.

"Shall '*Reveille*' be Continued?" *The Pentecostal Evangel*, 28 July 1945, 7.

Sheridan, Laura C. "Helping the Lord Against the Mighty." *The Pentecostal Evangel*, 30 June 1928, 8.

"Short-sleeve Religion." *The Pentecostal Evangel*, 9 November 1952, 11.

Simpson, W.W. "The Great War and its Results: The Man of Sin Soon to be Revealed." *The Weekly Evangel*, 3 March 1917, 2-3.

————. "Chinese Assemblies Prospering in War Zone." *The Pentecostal Evangel,* 11 June 1938, 7.

————. "Unharmed in China War Zone." *The Pentecostal Evangel*, 5 November 1938, 7.

Simun, Phil. "What Can We Do?" *The Pentecostal Evangel*, 17 March 1991, 8.

"The Sinister Education of War." *The Weekly Evangel*, 20 January 1917, 2.

Sisler, George T. "War 'Profits.'" *The Weekly Evangel*, 29 April 1916, 7.

Sitton, John W. "Ministering to Soldiers." *The Pentecostal Evangel*, 23 May 1942, 10.

"Sixth Assemblies Minister Becomes Navy Chaplain." *The Pentecostal Evangel*, 27 August 1961, 10.

Skipper, Vivian. "One Nation Under God." *The Pentecostal Evangel*, 5 July 1964, 6.

Slager, George C. "The Horrors of War in China." *The Pentecostal Evangel*, 14 March 1931, 10.

Slaybaugh, E. T. "Effect of Universal War." *The Weekly Evangel*, 15 May 1915, 3.

Sloan, Brenda. "We Never Close." *The Pentecostal Evangel*, 28 August 1988, 19.

Smales, Clarence P. "Visit with an Army Chaplain." *The Pentecostal Evangel*, 17 October 1942, 3.

―――. "Marks of a Good Soldier." *The Pentecostal Evangel*, 25 September 1943, 1, 13.

―――. "Problems of the Serviceman." *The Pentecostal Evangel*, 24 June 1944, 5, 8.

Smith, Gipsy. "Behind the Firing Line." *The Weekly Evangel*, 14 July 1917, 6-7.

Smith, Jim. "Making Disciples In the Armed Forces." *The Pentecostal Evangel*, 27 February 1983, 18.

"Soldiers in the Middle East Hunger for God's Word." *The Pentecostal Evangel*, 27 January 1991, 14.

"Soldiers on Canal Zone." *The Weekly Evangel*, 24 November 1917, 13.

"Somewhere in New Guinea." *The Pentecostal Evangel*, 1 July 1944, 12.

"Special Prayer for the Soldiers." *The Weekly Evangel*, 2 June 1917, 9.

Speer, Gary. "Revival in the Persian Gulf." *The Pentecostal Evangel*, 17 March 1991, 14.

Spence, John Rutherford. "Victories in Spite of the War." *The Pentecostal Evangel*, 4 August 1923, 12.

―――. "The War in South China." *The Pentecostal Evangel*, 22 July 1922, 13.

"Spiritual Conflict." *The Weekly Evangel*, 4 November 1916, 3.

"Spiritual Conflict and the Armor Needed." *The Pentecostal Evangel*, 10 November 1923, 4.

"Spiritual Victories for Our Fighting Men." *The Pentecostal Evangel*, 2 September 1944, 9.

"Spiritual Warfare." *The Pentecostal Evangel*, 30 June 1934, 8.

"Spiritual Warfare." *The Pentecostal Evangel*, 1 September 1945, 2.

Spratt, L.P. "How Dependable is your Conscience?" *Weekly Evangel*, 4 July 1965, 5.

"Spreading Gospel Light in Greenland's Long Night." *The Pentecostal Evangel*, 5 February 1961, 12.

"Stanley N. Millard Named to Chaplaincy." *The Pentecostal Evangel*, 26 December 1966, 29.

Steelberg, Wesley R. "Ministering in Veterans Hospitals." *The Pentecostal Evangel*, 21 June 1947, 11.

———. "The Stars and Stripes of Calvary." *The Pentecostal Evangel*, 4 July 1942, 1, 4-5.

Steil, Harry J. "Christian Warfare." *The Pentecostal Evangel*, 12 November 1938, 8.

Stephany, Marie. "In the War Zone." *The Pentecostal Evangel*, 21 January 1928, 7.

Stewart, Alice F. "On the War Path in Shansi." *The Pentecostal Evangel*, 20 October 1934, 7.

———. "News From China War Zone." *The Pentecostal Evangel*, 9 July 1938, 9.

Stewart, George P. "An Oasis in the Desert." *The Pentecostal Evangel*, 8 September 1945, 10.

St. Lawrence Annual Conference, Watertown, N.Y, 1847. Quoted in Donald W. and Lucille Sider Dayton. *An Historical Survey of Attitudes Toward War and Peace Within the American Holiness Movement*, 7. Winona Lake, Ind.: 1973.

"Stormy Days in China." *The Pentecostal Evangel*, 27 February 1926, 10.

Sturgeon, Inez. "In Formosa Today the Word is 'War!'" *The Pentecostal Evangel*, 9 November 1958, 13.

Sumrall, Lester F. "V Day." *The Pentecostal Evangel*, 23 September 1944, 2-3.

———. "The War is Not Over . . . Tho' the Boys are Coming Home." *The Pentecostal Evangel*, 27 October 1945, 1, 5.

———. "Ambassadors of Goodwill." *The Pentecostal Evangel*, 10 August 1946, 8.

Sutherlin, Dave. "Air Force Sergeant Excels in Dual Role." *The Pentecostal Evangel*, 29 June 1980, 10.

Swarztrauber, Vera I. "Pentecost in Cairo and Jerusalem." *The Pentecostal Evangel*, 3 March 1945, 1, 4.

"Take WARning." *The Christian Evangel,* 5 September 1914, 1.

Tangen, Richard. "Oasis in a Desert of Ungodliness." *The Pentecostal Evangel,* 26 August 1973, 11.

Taylor, Earl A. "'Pop, I've Got a Problem!'" *The Pentecostal Evangel,* 25 June 1972, 12.

"Testaments for the Soldiers." *The Weekly Evangel,* 29 September 1917, 3.

"'Thanks for Thinking About Us.'" *The Pentecostal Evangel,* 28 June 1970, 32.

"'That Thou Mightest War A Good Warfare.'" *The Pentecostal Evangel,* 27 November 1926, 1.

"There's a Job to be Done: Serving the Men in the Service." *The Pentecostal Evangel,* 19 February 1944, 12.

"This Ministry Must Continue." *The Pentecostal Evangel,* 13 July 1946, 1, 6-7.

Thompson, Fred A. "What Kind of Chaplain Are You, Sir?" *The Pentecostal Evangel,* 26 June 1994, 20.

"'Till the Boys Come Home.'" *The Pentecostal Evangel,* 8 December 1945, 12.

Tillis, Michael R. "Out Here in the Desert." *The Pentecostal Evangel,* 7 July 1991, 6.

Tilus, Tamara. "Military Deployment: the Prospect of Battle." *The Pentecostal Evangel,* 28 October 1990, 20.

"Time is Running Out." *The Pentecostal Evangel,* 14 January 1950, 8.

"Tithes and Free Will Offerings." *The Weekly Evangel,* 3 July 1915, 3.

"Topics of the Times." *The Pentecostal Evangel,* 6 August 1932, 6-7.

"Triumphing Over the Principalities and Powers of Darkness." *The Pentecostal Evangel,* 27 January 1917, 6.

Turnbull, Josephine E. "Strength for the Battle." *The Pentecostal Evangel,* 17 April 1943, 4-5.

Turner, Charles. "You Can Live for God in the Service." *At Ease* 6 (Winter 1966): 4.

Twamley, Jim. "When War Hits Home." *The Pentecostal Evangel,* 22 March 1992, 18.

"Twelve Million Men at Stake." *The Pentecostal Evangel,* 13 May 1944, 12.

"Twenty-five Assemblies Chaplains Now Serving." *The Pentecostal Evangel,* 7 July 1963, 10.

"Two from Florida Assembly Head for Military Academy." *The Pentecostal Evangel*, 25 October 1987, 27.

"Two Million Dollars an Hour." *The Weekly Evangel*, 31 July 1915, 3.

"Two Soldiers Talk." *The Pentecostal Evangel*, 5 August 1944, 1.

"Universal Military Training." *The Pentecostal Evangel*, 6 May 1951, 7.

"Universal Warfare." *The Pentecostal Evangel*, 19 April 1941, 4.

"Up Front with Reveille." *The Pentecostal Evangel*, 21 July 1945, 9.

Urshan, Andrew D. "The Sad Effects of the War on the Persian Pentecostal Saints." *The Weekly Evangel*, 17 November 1917, 5.

"U.S. Is 'Gamblingest' Nation." *The Pentecostal Evangel*, 7 February 1960, 11.

Vaudrey, Stephen J. "Retreat!" *The Pentecostal Evangel*, 16 December 1984, 16.

———. "Serving Those Who Serve." *The Pentecostal Evangel*, 28 June 1987, 22.

"Victorious in Captivity." *The Pentecostal Evangel*, 30 March 1946, 12.

"Victory." *The Pentecostal Evangel*, 24 June 1944, 1.

"Victory Service Center." *The Pentecostal Evangel*, 29 July 1944, 9.

"Voice of Conscience." *The Weekly Evangel*, 19 April 1959, 2.

Walfron, L. O. "Work Among the Soldiers." *The Pentecostal Evangel*, 1 November 1941, 16.

Wallis, William G. "London, Eng." *The Christian Evangel*, 31 October 1914, 4.

"War and Christianity." *The Pentecostal Evangel*, 23 September 1939, 10.

"War and Missions." *The Pentecostal Evangel*, 28 September 1940, 9.

"War Babies Counted in Japan." *The Pentecostal Evangel*, 18 January 1953, 2.

"War-Clouds." *The Pentecostal Evangel*, 31 July 1926, 6-9.

"War Horrors in China." *The Pentecostal Evangel*, 18 December 1937, 6-7.

"War is the Great Tragedy." *The Pentecostal Evangel*, 8 April 1951, 7.

"War Mercies." *The Pentecostal Evangel*, 12 January 1946, 10.

"War Paralyzed Us, Missionaries Write." *The Christian Evangel*, 10 October 1914, 4.

"War or Peace?" *The Pentecostal Evangel*, 6 January 1957, 2.

"The War-Stunned World." *The Pentecostal Evangel*, 16 August 1924, 4.

"War Takes Huge Share of Tax Money." *The Pentecostal Evangel*, 24 January 1960, 8.

"The War to End in September?" *The Weekly Evangel*, 7 July 1917, 11.

"War Toys, Children's TV Programs. . . ." *The Pentecostal Evangel*, 10 January 1988, 24.

"War! War!! War!!!" *The Christian Evangel*, 15 August 1914, 1.

"Wars and the Missionaries." *The Christian Evangel*, 12 September 1914, 1.

"Wars and Rumors of Wars." *The Pentecostal Evangel*, 17 February 1952, 2.

"War's Dread Realities." *The Weekly Evangel*, 16 December 1916, 2.

Ward, A. G. "Overcomer's Equipment." *The Pentecostal Evangel*, 21 July 1917, 2.

————. "A Postwar Revival." *The Pentecostal Evangel*, 10 May 1941, 3.

Ward, C. M. "The Cold War." *The Pentecostal Evangel*, 14 June 1959, 3, 28-31.

————. "What Can Stop War?" *The Pentecostal Evangel*, 16 July 1972, 12.

————. "GIs Rescue Missionaries in the Philippines During World War II." *The Pentecostal Evangel*, 26 March 1995, 29.

————. "Wartime Ministry in the 1940's." *The Pentecostal Evangel*, 9 April 1995, 29.

————. "Missions Meeting Focuses on Postwar Expansion (1943)." *The Pentecostal Evangel*, 25 June 1995, 27.

"Wartime Wages of the C.O.'s." *The Pentecostal Evangel*, 14 January 1950, 8.

Watt, Gordon. "Prayer – The Fighting Force." *The Pentecostal Evangel*, 6 January 1940, 2, 6.

Watts, John. "War and Missions." *The Pentecostal Evangel*, 13 January 1945, 6.

Way, Robert R. "Our Mission to the Military." *The Pentecostal Evangel*, 26 September 1965, 7.

————. "Christmas in Vietnam." *The Pentecostal Evangel*, 19 December 1965, 5-6.

————. "Prophets in Fatigues." *The Pentecostal Evangel*, 30 October 1966, 23.

————. "Serving God and Country Involves the Other War." *The Pentecostal Evangel*, 25 June 1967, 8.

————. "The Other War." *The Pentecostal Evangel*, 25 June 1967, 8-9.

————. "A Soldier's Concern Prompted . . . The Colonel's New Order." *The Pentecostal Evangel*, 28 June 1987, 12.

"Wayne Rowland Now Serving in Chief Chaplains Office." *The Pentecostal Evangel*, 30 April 1967, 30.

"Weapons of our Warfare." *The Pentecostal Evangel*, 5 September 1925, 1.

Webb, Bert, memorandum to Bob Cunningham, 31 May 1961. J. R. Flower Pentecostal Heritage Center, Springfield, Missouri.

———, memorandum to Bob Cunningham, 17 July 1961. J. R. Flower Pentecostal Heritage Center, Springfield, Missouri.

———. "Ministering to Servicemen in Europe." *The Pentecostal Evangel*, 5 July 1964, 6.

———. "Men with a Mission." *The Pentecostal Evangel*, 27 June 1965, 6.

The Weekly Evangel, 19 June 1915, 1.

Welch, J. W. "Stand in the Ways and See." *The Weekly Evangel*, 10 June 1916, 3.

———. "An Explanation." *The Weekly Evangel*, 19 May 1917, 8.

———. "Power of Apostolic Days for You in the Twentieth Century." *The Pentecostal Evangel*, 1 November 1919, 2.

Wesley, John. "The Moral State of Mankind." In *The Doctrine of Original Sin*. Quoted in James H. Potts, *Living Quotes of John Wesley*, 78. New York: Hunt and Eaton, 1891.

"What Future Wars Will Be Like." *The Pentecostal Evangel*, 18 June 1927, 3.

"What God Says to His Soldiers." *The Christian Evangel*, 21 September 1918, 2.

"What is War?" *The Weekly Evangel*, 21 April 1917, 2.

"When a Coconut Log Became an Altar." *The Pentecostal Evangel*, 14 October 1944, 9.

"When the Enemy Comes in Like a Flood." *The Pentecostal Evangel*, 13 September 1924, 1.

"When Shall We Rise to Meet the Lord?" *The Weekly Evangel*, 10 April 1917, 2-3.

Whitfield, George. "When War Shall Cease." *The Weekly Evangel*, 26 January 1918, 3.

"Who's Fighting in Viet Nam: A Gallery of American Combatants." *Time*, 23 April 1965, 22-26.

"Will Mankind Be Annihilated?" *The Pentecostal Evangel*, 28 January 1950, 10.

"Will the United States be Involved in the World War?" *The Weekly Evangel*, 25 March 1916, 5, 8.

Williams, Ernest S. "Christian Conflict." *The Pentecostal Evangel*, 13 December 1924, 2.

———. "Our Duty as Christian Citizens." *Pentecostal Evangel*, 28 November 1936, 1, 3.

———. ". . . In Case of War . . ." *The Pentecostal Evangel*, 19 March 1938, 4.

———. "The Conscientious Objector." *Pentecostal Evangel*, 14 June 1940, 4-5.

———. "Questions and Answers." *Pentecostal Evangel*, 27 July 1940, 5.

———. "Questions and Answers." *Pentecostal Evangel*, 22 November 1941, 16.

———. "Servicemen's Sunday." *The Pentecostal Evangel*, 13 January 1945, 2.

———. "The Whole World." *The Pentecostal Evangel*, 30 March 1946, 3.

———. "Now – the Harvest." *The Pentecostal Evangel*, 27 April 1946, 1, 12.

———. "The Hour Demands It!" *The Pentecostal Evangel*, 31 August 1946, 8.

———. "Haunted by conscience." *Pentecostal Evangel*, 11 October 1947, 6.

———. "Christ Invades the Military." *The Pentecostal Evangel*, 11 September 1948, 6.

———. "Your Questions." *The Pentecostal Evangel*, 22 June 1958, 23.

———. "Your Questions." *The Pentecostal Evangel*, 5 July 1959, 7.

———. "Your Questions." *The Pentecostal Evangel*, 7 February 1960, 11.

———. "Your Questions." *The Pentecostal Evangel*, 20 August 1961, 21.

———. "Your Questions." *The Pentecostal Evangel*, 25 March 1962, 15.

———. "Your Questions." *The Pentecostal Evangel*, 13 February 1966, 11.

———. "Your Questions." *The Pentecostal Evangel*, 28 May 1967, 15.

Wilson, R. A., Jr. "Nuclear Explosions and You." *The Pentecostal Evangel*, 7 January 1962, 32.

"Winning Men in the Desert Training Area." *The Pentecostal Evangel*, 29 April 1944, 7.

"Winning the War in the Spiritual Realm." *The Pentecostal Evangel*, 23 January 1943, 4.

Wohlert, E. Harold. "Heaven in a Foxhole." *The Pentecostal Evangel*, 13 January 1945, 1, 7.

Wolff, Roger D. "Serving Our Nation's Veterans." *The Pentecostal Evangel*, 8 November 1987, 17.

"Woman Chaplain Finds Army Work Rewarding." *The Pentecostal Evangel*, 23 January 1977, 23.

Wood, Jon and Nona. "Loving the Whosoevers." *The Pentecostal Evangel*, 31 July 1977, 15.

Woodall, Roy D. "Pentecost Afloat." *The Pentecostal Evangel*, 23 November 1940, 11.

Woodrum, Lon. "The Long War." *The Pentecostal Evangel*, 11 July 1965, 6-7.

———. "Long War." *The Pentecostal Evangel*, 29 July 1984, 12.

"Work Among the Services." *The Pentecostal Evangel*, 7 February 1942, 1.

"Work Among the Soldiers." *The Pentecostal Evangel*, 1 November 1941, 16.

"Working Among the Soldiers." *The Weekly Evangel*, 9 September 1916, 11.

"World Relief Assists Croatian Churches in War Relief Effort." *The Pentecostal Evangel*, 29 March 1992, 25.

"World Relief Calls War Relief Sunday." *The Pentecostal Evangel*, 21 April 1991, 25.

Ziese, Anna. "Peace in War Time." *The Pentecostal Evangel*, 28 January 1928, 10.

Zimmerman, Thomas F. "The Christian and His Country." *The Pentecostal Evangel*, 29 June 1975, 6.

Secondary Sources

Books

Anderson, Allan. *An Introduction to Pentecostalism*. Cambridge: Cambridge University Press, 2004.

Anderson, Robert Mapes. *Vision of the Disinherited: The Making of American Pentecostalism*. New York: Oxford University Press, 1979.

———. *Vision of the Disinherited: The Making of American Pentecostalism*. Peabody, Mass.: Hendrickson, 1992.

Bainton, Roland H. *Christianity*. Boston, Mass.: Houghton Mifflin Company, 1987.

Bangs, Nathan. *The Life of the Rev. Freeborn Garrettson*. New York: Mason & Lane, 1938.

Barbour, Hugh and J. William Frost. *The Quakers in Puritan England*. London, 1964.

———. *The Quakers*. Denominations in America. Westport, CN: Greenwood Press, 1988.

Beaman, Jay. *Pentecostal Pacifism: The Origin, Development, and Rejection of Pacific Belief Among the Pentecostals.* Forward by John Howard Yoder. Hillsboro, Kan.: Center for Mennonite Brethren Studies, 1989.

Bloch-Hoell, Nils. *The Pentecostal Movement: Its Origin, Development, and Distinctive Character.* New York: Humanities Press, 1964.

Blumhofer, Edith L. *The Assemblies of God: A Chapter in the Story of American Pentecostalism.* Vols. I and II. Springfield, Mo.: Gospel Publishing House, 1989.

Booker, Christopher B. *African-Americans and the Presidency.* New York: Franklin Watts, 2000.

Bowman, Carl F. *Brethren Society: The Cultural Transformation of a "Peculiar People."* Baltimore: The Johns Hopkins University Press, 1995.

Brensinger, Terry L. and E. Morris Sider. *Within the Perfection of Christ: Essays on Peace and the Nature of the Church.* Nappannee: Ind.: Brethren in Christ Historical Society, 1990.

Brock, Peter. *Pacifism in the United States from the Colonial Era to the First World War.* Princeton: Princeton University Press, 1968.

———. *The Quaker Peace Testimony, 1660-1914.* York, England: Sessions Book Trust, 1990.

Brock, Peter and Nigel Young. *Pacifism in the Twentieth Century.* Toronto, ON: University of Toronto Press Incorporated, 1999.

Brumback, Carl. *Suddenly. . . from Heaven: A History of the Assemblies of God.* Springfield, Mo.: Gospel Publishing House, 1961.

Burgess, Stanley M. and Gary B. McGee. *Dictionary of Pentecostal and Charismatic Movements.* Grand Rapids, Mich.: Zondervan, 1988.

Butler, Anthea. *Women in the Church of God in Christ: Making a Sanctified World.* Chapel Hill: North Carolina University Press, 2007.

Cameron, Richard. *Methodism and Society in Historical Perspective.* New York: Abingdon, 1961.

Campbell, Joseph E. *The Pentecostal Holiness Church: The First Fifty Years . . . Plus!* Raleigh, N.C.: World Outlook Publications, 1951.

Carter, John. *Donald Gee: Pentecostal Statesman.* Nottingham, England: Assemblies of God Publishing House, 1971.

———. *Howard Carter: Man of the Spirit.* Nottingham, England: Assemblies of God Publishing House, n.d.

Cleary, Edward L. and Hannah W. Stewart-Gambino, editors. *Power, Politics, and Pentecostals in Latin America*. Boulder, Colo.: Westview Press, 1998.

Clemmons, Ithiel C. *Bishop C. H. Mason and the Roots of the Church of God in Christ*. Lanham, Md.: Pneuma Life, 1996.

Curti, Merle Eugene. *Peace or War: The American Struggle*. The Garland Library of War and Peace. New Introduction by Merle Eugene Curti. New York: Garland Publishing, Inc., 1972.

Dayton, Donald W. *Theological Roots of Pentecostalism*. Peabody, Mass.: Hendrickson, 1987.

DuPree, Sherry Sherrod. *African-American Holiness Pentecostal Movement: An Annotated Bibliography*. New York: Garland Publishing, 1996.

Dupree, Sherry Sherrod, ed. *Biographical Dictionary of African-American, Holiness-Pentecostals, 1880-1990*. Washington, D.C.: Middle Atlantic Regional Press, 1989.

Faulkner, John Alfred. *Wesley as Sociologist, Theologian, Churchman*. New York: The Methodist Book Concern, 1918.

Faupel, D. William. *The Everlasting Gospel: The Significance of Eschatology in the Development of Pentecostal Thought*. Journal of Pentecostal Theology Supplement Series. Sheffield, England: Sheffield Academic Press, 1996.

Frodsham, Stanley. *With Signs Following: The Story of the Pentecostal Revival in the Twentieth Century*. Springfield, Mo.: Gospel Publishing House, 1946.

Goff, James R., Jr. *Fields White Unto Harvest: Charles F. Parham and the Missionary Origins of Pentecostalism*. Fayetteville, Ark.: The University of Arkansas Press, 1988.

Goff, James R., Jr. and Grant Wacker, editors. *Portraits of a Generation: Early Pentecostal Leaders*. Fayetteville: University of Arkansas Press, 2002.

Guth, James L., John C. Green, Corwin E. Smidt, Lyman A. Kellstedt, Margaret M. Poloma, *The Bully Pulpit: The Politics of Protestant Clergy*. Lawrence, Kan.: University Press of Kansas, 1997.

Harper, Michael. *As at the Beginning*. London: Hodder and Stoughton, 1956.

Hartzler, J. S. *Mennonites in the World War: or Nonresistance Under Test*. Scottdale, Pa.: Mennonite Publishing House, 1921.

Hauerwas, Stanley. *The Peaceable Kingdom*. Notre Dame, Ind.: University of Notre Dame Press, 1983.

————. "The Church as God's New Language." In *Christian Existence Today*. Durham, N.C.: Labyrinth, 1988.

Hershberger, Guy F. *War, Peace, and Nonresistance*. Scottdale, Pa.: Herald Press, 1969.

Hirst, Margaret E. *The Quakers in Peace and War: An Account of Their Principles and Practice*. London: The Swarthmore Press, 1923. Reprint, Jeremy S. Ozer, 1972.

Hocken, Peter. *The Glory and the Shame: Reflections on the 20th Century Outpouring of the Holy Spirit*. Guildford, Surrey, England: Eagle, 1994.

Hollenweger, Walter, J. *The Pentecostals: The Charismatic Movement in the Churches*. Minneapolis: Augsburg, 1972.

————. *Pentecostalism: Origins and Developments Worldwide*. Peabody, Mass.: Hendrickson Publishers, Inc., 1997.

Homan, Gerlof. *American Mennonites and the Great War*. Scottdale, Pa.: Herald Press, 1994.

Hunter, Harold D. and Peter D. Hocken, eds. *All Together in One Place: Theological Papers from the Brighton Conference on World Evangelization*. Melksham, Wiltshire, England: The Cromwell Press, 1993.

Jacobsen, Douglas. *Thinking in the Spirit: Theologies of the Early Pentecostal Movement*. Bloomington, Ind.: Indiana University Press, 2003.

James, Sydney V. *A People Among Peoples: Quaker Benevolence in Eighteenth-Century America*. Cambridge, Mass.: Harvard University Press, 1963.

Jones, Charles Edward. *Perfectionist Persuasion: The Holiness Movement and American Methodism, 1867-1936*. Metuchen, N.J.: The Scarecrow Press, 1974.

————. *Black Holiness: A Guide to the Study of Black Participation in Wesleyan Perfectionist and Glossolalic Pentecostal Movements*. The American Theological Library Association Bibliography Series. Metuchen, N.J.: The American Theological Library Association and The Scarecrow Press, 1987.

Jones, Rufus M. *Spiritual Reformers in the 16th and 17th Centuries*. London: 1914.

Kendrick, Klaude. *The Promise Fulfilled: A History of the Modern Pentecostal Movement*. Springfield, Mo.: Gospel Publishing House, 1961.

Lee, Jesse. *A Short History of the Methodists in the United States of America*. Baltimore, Md.: Magill and Clime, 1810.

Lindbeck, George. *The Nature of Doctrine.* Philadelphia: Westminster Press, 1984.

Loveland, Anne C. *American Evangelicals and the U.S. Military, 1942-1993.* Baton Rouge, La.: Louisianna State University Press, 1996.

Lynd, Staughton, ed. *Nonviolence in America: A Documentary History.* The American Heritage Series. Indianapolis: Bobbs-Merrill Company, Inc., 1966.

MacRobert, Iain. *Black Pentecostalism: Its Origins, Functions and Theology with Special Reference to a Midland Borough.* Edinburgh: St. Andrew's Press, 1993.

———. *The Black Roots and White Racism of Early Pentecostalism in the USA.* London: Macmillan, 1988.

The Man, Charles Harrison Mason (1866-1961). Memphis, Tenn.: Church of God in Christ, 1979.

Marchand, C. Roland. *The American Peace Movement and Social Reform 1898-1918.* Princeton, N.J.: Princeton University Press, 1973.

Marquardt, Manfred. *John Wesley's Social Ethics: Praxis and Principles.* Trans. John E. Steely and W. Stephen Gunter. Nashville, Tenn.: Abingdon Press, 1992.

McClendon, James, Jr. *Systematic Theology.* Vol. 2, *Doctrine.* Nashville, Tenn.: Abingdon Press, 1994.

McGee, Gary B. *This Gospel Shall be Preached.* Vol. 1, *A History and Theology of Assemblies of God Foreign Missions to 1959.* Springfield, Mo.: Gospel Publishing House, 1986.

———. *This Gospel Shall be Preached.* Vol. 2, *A History and Theology of Assemblies of God Foreign Missions since 1959.* Springfield, Mo.: Gospel Publishing House, 1989.

Mead, Frank S. *Handbook of Denominations in the United States,* 5th ed. Nashville: Abingdon Press, 1970.

Menzies, William W. *Anointed To Serve: The Story of the Assemblies of God.* Springfield, Mo.: Gospel Publishing House, 1971.

———. and Stanley Horton. *Bible Doctrines.* Springfield, Mo.: Gospel Publishing House, 1993.

Miller, Donald E. and Tetsunao Yamamori. *Global Pentecostalism: The New Face of Christian Social Engagement.* Berkeley, Los Angeles, London: University of California Press, 2007.

Moody, William. *The Life of Dwight L. Moody.* New York: Revell, 1900.

Moon, Jesse K. *War and the Christian.* Springfield, Mo.: by the author, 1988.

National Service Board For Religious Objectors. *Statements of Religious Bodies on the Conscientious Objector,* rev. Washington, D.C.: National Service Board for Religious Objectors, 1953.

Nichol, John Thomas. *Pentecostalism.* New York: Harper & Row Publishers, 1966.

Niebhur, H. Richard. *The Social Source of Denominationalism.* New York: Henry Holt, 1929.

Parham, Sarah T. *The Life of Charles F. Parham.* Joplin, Mo.: Tri-State Printing Co., 1930.

Paris, Arthur E. *Black Pentecostalism: Southern Religion in an Urban World.* Amherst, Mass.: The University of Massachusetts Press, 1982.

Perry, Shawn. *Words of Conscience: Religious Statements on Conscientious Objection.* Washington, D.C.: National Inter-religious Service Board for Conscientious Objectors, 1980.

Peterson, H. C. and Gilbert C. Fite. *Opponents of War 1917-1918.* Madison, Wis.: University of Wisconsin Press, 1957.

Playne, Caroline E. *Society at War 1914-1916.* Boston, Mass.: Houghton Mifflin Company, 1931.

Poloma, Margaret M. *The Assemblies of God at the Crossroads: Charisma and Institutional Dilemmas.* Knoxville, Tenn.: The University of Tennessee Press, 1989.

Raboteau, Albert J. *Slave Religion: The "Invisible Institution" in the Antebellum South.* New York: Oxford University Press, 1978.

Reay, Barry. *The Quakers and the English Revolution.* London, 1985.

Sandeen, Ernest R. *The Roots of Fundamentalism.* Chicago: University of Chicago Press, 1970.

Schlissel, Lillian, ed. *Conscience in America: A Documentary of Conscientious Objection in America, 1757-1967.* New York: E. P. Dutton Co. Inc., 1968.

Selective Service System. *Conscientious Objection.* Special Monograph no. 11, Vol. 1. Washington, D.C.: Government Printing Office, 1950.

Sernett, Milton C. *Black Religion and American Evangelicalism: White Protestants, Plantation Missions, and the Flowering of Negro Christianity, 1787-1865.* The American Theological Library Association Monograph Series. Metuchen, N.J.: The Scarecrow Press, 1975.

Sernett, Milton C., ed. *Afro-American Religious History: A Documentary Witness.* Durham, N.C.: Duke University Press, 1985.

Shannon, David T. and Gayraud S. Wilmore. *Black Witness to the Apostolic Faith*. Grand Rapids: Eerdmans, 1985.

Schwartz, Gary. *Sect Ideologies and Social Status*. Chicago: University of Chicago Press, 1970.

Simmons, Dale H. *E.W. Kenyon and the Postbellum Pursuit of Peace, Power, and Plenty*. Studies in Evangelicalism. Lanham, Md.: The Scarecrow Press, 1997.

Smith, Warren Thomas. *John Wesley and Slavery*. Nashville, Tenn.: Abingdon, 1986.

Sweet, William Warren. *Methodism in American History*. New York: Abingdon-Cokesbury Press, 1933

Synan, Vinson. *The Holiness-Pentecostal Movement in the United States*. Grand Rapids, Mich.: William B. Eerdmans Publishing Company, 1971.

————. *The Old-Time Power*. Franklin Springs, Ga.: Advocate Press, 1973.

Synan, Vinson., ed. *Aspects of Pentecostal-Charismatic Origins*. Plainfield, N.J.: Logos International, 1975.

Thomas, Norman. *Is Conscience a Crime?* New ed., Foreword by Charles Chatfield. New York: Garland Publishing, Inc., 1972.

Tuttle, Robert G. *John Wesley: His Life and Theology*. Grand Rapids, Mich.: Zondervan, 1978.

Wacker, Grant. *Heaven Below*. Cambridge, Mass.: Harvard University Press, 2001.

Washington, Joseph R., Jr. *Black Sects and Cults*. Garden City, N.Y.: Doubleday, 1972.

Wilmore, Gayraud S. *Black Religion and Black Radicalism: An Interpretation of the Religious History of African Americans*, 3rd. ed. Maryknoll, N.Y.: Orbis Books, 1998.

Woodson, Carter G. *The History of the Negro Church*. 2nd ed. Washington, D.C.: The Associated Publishers, 1921.

Wynkoop, Mildred Bangs. *A Theology of Love: The Dynamic of Wesleyanism*. Kansas City, Mo.: Beacon Hill Press of Kansas City, 1972.

X, Malcolm. *Malcolm X Speaks*. Compiled by Betty Shabazz. New York: Merit Publishers, 1965.

Yoder, John Howard. *Nevertheless: Varieties and Shortcomings of Religious Pacifism*. Scottdale, Pa.: Herald Press, 1971.

————. *Christian Attitudes To War, Peace, and Revolution: A Companion to Bainton*. Elkhart, Ind.: Goshen Biblical Seminary, 1983.

———. Foreward to *Pentecostal Pacifism*, by Jay Beaman. Hillsboro, Kan.: Center for Mennonite Brethren Studies, 1989.

———. *When War is Unjust*. Maryknoll, N.Y.: Orbis, 1996.

Yong, Amos. *The Spirit Poured Out on All Flesh: Pentecostalism and the Possibilities of Global Theology*. Grand Rapids, Mich.: Baker Academic, 2005.

Articles

Alexander, Paul. "Spirit-Empowered Peacemaking: Toward a Pentecostal Charismatic Peace Fellowship." *Journal of the European Pentecostal Theological Association* 22 (2002): 78-102.

Althouse, Peter. "Canadian Pentecostal Pacifism." *Eastern Journal of Practical Theology* 4 (Fall 1990): 32-43.

Casey, Michael W. "From Pacifism to Patriotism: The Emergence of Civil Religion in the Churches of Christ during World War I." *Mennonite Quarterly Review* 66 (1992): 376-390.

———. "The Closing of Cordell Christian College: A Microcosm of American Intolerance during World War I." *Chronicles of Oklahoma* 76 (Spring 1998): 20-37.

Casey, Michael W. and Michael Jordan. "Free Speech in Time of War: Government Surveillance of Churches of Christ in the First World War." *Free Speech Yearbook* 34 (1996): 102-111.

Cerillo, Augustus. "Moving Up: Some Consequences of the New A/G Social Status." *Agora 1* (Winter 1978): 8-11.

Clemmons, Ithiel. "Insidious Racism in American Religious Statistics." *The Whole Truth*, February 1983, 3.

"Compulsory Military Service: An English Conscientious Movement." *Mennonite Quarterly Review* LIII (July 1979): 219-234.

Cronin, H. S., ed. "The Twelve Conclusions of the Lollards." *The English Historical Review* 22:2 (April 1907) 302-303. Quoted in Peter Brock, *The Quaker Peace Testimony, 1660-1914*, 1. York, England: Sessions Book Trust, 1990.

Dayton, Donald W. "From Christian Perfection to the 'Baptism in the Holy Ghost.'" In *Asptect of Pentecostal-Charismatic Origins*, ed. Vinson Synan, 39-54. Plainfield, N.J.: Logos, 1975.

———. "Theological Roots of Pentecostalism." *Journal of the Society for Pentecostal Studies* 2 (Spring 1980): 3-21.

Dearman, Marion. "Christ and Conformity: A Study of Pentecostal Values." *Journal for the Scientific Study of Religion* (1974): 437-453.

Dempster, Murray W. "Peacetime Draft Registration and Pentecostal Moral Conscience." *Agora* 3 (Spring 1980): 2-3.

————. "Jay Beaman, *Pentecostal Pacifism: The Origins, Development and Rejection of Pacific Belief among the Pentecostals* (Hillsboro, Kansas: Center for Mennonite Brethren Studies, 1989), 142 pp. $10.00 paper. Reviewed by Murray W. Dempster," *Pneuma* 11, no. 1 (Fall 1989): 60-64.

————. "Reassessing the Moral Rhetoric of Early American Pentecostal Pacifism." *Crux* 26 (March 1990): 23-36.

————. "'Crossing Borders': Arguments Used by Early American Pentecostals in Support of the Global Character of Pacifism." *European Pentecostal Theological Association Bulletin* 10:2 (1991): 63-80.

————. "Pacifism in Pentecostalism: The Case of the Assemblies of God," in *Proclaim Peace: Voices of Christian Pacifism from Unexpected Sources,* ed. Theron F. Schlabach and Richard T. Hughes (Champaign, Ill.: University of Illinois Press, 1997), 31-57.

George, Timothy. "Between Pacifism and Coercion: The English Baptist Doctrine of Religious Toleration." *The Mennonite Quarterly Review* 58:1 (January 1984): 38.

Gerloff, Roswith I. H. "The Holy Spirit and the African Diaspora. Spiritual, Cultural and Social Roots of Black Pentecostal Churches." Society for Pentecostal Studies Conference, Mattersey, England, July 1995.

Hollenweger, Walter, J. "Black Pentecostal Concept." *Concept* 30 (June 1970).

Johnson, Donald O. "Wilson, Burleson, and Censorship in the First World War." 28:1 (1962): 46-58.

Jones, Charles Edward. "Holiness Movement." In *Dictionary of Pentecostal and Charismatic Movements*, ed. Stanley M. Burgess and Gary B. McGee, 406-409. Grand Rapids, Mich.: Zondervan, 1988.

Liias, Jurgen W. "Charismatic Power or Military Power?" *Christian Century* 100 (November 1983): 1110-1113.

Lovell, John. "The Social Implications of the Negro Spirituals." *Journal of Negro Education*, 8 October 1939, 634-643.

Lovett, Leonard. "Black Origins of the Pentecostal Movement." *Aspects of Pentecostal-Charismatic Origins*, ed. Vinson Synan, 123-142. Plainfield, N.J.: Logos International, 1975.

————. "Black Holiness Pentecostalism." In *Dictionary of Pentecostal and Charismatic Movements*, ed. Stanley M. Burgess and Gary B. McGee, 76-84. Grand Rapids, Mich.: Zondervan, 1988.

————. "Black Theology." In *Dictionary of Pentecostal and Charismatic Movements*, ed. Stanley M. Burgess and Gary B. McGee, 84-86. Grand Rapids, Mich.: Zondervan, 1988.

Mason, Elsie W. "Bishop C. H. Mason, Church of God in Christ." In *Afro-American Religious History: A Documentary Witness*, ed. Milton C. Sernett, 286. Durham, N.C.: Duke University Press, 1985.

McGee, Gary B. "The Debate over Missionary Tongues Among Radical Evangelicals, 1881-1897." In *Toward Healing Our Divisions: Reflecting on Pentecostal Diversity and Common Witness, The 28th Annual Meeting of the Society for Pentecostal Studies Held in Springfield, Missouri 11-13 March 1999*. Society for Pentecostal Studies, 1999.

Pankratz, Herbert L. "The Suppression of Alleged Disloyalty in Kansas During WWI." *Kansas Historical Quarterly* 42:3 (1976): 277-307.

Robins, Roger. "A Chronology of Peace: Attitudes Toward War and Peace in the Assemblies of God: 1914-1918." *Pneuma* 6 (Spring 1984): 3-25.

————. "Our Forgotten Heritage: A Look at Early Pentecostal Pacifism." *Assemblies of God Heritage* 6 (Winter 1986-1987): 3-5.

Shuman, Joel. "Pentecost and the End of Patriotism: A Call for the Restoration of Pacifism Among Pentecostal Christians." *Journal of Pentecostal Theology* 9 (1996): 70-96.

Warner, Wayne E. "Church of God in Christ (White)." In *Dictionary of Pentecostal and Charismatic Movements*, ed. Stanley M. Burgess and Gary B. McGee, 203.

Grand Rapids, Mich.: Zondervan, 1988.

————. "Eudorus N. Bell." In *Dictionary of Pentecostal and Charismatic Movements*, ed. Stanley M. Burgess and Gary B. McGee, 53-54. Grand Rapids, Mich.: Zondervan, 1988.

Wilson, Dwight J. "Pacifism." In *Dictionary of Pentecostal and Charismatic Movements*, eds. Stanley M. Burgess and Gary B. McGee. Grand Rapids, Mich.: Zondervan, 1988.

Ytterock, Dave. "Probing Our Moral Identity." *Agora* 1 (Fall 1977): 6-9.

Dissertations, Theses, Unpublished Works, and Interviews

Assen, David L. "Forty Years of New Testament Teaching and Preaching in the General Council of the Assemblies of God, 1914-1954." Ph.D. diss., Southwestern Baptist Theological Seminary, 1956.

Beals, Michael J. "Toward a Constructive Pentecostal Perspective of the Just War Tradition: New Direction for the Moral Migration of the Assemblies of God." Ph.D. dissertation, Fuller Theological Seminary, 2002.

Beaman, Jay. "Pentecostal Pacifism: The Origin, Development, and Rejection of Pacific Belief among Pentecostals." M.Div. thesis, North American Baptist Seminary, 1982.

———. "Pacifism and the World View of Early Pentecostalism." Paper presented to The Society for Pentecostal Studies, Cleveland, Tennessee, November 1983.

Bird, Charnal Adrian. Interview by author, 20 December 1999, Hawkins, Texas. Video tape recording. Personal files of author.

Collins, Johnnie Andrew. "Pacifism in the Churches of Christ: 1866-1945." DA diss., Middle Tennessee State University, 1984.

Cummings, Howard. Interview by author, 12 April 2000, by letter. Personal files of author.

Dawes, Stuart Wayne. "Toward a Biblical and Pneumatic Theology of Social Concerns for the Pentecostal Movement." Ph.D. diss., Universite Laval (Canada), 1994.

Dayton, Donald W. and Lucille Sider Dayton. *An Historical Survey of Attitudes Toward War and Peace Within the American Holiness Movement.* Winona Lake, Ind.: 1973.

Dempster, Murray W. Address, "From Conscientious Objection to the Just War: The Ironic Journey of Pentecostal Social Conscience," Special Vietnam Moratorium Day Assembly, Southern California College, 1970.

———. "Pacifism in Pentecostalism: The Case of the Assemblies of God" at Conference on "Pacifist Traditions in American Churches (other than historic Peace Churches)," jointly sponsored by Goshen College and Pepperdine University at Goshen College, Goshen, Indiana, September 24-26, 1992.

———. "Pacifism as a Divisive Issue in the Pentecostal Tradition," at A Consultation on "The Fragmentation of the Church and its Unity in Peacemaking," sponsored by the Faith and Order Working Group of the National Council of Churches/USA and by the Joan B. Kroc Institute for International Peace Studies at Notre Dame, held at the University of Notre Dame, Notre Dame, Indiana, June 13-17, 1995.

Derrick, Louise Willard. Interview by author, 3 March 2000, by telephone.

Elrod, Mark Alan. "The Churches of Christ and the 'War Question': The Influence of Church Journals." Ph.D. diss., Vanderbilt University, 1995.

Fourqurean, David N. "The Politics of Christian Perfection as Peace: Karl Barth and John Wesley in Dialogue." Ph.D. diss., Duke University, 1997.

Francisco, Noel. "Pacifism as a Social Movement." Ph.D. diss., Duke University, 1954.

Frodsham, Stanley, to Leslie C. Wattenburger, 26 November 1941. Frodsham file, J. R. Flower Pentecostal Heritage Center, Springfield, Missouri.

———, to T. L. Ward, 30 December 1941. Frodsham file, J. R. Flower Pentecostal Heritage Center, Springfield, Missouri.

Grob, Bruce Russell. "*The Christian Century*'s 'How My Mind Has Changed' Series: A Study of Theology and Ethics in Transition, 1930-1980." Ph.D. diss., Drew University, 1984.

Harrison, John Irvine. "A History of the Assemblies of God." Th.D. diss., Berkley Baptist Divinity School, 1954.

Heath, Robert Wever. "Persuasive Patterns and Strategies in the Neo-Pentecostal Movement." Ph.D. diss., The University of Oklahoma, 1973.

Holloway, Vernon H. "American Pacifism Between Two Wars, 1919-1941." Ph.D. diss., Yale University, 1949.

Holm, Randall. "A Paradigmatic Analysis of Authority Within Pentecostalism." Ph.D. diss., Universite Laval, 1996.

Holtzman, Donald Ray. "The Transdenominational Nature of Neo-Evangelicalism and Pentecostalism and its Effect on Religious Denominational Identity Between 1900 and 1960." Ph.D. diss., Temple University, 1995.

Jackson, Mary Elizabeth Jones. "The Role of Women in Ministry in the Assemblies of God." Ph.D. diss., The University of Texas at Arlington, 1997.

Kenyon, Howard. "An Analysis of Ethical Issues in the History of the Assemblies of God." Ph.D. diss., Baylor University, 1988.

———. Interview by author, 26 February 2000, by telephone.

Kircher, Leon G. "The History of the Organizational Development and Ministry to the Military by the Assemblies of God December 1941-December 1979." Springfield, Mo.: Assemblies of God Theological Seminary, 1979.

Linzey, Stanford. E. Interview by author, 13 February 2000, by telephone.

Lovett, Leonard. "Black Holiness-Pentecostals: Implications for Ethics and Social Transformation." Ph.D. diss., Emory University, 1979.

Mason, C. H. "The Kaiser in the Light of the Scripture." Sermon of 23 June 1918, 4. Quoted in Howard Kenyon, "An Analysis of Ethical Issues in the History of the Assemblies of God," 64. Ph.D. diss., Baylor University, 1988.

McElhany, Gary Don. "The South Aflame: A History of the Assemblies of God in the Gulf Region, 1901-1940." Ph.D. diss., Mississippi State University, 1996.

McGee, Gary B. Interview by author, 24 April 2000. By e-mail. Personal files of author.

Menzies, William W. "The Assemblies of God: 1941-1967, The Consolidation of a Revival Movement." Ph.D. diss., The University of Iowa, 1968.

Millner, Marlon. "Send Judah First: A Pentecostal Perspective on Peace." Letter to President George Bush, 3 March 2003, www.pcpj.org.

Moore, Everett LeRoy. "Handbook of Pentecostal Denominations in the United States." M.A. Thesis, Pasadena College, 1954

Morris, Valarie Ziegler. "The Advocates of Peace: Theological Foundations of the Nineteenth-Century American Peace Movement." Ph.D. diss., Emory University, 1987.

Robertson, William H. Interview by author, 12 February 2000. By telephone. Personal files of author.

Rosengartner, Helen. Interview by author, 30 May 2000, Garland, Texas. Personal files of author.

Smith, Evelyn. Interview by author, 30 May 2000, Garland, Texas. Personal files of author.

Smith, Walter B. Interview by author, 18 December 1999, Mt. Pleasant, Texas. Video tape recording. Personal files of author.

Tracy, James Russell. "Forging Dissent in an Age of Consensus: Radical Pacifism in America, 1940 to 1970." Ph.D. diss., Stanford University, 1994.

Waldvogel, Edith Lydia. "The 'Overcoming Life: A Study in the Reformed Evangelical Origins of Pentecostalism." Ph.D. diss., Harvard University, 1977.

White, Allen. "Spirit Baptism and the Initial Evidence in the Writings of the 'Apostle of Balance:' Donald Gee." Assemblies of God Theological Seminary, 1990.

Wessels, Roland. "Charles Parham's Exegetical Journey to the Biblical Evidence of the Spirit Baptism." Paper presented to the Society for Pentecostal Studies, 1993.

Witte, William Darwin Swanson. "Quaker Pacifism in the United States, 1919-1942, With Special Reference to its Relation to Isolationism and Internationalism." Ph.D. diss., Columbia University, 1954.

Wood, William Woodhull. "Culture and Personality Aspects of the Pentecostal Holiness Religion." Ph.D. diss., University of North Carolina Chapel Hill, 1961.

THE INDEX

P

THE AUTHOR

Paul Alexander is a Pentecostal farm boy from Kansas who attended his local Assembly of God at least three times a week while growing up and never missed a summer church camp. All four of his grandparents were Pentecostal, and he has a four-generation heritage that reaches back to the years right after the Azusa Street Revival (Los Angeles, 1906-1909). He was "saved" repeatedly and baptized in the Spirit at the age of twelve and began praying in tongues.

As a freshman Cross-Cultural Missions major at Southwestern Assemblies of God University in Waxahachie, Texas, he cheered and sang "bomb, bomb, bomb . . . bomb, bomb, Iraq" during the Gulf War in 1991. After serving as Student Congress president and Missions Association president, marrying Deborah, being named Mr. Southwestern, and graduating summa cum laude, Alexander attended the Assemblies of God Theological Seminary in Springfield, Missouri, as the recipient of the full tuition "Distinguished Assemblies of God Scholar" award. While in Springfield, Alexander's favorite three hours of each weekday was listening to Rush Limbaugh; he even tried to sell anti-Bill Clinton t-shirts that said "Don't blame me, I didn't vote for the dope smoking, womanizing, draft dodging governor of a backwater state." He also preached regularly and worked with Deborah in the Peanut Butter and Jelly Preschool at their church.

After graduating with his M.Div. at age twenty-three, Alexander was hired as an Assistant Professor at Southwestern to teach Bible and theology classes. The following year he started his Ph.D. in Religion (Theological Ethics) at Baylor University in Waco, Texas. While at Baylor, he day-traded stocks with borrowed money and invested in real estate. He also accidentally found out that the Assemblies of God had been a peace church full of conscientious objectors (as had most other early Pentecostal denominations). Although such a position made no sense to him, he decided to devote his dissertation to exploring the story. Along the way he discovered that his grandfather (as a conscientious objector) and his wife Deborah's grandfather (as a noncombatant) had both followed the Assemblies of God teaching on nonviolence during World War II. He also studied with John Howard Yoder in summer 1997 and began reading Anabaptist theology alongside his Pentecostal history.

In 1998 Alexander went back to Southwestern to teach full time and write his dissertation, which years later has become this book. After working through almost one hundred years of Assemblies of God history, theology, and ethics regarding peace, war, and nation, Alexander realized he needed friends to talk with about these identity shattering and life transforming issues. He scoured the web and couldn't find an organization of Pentecostals or Charismatics devoted to peacemaking and justice, so in July 2001 he proposed the formation of what is now Pentecostals and Charismatics for Peace and Justice (www.pcpj.org).

Alexander continued to preach and teach Sunday school classes at his local Assembly of God and taught Greek, biblical studies, theology, and ethics at Southwestern. He and others have worked together and slowly followed the leading of the Spirit to raise a voice for Jesus' way of peace with justice. In 2006 his alma mater did not renew his faculty contract, but Azusa Pacific University welcomed him, so he and his family moved to southern California, where he serves as Professor of Theology and Ethics and Director of the Doctor of Ministry program.

Alexander is a licensed Assemblies of God minister and also serves as an editor for the *Pentecostals, Peacemaking, and Social Justice* series with Wipf & Stock Publishers.

Printed in the United States
207953BV00004B/268-312/P